Illegal Annexation and State Continuity

The Case of the Incorporation of the Baltic States by the USSR

Second Revised Edition

By

Lauri Mälksoo

BRILL
NIJHOFF

LEIDEN | BOSTON

The Library of Congress Cataloging-in-Publication Data is available online at https://catalog.loc.gov
LC record available at https://lccn.loc.gov/2022024658

Typeface for the Latin, Greek, and Cyrillic scripts: "Brill". See and download: brill.com/brill-typeface.

ISSN 1568-2765
ISBN 978-90-04-46488-9 (hardback)
ISBN 978-90-04-46489-6 (e-book)

This book is printed on acid-free paper and produced in a sustainable manner.

Illegal Annexation and State Continuity

The Erik Castrén Institute Monographs on International Law and Human Rights

The Series of *International Law Monographs* by the *Erik Castrén Institute of International Law and Human Rights* seeks to bring to the reader high-quality research in international law with particular emphasis on the theoretical and historical aspects of the topics dealt with. The Series encourages doctrinal and practical criticism, a multidisciplinary approach and broad syntheses. Manuscripts that seek to renew the field's intellectual energy and political commitment are welcome. The Series is based on a conviction that theoretical ambition and practical relevance cannot be dissociated from each other and that even as it looks for a rejuvenation of the field it insists on speaking to both academic and practising lawyers.

VOLUME 20

The titles published in this series are listed at *brill.com/ilmc*

Contents

Preface to the First Edition

The depth and intensity of the transformation in Eastern and Central Europe in the 1980's and 1990's took most diplomats and political commentators by surprise. Needless to say, European politics now looks completely different from how it did during the stale years of the Cold War. For those who think that international law may be a useful instrument for regulating diplomatic privileges or the minutiae of the law of the sea, but that it cannot (and should not) play a role in questions about the life and death of States, it may come as a surprise to what extent the application of legal doctrines—even quite classical and formal doctrines—was taken for granted by practically all the protagonists during the demise of the Soviet Union. These doctrines had to do with State succession, recognition and the creation and continuity of statehood. Yet this may not be too surprising. As political truths, concepts and entities collapsed, little else was available apart from the language and principles of international law through which to address the changes in an organised way. The fall of the Soviet Union did not lead into a conceptual or political vacuum. And the fact that it did not was in part dependent on the presence of a legal language about statehood and State succession through which both new and old entities in the area of the former USSR could articulate their claims of identity and manage the transformation in a peaceful fashion.

None of this is to say that legal rules would have offered a set of pre-existing solutions to the political conflicts and disagreements that surfaced between the different players during the peak years of the transformation. Some of those disagreements have been settled, while others persist today. What was offered by international law was a language and a set of concepts through which political conflicts could be articulated, claims and counterclaims could be made and political negotiation could be conducted through a more or less non-biased means. Precedents could be (and were) invoked, analogies were drawn and all the standard legal arguments entered to provide a set of conceptual instruments through which political interests could receive shape and the outlines of political settlement be perceived. Law did not create a new status quo in the area of the former Soviet Union—but one wonders whether the transformation could have taken place so peacefully without the availability of law to provide a relatively uncontested point of reference for political struggles.

Lauri Mälksoo's study is an in-depth analysis of one aspect of that transformation—namely the Baltic States' struggle to regain the statehood they had lost due to Soviet occupation in August 1940. The Baltic States, of course, insisted that the occupation had been illegal; that this meant that they—Estonia, Latvia, Lithuania—had been under illegal occupation for some fifty years; and that as they now realised their right of self-determination, this took place not through the creation of new States, but through re-establishment of the old ones. These were not uncontested claims when they were made. But, as Mälksoo carefully shows, they articulated moral and political considerations that were of great importance not only for the Baltic populations, but for all self-determining entities and the international system as such. And the Baltic case was largely vindicated by subsequent diplomatic practice. Most States have now recognised the Baltic 'continuity thesis'—though this has not meant automatic re-establishment of the status quo of 1940 in the relevant bilateral relationships. The requirements of the intervening half century have in various ways been taken account of as the Baltic States have taken anew their place in international life. Mälksoo details some of those techniques under the provocative title '*ex factis jus oritur*'.

The present work analyses the claim of illegality of the Soviet occupation, arguments about possible prescription, the legal consequences of illegality, as well as restoration of the statehood of the three Baltic States after 1990. The relevant facts are well described, and the application of legal rules is skilfully based on arguments from precedent and legal principle. Mälksoo also discusses the question of the significance of (pure) legal status, detached from the enjoyment of rights and obligations that status entails in law. He writes as an Estonian for whom the symbolic substance of the independence of his mother country is indeed separable from whatever legal rights or duties might be associated with it—thus reminding us that all legal positions are a 'politics of law' but none the worse for being so, and indeed receive significance beyond the small circle of legal specialists only through their quality as such.

Martti Koskenniemi, Series Editor
Professor of International Law

Preface to the Second Edition

In 2018, the three Baltic States – the Republics of Estonia, Latvia and Lithuania - celebrated the 100th anniversary of their existence and in 2021 the 30th anniversary of the restoration of their independence. This book is about how before, during and after 1991 international law shaped the restoration of independence of these three States and how, in turn, the case of Soviet illegal annexation and yet successful restoration of the Baltic States reflects important 20th century developments in international law, and what would be the precedent value of this case in the future. Thus, it is also a book about the importance of international law and international legal arguments, and about the tremendous impact that international law can sometimes have on the fate of smaller nations. International law does its work sometimes (too) slowly; but the Soviet annexation case demonstrates that it eventually does. May this give hope for smaller States should they become victims of aggression now and in the future!

This book was defended as a doctoral dissertation at the Faculty of Law of the Humboldt University Berlin in July 2002 and published in its first edition at Martinus Nijhoff/Brill in 2003. Thus, it was written before 2004, when Estonia, Latvia and Lithuania became members of both the EU and NATO. Both the Estonian and Russian language translations of the book were published by Tartu University Press in 2005 and the Lithuanian translation in 2021.

Beside its continued relevance in the Baltic-Russian historical and legal-political contexts, the most surprising element of the reception of this book for me was that individuals were looking for inspiration in the Baltic precedent in places that I was initially not even able to foresee. For example, I was contacted by scholars from Hawaii who had noticed my book and were eager to discuss what the similarities and differences between these annexations may have been. However, the US annexation of Hawai happened in 1898 and it was a central argument in my book that the important legal developments concerning the Baltic case happened in international law in 1928–1945, not covering previous annexations in the legal positivist sense.

When Brill's international law editor Lindy Melman raised the perspective of the second edition of this book, I saw it as an opportunity to update the information in some aspects, for example regarding new developments on the Baltic-Russian border treaties. Also, I have tried to include more Russian perspectives and sources for the second edition. At the same, I have deleted several passages which seemed much less relevant to me now than when working on the dissertation.

One of the main reasons which motivated me to work on the second edition of this book was the opportunity to publish it open access. The production of the second edition overall, including the open access fees, was made possible thanks to grant PRG969 of the Estonian Research Council. Moreover, I very much benefted from a short-term research fellowship at Stanford University for Estonian Scholars which was funded by the University of Stanford libraries and the Estonian MFA. This opportunity enabled me to prepare the second edition in Palo Alto, California, in early 2022, and I would particularly like to thank Dr Liisi Esse for her support. Especially visits to Hoover Institute's archive at Stanford, for instance examining the personal archive of the Estonian diplomat Kaarel Robert Pusta made the topic of my dissertation very alive for me again. In Estonia, former diplomat Peeter Reštšinski supported me with valuable historical materials. I am also very grateful to Christopher Goddard for checking the quality of English language in this book.

Finally, in retrospect, I am most grateful that this book started a life-long conversation with two extraordinary international lawyers; both have remained great role models for me - Christian Tomuschat and Martti Koskenniemi.

Acknowledgments

I would like to thank the individuals who have helped me most while I was working on this PhD thesis. In the first place, thanks are due to my *Doktorvater,* Professor Christian Tomuschat. He was a constant source of inspiration and encouragement for me, and I feel really fortunate that I could be Professor Tomuschat's doctoral student. To Professor Gerd Seidel, the second corrector of my thesis, I am also thankful for his positive appraisal of my dissertation. In addition, I would like to acknowledge my intellectual debt to my former teachers of international law: Professor Dietrich Rauschning from Göttingen and Professors David P. Stewart, Edith Brown Weiss and Anthony Clark Arend from Georgetown University.

I would also like to thank Bardo Fassbender, Christian Fulda, Edgar Lenski, Ian Pepper, Moritz von Plate, Tilmann Röder, Sebastian von Schweinitz and Carola Wolprecht for their friendship and support during my three years of PhD studies in Berlin. My family in Estonia, and especially my sister Maria, always sent me positive energy waves while I was writing the thesis.

The writing of this dissertation would not have been possible without generous help from two institutions. During the first year of my PhD studies, I was a recipient of a scholarship awarded by the Foundation of the Parliament of Berlin. I would like to thank Professor Arnulf Baring for this scholarship. During the second and third years, I was supported by a scholarship from the Konrad Adenauer Foundation—for which I would like to express my gratitute to Dr. Detlev Preusse.

Last but not least, I am very grateful to Professor Martti Koskenniemi both for accepting my dissertation for publication in the Erik Castrén Institute's series and making valuable suggestions for improvement of the manuscript. Nevertheless, it goes without saying that I am solely responsible for any errors or omissions in this book.

Lauri Mälksoo

Abbreviations

A.D.	Annual Digest
AFDI	Annuaire français de droit international
AJIL	American Journal of International Law
Art.	Article
ASIL	American Society of International Law
ASIL Proc.	Proceedings of the American Society of International Law
Aufl.	Auflage
AVR	Archiv des Völkerrechts
Bd.	Band
BDGV	Berichte der Deutschen Gesellschaft fur Völkerrecht
BverfG	Bundesverfassungsgericht
BYBIL	British Yearbook of International Law
ch.	Chapter
CP	Communist Party
CSCE	Conference on Security and Co-operation in Europe
EC	European Communities
ed.	Editor
EJIL	European Journal of International Law
EPIL	Encyclopedia of Public International Law
EU	European Union
EÜS	Eesti Üliõpilaste Selts (Estonian Students' Society)
FAO	Food and Agriculture Organization of the United Nations
FRG	Federal Republic of Germany
FRUS	Foreign Relations of the United States of America
FS	Festschrift
FYROM	Former Yugoslav Republic of Macedonia
GA	General Assembly
GYBIL	German Yearbook of International Law
Hrsg.	Herausgeber
IAEA	International Atomic Energy Agency
IBRD	International Bank for Reconstruction and Development (World Bank)
ICAO	International Civil Aviation Organization
ICJ	International Court of Justice
ICLQ	International and Comparative Law Quarterly
ICRC	International Committee of the Red Cross
ILA	International Law Association
ILC	International Law Commission

ILJ	International Law Journal
ILM	International Law Materials
ILO	International Labor Organization
ILR	International Law Reports
IMF	International Monetary Fund
IMO	International Maritime Organization
Inst.	Instalment
Int'l Aff.	International Affairs
ITU	International Telecommunication Union
JBS	Journal of Baltic Studies
JIL	Journal of International Law
JTL	Journal of Transnational Law
LNOJ.	League of Nations Official Journal
LNTS	League of Nations Treaty Series
Loy.L.A.Int'l & Comp.L.J.	Loyola Los Angeles International and Comparative Law Journal
MDR	Monatsschrift für Deutsches Recht
MP	Member of Parliament
mtg.	Meeting
NATO	North Atlantic Treaty Organization
NGO	Non-governmental organization
NY	New York
N.Y.L.Sch.J.Int'l&Comp.L.	New York University Law School's Journal of International and Comparative Law
OJ	Official Journal
ÖJZ	Österreichische Juristenzeitung
orig.	Original
OSCE	Organization for Security and Cooperation in Europe
Parl. Deb.	Parlamentary Debates
PCIJ	Permanent Court of International Justice
RBDI	Revue belge de droit internationale
RCADI	Recueil des Cours de l'Académie de Droit International de la Haye
Rdnr.	Randnummer
Res.	Resolution
RGDIP	Revue générale de droit international public
RIAA	Reports of International Arbitral Awards
RSFSR	Russian Socialist Federalist Soviet Republic
SCOR	Official Records of the United Nations Security Council
Ser.	Series
SIPRI	Stockholm International Peace Research Institute

SSR	Socialist Soviet Republic
t.	Tome
transl.	Translated
TRNC	Turkish Republic of Northern Cyprus
UK	United Kingdom
UKTS	United Kingdom Treaty Series
UN	United Nations Organization
UNCIO	United Nations Conference on International Organization
UNESCO	United Nations Educational, Scientific and Cultural Organization
UNIDO	United Nations Industrial Development Organization
UNTS	United Nations Treaty Series
UP	University Press
UPU	Universal Postal Union
USA	United States of America (noun); US (adjective)
USSR	Union of Soviet Socialist Republics
Va.J.Int'l L.	Virginia Journal of International Law
vol.	Volume
WHO	World Health Organization
WIPO	World Intellectual Property Organization
WMO	World Meteorological Organization
WTO	World Trade Organization
YBEL	Yearbook of European Law
YBIL	Yearbook of International Law
ZaöRV	Zeitschrift für ausländisches öffentliches Recht und Völkerrecht
Z für VR	Zeitschrift für Völkerrecht
ZÖR	Zeitschrift für öffentliches Recht
ZvglRWiss	Zeitschrift für vergleichende Rechtswissenschaft

Introduction

In a fairytale narrated by Jacob and Wilhelm Grimm, Snow White or *Schneewittchen* tastes a poisoned apple offered by the envious queen, and falls into a deep sleep lasting for many years. Although many consider Snow White to be dead, a kiss from the Gentle Prince finally wakes her up. The three Baltic States have claimed that their stories were similar to that of Snow White. They were forcibly erased from the world map in 1940, but awoke in 1991 as though from a long comatose sleep upon receiving kisses from third States recognizing their identity with pre-1940 Estonia, Latvia and Lithuania. Recognition of the 'sameness' of the Baltic States fifty-one years after their *de facto* disappearance became a unique precedent in international relations, a remarkable 'world record' of its kind. The Baltic republics could not be added to any historical atlas of vanished countries.[1]

However, for some international lawyers, this outcome in State practice came almost out of the blue. In 1940, authors already started to bid farewell to the Baltic republics that had existed during the interwar period. Although the emergence and the legal status of the Baltic States had deserved some academic attention before World War II,[2] one scholar nevertheless wrote in 1957 that '[*e*]*n 1917, les Etats baltes sort de l'ombre pour prendre leur place parmi une communauté européenne qui jusque là les avait ignorés à peu près complètement. Aujourd'hui, ils sont en train de disparaître de nouveau dans le brouillard de la légende.*'[3] The Baltic *Schneewittchen* were thus already seen to inhabit the 'mists of legend.' No trace remained of the existence of the Baltic States in legal minds when Martti Koskenniemi wrote in early 1991, with reference to the Iraqi annexation of Kuwait, that '*war had begun in the Gulf, and the Soviet Union had increased military pressure on the Baltic republics. Both crises involved statehood:*

1 See B. Bjerge, *Nowherelands. An Atlas of Vanished Countries 1840–1985*, New York: Thames & Hudson, 2017.

2 See e.g. G. Heumann, *Aspects juridiques de l'indépendence estonienne*, Anvers: Lloyd, 1937; M.W. Graham, 'The Diplomatic Recognition of the Border States. Part II: Estonia', in: 3 *Publications of the University of California at Los Angeles in Social Sciences*, Berkeley, CA: University of California Press, 1939, pp. 231–398.

3 S.R. Schram, 'L'Union soviétique et les États Baltes', in: J.-B. Duroselle (ed.) *Les frontières européennes de l'U.R.S.S. 1917–1941*, Paris: Librairie Armand Colin, 1957, p. 25. ("In 1917, the Baltic States emerged from he shadow to take their place among a European community that until then had been virtually unaware of them. Today, they are once again on the way to disappearing into the mists of legend.")

the former involved an attempt to restore it, the latter an effort to preserve the boundaries claimed by one state and to prevent the creation of a new state.'[4]

Thus, a scholarly intrigue is clearly visible. What happened in reality? What role did international law play? What can international lawyers know, or indeed predict? Were the legal concepts employed by international law doctrine adequate? Did we miss some old legal rules or witness the creation of new ones in the Baltic case that should be noted for future purposes? The goal of this book is to find answers to these questions.

To the extent that the situation in the Baltic States could be analyzed within the dilemma 'legal fiction *versus* effectiveness', the question was raised: was it correct to recognize their identity? To be sure, the poisoned apple from the malevolent queen was an act to condemn, but was it a sufficient reason to pretend that the awakened lady was the same *Schneewittchen* who had been away for so long? Several scholars of international law, referring to the long period of factual non-existence of the Baltic republics, have sceptically characterized confirmation of the continuity/identity of those States as 'problematic',[5] or as 'dogmatically not undoubtful.'[6] Other authors have insisted that recognition of the continuity of the Baltic States was a symbolic or political decision, not necessarily a result of reasoned application of international law.[7] For example, Oliver Dörr concludes perplexedly that 'this politically motivated fiction cannot be explained with the rules of positive international law.'[8]

Thus quite a wide array exists of competing scholarly views and interpretations of the case of the Baltic States. Among the questions it raises, the most challenging may well be: to what extent has State practice, and hence the outcome of the question of the Baltic republics, been determined by law, and to what extent by politics? How important has international *law* been, or—for that matter—what *is* international law? The case of the annexation and restoration of the Baltic States concerns the very fundamentals of international law,

4 M. Koskenniemi, 'The Future of Statehood', 32 *Harvard ILJ* 1991, p. 410.

5 A. Zimmermann, *Staatennachfolge in völkerrechtliche Verträge. Zugleich ein Beitrag zu den Möglichkeiten und Grenzen völkerrechtlicher Kodifikation,* Berlin: Springer, 2000, p. 50.

6 O. Dörr, *Die Inkorporation als Tatbestand der Staatensukzession,* Berlin: Duncker & Humblot, 1995, p. 49.

7 See e.g. M. Koskenniemi and M. Lehto, 'La succession d'états dans l'ex-URSS, en ce qui concerne particulièrement les relations avec la Finlande', 38 *AFDI* 1992, pp. 197–8 ('*La thèse de la continuation implique ici une fiction juridique. Ni les Etats baltes ni le monde politique dans lequel its évoluent ne sont les 'mêmes' qu'en 1940. (…) On peut doubter qu'il faille recourir à la fiction de la continuité pour parvenir aux conséquences juridiques découlant déjà de la reconnaissance de l'illégalité de l'occupation.*')

8 See Dörr, *op. cit.*, p. 355.

its nature, its limits and its possibilities. During the Soviet annexation, leading political scientists, among them Raymond Aron, referred to the Baltic case to point out the limits of international law when confronted with factors such as power.[9]

In the course of this study, we may be reminded of the words of the German international lawyer Friedrich Berber, who spoke of 'the revenge of politics on international law' for taking up highly politicized issues.[10] Traditionally, international law experts have been quite fearful of such a revenge. Louis Henkin once observed critically that '(s)tudents of international law (…) tend to begin [their analysis] with international law, and often they end there (…)'[11] The author of the present book aspires to examine the subject in the spirit of Professor Henkin, for whom it is not sufficient to reduce international legal analysis to a formal discussion of 'pure' legal norms, to dogmatic analysis. The case of the legal status of the Baltic States cannot be properly understood within such a constrained approach.

Nevertheless, the underlying assumption of this study is that international law and international politics remain separate, although necessarily inter-related phenomena and fields of study. Legal explanations of the Baltic case are therefore not only possible, but inevitable and necessary. The varying explanations of the Baltic case given by legal authorities only demonstrate the (sometimes hidden) relevance of values and of politics. It is evident that doubts and questions presented by international lawyers are not just about a particular case—that of the legal status of the Baltic States—but about some of the most fundamental concepts of international law, about changes and dilemmas that the international community has been facing. What values does and should international law protect when such changes occur? Lawyers cannot deceive themselves about the fact that international law is based upon

---

9 R. Aron, *Peace and War: A Theory of International Relations*, transl. R. Howard and A. Baker Fox, Garden City, NY: Doubleday, 1966, p. 108: 'Major historical events, those by which the states are born and die, are external to the judicial order. The Baltic States have ceased to exist, they are no longer subjects of law; nothing the Soviet Union does on the territories that, in 1939, were subject to the Estonian or Lithuanian sovereignty any longer relates to international law, at least in the eyes of those of the states that have ceased to 'recognize' Estonia, Lithuania, and Latvia (that is, almost every state). When a state is crossed off the map of the world, it is the victim of the violation of international law. If no one comes to its aid, it will soon be forgotten and the state that has delivered the *coup de grace* will be no less welcome in the assemblies of so-called peaceful nations.'

10 Quoted from B. Simma, 'Comments on Global Governance, the United Nations Reform and the Place of Law', in: 9 *Finnish YBIL* 1998, p. 64.

11 L. Henkin, *How Nations Behave. Law and Foreign Policy*, New York et al: Frederick A. Praeger, 1968, p. 5.

values, and that the determination and choice between values in the process of creation and application of international legal norms is never purely legal, but also an ethical, moral,[12] and thus inevitably also a political, matter.

One fundamental choice between conflicting values has been well known to the international community since the origins of *ius gentium*: how much weight ought to be attributed to the principle of legality (*ex injuria ius non oritur*), and how much to the principle of effectiveness (*ex factis oritur ius*)? While international law must take both of these principles into account—in order to be *law* and to be *effective*—it must also decide which of the two is to be preferred in a particular type of conflict. Thomas M. Franck has convincingly postulated that '(t)he questions to which the international lawyer must now be prepared to respond, in this postontological era, are different from the traditional inquiry: whether international law is law. Instead, we are now asked: is international law effective? (...) And, the most important question: is international law fair?'[13]

À propos values, a few words must be said at the outset about what entitles the author to write about the topic chosen. This author comes from one of the Baltic States—Estonia—and intends to write about the Baltic States. Can one be objective in such a situation? Boris Meissner regretted in 1995 that there exists 'not a single really objective critical treatment of the Baltic case by Russian international lawyers.'[14] But is there a 'really objective' answer at all, and how can we know it? Josef Kunz has raised the problem of the possible bias of authors writing on particularly controversial cases of statehood, namely that 'political influences sway many writers on this topic, so that they approach the problems with preconceived solutions corresponding to their political wishes.'[15] Alfred Verdross was clearly confronted with the same legitimacy problem when, presenting his thoughts on the legal status of Austria in 1938–1945 as a consequence of Nazi rule, he emphasized that he intended to do so *sine ira et studio*.[16] Krystyna Marek revealed something important about her identity as a human being when she decided on *manibus Patris mei* as the motto of her influential study of State identity and continuity.[17]

---

12 For the relationship between law and morality, see generally C. Tomuschat, 'Ethos, Ethics and Morality in International Relations', EPIL 9, 1986, pp. 127–134.

13 T.M. Franck, *Fairness in International Law and Institutions*, Oxford UP, 1995, p. 6.

14 See Professor Meissner's remark in: BDGY, Bd. 35. *Das Recht der Staatensukzession. Referate und Thesen von U. Fastenrath etc*, Heidelberg, 1996, p. 359.

15 J.L. Kunz, 'Identity of States under International Law', 49 AJIL 1955, p. 70.

16 A. Verdross, 'Die vökerrechtliche Identität der Staaten', in: *Festschrift H. Klang*, Wien: Springer Verlag, 1950, p. 18 at 20.

17 K. Marek, *Identity and Continuity of States in International Law*, Genève: E. Dros, 1954.

This author believes that any researcher's biographical background *nolens volens* influences their thinking and perception.[18] The only way to approach objectivity is, as Swedish economist and Nobel prizewinner Gunnar Myrdal said, to reveal one's own subjectivities.[19] The quest for objectivity thus acquires a more realistic meaning in the sense of Richard Rorty, who argued that 'the desire for objectivity is not the desire to escape the limitations of one's community, but simply the desire for as much intersubjective agreement as possible, the desire to extend the reference of 'us' as far as we can.'[20]

One further explanation is due, concerning the notion of the Baltic States, or Baltic republics. The very concept of the Baltic countries has been subject to fluctuations in history. Originally, only today's Estonia and Latvia (then provinces of Estonia, Livonia and Curonia) composed the Baltics. At the beginning of the 20th century, Finland and even Poland were sometimes counted alongside Estonia, Latvia and Lithuania as 'the Baltic countries.' However, nowadays the Baltic States has come to signify the republics of Estonia, Latvia and Lithuania. This is also the usage employed in this book.

The common experience of having been occupied and annexed by the Soviet Union does not therefore make the three Baltic republics, their policies and identities, the same.[21] What is true of Lithuania may or may not be true for Estonia, and *vice versa*. What is common to all three is that in terms of population, those States and their predominant ethnic groups are quite small—comprising fewer people than global cities.[22] Ethnic Latvians and Lithuanians speak languages which belong to the Baltic linguistic family, while ethnic Estonians speak a Finno-Ugric language which is close to Finnish. While Lithuania is a predominantly Catholic country, most people among the titular nations in Latvia and in Estonia are historically Lutherans.

Although this book deals with the problem of illegal Soviet annexation of the Baltic States in 1940–1991 (with the interlude of Nazi German occupation in 1941–1944), the encounter of the Baltic territories with Muscovy and the Russian Empire in the context of international law and legal arguments

---

18 See further O. Korhonen, *International Law Situated. An Analysis of the Lawyer's Stance Towards Culture, History and Community*, The Hague: Kluwer, 2000, a book which inter alia also analyzes Finnish-Russian relations at the time of the birth of Finland's statehood.

19 Quoted from A. Cassese and J.H.H. Weiler (eds.), *Change and Stability in International Law-Making*, Berlin: de Gruyter, 1988, p. 152 (from the remarks of Georges Abi-Saab).

20 R. Rorty, *Objectivity, Relativism, and Truth*, Cambridge University Press, 1996, p. 23.

21 For the history of the Baltic States and countries, see A. Kasekamp, *A History of the Baltic States*, 2nd ed., London: Bloomsbury, 2017.

22 As of 2019, Estonia's population was 1.325 million, Latvia's 1.92 million, Lithuania's 2.79 million.

goes further back in time. The biggest 'continuity' question related to the Baltic States (formerly territories) is whether they belong geopolitically to the West or the East. With an iron law, when Muscovy/Russia has strengthened, it has referred to the changed balance of power, renounced existing treaties and invoked doubious proofs from its own chronicles when submitting its claims about the Baltic States (formerly territories). During the Middle Ages, there were Teutonic (German) crusader States in what is today's Estonia and Latvia; in turn, Lithuania was part of the powerful Commonwealth with Poland. When Muscovy's Tsar Ivan Gorny made claims over today's Estonian and Latvian territories before he started the Great Livonian War (1558–1583), Russian diplomats referred to a 'tribute of Yur'ev (Tartu)' which they said Livonian cities had failed to pay for some centuries.[23] The Livonian representaties had not heard of such a tribute but they learned that with Muscovy, certain 'continuity' claims can even be raised over centuries. Similarly, when Muscovy's Tsar Peter attacked Sweden in Narva in 1710 and the Great Nordic War (1700–1721) broke out, the Russian diplomat Petr Shafirov produced a writing in the context of propagandistic lawfare with Sweden in which he tried to justify Muscovy's war aims with an idiosyncratic interpretation of previous treaties concluded with Sweden.[24] With this writing, sometimes referred to as the first Russian writing in the tradition of European international law,[25] Shafirov responded *inter alia* to the Swedish State historian Olaus Hermelin who had previously been natural law and rhetoric professor at the University of Tartu (Dorpat);[26] thus making international legal arguments in times of geopolitical adversity also happens to be an old Baltic tradition. In 2022 and subsequently, similar 'continuity-based' arguments cannot be ruled out coming from Moscow: for example, that in 1991, the Soviet Union was not ended 'properly' or at least according to its constitution. In his 2022 declaration of war against Ukraine, Russia's

23 M. Laidre, *Domus belli. Põhjamaade Saja-aastane sõda Liivimaal 1554–1661*, Tallinn: Argo, 2015.

24 P.P. Shafirov, *A Discourse Concerning the Just Causes of the War Between Sweden and Russia: 1700–1721*, with an introduction by William E. Butler, Dobs Ferry, N.Y.: Oceana Publications, 1973. (The title of the English translation is not chosen well because in this war, Russia (Muscovy) attacked Sweden; not vice versa.)

25 Cf V.E.Grabar, *The History of International Law in Russia 1647–1917. A Bio-Bibliographical Study*, translated by W.E. Butler, Oxford: Clarendon Press, 1990, p. 76.

26 See O. Hermelin, *Gerechte Ablehnung derer lassterhafften Beschuldigungen womit der moscowitische Czar seinen Krieg damit er Schweden wieder Eyd und noch neulich versicherte Treu und Glauben angegriffen zu beschönigen gesuchet hat*, Stockholm, 1701. On Hermelin, see also G. von Rauch, *Die Universität Dorpat und das Eindringen der frühen Aufklärung in Livland 1690–1710*, Essen: Essener Verlagsanstalt, 1943, p. 269 *et seq.*

President Putin challenged the record of Bolsheviks for the Russian Empire more generally so the main question, from that imperial viewpoint, was no longer whether the Soviets annexed the Baltic States illegally but whether the Baltic States even had a right (morally, etc) to secede from (Soviet) Russia in 1918 in the first place. The easiest way for post-Putin Russia to renounce such trends challenging previous international legal obligations of Russia and the Soviet Union would be to unequivocally admit to the illegality of the Soviet occupation and annexation of the Baltic States in 1940, and to recognize their State continuity since 1991.

Beside publications written in major languages, including Russian, the author has tried to use as many Baltic sources as possible; however, not commanding the Latvian and Lithuanian languages, he was prevented from considering some of the legal literature published in those countries. Nevertheless, at least during the period of Soviet annexation, the most relevant literature written on this topic by Baltic exiles was in English.

The present study is divided into three substantive parts. In the first part, titled '*Ex injuria ius non oritur*,' we examine at length the legal status of the present-day Baltic republics. In the first chapter, we start by introducing the history of the legal concepts employed as well as earlier cases of restoration of States. This is the most theoretical chapter of the book, laying out the conceptual ramifications of the legal debate about State continuity and/or succession. With the help of the theoretical and terminological knowledge gained in the first chapter, we ten examine the applicability of existing general concepts of international law—such as aggression, the illegality of annexation, prescription, occupation and State continuity—to the facts in the case of the Baltic republics. The analysis moves from the general to the particular, so that the analytical method employed is primarily deductive. The goal of the second chapter is to clarify—with the help of existing legal concepts—the nature of the fiction of the 'sameness' of the Baltic States. Do State practice and existing concepts support the fiction of the uninterrupted existence of the Baltic States (State continuity) or not? The case of the Baltic States demonstrates that this dilemma, of a seemingly only metaphysical character, has significant practical relevance, raising, *inter alia*, questions of State responsibility for the period of hibernation.

In the second part of the study, titled '*Ex factis oritur ius*,' we discuss the legal implications of the discrepancy between the legal status of the Baltic republics, on the one hand, and their partly unsuccessful attempts to restore pre-annexation legal relationships (rights) on the other. We conclude with Part III, which deals with the implications of the Baltic case for international law and legal doctrine. The analytical method employed here is primarily inductive. Does State practice in the Baltic case, seen together with parallel developments in international law practice, bear witness to changes or developments concerning statehood in international law? The potential precedential value of the Baltic case can already be inferred from the fact that James Crawford, in the first edition of his important study 'The Creation of States in International Law,' could not offer definitive conclusions on State continuity or extinction in cases of prolonged illegal annexations.[27] So, then: what can we learn from the Baltic case about State continuity for the purposes of international law doctrine? The debated question involves more than whether certain abstract concepts (such as State continuity) should be employed in the Baltic context, but also the question what *is* the content of those concepts, based on practical experience. This author's project is thus to contribute, by analyzing the facts in one particular scarce precedent, to clarifying some fundamental doctrinal questions and concepts pertaining to the existence and restoration of the States in cases of illegal annexation.

27 J. Crawford, *The Creation of States in International Law*, Oxford: Clarendon Press, 1979, p. 420.

PART 1

Ex Injuria Ius Non Oritur

CHAPTER 1

Illegal Annexation, State Continuity and Identity: Concepts and Controversies

1 The Changing Status of Statehood in Contemporary International Law and Society: Starting Point for Analysis

The present time is an interesting one for the study of States in international law since it is widely perceived that both domestically and internationally, the role of the nation State is diminishing and in any case changing. Often disregarded today, however, is that predictions about the end of the State are not so new. During the 20th century, the disappearance of the State has been suggested by both Marxist and conservative legal thinkers alike. Edouard Berth declared in 1907: '*L'État est mort*'[1] Vladimir Lenin predicted in 1917 that the State would wither away.[2] Carl Schmitt suggested in 1963 that there is 'little remaining doubt' about the approaching end of the era of statehood.[3]

At the same time, international law experts have obviously had conceptual difficulties with this development since classical international law has centered round the maxim 'the State is the main subject of international law.' Nevertheless, international lawyers, too, have occasionally taken up the theme of the decline of statehood,[4] even though the fashionable thesis

1 Quoted from W Rudolf, *Wandel des Staatsbegriffs im Völkerrecht?,* Bonn: Europa Union Verlag, 1986, p. 45.

2 В.И. Ленин, *Государство и революция. Учение марксизма о государстве и задачи пролетариата вреволюций,* Москва: Издательство политической литерературы, 1952 (orig. 1917). (VI. Lenin, The State and Revolution).

3 C. Schmitt, *Der Begriff des Politischen. Text von 1932 mit einem Vorwort und drei Corollarien,* Berlin: Duncker & Humblot, 1963, p. 40.

4 See e.g. L. Ali Khan, *The Extinction of Nation-States. A World without Borders,* The Hague: Kluwer, 1998; C. Schreuer, 'The Waning of the Sovereign State: Towards a New Paradigm for International Law?', 4 EJIL 1993. pp. 447–471; S. Sur, 'The State between Fragmentation and Globalization', 8 EJIL 1997, pp. 421–432; O. Schachter, 'The Decline of the Nation-State and its Implications for International Law', in: J.I. Charney, D.K. Anton, M.E. O'Connell (eds.) *Politics, Values and Functions. International Law in the 21st Century. Essays in Honor of Professor Louis Henkin,* The Hague: Nijhoff, 1997; A.-M. Slaughter, 'Governing the Global Economy through Government Networks', in: M. Byers (ed.) *The Role of Law in International Politics,* 2000, pp. 177–205.

© LAURI MÄLKSOO, 2022 | DOI:10.1163/9789004464896_003

of the decline of the State has also been criticized by other international lawyers.[5]

In any case, it is clear that statehood is not a static phenomenon. In the modern era, the social perception of States has become less and less value neutral, just as individuals and peoples, legitimacy and even democracy, have started to march into the international law arena. Such changes in the perception of States have challenged—and are likely to further challenge—the traditional concept of international law which has blindly accepted the existence of States as a social fact, without ever asking whether a particular effective entity is a democracy or a dictatorship, whether it accepts fundamental norms of international law, how a given State was created or by what means its existence is challenged.

The task of legal scholarship is to re-evaluate the validity of certain perennial analytical tools by analyzing recent trends in practice and in social perceptions. A State is by nature an abstraction, a concept[6]—but how far can statehood for normative reasons be recognized at variance with the principle of effectiveness? The problem of illegally annexed States can be analyzed in this paradigmatic framework of changes and uncertainties regarding statehood. The historical events of the restoration of States are most of all characterized by changes in international relations. It is because of the difficulty in classifying the relevant changes that international law of State succession and continuity has traditionally been characterized by legal scholars as 'uncertain', 'not suitable for codification', and so on.

2 Re-established States in the Practice of International Relations: Historical Perspective

The phenomenon of re-established States is relatively old. As long ago as the eighteenth century, Emer de Vattel used the case of Portugal as an example.[7] In 1580, the ruling dynasty of Portugal died out and the country was incorporated into the Kingdom of Spain. However, following an insurgency in 1640, the independence of Portugal was re-established. This is possibly the first case

5 See e.g. M. Koskenniemi, 'The Wonderful Artificiality of States', in: 88 *ASIL Proc.* 1994, p. 29; B. Stern, 'How to Regulate Globalization?', in: M. Byers (ed.) *The Role of Law in International Politics*, Oxford UP, 2000, pp. 247–268.

6 See L. Henkin, 'International Law: Politics, Values and Functions, General Course on Public International Law', in: 216 *RCADI* 1989, p. 23.

7 E. de Vattel, *Droit des Gens,* 1758, Book III, Chapter XIV, para. 213.

of a resurrected State in international relations,[8] even predating the birth of the Westphalia system. Another historic case mentioned in this context is the resurrection of the Republic of Genoa.[9]

The Vienna Congress of 1815 re-established the independence of certain German and Italian States, restoring power to dynasties that had been ousted by Napoleon. Among the States re-established were also The Netherlands, which had been incorporated into the French Empire in 1810.[10]

The first modern case of State re-establishment is Poland, which lost its independence as a consequence of the third Polish partition in 1795 but regained it after World War I, in 1918. Poland was the first State to claim in contemporary legal concepts—notwithstanding that it had not *de facto* existed for one hundred and twenty-three years—that as a subject of international law it was identical with the previous State.[11] However, notwithstanding the arguments advanced by Polish jurists,[12] internationally the Polish claim found no specific recognition beyond the domestic sphere.[13] Similarly, the claim of post-1918 Lithuania to be the same State as the Lithuanian part of the Polish-Lithuanian Commonwealth before 1795 was not considered at the international level.[14]

A major change in this respect occurred before and in the course of World War II. On October 5, 1935, the Italian army invaded Ethiopia; the annexation of the country followed on May 9, 1936. After some hesitation, other States recognized this forcible annexation. However, after Italy declared war on the allies on June 11, 1940, the attitude of other States with respect to the legal status of Ethiopia changed. When Ethiopia was liberated by the British, its continuous identity with pre-annexation Ethiopia was recognized. On February 10, 1947,

---

8 See V.-D. Degan, 'Création et disparition de l'État (à la lumière du démembrement de trois fédérations multiethniques en Europe', 279 *RCADI* 1999, p. 293.

9 See W.E. Hall, *A Treatise on International Law*, 8th ed., ed. by A.P. Higgins, Oxford, 1924, pp. 580–581.

10 V.-D. Degan, *op. cit.*, p. 294.

11 In the following cases, the Polish courts claimed identity: *Republic v. Felsenstadt* (1922), I AD No. 16; *Republic v. Weisholc* (1919), ibid., No. 17; *Republic v. Pantol* (1922) ibid., No 18. See further about these cases A. Uschakow, 'Die Wiederherstellung Polens im Lichte des Völkerrechts', in: B. Meissner, G. Zieger (Hg.), *Staatliche Kontinuität unter besonderer Berücksichtigung der Rechtslage Deutschlands*, Köln: Verlag Wissenschaft und Politik, 1983, p. 107 at 113.

12 See e.g. S. Cybichowski, 'Das völkerrechtliche Okkupationsrecht', 18 *Z. für VR* 1934, p. 318.

13 Crawford, *op. cit.*, p. 408. See also Kunz, *op. cit.*, p. 71; Marek, *op. cit.*, p. 581 and W. Fiedler, *Das Kontinuitätsproblem im Völkerrecht. Zum funktionalen Zusammenhang zwischen Völkerrecht, Staatsrecht und Politik*, Freiburg: Karl Alber, 1978, p. 36.

14 See I. Ziemele, *State Continuity and Nationality in the Baltic States: the Baltic States and Russia. Past, Present and Future as Defined by International Law*, Leiden: Brill, 2005, p. 40.

the Allied and Associated Powers signed a Peace Treaty with Italy, in which Italian actions in Ethiopia were declared null and void *ex tunc*, that is, operating retroactively from the very moment of Italian aggression.[15] Post-war Ethiopa was thus recognized as being the same State as before 1936—moreover, it was implied that the Italian annexation had not caused the extinction of Ethiopia in the meantime.

Another case was Czechoslovakia which, after it had already been forced to surrender the Sudetenland to Germany in 1938, was occupied by the German military on March 16, 1939. A day earlier, Hitler and Göring had presented Czechoslovak President Hacha with an ultimatum, threatening to bomb Prague if the German demand to occupy Bohemia and Moravia was rejected. President Hacha accepted the ultimatum. The USA never recognized the status of Bohemia and Moravia as a German protectorate, and continued to recognize the statehood of Czechoslovakia. However, the majority of the international community either explicitly or implicitly recognized Czechoslovakia's extinction.[16] During the course of World War II, the Czechoslovak government in exile was founded by Edvard Beneš, former President of Czechoslovakia. In the Peace Treaties of February 10, 1947, the identity of the post-war Czechoslovak Republic with the pre-1939 Czechoslovak Republic was confirmed.[17]

A similar case was Albania. The Italian army attacked Albania on April 7, 1939. The Albanian crown was 'offered' to the King of Italy, and on April 14, 1939 a 'personal union between the two Kingdoms' was proclaimed. In other words, Italy had annexed Albania. Most countries, except the USA and some other States, recognized the results of the Italian act of force. As no Albanian government in exile was established, Albania appeared to be extinguished as a State. However, in the Italian Peace Treaty of February 10, 1947, the Italian operation against Albania was qualified as aggression and Albanian State continuity with pre-1939 Albania was confirmed.

Last but not least, there is the perhaps most famous—or at least most discussed—case, that of Austria. On March 11, 1938, Germany presented an ultimatum to the Austrian Government in which it demanded that Austria should cancel a planned plebiscite on the issue whether Austria should remain independent or join Germany.[18] After Austria complied with this ultimatum, Germany further demanded that Austria form a new, German-friendly

---

15 See Marek, *op. cit.*, p. 277.

16 Marek, *op. cit.*, p. 290.

17 See Marek, *op. cit.*, pp. 318–9; See also G. Cansacchi, 'Identité et continuité des sujets intenationaux', *RCADI* 1970, p. 55.

18 See Marek, *op. cit.*, pp. 340–1.

government under the leader of the Austrian Nazis, Arthur Seyss-Inquardt. Austria accepted this ultimatum, too, although the resigning Chancellor succeeded in broadcasting a speech in which he declared that Austria was yielding to force. The new Austrian Chancellor, Seyss-Inquart, immediately requested that Germany send troops into Austria 'to prevent bloodshed.' Germany met this 'request.'[5] On April 10, 1938, a plebiscite was arranged in Austria in which the population was to express its opinion on incorporation into Germany. According to official figures, of 4 284 795 voters 4 273 884 approved of incorporation.[19]

No Austrian government in exile was formed; nor did Austrian diplomatic missions abroad remain functional. It seemed that the international community took Austria's extinction for granted. Even the most ardent follower of the non-recognition principle, the USA, recognized Austria's extinction.[20]

However, the positions changed after World War II had broken out. On November 1, 1943, Great Britain, the USA and the Soviet Union adopted a declaration in Moscow in which they declared the annexation of Austria null and void. In April 1945, Vienna was captured by the Soviet army and the restoration of the Austrian Republic was proclaimed by Austrian politicians. Instead of recognizing Austria as a new State, the Allies accorded their recognition to the new Austrian government.

As a consequence of the restoration of the Austrian State, the Allied Powers agreed at the Potsdam Conference of 1945 that 'reparations should not be exacted from Austria.' Finally, the continuity of the Republic of Austria with pre-1938 Austria was recognized in the Austrian State Treaty of May 15, 1955.[21] Therefore, it can be concluded that the thesis of Austria's continuity was accepted in State practice.[22]

However, far from every claim of sameness with historic States has been recognized in post-World War II State practice. For instance, after Algeria became independent in 1958, it claimed to be legally identical with the Algeria that had

19 Dahm points out that the mood of the Austrian population may have supported the *Anschluß*, even if this did not change the illegality of the German action from the point of view of international law: *'Damit wurde dieses Ereignis, obwohl der damaligen Voksstimmung entsprechend, zu einem völkerrechtswidrigen Vorgang.'* See G. Dahm, *Völkerrecht*, Band I, Stuttgart, 1958, p. 592.

20 Cf. D.P. O'Connell, *State Succession*, Vol. II, 1967, pp. 38–39.

21 See *Austrian State Treaty (Staatsvertrag)*, Vienna (Belvedere), 15.5.1955, BGBI 1955/152, Arts I and 21.

22 Cf. also with R.E. Clute, *The International Legal Status of Austria*, 1938–1955, The Hague: Nijhoff, 1962, p. 111. For a recent brief account, see P. Oberhammer/A. Reinisch, 'Restitution of Jewish Property in Austria', *ZaöRV* 2000 60/3–4, p. 739 *et seq.*

been subjugated by France in 1830.[23] Although the old Algeria had disappeared from the political map of the world 130 years ago, Algeria claimed 'résurrection légale d'un état préexistant.'[24] Thus, the Algerian government suggested that no recognition as a new State was necessary.[25] However, the Algerian claim to be the same State as 130 years ago did not find recognition in State practice. Similarly, today's Republic of Korea has argued that the annexation of Korea by Japan in 1910 was illegal, since the Agreement of Annexation of 1910 was concluded under duress. Korea has therefore insisted that it did not cease to exist as a State and is identical with the old Korean Empire. This position has not found specific recognition in international practice.

Already a first glance at this summary of State practice reveals that a claim of State identity does not guarantee recognition of such an identity as a subject of international law. Clearly, for reasons to be studied, important legal and political factors have confirmed State identity in some cases and denied it in others. Why, then, were the cases of Poland (1795–1918) and Algeria (1830–1958) on the one hand, and those of Ethiopia, Czechoslovakia, Albania and Austria on the other hand, treated so differently? And what really was the legal status of Ethiopia, Czechoslovakia, Albania and Austria during their *de facto* nonexistence? How did international legal doctrine interpret and classify these cases and what consequences did it draw from them for the concept of statehood in international law?

3 State Continuity, Identity and Extinction in International Law Doctrine

It is in the fundamental interest of every legal order to establish rules which would help to determine who its subjects are, how they are created, and how they become extinguished. The identity of the subjects of international law is directly related to their rights and obligations, respect for or disregard of which would directly affect the stability of international relations. On that basis, international law has traditionally distinguished between two different, even opposing concepts: State succession and State continuity (or identity). In the

23 See generally J.A. Frowein, 'Die Abmachung von Evian und die Entstehung des algerischen Staates', in: 23 *ZaöRV* 1963, pp. 20–48. See also I. Seidl-Hohenveldern, T. Stein, *Völkerrecht*, C. Heimann Verlag, 2000, p. 254.

24 See also M. Bedjaoui, *La Rèvolution algérienne et le droit*, Bruxelles: Association internationale des juristes démocrates, 1961, p. 18 *et seq* where the author argues that Algeria's sovereignty was never extinguished, and was revived with the belligerency.

25 O. Döff, *Inkorporation...*, p. 48.

case of State succession, the former State becomes extinct and the continuity of its legal relations by its successors is yet to be determined by the parties and under relevant rules of international law.[26] In the case of State identity, however, the former legal subject continues to exist notwithstanding certain changes which may be significant, and continuity of legal relations is generally presumed. As international law seeks to safeguard the stability of international relations, it is natural that in State practice, there is a strong presumption in favour of the continuity of established States.[27] Authors have spoken of the principle of the 'greatest possible continuity of States.'[28]

But what is a State for the purposes of international law? The answers to this question determine, more or less directly, when a State becomes extinguished.

Theoretical explanations of the classic notion of statehood in international law lie in 19th century German State law theory. The German legal scholar Georg Jellinek identified three constitutive elements of statehood: territory, population, and government.[29] Jellinek distinguished between two sides of a State: social-factual and normative-ideal.[30] While he suggested that the birth and extinction of States are metajuridical phenomena beyond juridical constructions, he linked the identity of a State to its 'social side', to the 'historical-political facts.' This enabled him to argue that restoration of the same State is possible, where the elements of association join forces anew.[31]

Since at least the 19th century, there have been two competing schools of thought on the matter of the creation and existence of States in international law doctrine: one arguing that the existence of States is a matter of fact, the other claiming that States become States as legal persons only through admission, recognition by the international community—the declaratory and constitutive theories of recognition. The relevance to be attributed to recognition by other States, members of the international community, has also been a controversial issue in the cases of State extinction.

---

26 See *Vienna Convention on Succession of States in Respect of Treaties*, August 23,1978, UN Doc. A/CONF. 80/31 (1978); ILM, Vol. 17 (1978), pp. 1488–1517 and *Vienna Convention on Succession of States in Respect of State Property, Archives and Debts*, April 8, 1983, UN Doc. A/CONF. 117/14 (1983).

27 Marek, *op. cit.*, p. 548; Crawford, *op. cit.*, p. 417; W. Czaplinski, 'La continuité, l'identité et la succession d'états—évaluation de cas récents', 26 *RBDI* 1993, p. 375.

28 In German: *Grundsatz der größtmöglichen Kontinuität des Staates*. See G. Dahm, *Völkerrecht*, Bd. I, Stuttgart, 1958, p. 85.

29 See G. Jellinek, *Allgemeine Staatslehre*, 3rd ed., 1920, pp. 394–434.

30 G. Jellinek, *Allgemeine Staatslehre*, 3. Aufl., 1920, p. 281. For a critique, see H. Herz, 'Beiträge zum Problem der Identität des Staates', 15 *ZÖR* 1935, p. 247.

31 G. Jellinek, *Allgemeine Staatslehre*, 3. Aufl., 1920, p. 286.

A certain victory of the declaratory theory of State recognition seemed to be reflected in the 1933 Montevideo *Convention on the Rights and Duties of States*.[32] At the Montevideo Convention, the 'three-elements theory' was accommodated for the purposes of international law as 'four-elements-theory.' Article 1 of the Convention reads: 'The State as a person of international law should possess the following qualities: (a) a permanent population; (b) a defined territory; (c) government; and (d) capacity to enter into international relations with other States.' The distinction between the third and fourth elements has been criticized as superfluous since an effective government would automatically have the capacity to entertain international relations with other States.[33] Generally, however, there developed a certain agreement among the lawyers of that time that the Montevideo elements reflected the state of customary international law.[34]

The Montevideo criteria reflect the understanding that a State is in the first place a sociological reality; it is neither created nor destroyed by international law—a State is simply there when it is.[35] Among legal scholars, Hans Kelsen has been the most distinguished proponent of this concept of statehood:

> [I]f a power is established anywhere, in any manner, which is able to ensure permanent obedience to its coercive order among the individuals whose behavior this order regulates, then the community constituted by this coercive order is a state in the sense of international law. The sphere in which this coercive order is permanently effective is the territory of the state; the individuals who live in the territory are the people of the state in the sense of positive international law.[36]

It is striking how strongly Kelsen's thinking about statehood in international law was influenced by the sociological conception of the State. This emphasis on sociological reality is almost in question-begging contradiction with the distinction that is otherwise so characteristic of Kelsen's State theory: the distinction between the social and the juridical conception of the State, and the

32 165 LNTS 19.

33 See C. Tomuschat, 'General Course on Public International Law', 281 *RCADI* 2001, p. 96.

34 H. Lauterpacht, L. Oppenheim, *International Law. A Treatise*, 5th ed., London: Longmans, Green, vol. I, 1935, p. 121.

35 Martti Koskenniemi calls this approach to statehood 'pure fact view.' See M. Koskenniemi, 'The Politics of International Law', 1 *EJIL* 1990, p. 14.

36 H. Kelsen, 'The Pure Theory of Law and Analytical Jurisprudence', 55 *Harvard L. Rev.* 1941–42, p. 44 at 64–65.

priority of the latter for the lawyer.[37] If a State is for a lawyer a pure form, a normative system—a fiction in a way—why should the sociological reality so strongly determine the legal concept of statehood?

That the Montevideo definition of the State reflects the concept of statehood in international law has also been suggested by contemporary legal scholars.[38] The Montevideo definition of statehood is generally provided in most casebooks of international law as the definition of statehood.[39]

Along the lines of the Montevideo elements of statehood, it has then only been logical to argue that the disappearance of any one of these constituting elements brings about the extinction of the State itself.[40] Following this thinking, should the flooding over of an island State as a consequence of climate change or other natural catastrophe bring about the disappearance of the State's territory, the State itself would become extinguished.[41] In another theoretical construction, the total disappearance of a people—for example, in the result of natural catastrophe or genocidal acts—would also bring about the extinction of their State.

The most topical and challenging cases in international practice are those connected to changes or even to the disappearance of an (independent and effective) State power. Some rules of customary international law which specify what occurs with State personality when changes in State government take place are already relatively old and well-established. According to the first rule, the continuity of a State will *per se* not be affected by territorial changes, by acquisition or loss of territory.[42] After World War I, the Republic of Turkey was recognized as the continuation of the Ottoman Empire, although the territory had shrunk considerably. Similarly, conquests and acquisitions during the 15th–20th centuries did not alter the international legal personality of Muscovy/Russia.[43]

37 H. Kelsen, *Der soziologische und der juristische Staatsbegriff. Kritische Untersuchung des Verhältnisses von Staat und Recht*, 2. Aufl., Tübingen: Mohr, 1928, p. 3

38 See e.g. S.V. Tchernichenko, 'State as a Personality, Subject of International Law and Bearer of Sovereignty', *Russian YBIL* 1993–1994, p. 15 *et seq.*

39 See e.g. Dahm/Delbrück/Wolfrum, Völkerrecht, Bd. I/1, 2. Aufl., 1989, Berlin, pp. 125–137, esp. at 133; Hailbronner in Vitzthum (ed.) *Völkerrecht*, Berlin, 1997, 3. chapter, Rdnr. 63–68.

40 See e.g. U. Fastenrath, 'States, Extinction', in: *EPIL* 1987, Vol. 10, p. 465 and Cansacchi, *op. cit.*, pp. 9–10. But see A. Verdross, 'Untergang von Staaten', in: K. Strupp, H.-J. Schlochauer (eds.) *Wörterbuch des Völkerrechts*, Band III, Berlin: Springer, 1962, p. 479.

41 See e.g. K. Doehring, *Völkerrecht*, 1999, p. 70.

42 See Fiedler, *Das Kontinuitätsproblem*, pp. 52–54

43 See Crawford, *op. cit.*, p. 404 *et seq.*

According to the second well-established rule of customary international law, changes in the government, whether of a constitutional or a revolutionary nature, do not as such affect the continuity of the State.[44] Therefore, internal changes do not justify abandoning international obligations. This rule was seriously challenged when, following the October revolution of 1917, Russia's communist government claimed discontinuity with Tsarist Russia, at least with respect to financial and other obligations that Tsarist Russia had taken on. Other States did not accept this claim and although the question of Tsarist Russia's debts remained unresolved, other European States considered Soviet Russia as the continuator State of Tsarist Russia.[45]

The third well-established rule of customary international law is the most interesting for our case study. It establishes that when a State temporarily comes under military occupation (*occupatio bellica*), it does not become extinguished, so that its continuity remains preserved.[46] The limits to this rule have been set by the principle of effectivity. According to classic understanding, the legal institute of military occupation has in itself temporary limits, or a provisional character.[47] Military occupation comes to an end either with the legally valid incorporation of the occupied State's territory (such as *qua* peace treaty), or with restoration of the original sovereign's power.[48]

Although the legal regime of occupation has thus by definition been temporary, it demonstrates that a State can—temporarily—survive without effective government over the citizens living in a State's territory (under occupation). Annexation of territory seized *durante bello* was therefore without legal effect upon the status of the occupied territory. From the strict point of view of the Montevideo requirements for statehood, legal fictions on the question of extinction or survival of State personality were already accepted in customary international law.[49]

---

44 Cansacchi, *op. cit.*, p. 22 et seq; Fiedler, *Das Kontinutätsproblem*, pp. 46–51.

45 See e.g. Cansacchi, *op. cit.*, p. 22 *et seq.*

46 See Marek, *op. cit.*, p. 15; Cansacchi, *op. cit.*, pp. 26–7; Fiedler, p. 55 *et seq;* Ipsen, *Völkerrecht*, p. 59.

47 See generally A. Gerson, 'War, Conquered Territory, and Military Occupation in the Contemporary International Legal System', in: 18 *Harvard ILJ* 1977, p. 525 *et seq*; E. Benvenisti, *The International Law of Occupation*, Princeton: Princeton University Press, 1993, p. 3 *et seq.* See also N. Ando, *Surrender, Occupation, and Private Property in International Law. An Evaluation of US Practice in Japan*, Oxford: Clarendon Press, 1991, p. 34 *et seq.*

48 See Sir A.D. McNair, *Legal Effects of War*, 2nd ed., Cambridge: University Press, 1944, pp. 318–320.

49 State continuity, although recognized in customary international law, is similarly 'fictitious' in cases of anarchy or insurgency, i.e. when the State government is missing or lacks effectivity. See Cansacchi, p. 40 *et seq.* See also Marek, p. 365. For instance, it is today

These were the three recognized customary international legal rules that prevented extinction of a given State at the time when the cases of Ethiopia, Czechoslovakia, Austria and Albania challenged the exclusiveness of the three customary rules protecting States from extinction.

4 Issues Raised in Legal Doctrine by World War II Annexation Cases

Recognition of State continuity in the Ethiopian, Czechoslovakian, Austrian and Albanian cases became a new development in international law. According to strict application of the Montevideo criteria and the principle of effectiveness, those annexed States should have become extinct at the moment of annexation; their re-establishment after liberation could only have created new States from the point of view of international law.[50] In the cases of Austria and Czechoslovakia, since no military hostilities had occurred, there were not even military occupations in the narrower sense. All of those States were *de iure* or *de facto* annexed following occupation; moreover, their annexation was, after some hesitation, recognized by almost all members of the then international community, with the exception of Czechoslovakia. It was a difficult task to explain convincingly the status of those States as subjects of international law.

Correspondingly, highly diverse legal opinions evolved. The discussion has been most vivid in the Austrian case. Here, two opposing theories were presented—the occupation theory and the annexation theory. One group of writers, led by Hans Kelsen, insisted that Austria became extinguished upon its annexation by Germany and after World War II was created as a new State (annexation theory). According to the occupation theory, however, Austria fell under illegal occupation in 1938, was therefore not extinguished as a subject of international law and in 1945 re-established its capacity to act.[51]

The annexation theory was at variance with the final outcome in State practice because re-established Austria claimed identity with pre-*Anschluß* Austria and its identity was generally recognized by the international community.[52]

---

widely recognized that the State of Somalia has not become extinct, notwithstanding the anarchical situation in that country.

50 See e.g. Kunz, *op. cit.*, p. 75.

51 For a concise summary, see W. Hummer, 'Der internationale Status und die völkerrechtliche Stellung Österreichs seit dem Ersten Weltkrieg', in: H. Neuhold *et al*, *Österreichisches Handbuch des Völkerrechts*, 3. Aufl., Wien, 1997, p. 500. See also H. Miehsler/C. Schreuer, Austria, in: *EPIL* 12, 1990, pp. 28–33.

52 Ulrich Scheuner, who had 'serious doubts' about such an 'expansion' of State continuity, admitted that '[u]nzweifelhaft hat in den genannten Fällen die internationale Praxis

Therefore, the scholarly discourse has rather centred around three main questions: first, did recognition of Austria's, Czechoslovakia's (and others') State identity inevitably imply their State *continuity*; second, what are the normative consequences of State identity; and third, on what legal basis was State identity/continuity in those cases preserved? These theoretical questions are still open in doctrine and as they will have major importance in analysis of the Baltic situation, we will discuss each of them separately.

a *Does State Identity Always Imply State Continuity?*

When it comes to this question, the very way of putting it was new in doctrine. Both concepts of State continuity and identity had been used to mean basically the same thing, as synonyms.[53] Krystyna Marek defined State identity as the identity of its international rights and obligations, and State continuity as 'the dynamic predicate of State identity.'[54] For Marek, there can be no continuity without identity (and *vice versa*)—'unless the possibility of legal miracles is accepted.'[55] A State either exists continuously or becomes extinguished. According to this—until today probably predominant—understanding, it is, at least in legal terms, impossible for a State to temporarily disappear, and then reappear as the same State.

Later writers have challenged this view.[56] In contrast to Marek, these authors argue that, indeed, it has happened in State practice that the identity of a State is recognized after the event which called that identity in question is recognized—and thus that identity was preserved—although the *continued* existence of the State during the critical time must be denied. James Crawford, for instance, has suggested that identity without continuity, a kind of resurrection of the same legal entities, is indeed possible in international law.[57] Ian Brownlie's approach is quite similar to Professor Crawford's. In Professor Brownlie's view, a 'functional approach'[58] was taken in the cases of Ethiopia, Albania, Austria and Czechoslovakia, since 'the insistence on continuity

---

die Kontinuität weitgehend anerkannt.' See his book review of Marek, 17 *ZaöRV* 1956/57, pp. 174–5.

53 Bernhardt: '*Beide Begriffe bezeichnen nach der in der Völkerrechtslehre überwiegenden Ansicht denselben Sachverhalt.*' Bernhardt, *Kontinuität,* p. 295. See also Thurn, *Die Kontinuitätsfrage...*, p. 30.

54 Marek, *op. cit.,* p. 5–6. Kelsen adheres to the same view, calling continuity 'identity in time.' See H. Kelsen, *Principles of International Law,* 2nd ed., New York, 1967, p. 384

55 Marek, *op. cit.,* p. 6.

56 See Cansacchi, *op. cit.,* p. 9 *et seq.* and 59 *et seq.;* Fiedler, *Das Kontinutätsproblem ...,* p. 35 *et seq.*

57 Crawford, *The Creation ...,* p. 690 et seq.

58 Brownlie, *Principles of Public International Law,* Oxford: Clarendon Press, p. 81.

[was] theoretical in these cases: what occurred upon liberation was the restoration, re-establishment of former States.'[59] Brownlie therefore speaks of 'qualified continuity.'[60] Wilfried Fiedler[61] and Giorgio Cansacchi[62] suggest that the extinction of an effectively annexed State should still be accepted once the extinction is recognized by the State community, as in the Austrian case. Among German international law scholars, for example Ulrich Scheuner was highly critical of the theory of the continued legal personality of Austria and instead proposed the introduction of a new legal institution—'the re-establishment of States.'[63] This legal theory has been re-presented by Ulrich Fastenrath, who suggests that a 'once-extinct State may be resurrected as the same legal person, and thus regain its previous position with regard to its former rights and obligations, if the actual extinction was caused by an unlawful act and is, therefore, legally negated.'[64] Note, however, that the provision referring to the re-establishment of States in the ILC's draft of the Convention on State succession[65] was deleted in the working process.[66]

A modified theory of identity without continuity by Werner Jakusch[67] invoked the old Roman legal concept *postliminium*. In ancient Rome, *postliminium* designated the legal process of restoration to former status when prisoners of war returned home.[68] Although in legal terms such a person had been considered dead during his disapperance or captivity, he could now regain his former legal status. Thus Jakusch rejects the fiction of the continued legal existence of Austria between 1938 and 1945, as the three constitutive elements set for a State—population, territory, and State power—were not all present during this period.[69] However, drawing parallels with the ancient *ius postliminii*

59 Brownlie, *Principles ...*, p. 82.

60 Brownlie, *Principles ...*, p. 82.

61 Fiedler, *Das Kontinuitätsproblem...*, p. 105.

62 Cansacchi, *op. cit.*, p. 47 *et seq.*

63 See U. Scheuner, 'Die Funktionsnachfolge und das Problem der staatsrechtlichen Kontinuität', in: FS *Nawiasky*, 1956, p. 9–48 at 19 *et seq.* and in: Marek's book review, *ZaöRV* 17 (57), 1956/p. 173–4.

64 U. Fastenrath, 'States, Extinction', in: *EPIL* 10, 1987, pp. 465–467 at 465.

65 See Art. 7, *ILC Yearbook* 1973, vol. I, p. 137.

66 *ILC Yearbook* 1973, vol. 1, 1239th mtg., para. 21.

67 See W Jakusch, 'Okkupationstheorie, Annexionstheorie und das ius postliminii', *25 ÖJZ* 1970, pp. 258–263.

68 See P. Kunig, Postliminium, *EPIL* 4, 1982, p. 140. See for further discussion: G. von Glahn, *The Occupation of Enemy Territory. A Commentary on the Law and Practice of Belligerent Occupation,* Minneapolis: The University of Minnesota Press, 1957, p. 257 *et seq;* G. Cansacchi, *op. cit.*, p. 50–51.

69 See Jakusch, *op. cit.*, p. 262.

concept, Jakusch accepts the extinction of Austria in 1938—*and* still accepts post-1945 Austria as the same State.[70]

Both Marek's and Crawford's (or Jakusch's) opposing theories contain a fiction—albeit of different kinds. Marek's own 'legal miracle' happens when she lets a State continue to exist in the case of effective annexation, or when the requirements of the three elements theory are not fulfilled, as there is no effective government. While the theory of identity without continuity seems more realistic (Austria *did not* exist during 1938–1945 and its exctinction was widely accepted, yet Austria *was* recognized as the same State later on), it lets another 'miracle' happen, by recognizing the sameness with a State that has become extinguished.[71]

The logical consequence of the theory of identity without continuity is the conclusion that recognition status accorded by third States largely determines whether or not a re-established State is the same.[72] The inherent difficulty here is that State recognition can be arbitrary and has often been non-unanimous. Marek, relying on a 'pure' legal principle (or fiction), is deeply critical with respect to use of recognition by other States as the ultimate test of State personality.

As an example of identity without continuity, Crawford uses the case of Syria (1958–1961).[73] This was a case of voluntary yet failed short-term unification. On November 1, 1958, Syria had united with Egypt, together constituting a State named the United Arab Republic. On September 28, 1961, following a military coup d'état, Syria again broke away from Egypt. During more than three years of the existence of the United Arab Republic, Syria had disappeared from the international community; it was no longer a member of the United Nations.[74] Yet after 1961 Syria was regarded by the State community as the same entity as before unification with Egypt (for example, its membership in the UN was 'revived' on October 19 1962.)[75]

70 See *ibid.*

71 Jakusch explicitly emphasizes the element of fiction in his application of *ius postliminii: 'Der Preis ist das offene Eingeständnis, mit einer Fiktion zu arbeiten—eine... der Jurisprudenz nicht fremde Denkweise!'* p. 263.

72 Crawford seems to recognize this difficulty when he states that 'where State existence is terminated either by consent of the entities concerned ... or validly in accordance with international law at the time, any subsequent assertion of 'identity' takes decidedly fictional overones, and may very well be non-opposable.' See Crawford, *The Creation...*, p. 408.

73 See Crawford, *The Creation...*, p. 407–8.

74 See Cansacchi, *op. cit.*, p. 56. See R. Young, 'The State of Syria: Old or New?', 56 *AJIL* 1962, p. 482.

75 Cf. Crawford, *The Creation...*, p. 407. See also Cansacchi, *op. cit.*, p. 57 and C. Rousseau, 'Syrie', 33 *RGDIP* 1962, p. 413 *et seq.*

Since nobody seriously doubted that Syria had not existed between 1958 and 1961 as a separate State, the Syrian case demonstrates that 'identity without continuity' is indeed possible in State practice. For adoption of this fiction, it was crucial that relatively little time had passed since the extinction of Syria in 1958, and that accepting the fiction of Syria's identity did not bring about legal or political disputes between the affected States. This was the very reason why other States voted in favour of the fiction of Syria's identity. The view of the President of the UN General Assembly in the respective plenary meeting highlights the special circumstances of the case:

> I have consulted many delegations on this question and the consensus seems to be that, in view of the special circumstances of this matter, Syria, an original Member of the United Nations, may be authorized to be represented in the General Assembly as it has specifically requested.[76]

Recognizing the State identity of Syria did not seem to harm anybody and offered a way out of a politically delicate situation. Nevertheless, the Syrian case must be distinguished from the Austrian, Czechoslovakian, and other cases. As the arguable loss of the Montevideo criteria for statehood occurred for very different reasons in those cases—voluntary union with Egypt in Syria and the illegal use or threat of force in the other cases—the protected values and the fictions employed by recognition of State identity were of a completely different kind. According to Joe Verhoeven, the fiction of Syrian 'suspension has no basis in law: it is either a matter of fantasy or politics.'[77]

Moreover, in defence of Marek's argument that identity always implies continuity, it is still arguable that the fiction of Syria's identity also implies the fiction of Syria's continuity—especially as the issue about Syria's continuity did not practically even arise. Konrad Bühler has analyzed the respective State practice and come to the conclusion that Syria was considered to continue to exist as an international person with restricted capacities even after unification.[78] The Syrian case would fit only with considerable difficulty into the predominant thesis that State identity implies continuity, but it is questionable whether the Syrian case should therefore constitute any new rule, or inevitably

76 Quoted in Young, *op. cit.*, p. 486.

77 J. Verhoeven, *La reconnaissance internationale dans la pratique contemporaine*, Paris: Pedone, 1975, p. 32.

78 K. Bühler, *State Succession and Membership in International Organizations. Legal Theories versus Political Pragmatism*, The Hague: Kluwer, 2001, p. 101. See also pp. 57–61, 97–102, 295–297.

lead to rejection of Marek's concept that, as a rule, State identity also implies State continuity.

However, it appears that the 'identity equals continuity?' dispute is in essence not a purely terminological or metaphysical one; rather, it is about the question: when do States become extinguished and under what conditions will/may they survive in international law? For the purposes of analyzing the Baltic case, the confusion may be primarily terminological: how to use both words: identity and continuity. Many authors, departing from the unity of the two concepts, have preferred to employ the word continuity for both phenomena simultaneously. This identification cannot be accepted for the purposes of further analysis. Therefore, the possible distinction between identity and continuity will lie at the very heart of this study of the Baltic case. For this reason, we accept the terminological specification introduced by Crawford and speak—until any further conclusions—about State identity in contexts when it is inconclusive whether identity without continuity or identity *and* continuity are implied.

b *What Are the Normative Consequences of State Identity?*

The hairsplitting in the debate 'identity and/or continuity' may seem quite metaphysical at first glance. However, it is directly related to the fundamental question: what are the normative consequences of State identity and continuity or succession? What does it mean to be the same State? Rudolf Bernhardt presents a circular definition of State continuity when he writes that State continuity is the continuation of a State as a subject of international law, notwithstanding external or internal changes.[79] Krystyna Marek, on the other hand, defines the identity of a State as the identity of its international rights and obligations, before and after the event which called that identity into question.[80] In other words, whenever there is State identity, there is also the identity of legal rights and obligations, and *vice versa*. Although Marek of course admits that in practice concessions have to be made from this proposition, she is certain about the basic trend: State identity means the identity of rights and duties.

79 See R. Bernhardt, 'Kontinuität', in: K. Strupp, H.-J. Schlochauer (Hg.) *Wörterbuch des Völkerrechts*, 1961, pp. 295–297 at 295 ('Völkerrechdiche Kontinuität bedeutet Fortbestand eines Völkerrechtssubjekts trotz äußerer oder innerer Wandlungen.')

80 Marek, *op. cit.*, p. 14.

Crawford is polemical about this view and argues that particular rights, duties and powers are rather consequences of statehood: the existence of a State is separate from the legal relations of that State.[81]

In the case of re-established States, these different views may involve important consequences. Following the position of Marek, there is a strong normative presumption for the restoration of former legal relations, rights and duties. Crawford's argument, on the other hand, seems to leave questions of the fate of former rights and duties more open. State identity would still exist independently from whether it was possible or necessary to restore specific legal relations from beforehand.

From the standpoint of rights and duties, it is evident that, according to international law, only a State which existed—'really' or fictionally—at a certain point in time can be subject to rights and duties, for example as an illegally occupied country. Depending on whether a State is held to be illegally annexed—and therefore further existing in international law—or extinct, it either can or cannot be an object of for example internationally wrongful acts during the period of its *de facto* non-existence. Another way to look at it would be to equate existence with the validity of rights and duties.

c *The Basis in International Law for State Identity in World War II Annexation Cases*

i *Occupatio Quasi Bellica* and Other Auxiliary Theories

Offering legal explanations for World War II State continuity/identity cases, international law scholars have tried *inter alia* to accommodate arguments derived from established customary rules preserving State identity. In the Austrian discussion, Alfred Verdross coined the term *occupatio quasi bellica* and argued that the rule protecting States from extinction in cases of *occupatio bellica* also expands to similarly forcible, quasi-belligerent occupation, even though a state of war was not established.[82] At the same time, Wilfried Fiedler has persistently rejected this expansion of the 'continuity under occupation' rule to quasi-belligerent occupation.[83] However, later parallel developments in

81 Crawford, *The Creation...*, pp. 401–2.

82 See A. Verdross, 'Die völkerrechtliche Identität von Staaten', in: *FS H. Klang*, Wien: Springer-Verlag, 195, p. 20.

83 See Fiedler, *Das Kontinuitätsproblem ...*, p. 57 and Fiedler, 'Continuity', *EPIL*, 1987, pp. 806–809 at 808. See also Fiedler, *Staatskontinuität und Verfassungsrechtsprechu ng. Zum Begriff der Kontinuität ...*, p. 53: '*Diese Ausdehnung hat sich jedoch nicht allgemein durchgesetzt. Sie ist insoweit abzulehnen, als rein subjektive Erwägungen, Absichten und Pläne einzelner Staatsmänner oder Regierungen zu irgendeiner Zeit vor dem Kriegsausbruch herangezogen*

international humanitarian law seem to confirm—at least retrospectively—the correctness of Verdross's analogy.[84]

The main difficulty in the Austrian case, however, was not whether Austria was occupied militarily or not, but that Austria was also effectively annexed. Continuity under occupation rule, as established in earlier practice and doctrine, was previously not used to cover cases where the occupied country had been effectively subsumed.

ii Illegality of Annexation Due to Use of Force

Inevitably, the legally relevant essence of the Ethiopian, Austrian, Albanian and Czechoslovakian cases appeared to be located elsewhere and clearly had something to do with the illegality of those annexations pursued by the Axis powers. In 1928 and afterwards, international law had experienced a true normative revolution which prohibited States any recourse to war, except in self-defence. Before 1928, recourse to military force had been legal under international law—a true continuation of politics by other means', as Prussian general Carl von Clausewitz maintained. By accepting the legality of war, it was only natural that international law would accept the legality of its fruits—that is, of conquest and annexation. In 1896, Alphonse Rivier, a Swiss international lawyer working in Brussels declared: '*Conquest justifies itself by its very existence, like war, of which it is a natural consequence. The source of the law of nations is positive, constrained to take into account of what is.*'[85] This changed after 1928, and the impact of this change in international law is, by its revolutionary nature, comparable only to the introduction of the concept of human rights as part of international law, not merely domestic jurisdiction, in the decades following World War II.[86]

Paris on August 27, 1928, saw the adoption of the so-called Kellogg-Briand Pact, an international treaty in which States banned 'war as instrument of

---

und für rechtlich maßgebend erklärt werden, so daß der unmittelbare Zusammenhang zur effektiven militärischen Inbesitznahme fehlt.'

84 See common Art. 2 para 2 of four 1949 Geneva Red Cross Conventions: 'The Conventions shall also apply to all cases of partial or total occupation of the territory of a High Contracting Party, even if the said occupation meets with no armed resistance.' This provision makes it unreasonable to make a further distinction between 'belligerent' and 'quasi-belligerent' occupations. There is no reason why this should make a difference in the field of State continuity.

85 A. Rivier, *Principes du droit des gens*, 1896, I Tome, Paris: A. Rousseau, p. 181. (transl.)

86 For a recent positive appraisal of the prohibition of the use of force, see also: G. Seidel, 'Die Völkerrechtsordnung an der Schwelle zum 21. Jahrhundert', 38 *AVR* 2000, p. 23.

national politics.'[87] The Pact entered into force on July 24, 1929. By the end of 1938, 63 States, that is, almost all States in existence at the time, had become members of the Pact.[88] The example of the Kellogg-Briand Pact was followed by similar regional commitments such as the Saavedra Lamas Treaty which was signed on October 10, 1933 by Latin American States.[89]

Notwithstanding these developments, debate has been ongoing in international legal literature about when exactly prohibition of the use of military force became a recognized part of general international law. It has been suggested by some authors that the years between adoption of the Kellogg-Briand Pact in 1928 and adoption of the UN Charter in 1945[90] still remained a sort of legal transition period in this respect. Those scholars have argued that notwithstanding legal commitments such as the 1928 Kellogg-Briand Pact, State practice and review of international law manuals published at the time confirm that general international law did not prohibit recourse to military force during the late 1930s or generally during World War II.[91]

This is clearly a minority view and seems to have been convincingly rejected in post-World War II State practice and legal pronouncements, such as those made at the Nuremberg war crimes trials. The case has been convincingly argued by Ian Brownlie.[92] The legal character of an international legal norm cannot be denied on the basis that this norm has been violated—even though violations of the Kellogg-Briand Pact during World War II certainly brought under attack not only this newly created norm but the relevance of international law itself.

87 *General Treaty for Renunciation of War as an Instrument of National Policy*, LNTS, Vol. 94 (1929), pp. 57–64.

88 See further O.A. Hathaway, S.J. Shapiro, *The Internationalists. How a Radical Plan to Outaw War Remade the World*, New York: Simon & Schuster, 2017.

89 *Anti-war Treaty of Non-Aggression and Conciliation* (*Saavedra Lamas Treaty*); October 10, 1933; 49 Stat. 3363; Treaty Series 906.

90 *The Charter of the United Nations of June 26, 1945*, XV UNCIO, 355.

91 See e.g. G.-H. Gornig, *Der Hitler-Stalin-Pakt. Eine völkerrechtliche Studie*, Frankfurt: Peter Lang, 1990, pp. 65–6.

92 I. Brownlie, The *Use of Force in International Law*, Oxford: Clarendon Press, 1963, pp. 107–111, but also pp. 84–88, 88–89—in which the author proves that measures short of war and the threat of the use of force were prohibited in 1939. Among recent authors writing on State continuity and succession, Vladimir-Djuro Degan starts with the presumption that 'after the Kellogg-Briand Pact of 1928' annexation via subjugation was no more legal. See V.-D. Degan, 'Création et disparition de l'État (À la lumière du démembrement de trois fédérations multiethniques en Europe)', 279 *RCADI* 1999, p. 283.

The legality of annexation depends upon whether the use of force appears to be legal.[93] Although the predominant view holds that the use of military force was outlawed in post-1928 general international law, it has nevertheless been disputed whether the rule unconditionally prohibiting forcible annexations is equally old.[94] For example, Oliver Dörr has extensively elaborated upon the thesis that, before 1945, forcible annexation could still be legal under international law, and thus create legal title over territory seized.[95] This view about annexation can logically be maintained only when the use of force in the late-1930s is held to be legal under general international law. Otherwise, in the words of Sir Hersch Lauterpacht:

> ...admettre qu'un acte illégal, ou ses conséquences ou manifestations immédiates, puisse devenir une source de droits juridiques pour le transgresseur de la loi, c'est introduire dans le systéme juridique une contradiction qui ne peut être résolue que par la négation de son caractère juridique.[96]

A situation when the use of military force would be illegal, but incorporation of the territory seized by the aggressor (annexation) might become legal, is illogical. Why bother to prohibit aggression when the aggressor knows that

---

93 See R.L. Bindschedler, 'Annexation', in: *EPIL*, 1992, Inst. I, p. 169. See generally: G. Schulz, 'Die Entwicklung des völkerrechtlichen Annexionsverbots', in: *Jahrbuch der Albertus-Universität zu Königsberg/Preußen*, Band XII, 1962.

94 See Langer, *op. cit.* p. 95 *et seq.*

95 See O. Dörr, *Inkorporation als Tatbestandsmerkmal der Staatensukzession*, 1995, p. 350–355 and p. 67: '*Für die Zeit bis 1945 ist dementsprechend davon auszugehen, daß (nicht-kriegerische) Annexionen nicht schon* eo ipso, *d.h. als Emanation des ihnen inhärenten Elements der Gewalt, völkerrechtswidrig waren.*' p. 82: '*Das aus der Zeit des sog. klassischen Völkerrechts stammende Eroberungs- und Annexionsrecht war als Bestandteil des geltenden Völkergewohnheitsrechts bis zum Ende des 2. Weltkrieges nicht wirklich überwunden, auch wenn sich im partikulären Völkervertragsrecht bereits weitgehende Einschränkungen fanden und der Annexion unter Geltung von Völkerbundsatzung und Briand-Kellogg-Pakt über ihre partielle rechtliche Ächtung hinaus gewiß auch ein allgemeiner Makel des moralisch-ethisch verwerflichen anhaftete.*' p. 94: '*nach Inkrafttreten der UN-Charta Raum gewinnende Rechtsüberzeugung von der Unzulässigkeit jeder Annexion sich in der gerichtlichen Praxis der unmittelbaren Nachkriegszeit noch nicht wirklich durchgesetzt hatte—jedenfolls nicht insoweit, als Handlungen vor Ende des 2. Weltkrieges in Frage standen.*'

96 H. Lauterpacht, 'Règles générales du droit de la paix', 62 *RCADI* 1937, p. 291. "To admit that an illegal act, or its immediate consequences or manifestations, may become a source of legal rights for the transgressor of the law, is to introduce into the legal system a contradiction that can only be resolved by denying its legal character."

the ultimate goal of its aggression—acquisition of foreign territory—could still acquire legal quality?[97] What would be the meaning of an international legal norm prohibiting the use of force, but allowing enjoyment of its fruits? Without the sanction of unconditional illegality of annexation, prohibition of the use of force would also not not fulfill its preventive function, namely of deterring future aggressors.

Following adoption of the League of Nations Statute, German international law scholar Walter Schätzel argued that annexation had become illegal in international law, and that the only way to turn annexation into legal title would be recognition of the illegal situation by the international community.[98] But why would other States recognize such an illegal situation at all? At the same time, another German scholar, Boris Meissner argued that a norm that would have rendered annexation of seized territory null and void in all circumstances had not yet emerged with adoption of the Kellogg-Briand Pact in 1928. At least initially after adoption of the prohibition of use of force, in the years following 1928 (that is, before the rule *eo ipso* prohibiting annexation had crystallized in international law), the legal consequences were ultimately left for the rest of the international community to decide.[99] Recognition of forcible seizure by the international community could 'cure' the initial illegality of the conquest and give rise to legal title for the invader. Logically, such acceptance of the annexation by the community of States brought about the extinction of the annexed State.[100] And *vice versa*—refusal by a considerable number of States to accord full recognition to annexation served as conclusive evidence of its illegality, proving that the invader had not succeeded in acquiring legal title over the seized territory, and, moreover, that the conquered State had not been extinguished in terms of international law.[101]

---

97 Cf. Jennings, *The Acquisition of Territory…*, p. 54 and M.M. McMahon, *Conquest in Modern International Law*, Washington, DC: Catholic University of America Press, 1940, p. 13.

98 See W. Schätzel, *Völkerbund und Gebietserwerb*, Berlin, 1919, pp. 11–34; W. Schätzel, *Die Annexion im Völkerrecht*, Berlin, 1920, pp. 91, 143, 164. Both reprinted in and quoted from W. Schätzel, *Das Recht des völkerrechtfichen Gebietserwerbs*, Bonn: Ludwig Röhrscheid Verlag, 1959.

99 See B. Meissner, *Die Sowjetunion, die baltischen Staaten und das Völkerrecht*, Köln: Verlag Politik und Wirtschaft, 1956, p. 288–289.

100 So Repečka, *op. cit.*, p. 255.

101 Arnold Raestad argued in 1939 that a State can exist in international law in two ways: '*par les propres moyens, et par la volonté des autres Etats de ne pas reconnaître une débellatio.*' See A. Raestad, 'La cession des États d'après le Droit des Gens', 66 *Revue de Droit International et et de législation comparée*, 1939, p. 449. (Even when '*existence effective*' is destroyed, '*existence actualisée*' can continue.)

Sir Hersch Lauterpacht also attributed importance to the act of nonrecognition by the community of States:

> When the acts in question are in breach of general international law, such recognition... assumes the character of a quasi-legislative measure in the general interest of international society and international peace.[102]

Recognition of conquest by the community of States was not completely ruled out by British international lawyer Robert Jennings even as late as 1963:

> ... [the] international community may (...) eventually signify assent to the new position and thus by recognition create a title. This possibility in no way contradicts the main proposition that force does not of itself create a title, because the international community would from this point of view be exercising a quasi-legislative function.[103]

It is realistic to attribute a certain 'law-creating-power' to recognition by third States of an illegal situation during the years immediately following 1928. This, however, does not alter the basic presumption following 1928—the *prima facie* illegality of an annexation resulting from the use of force. Several renowned lawyers, such as Hans Wehberg, general secretary of the Institut de Droit International, even argued in the pre-World War II context that annexation was *ipso iure* null and void, and that even recognition by third States would not alter such nullity.[104]

In conclusion, the illegality of forcible annexations after the almost universal adoption of the Kellogg-Briand Pact in 1928 has been a presumption in international law. However, during a transition period following adoption of the Pact, the eventual recognition of conquest by the State community was still legally an option, at least in terms of *Realpolitik*. There did not yet exist *opinio iuris* that recognition of a situation illegally brought about is itself illegal or even that is violates a peremptory norm of international law (*jus cogens*). Recognition of forcible annexation by all or almost all members of the community of

102 H. Lauterpacht, *Recognition in International Law,* Cambridge, 1947, p. 412. See also p. 429.

103 Jennings, *The Acquisition ...*, p. 62.

104 H. Wehberg, *Krieg und Eroberung im Wandel des Völkerrechts,* Frankfurt a.M.: Alfred Metzner Verlag, 1953, pp. 105–107 (writing that recognition of the Italian annexation of Ethiopia was illegal, and May 12, 1938, the day when the League of Nations gave up its non-recognition policy 'one of the saddest hours of the League of Nations', p. 107.)

States did have the capacity to 'cure' the initial illegality of annexation. Annexation could thus only become legal in cases when the annexation would have been steady and undisputed.[105] When the annexation was still disputed by other powers, it was not 'firmly established',[106] and therefore could not create a legitimate title under international law. In 1939, this position was convincingly maintained by the Norwegian internationalist Arnold Ræstad, according to whom:

> pour décider si un État a cessé d'exister ou non, il faut se rapporter à l'attitude de la collectivité des États, de cette même collectivité a laquelle incombe la reconnaissance d'un nouveau État.[107]

However, non-recognition of illegal acts *per se* did not *make* those acts illegal; it was only a further indication of their illegality, which originated from international law. In determining the illegality of forcible annexation, the non-recognition policy exercized by the State community therefore played only a supportive role, further confirming the illegality of the acts in question. It follows from this view that even politically motivated recognition of an illegal situation—there was no duty of non-recognition in international law as of 1939[108]—could not give title to the annexing State unless accorded to by the whole community of States.

The crucial aspect of the illegality of annexation explains why State identity was not recognized, as in the Algerian case. Because the illegality of annexation has been the key element in the confirmation of identity and continuity of resurrected States, attempts to expand resurrection of the same subject to cases

105 Verdross, *Die völkerrechtliche Identität...*, p. 20. See also Repečka, *op. cit.*, p. 94 and Marek, p. 329 ('The effectiveness of the illegal act must be beyond doubt and every reasonable chance of a *restitutio ad integrum* must be excluded.')

106 According to Kelsen, in order for an annexation to become legal, it should have been 'firmly established.' See H. Kelsen, *General Theory of State and Law*, 1946, p. 214 *et seq.* Verdross uses this argument in favour of his own position, pointing out that an annexation can only be 'firmly established' when it is no longer disputed by other powers. See Verdross, *op. cit.*, p. 20.

107 Raestad, *La cession des États...*, p. 447. "In deciding whether a State has ceased to exist or not, it is necessary to refer to the attitude of the collectivity of States, of the same collectivity to which the recognition of a new State is incumbent upon it."

108 Ulrich Scheuner wrote in 1951 that in international law 'darf (...), da es an einer übergeordneten internationalen Macht fehlt, jeder Staat für sich entscheiden, ob und zu welchem Zeitpunkt er (...) der Annexion eines Staates durch einen anderen seine Anerkennung geben will.' See Scheuner 'Entstehung, Altersstufen...', *Kölner ZfSoz* 1951/1952 p. 210.

of the independence of colonies were rejected in both State practice and legal literature.[109] In jurisprudence, such a concept has only been employed in the dissenting opinion of Judge Moreno Quintana in the Indo-Portugese dispute at the ICJ.[110] In elaborating on this concept, the international law scholar of Polish origin, Charles H. Alexandrowicz, suggested that Ceylon (now Sri Lanka), Burma (now Myanmar), India or Indonesia would not be new subjects in the community of States, but that they simply 'reverted to sovereignty' in the post-World War II process of decolonization.[111] According to Alexandrowicz, such a reversion to sovereignty would create a special presumption in favour of the reverting State which ordinary succession would not create—'the reverting State can rely on a presumption of reversion to the same quantum and measure of sovereignty as that which it had to abandon at the moment of elimination from the Family of Nations in the past.'[112] Contrary to Alexandrowicz' position, there are not many indications in State practice that those colonies which had been independent prior to colonialization had received preferential treatment compared with colonized peoples unable to look back to a pre-colonial period of statehood with the same name and identity. Generally, all such States could start their post-colonial existence as 'clean slates'—no automatic succession of the legal obligations of the colonial time took place. This, however, is not to deny that denial of reversion to sovereignty in such cases in international law was an expression of the Eurocentrism of international law at the time.[113]

iii The Relevance of the People in Determining the Illegality and Continuity of Statehood

In the cases analyzed here involving World War II, illegality of the use of force was also connected with violation of the rights of the affected peoples. Several authors, most notably from Austria, have explained the continuity of

---

109 See Crawford, *The Creation*.... See also I. Seidl-Hohenveldern, *Völkerrecht*, 9. Aufl., 1997, Rdnr. 1394 and H. Krieger, *Das Effektivitätsprinzip*..., p. 173.

110 'India made no fundamental change in the established system.... We must not forget that India, as the territorial successor, was not acquiring the territory for the first time, but was recovering an independence (sovereignty) long lost since. Its legal position at once reverted to what it had been more than a hundred years before, as though British occupation had made no difference.' See *Case Concerning Right of Passage over Indian Territory (Merits)*, Judgment of 12.4.1969 ICJ Reports 1960, p. 6 at 95.

111 C.H. Alexandrowicz, 'New and Original States. The Issue of Reversion to Sovereignty', 45 *Int'l Aff.* 1969, p. 471.

112 See Alexandrowicz, *op. cit.*, p. 478.

113 See also J.J.G. Syatow, 'Old and New States—a Misleading Distinction for Future International Law and International Relations', in: *Le droit international demain*. Université de Neuchatel, Série juridique No. 8, Neuchatel: Éditions Ides et Calendes, 1974.

the illegally annexed State with another aspect: the continuity of its people (population). Alfred Verdross argued that not a government, but in the first place a people forms a State.[114] It is interesting to note that Soviet international law doctrine also accepted the special role of the people for the State—thus, Roman L. Borbov argued that the people of the State are the 'essence of the international legal subjectivity of a given State.'[115]

Alfred Verdross traced this concept back to Hugo Grotius, who had emphasized the continuity of international legal responsibility because of the continuity of the people. For Verdross, this was the reason '*warum nach Völkerrecht die Identität des Staates nicht von der Identität seiner Verfassung, sondern von der Kontinuität seiner sich ständig in der Geschlechterfolge erneuernden Personengemeinschaft abhängt.*'[116] A similar argument was made by another Austrian scholar, Stephan Verosta.[117] However, the German international law professor Ulrich Scheuner criticized this position by pointing out that the 'real identity' of the population would also continue in the case of (legal) annexation; what must be meant (by Verosta) is the continuity of the will to maintain national unity (*Fortbestand eines nationalen Einheitswillens;* continuation of a national will to form a whole/be as one). The theory that the people of a State are the 'guardians' of an (illegally annexed) State has its roots in an unconventional theory of State which suggests 'the living mental-political unity of the people in the sense of a national consciousness' as a crucial element of the State.[118]

---

114 A. Verdross, *Die völkerrechtliche Identität von Staaten...*, p. 19. ('Hingegen geht das moderne Völkerrecht bei der Beurteilung der Identität der Staaten von ihrer Bevölkerungaus. (...) nicht die Regierung, sondern das Staatsvolk das Völkerrechtssubjekt 'Staat' konstituiert.')

115 Р.Л. Борбов, *Основные проблемы меорцц межбународиого права,* Москва: Международные отношения, 1968, p. 64.

116 Verdross, *op. cit.*, p. 19. See also Verdross/Simma, *Universelles Völkerrecht,* 3. Auflage, Berlin: Ducker & Humblot, 1984, § 390 *et seq.*, p. 231. "Why, according to international law, the identity of the state does not depend on the identity of its constitution, but on the continuity of its community of persons, which is constantly renewing itself in the sequence of persons."

117 See Verosta, *Die internationale Stellung Österreichs 1938–1947,* Wien, 1947, p. 9.

118 Such as e.g. the theory of Nikolai Hartmann of the 'objective common spirit that lives in the State' (*im Staate lebendiger objektiver Gemeingeist*). See for references and critique U. Scheuner, 'Die Funktionsnachfolge...', in: *F.S. Nawiasky*, p. 21 One historic example of how such an argument is taken to the extreme, is the explanation of S. Cybichowski about the continuity of the Polish State from 1775–1918, a doubtful attempt to make the case for the Polish continuity to the national socialists in their language: '*Dies ist besonders klar, wenn man sich auf den Standpunkt der nationalsozialistischen Rechts- und Staatsauffosung stellt, die dem Volke den Vorrang vor dem Staate einräumt.* (...) *In der Genesis des Völkerrechts ist nicht der Staat, sondern das Volk die elementare Einheit, die rationale Monade der Wissenschaft.* (...) *Der Schöpfer des Völkerrechts Grotius kannte dieses Prinzip noch nicht*

Scheuner argues that in order not to become a mere fiction, such a 'will to mental continuity' must be confirmed by acts of the population (resistance, fighting, and the like).[119]

The impact of the people and its right to self-determination upon statehood was extensively discussed in the case of Germany's legal status after its defeat in World War II. The debated issue was, in particular, whether the German State had become extinct or continued to exist. At least from the point of view of the 'three-elements-theory', lack of a German government after the arrest of the members of the Dönitz government in May 1945 spoke against the continued existence of the German State. Hans Kelsen, among other scholars, argued that Germany had become extinct.[120] Following the allied decisions at the Potsdam conference, the eastern parts of pre-1938 Germany were annexed by Poland and the USSR. At the same time, the victorious Allies did not intend to annex the whole territory of the defeated *Reich*, and there was thus no *animus* which would operate as a precondition for effective annexation.

In 1949, two German States, one in the West and the other in the East, were proclaimed in the occupation zones of the Western Allies and the USSR. This was another factor which seemed to suggest that the previous German State had become extinct. However, the Federal Republic of Germany claimed that this was not the case and that the legal personality of the German *Reich* continued in the shape of the FRG.[121] West German international law scholars based the State continuity claim in particular upon the argument that the division of Germany was brought about in violation of the German people's right to self-determination.[122] Until the admission of both German States to the UN

(...) *Man wird hervorheben müssen, dass das polnische Volk als politische, moralische und rechtliche Einheit* (...) *niemals seine Existenz eingebüßt hat. Die polnische Nation ist nicht nur eine politische und moralische, sondern auch eine rechtliche Einheit, wobei das Wort Recht nicht eine Summe von formalen Normen, sondern den Inbegriff auf tiefster sittlicher Grundlage ruhender, vom Boden, Blut und Rasse abhängender Lebensregeln bedeutet* (...)' See S. Cybichowski, 'Das völkerrechtliche Okkupationsrecht', 18 *Z. für VR* 1934, pp. 318–319.

119 Scheuner, 'Die Funktionsnachfolge...', in: FS *Nawiasky*, 1956, p. 21.

120 See H. Kelsen, 'The Legal Status of Germany to be Established Immediately upon Termination of War', 38 *AJIL* 1944, p. 680 *et seq* and in particular 'The Legal Status of Germany According to the Declaration of Berlin', 39 *AJIL* 1945, p. 518 *et seq.*

121 *GLV*-Urteil, BVerfGE 36, 1973, I, 15–16; *Teso*-Urteil, BVerfGE 77, 137. See for an overview of the respective doctrinal issues G. Ress, *Die Rechtslage Deutschlands nach dem Grundlagenvertrag vom 21. Dezember 1972*, Berlin: Springer, 1978 and D. Blumenwitz, *What is Germany? Exploring Germany's Status after World War II*, Bonn: Kulturstiftung der dt. Vertriebenen, 1989.

122 See e.g. C. Tomuschat, 'Staatsvolk ohne Staat? Zum Teso-Urteil des Bundesverfassungs gerichts (BverfGE 77, 137)', in: FS *Karl Doehring*, Heidelberg: Springer, p. 1000 and E. Klein, *Das Selbstbestimmungsrecht der Völker und die deutsche Frage, 1990.*

in 1973, the Western powers often contended that as the GDR was created and supported by the Soviet occupation regime, it lacked the essentials of a State.[123] Moreover, in West German legal scholarship and case law, different theoretical interpretations emerged as to this identity and continuity claim.

During the following decades when the FRG controlled only a part of the *Reich*'s former territory, and another German State, the GDR, was admitted to the UN and recognized as a sovereign State by the FRG and other States, the claim of the continuity of the German State included a considerable element of legal fiction.[124] In any case, it was a quite unorthodox doctrine when it was argued, on the basis of the jurisprudence of the German Constitutional Court and in the words of Professor Georg Ress, that on the one hand, 'the FRG recognized the GDR at the international level as a State in the same way as the Federal Republic is itself a State under international law', but at the same time, 'the relations between the FRG and the GDR are not only of an international law nature, but a mixture of State law (internal law) and of international law.'[125] It was also from the point of view of effectiveness that Soviet and East German legal scholars criticized the Western 'imperialistic' doctrine of one indivisible Germany.[126]

Yet the German continuity claim subsequently found recognition in State practice, and today's unified Germany is, in terms of international legal personality, considered to be identical with the German *Reich*. Certain elements of fiction in this legal claim have already been pointed out; none the less, this claim has been recognized. In a way, it can be argued that history gave the right to the (West) German view.

The lessons to be drawn from the discussion of Germany's legal status are twofold. On the one hand, the success of claims to statehood in difficult cases has a lot to do with political developments: who prevails and who does not. The claim of the continuity of the German State was not only a legal, but also a political claim as it was aimed at the re-unification of Germany. This theory proved to be successful *inter alia* because the German claim for re-unification proved to be successful, not only because of the inherent supremacy of its legal arguments over the effectiveness doctrine.

On the other hand, the acceptance of Germany's legal position in State practice still demonstrates that after World War II, international legal practice had started to accept certain 'fictitious' claims to statehood when backed by some

123 See e.g. C. Tomuschat, *General Course...*, 2000, p. 97.

124 See C. Tomuschat, *Staatsvolk ohne Staat?...* 1990, p. 998.

125 See G. Ress, 'Germany, Legal Status after World War II', 10 *EPIL* 1987, p. 199.

126 See e.g. D.I. Feldman, 'Illegality of the Hallstein Doctrine', *Soviet YBIL* 1962, pp. 158–165.

of the emerging fundamental norms of international law, such as the right of peoples to self-determination.[127]

The relevance of the people and the departure from the formalistic application of the Montevideo criteria is also highlighted by Wilfried Fiedler, who was otherwise quite critical of 'fictional' continuity claims:

> More recent developments in international law tend to accentuate material elements. While already in the 19th century international law often recognized the existence of nations or peoples in spite of foreign occupation, this aspect gained further significance with the development of the right of self-determination in the 20th century. The turning away from formal criteria was strengthened by the prohibition of the use of force and annexation. This general trend in international law, which has also become evident in the work of the United Nations, justifies giving priority to the right of self-determination in the solution of problems of continuity, provided that this right is actually exercised in an internationally perceptible manner.[128]

5 Implications of the Illegality of Annexation for State Personality

In the light of the illegal annexation cases, international lawyers started to argue that illegality of annexation prevents extinction of the annexed State.[129] Starting from the illegality of the Axis annexations in the cases of Ethiopia, Austria, Albania and Czechoslovakia, Krystyna Marek has derived a legal explanation for the survival of those States from the maxim *ex injuria ius non oritur*.[130]

---

127 According to Christian Tomuschat: '*At first glance, it seems awkward that all of the citizens of one State are considered by another State to be at the same time its citizens. But there existed still a powerful interlocking factor holding the Germans in East and West together, to wit the right of self determination.*' See *General Course*, 2000, p. 99.

128 Fiedler, 'Continuity', *EPIL*, p. 808 *et seq.* Similar ideas were expressed by Fiedler already in 1970 ('*Staatskontinuität und...*'): '*Die Nation ist nach geltendem Völkerrecht der wichtigste Träger staatlicher Kontinuität (...) Die Kritik... wird jedoch an der Tatsache nicht vorbeigehen können, daß das geltende Völkerrecht im Rahmen des Identitätsproblems besonderen Wert auf den Fortbestand des Staatsvolkes—nicht zuletzt auch aus Haftungsgründen—legt und die Identitätsentscheidung hiernach mit ausrichtet.*' p. 67.

129 See e.g. G. Scelle, 'Die Annexion Abessiniens durch Italien und der Völkerbund', in: 3 *Völkerbund und Völkerrecht* 1936/37, pp. 167–172.

130 See Marek, *op. cit.*, with respect to Ethiopia p. 279, Czechoslovakia p. 328 *et seq.*, Albania p. 337, Austria p. 367–368.

> It is this principle alone which—throughout all changing attitudes of third States—can provide a legal explanation of that survival, which indeed *makes* it a legal survival and not an arbitrary political fiction.[131]

Marek points out that if mere recognition by other States were to be the decisive criterion, one would be forced to accept the extinction of these States through a 'death sentence' pronounced by other States, that is, those that initially recognized the extinction of Austria and Czechslovakia in 1938/1939.[132] Otherwise, it:

> ...would follow that the Czechoslovak Republic passed through some very peculiar vicissitudes indeed as regards her international status: it existed for some time after March 15, 1939, then it ceased to exist, then it was in existence again and, what is supremely puzzling, not as a new State but precisely as the old one. Moreover, even then it existed in relation to the Allied countries, while it did not exist in relation to the Axis and some of the neutrals (e.g. Switzerland).[133]

But would not the principle *ex injuria ius non oritur* be too abstract and general to preserve a State from extinction in a case of illegal annexation? A substantive segment of post-World War II international legal scholarship remained critical of the explanations and justifications given for Austrian, Czecholovakian and other continuity. Hans Kelsen even went as far as to deny the legal value of the principle *ex injuria ius non oritur* in international law.[134] Not surprisingly, similar dismissive views with respect to the '*ex injuria*' principle had been taken *inter alia* by Italian legal scholars during the fascist period.[135]

---

131 Marek, *op. cit.*, p. 329.

132 On the (ir)relevance of recognition by other States, see Marek, *op. cit.*, generally p. 130–161, but in particular pp. 279–281 (Ethiopia), p. 327 (Czechoslovakia). For the contrary argument that indeed, the general recognition of e.g. Austrian incorporation by Germany *meant* the extinction of Austria, see Cansacchi, *op. cit.*, p. 48.

133 Marek, *op. cit.*, p. 328.

134 '*Under general international law, the states are obliged to respect the territorial integrity of the other states; but a violation of this obligation does not exclude the change of the legal situation. The principle advocated by some writers—ex injuria jus non oritur ('a right cannot originate in an illegal act')—does not, or not without important exceptions, apply in international law.*' See H. Kelsen, *Principles of International Law,* 2nd edn., rev. and ed. by R. W. Tucker, New York: Holt, Rinehart, and Winston, 1967, p. 316 *et seq.*

135 See e.g. G. Ottolenghi, 'Il principo di effictività e la sua funzione nell' ordinamento internazionale', 15 *Rivista di diritto internazionale* 1936, esp. pp. 3–33 and Condorelli, 'Ex facto jus oritur', *Rivista internazionela di filosofia del diritto*, 1931, pp. 115–139.

The application and legal consequences of the principle *ex injuria ius non oritur* have remained disputed until our times. Most international lawyers would agree that the principle of effectiveness remains central to the system of international law.[136] Walter Rudolf argued in 1986 that '(*d*)*er Verzicht auf das* ius ad bellum *und auf die Anwendung jeder Gewalt berührt den Staatsbegriff* (*wenig*).'[137] In the context of State identity and continuity in the Austrian case, Wilfried Fiedler criticized the validity of the principle *ex injuria ius non oritur*:

> Aus dem Rechtswidrigkeitsurteil (...) folgt jedoch nicht notwendig der *ununterbrochene* Fortbestand eines Staates als Völkerrechtssubjekt. (...) Daher kann auch das von Marek herangezogene Prinzip *ex injuria ius non oritur* die *ununterbrochene* Identitat Österreichs nicht nachweisen, mochte die Rechtswidrigkeit des Anschlusses auch Motiv und politische Triebfeder fur die Wiederherstellung des Staates abgegeben haben.[138]

Here, the fundamental conceptual disagreement among international lawyers becomes evident: can the illegality of annexation compensate for lack of effectivity in terms of the continued existence of States?[139] Should the Montevideo requirements for statehood be put aside when the act of annexation is illegal? Is international law strong enough to uphold such an approach? If so, then under what circumstances; and for how long? Ulrich Scheuner sums up the critique from the point of view of realists: '*Da aber der Fortbestand eines Staates einen Tatbestand darstellt, der sich auf eine soziologische Realität gründet, wird dadurch* [*der Rechtswidrigkeit der Annexion*] *an dem Untergang des Staates als faktischem Vorgang nichts geändert*.'[140] It was always the presumption of the

136 See J. Stone, 'What Price Effictiveness?', 50 *ASIL Proc.* 1956, pp. 198–206 at 198.

137 See W. Rudolf, *Wandel des Staatsbegriffs im Völkerrecht?*, Bonn: Europa Union Verlag, 1986, p. 40. "Renunciation of *jus ad bellum* and the use of all force has little effect on the concept of he State."

138 W. Fiedler, *Das Kontinuitätsproblem*..., p. 100–101. "However, the judgment of illegality (...) does not necessarily result in the uninterrupted continued existence of a state as a subject of international law. (...) Therefore, even the principle *ex injuria ius non oritur* used by Marek cannot prove the uninterrupted identity of Austria, even if the illegality of the annexation may have given rise to the motive and political driving force for the restoration of the State."

139 U. Scheuner, 'Entstehung, Altersstufen und Untergang von Staaten im Lichte des Rechts', in: 4 *Kölner Zeitschrift für Soziologie* 1951/52, pp. 208–221 at 209.

140 U. Scheuner, 'Die Funktionsnachfolge und das Problem der...', *FS Nawiasky*, 1956, p. 20. "However, since the continued existence of a State constitutes an offence based on a sociological reality, it [the illegality of annexation] does not alter the demise of the State as a de facto operation/process."

classic doctrine that law does not govern either the coming into existence or the disappearance of States.

Altogether, however, the fiction of the legal identity of Austria and other illegally annexed States, was there (in State practice), and traditional theory failed to explain this phenomenon in legal terms. The conservative segment of legal doctrine seemed to be a prisoner of the Montevideo legacy, of a too literal application of the three constitutive elements of statehood, and of the effectiveness principle. It regarded cases where State identity was recognized notwithstanding effective annexation with realist suspicion, as uneasy and strange anomalies, products of fictional politics. It was more worried about the 'relevance' of international law when State identity was recognized notwithstanding the temporary *de facto* disappearance of a State than when a State was annexed following the illegal use of force. The German international lawyer Walter Rudolf maintained that the concept of a State has not substantially changed in international law,[141] and that—one realizes *why* international lawyers should defend the existing definition of statehood, almost like medieval knights a castle against the infidels—'*Mit dem Staatsbegriff steht und fällt die Völkerrechtsordnung*.'[142]

For international lawyers who did not see certain departures from the Montevideo criteria as a heresy, the question has been instead: what is the content of new international law rules; how far has international law gone — and how far can it go—in defence of legality and in rejecting the argument of effectiveness when effectiveness was created illegally? Modern practice has supported the proposition that statehood need not always be equated with effectiveness; statehood is no longer simply 'a factual situation but a legally defined claim of right, specifically to the competence to govern a certain territory.'[143] This means not only that State practice has started to make important qualifications to the Montevideo criteria, but also that in international law 'there is (...) no generally accepted and satisfactory legal definition of statehood,'[144] even though most lawyers seem to agree that the Montevideo criteria have at least remained a useful starting point for analysis of statehood.

Soviet legal doctrine did not have problems with the idea of the continued existence of illegally annexed States. For example, Natalya Zakharova strongly

---

141 W Rudolf, *Wandel des Staatsbegriffi im Völkerrecht?*, Bonn: Europa Union Verlag, 1986, p. 48.

142 See *ibid.* at 48. "The international legal order stands and falls with the concept of a State."

143 See Crawford, 'The Criteria for Statehood in International Law', 48 *BYBIL* 1976/77, pp. 119 and 144.

144 See Crawford, 'The Criteria...', pp. 107 and 111.

supported the continuity of Austria (notwithstanding the German annexation in 1938–1945):

> It is known that the existence of an international treaty that foresees the creation of, or whose goal is the creation of one or another 'factual situation', does not yet in any way witness its legality. Among such treaties not a few are legally void (an example—the Munich agreement of 1938). The aggressor State, of course, does not have any rights of the successor. Its activities that are directed towards the acquisition of 'rights' to the conquered territory, or equally of any rights of the State to whom this territory belongs, remain legally void... [o]nly legal factual situations may predetermine the succession... This thesis is undisputed in the doctrine. From this follows that the conquest of State territory by the aggressor not only fails to deprive that State of the international rights belonging to it, but also to interrupt their attribution to it. Therefore, after the liberation of the territory, the problem of succession does not arise for it—it continues to enjoy the rights, acquired earlier... Of the illegality and criminality of the aggression also follows that all agreements that the aggressor expanded to the conquered territory will terminate their effect upon reestablishment of the independence of the State.[145]

Thus, notwithstanding differences in legal doctrine, the Australian scholar James Crawford seemed to represent the majority view when, having analyzed World War II State practice, he postulated in 1978 that:

> State practice in the period since 1930 has established, not without some uncertainty, the proposition that annexation of the territory of a State as a result of the illegal use of force does not effect the extinction of the State.[146]

Some of the 'uncertainties' referred to by Professor Crawford were due to—at that time—the still unresolved case of the Soviet annexation of the Baltic States. Did this case fall under the rule postulated by Crawford or not, and if so, then what were the legal implications of the fact that the solution to the Baltic problem was still frozen in the icy winds of the Cold War? How long can international law, and the international community, uphold a legal fiction

---

145 Н.В. Захарова, *Правопреемсмво госубарсв,* Москва: Международные отношения, 1973, pp. 9–10. (Translated from Russian.)

146 Crawford, *The Creation...,* p. 407.

on statehood which is not supported by reality on the ground? With time, the whole legal debate had become somewhat 'meta-physical' and 'centere[d] on the scholars' paradigms and not the behavior of the international actors that they [were] supposed to be evaluating.'[147]

At the end of the day, one of the last remnants of World War II, the Baltic question, found a peaceful solution in August 1991, and did so in a way that reconfirmed several earlier normative expectations, pushed aside some old uncertainties, but also managed to revive others.

147 So characterizes Anthony Clark Arend a fallacy of the post-World War II international law scholarship. See A.C. Arend, *Legal Rules and International Society,* New York: Oxford University Press, 1999, p. 7.

CHAPTER 2

The Legal Status of the Baltic States in International Law After 1991: Claims and Responses

1 The Baltic Thesis

The Baltic thesis of their unbroken continuity has not only been a legal theory, it also used to be—to quote Krystyna Marek's characterization of Czechoslovakia's case during and after World War II—'a political fighting program.'[1] What Estonian president (1992–2001) Lennart Meri said about Estonia, applies *mutatis mutandis* to the other two Baltic republics as well: '*State power in Estonia or the Estonian conception of the State—or, if one wishes: State philosophy—is based on the continuity of the State*.'[2]

During five decades of Soviet rule in Estonia, Latvia and Lithuania, the State continuity doctrine undermined the legality and legitimacy of Soviet rule in the Baltic States, and supported the independence claims of Baltic refugees in the West and of dissidents[3] at home. When Soviet leaders attempted to dictate conditions for the Baltic republics' secession from the Soviet Union in 1991,[4] Estonian, Latvian, and Lithuanian politicians claimed that one who has not voluntarily and legally married cannot discuss divorce, claiming simply that the illegal situation created by the USSR had to be terminated.[5]

1 K. Marek, *op. cit.*, p. 311.

2 See A. Oplatka, *Lennart Meri. Ein Leben fur Estland. Dialog mit dem Präsidenten*, Zürich: Verlag Neue Zürcher Zeitung, 1999. (Quoted from the Estonian edition, Tartu: Ilmamaa, 2000 p. 58).

3 Enn Sarv has argued against the use of the concept of 'dissidents' in the Baltic case, since individuals who fight for freedom in an *occupied* country do not fight against their 'own' regime and cannot be called 'dissidents', i.e. 'persons who think differently.' See E. Sarv, *Õiguse vastu ei saa ükski* (No One Can Withstand the Law), Tartu, 1997, p. 75. The semantic dilemma between a 'dissident' and a 'freedom (or: resistance) fighter' illustrates the difficulties of adequately characterizing an illegally created period with as long a duration as Soviet rule in the Baltic republics.

4 See C. Gray, 'Self-Determination and the Breakup of the Soviet Union', 12 *YBEL* 1992, p. 466. Under the April 7, 1990 Soviet law on secession, the secession of a union republic required approval by a two-thirds majority. Latvia and Estonia, who had suffered more from Soviet migration policies, might have had difficulty in fulfilling the requirements of this Soviet law. See also A. Cassese, *Self-determination of Peoples. A Legal Reappraisal*, Cambridge: Cambridge University Press, 1995, p. 261.

5 Of the common efforts of that period, note the May 26, 1990, Declaration of Foreign Ministers of the three Baltic States in Riga, which declared that 'the Republic of Estonia, the Republic

According to the view presented by the Baltic States, the Soviet Union committed acts of aggression against the republics of Estonia, Latvia, and Lithuania in June 1940. Since Soviet aggression violated bi- and multilateral treaties in force between those countries, the occupation of Estonia, Latvia and Lithuania by the Red Army on June 17, 1940, the subsequent communist takeover and the annexation of the Baltic republics by the Soviet Union in August 1940, must be qualified as illegal acts, and are therefore null and void *ab initio.* While the Soviet annexation of the Baltic States terminated the independence of those States *de facto,* they did not lose their international legal personality, and continued to exist *de iure.* During the years of Soviet rule, the Baltic States were 'only seemingly dead.'[6] Most Western countries never recognized the legality of Soviet annexation, at least not *de iure.* Therefore, the Soviet Union never acquired sovereign title over the Baltic States, and thus remained solely an occupying power until the independence of the *de iure* existing Baltic republics was *de facto* restored in 1991.

Accordingly, the present-day Republic of Lithuania celebrates its independence on February 16, the day independence was proclaimed in 1918. The independence days of the Republic of Estonia (February 24) and the Republic of Latvia (November 18) are the days of proclamation of their independence in 1918.[7] The renewed proclamations of independence from the Soviet Union by the Baltic parliaments—on March 11, 1990 by Lithuania and on August 20, 1991 by Estonia and Latvia—are seen as restoring the independence of already existing States. It follows from the above that the Baltic States do not regard themselves as successor States to the Soviet Union.

In the following, a more precise account is given of the continuity claim, as manifested in each of the Baltic States.

a *The Republic of Estonia*

On February 2, 1990, on the 70th anniversary of the Peace Treaty of Tartu in which Soviet Russia recognized the independence of the Republic of Estonia,

of Latvia, and the Republic of Lithuania still continue to exist.' The substantive part of the declaration was supplemented by the following quest for symbolism: '*This declaration is signed in Riga in accordance with the trilateral agreement signed in Geneva in 1934, registered in the League of Nations and renewed in Tallinn on May 12, 1990.*' Quoted in Jaakson, *Eestile,* pp. 274–275.

6 The relevant notion in German legal language is '*scheintot.*' See e.g. Neuhold/Hummer/Schreuer, *Österreichisches Handhuch des Volkerrechts,* Band 1: Textteil, 2. Auflage, 1991, p. 152.

7 On the creation and recognition of the Baltic States by the international community, see C. Hillgruber, *Die Aufizahme neuer Staaten in die Völkerrechtsgemeinschafi. Das völkerrechtliche Institut tier Anerkennung von Neustaaten in der Praxis des 1p. and 20. Jahrhunderts,* Frankfurt a.M.: Peter Lang, 1997, p. 236 et seq.

the specially convened General Assembly of all the people's representatives in the then Estonian Soviet Socialist Republic (SSR) declared '*that democratic statehood, based on the continuity of the Republic of Estonia, remains to this day the undisputed political ideal of the Estonian people.*'[8] In March 1990, when Estonia was still controlled by the Soviet Union, the election of the Congress of Estonia by Estonian citizens (namely, the citizens of the pre-1940 Republic of Estonia and their successors), clearly manifested the will of the Estonian people for restoration of independence according to the principle of State continuity.

On March 30, 1990, the Supreme Soviet of the Estonian SSR, a legislative body elected according to the constitution of the Estonian SSR of 1978, adopted the *Resolution On the State Status of Estonia.* This document, which was proclaimed by a legislative body that was—by its own logic—technically speaking still an institution of the occupying power, asserted '*that the occupation of the Republic of Estonia by the Soviet Union in June 17, 1940 has not suspended the existence of the Republic of Estonia* de jure. *The territory of the Republic of Estonia is occupied to this day.*' Moreover, the Supreme Soviet declared the '*state power of the USSR in Estonia to be unlawful from the moment of its enactment*' and proclaimed '*the restoration of the Republic of Estonia* (*restitutio in integrum*).' A period of transition which '*shall terminate with the formation of constitutional organs of state power of the Republic of Estonia*' was proclaimed.[9]

The *Resolution On the National Independence of Estonia* was adopted by the Supreme Council on August 20, 1991, in connection with the attempted communist coup d'état in Moscow. This document clearly proceeded from the assumption that the Republic of Estonia continued as a subject of international law. It referred to the March 3, 1991, referendum, in which the people of Estonia had overwhelmingly supported the idea of 'restoring the national independence of the Republic of Estonia', affirmed the national independence of the Republic of Estonia and sought 'restoration of [...] diplomatic relations.'[10]

On June 28, 1992, the new Constitution of the Republic of Estonia was adopted by popular referendum in accordance with Article 1 of the 1938 Estonian Constitution. The preamble to the 1992 Constitution stresses that the

8 See the text of the declaration in A. Kiris, *Restoration of the Independence of the Republic of Estonia. Selection of Legal Acts (1988–1991)*, Tallinn: Ministry of Foreign Affairs of the Republic of Estonia and Estonian Institute for Information, 1991, p. 19.

9 See the text in A. Kiris, *op. cit.*, pp. 22–23. See the original Estonian text in 12 Eesti Vabariigi Ülemnõukogu ja Valitsuse Teataja, p. 269.

10 See the text in A. Kiris, *op. cit.*, p. 101.

present Estonian State had been proclaimed on February 24, 1918.[11] Another provision, Article 122, referring to the continuity of the Estonian Constitution of 1992, stipulates that 'the Estonian land borders are determined by the February 2, 1920, Peace Treaty of Tartu and other interstate border treaties.'

When the parliament of the Republic of Estonia, the 7th (*sic*) *Riigikogu,* was finally elected and convened under the Constitution of 1992, it adopted the following declaration on October 7, 1992:

> The present Republic of Estonia is as a subject of law identical with the Republic of Estonia that was proclaimed on February 24, 1918, fell victim to the aggression of the Soviet Union in 1940, and was illegally incorporated into the Soviet Union.
>
> Riigikogu expresses its gratitude to those States which continued to recognize the Republic of Estonia during the difficult years of occupation. This made the *de facto* restoration of independence possible on August 20, 1991.[12]

b *Republic of Latvia*

On May 4, 1990, the *Declaration on the Renewal of the Independence of the Republic of Latvia* was adopted by the Supreme Soviet of the Latvian SSR. It declared that the incorporation of the Republic of Latvia into the USSR never acquired legality, and that the Republic of Latvia had continued to exist *de jure* as a subject of international law, a fact that was 'recognized by more than 50 States.'[13] According to the Declaration, the legal nature of the independence process was the restoration of the independence of the Republic of Latvia *de facto.* The authority of the 1922 Constitution was reintroduced throughout the whole of Latvia. Article 5 of the Declaration provided a transition period until *de facto* control of Latvian State power could be established in the territory concerned. At the same time, however, the illegal occupation and annexation of Latvia continued, as Soviet troops were present in Latvia, and its then

11 The Preamble of the 1992 Põhiseadus reads: '*Unwavering in their faith and with an unswerving will to safeguard and develop a State which is established on the inextinguished right of the Estonian people to national self-determination and which was proclaimed on February 24, 1918... the Estonian people adopted, on the basis of Article I of the Constitution which entered into force in 1938, by referendum held on June 28, 1992, the following Constitution:...*' See *Eesti Vabariigi Põhiseadus,* RT 1992, 26, 349; 36.

12 Riigi Teataja (State Gazette) 1992/40/533. The translation from Estonian is by this author.

13 See a French translation of the text in A. Reinhards (ed.) *Lettonie-Russie. Traités et documents de base* in extenso, Lausanne, 1998, p. 202.

functioning State institutions, including the Supreme Council, lacked legitimate authority from the point of view of the 1922 Latvian Constitution.[14]

On August 21, 1991, in connection with the coup d'état in Moscow, which was directed against Mikhail Gorbachev, the Constitutional Law On the Republic of Latvia'a Status as a State was adopted. The Law provided that Latvia's 'sovereign State status is determined by the Republic of Latvia Constitution of February 15, 1922.'[15]

In 1993, the 5th (*sic*) Saeima (Parliament) was elected in Latvia, and the constitutional organs of the Republic of Latvia restarted their activities.

c *Republic of Lithuania*

The history of Lithuania has differed significantly from its Northern neighbours, Latvia and Estonia.[16] While the territories of Estonia and Latvia were conquered by German and Danish crusaders at the beginning of the 13th century, the Lithuanians managed to withstand foreign attacks and established their own State in 1263. In medieval times, the Lithuanian State, later in personal union with Poland, was one of the most powerful States in Central and Eastern Europe, reaching as far as the coasts of the Black Sea. So Lithuania's statehood can be traced many centuries back.

The Supreme Council of the Republic of Lithuania adopted the *Act On the Restoration of the Lithuanian State* on March 11, 1990. The act declared that the Lithuanian government took full control over its territory once more within the historical boundaries of the State, and emphasized that the 1918 Act of Independence and the 1920 Decree on the Re-established Democratic State of Lithuania never lost their legal effect.[17] On the same day the Supreme Council of the Republic of Lithuania adopted the *Law On the Reinstatement of the May 12, 1938, Lithuanian Constitution* on the basis that the Constitution had been illegally suspended. At the same time, some articles regulating the status and powers of political institutions in the 1938 Constitution were suspended because of their authoritarian character.[18]

As can be seen from the laws and declarations referred to above, today's Republics of Estonia, Latvia and Lithuania claim to have preserved their identity

---

14 I. Ziemele, *op. cit.*, pp. 252–253.

15 See the *Constitutional Law of the Republic of Latvia On the Republic of Latvia Status as a State* of August 21, 1991, in Human Rights Issues (5th Saeima Human Rights Committee eds.) Riga, 1993, p. 65.

16 For a succinct overview, see B. Meissner, 'Baltic States', *EPIL* 1, p. 328 *et seq.*

17 This Act of the Supreme Council of Lithuania is translated and published in English. See Lithuanian Foreign Policy Review 1999/4, p. 179.

18 See I. Ziemele, *op. cit.*, p. 253.

with the pre-World War II Baltic States. Latvia even continued to apply parts of its pre-World War II Constitution. Although Estonia and Lithuania adopted new Constitutions in 1992, both countries have strictly adhered to the State continuity thesis when making changes in their respective constitutional systems.

2 Responses to the Baltic Continuity Thesis in the Practice of the International Community

a *Restoration of Diplomatic Relations with Western Countries in 1991*

Iceland was the first country to recognize the restoration of independence of the Baltic States, based on the principle of State identity. Already on February 11, 1991, the Althing (the Parliament) of Iceland passed a resolution confirming that recognition of the independence of the Republic of Lithuania granted by Iceland in 1922 was still in force.[19] A similar position with respect to Estonia and Latvia was taken by Iceland after those countries had re-proclaimed their independence in August 1991.[20]

Other Western countries gave their support and recognition to the idea of State identity when they announced, in late summer 1991, that they would restore diplomatic relationships with Estonia, Latvia and Lithuania.[21] As a matter of fact, the term 'recognition' was even not used in the wording of the declarations by the countries of the European Community and the USA[22] On August 27, 1991, an Extraordinary Meeting of the Foreign Ministers of the EC countries warmly welcomed 'the restoration of the sovereignty and independence of the

---

19 See D. Zalimas, 'Legal and Political Issues on the Continuity of the Republic of Lithuania', in: *Lithuanian Foreign Policy Review* 1999 No. 4, p. 107 at 114.

20 See information provided on the website of the Foreign Ministry of the Republic of Estonia, at http://www.vm.ee/eng/estoday/2000/Eesti-Island.htm, visited on November 20, 2000. On the re-establishment of diplomatic relations between Iceland and Latvia, see Reinhards, *op. cit.*, p. 240.

21 See R. Müllerson, *International Law, Rights and Politics. Developments in Eastern Europe and the CIS*, London: Routledge, 1994, p. 120. For a comparative analysis, see J.A. Trapans, *The West and the Recognition of the Baltic States: 1919 and 1991. A Study of the Politics of the Major Powers*, 25 JBS, 2, pp. 153–173.

22 See e.g. the practice with regard to France: 40 *AFDI* 1091 (1994) and P. Daillier, A. Pellet, Nguyen Quoc Dinh, *Droit international public*, Paris: L.G.D.J, 1999, p. 559; with regard to Austria: H. Tichy, 'Two Recent Cases of State Succession—An Austrian Perspective', 44 *Austrian JPIL* 1992, p. 117 at 127; with regard to Germany: O. Dörr, *Die Inkorporation...*, p. 354. See also the declaration by the Government of Belgium of March 29, 1990, *RBDI* 1991, p. 262; Norway: see 65 *Nordic JIL* 289, at 290 (1996). Of other Western States, see Australia: 13 *Australian YIL* 223 (1992).

Baltic states which they lost in 1940', and confirmed the decision of its members 'to establish diplomatic relations (...) without delay.'[23]

The US President, George Bush, announced on September 2, 1991, that *'the United States has always supported the independence of the Baltic States and is now prepared immediately to establish diplomatic relations with their governments.'*[24] According to Bush, this marked *'the culmination of the United States' 52 year refusal to accept the forcible incorporation of the independent Baltic States by the USSR.'*[25]

Only a few Western countries recognized the Baltic States and established diplomatic relations anew, since they had earlier accorded *de iure* recognition to the incorporation of the Baltic republics in the Soviet Union.[26] Some other countries which had had diplomatic relations with the Baltic States before 1940, such as Japan, apparently still formally recognized the Baltic States as new States in 1991.[27]

It is also interesting to note that States which were formerly part of the 'socialist bloc' (Czechoslovakia, Poland, Romania, and Hungary) recognized the independence of the Baltic republics, based on the principle of State identity.[28]

In conclusion, most—although not all—States in 1991 recognized the claim of the Baltic States to be identical with the pre-1940 Baltic States.

---

23 Declaration of European Community Foreign Ministers on the Baltic States, Brussels, August 27, 1991, EPC Press Release, P 81/91. It is interesting to note, though, that for the Netherlands and Spain, this declaration ultimately meant the (second) recognition of the Baltic States, as both had recognized the incorporation of the Baltic States into the USSR. See 23 *Netherl. YBIL* XXIII (1992), p. 298. Even more interesting is the British position: 'The British Government, unlike some other Member States, regards this statement as an act of recognition.' See the statement of Mr Douglas Hogg, Minister of State, Foreign and Commonwealth Office: 'Following the Government's recognition of the independence of the Baltic states on 27 August 1991, I immediately visited the three states...' See 63 *BYBIL* 1992, p. 258 fn. 154.

24 Quoted in R. Yakemtchouk, 'Les Républiques baltes en droit international. Echec d'une annexion opérée en violation du droit des gens', 37 *AFDI* 1991, p. 281.

25 State Department Press Statement, Washington, DC, September 2, 1991.

26 See Netherlands: 13 *NYIL* 298 (1992) and Spain: 1 *Spanish YIL* 48 (1991). Sweden had also recognized the incorporation of the Baltic States by the Soviet Union. For the whole list of recognitions, see R. Pullat, *The Restauration of the Independence of Estonia, 2 Finnish YBIL* 1991, p. 529.

27 See Satkasuskas, master's thesis, pp. 64, 75.

28 See for further references: I. Ziemele, *op. cit.*, , p. 188 and D.A. Loeber, 'Consequences of the Molotov-Ribbentrop Pact for Lithuania of Today International Law Aspects', *Lithuanian Foreign Policy Review* 1999 No. 4, p. 95 at 99. See with regard to the Polish position: R. Szafarz, 'The Practice of Poland as the 'Other State Party' and as a Depositary—as Regards Succession of Recently Established States in Respect of Treaties (a Case Study)', 22 *Polish YBIL* 1995–1996, pp. 221–235 at 222–224.

b *Subsequent Treaty Practice: Multilateral Treaties*

Initial recognition of the identity of the Baltic republics by Western countries found subsequent confirmation in treaty practice. This is an area where problems pertaining to the legal identity of those States found a practical manifestation. As the legal identity of a State implies, unless otherwise decided, the identity of the sum total of its rights and obligations under both customary and conventional international law,[29] meaning that which obligations were going to bind the restored Baltic States and their treaty partners had to be defined.

The following general pattern was accepted: the treaty obligations that the Soviet Union had entered into were not considered to be automatically binding on the republics of Estonia, Latvia and Lithuania.[30] The Estonian, Latvian and Lithuanian governments officially notified the Secretary General of the UN that they did not consider themselves to be bound via succession to any treaties concluded by the Soviet Union:

> Estonia [Latvia] does not regard itself as party by virtue of the doctrine of treaty succession to any bilateral or multilateral treaties entered into by the USSR.[31]

Lithuania's declaration had the following wording:

> Having restored its independence on the 11th of March 1990, the Republic of Lithuania neither is nor can be the successor state of the former USSR. The Republic of Lithuania can not take responsibility for treaties concluded by the former USSR, for it neither participated in making those treaties nor influenced them.[32]

---

29 K. Marek, *op. cit.*, p. 3; Cf. e.g. with D.P. O' Connell, *International Law*, Volume One, London: Stevens & Sons Limited, 1965, p. 128. See also Н.В. Захарова, *Правопреемство государсв, Мосва*: Международные отношения, 1973, p. 35.

30 See the evidence in: ILA, Helsinki Conference, *Rapport préliminaire sur la succession d'États en matiere de traités*, 1996, for Germany p. 25, Austria p. 26, Finland p. 28, Poland p. 29, the Netherlands p. 29. From the practice of Great Britain see e.g. the UK-USSR Treaty on Merchant Navigation of 1968 that was not deemed to be binding on the Baltic States. See *BYBIL* 69 (1998), p. 457. See also L. Love, 'International Agreement Obligations After the Soviet Union's Break-up: Current United States Practice and Its Consistency with International Law', *Vanderbilt JTL*, vol. 26, 1993, no. 2, p. 198.

31 Multilateral Treaties Deposited with the Secretary General (Status as of 31 Dec. 1994), p. 9. Moreover, the declaration by Estonia continues as follows: *The Republic of Estonia has begun careful review of multilateral treaties in order to determine those to which it wishes to become a party. In this regard it will act on a case-by-case basis in exercise of its own sovereign right in the name of the Republic of Estonia.', ibid.*

32 Multilateral treaties Deposited with the Secretary General (Status as of 31 Dec. 1995), p. 9.

As such, this virtually meant, practically speaking, application of a 'clean slate' or *tabula rasa* policy with respect to multilateral treaties concluded during the decades of Soviet annexation of Estonia, Latvia and Lithuania.[33] Of course, the Baltic States, while in principle standing for their right not to automatically inherit treaties to which the Soviet Union had been a party, quickly accepted major multilateral treaties which had been negotiated in the framework of the United Nations.

Especially with respect to human rights treaties (to which the USSR had been and was in 1991 a party), it was doubtful whether the international community would have looked favourably on the Baltic States had they left it uncertain whether they felt themselves bound by such treaties and ideas underlying them. Practically speaking, this question was resolved before it could be seriously raised by anyone. The Supreme Council of the Republic of Latvia declared the accession of Latvia to major human rights treaties even before the country's independence was *de facto* established, on May 4, 1990.[34] Estonia waited until its independence was *de facto* re-established and on October 21, 1991, acceded to 28 major international conventions in the fields of treaty law, peaceful settlement of disputes, human rights, diplomatic and consular matters.[35]

Significant from the point of view of State identity, however, has been the symbolic practice of declaring the renewed application of multilateral treaties of which the Baltic States were members before 1940.[36] In a declaration signed on June 26, 1992, and addressed to the Secretary General of the UN, the Estonian Minister of Foreign Affairs announced that Estonia continues to consider itself bound by the *Convention on Non fortification and Neutralization of the Aaland Islands*.[37] (Both Estonia and Lithuania had been countries among the original signatories in 1921.) In 1993, Estonia, Latvia and Lithuania restored their membership to the 1925 *Geneva Protocol for the Prohibition of the Use of Poisonous or other Gases* with a specification that in respect of these countries,

---

33 Cf. M. Kaljurand, *Some Aspects of Succession of Estonia to the International Treaties Concluded in* 1918–1940, Master's Thesis at The Fletcher School of Law and Diplomacy, 1995 (on file with the author), p. 37.

34 See the text of the respective declaration in Reinhards, *op. cit.*, p. 206 *et seq.* Accession to fifty-one multilateral human rights treaties was declared this time.

35 35 Riigi Teataja (*The Official Gazette*), Art. 428 (1991).

36 See League of Nations Multilateral Treaties, in *Multilateral Treaties Deposited with the Secretary-General* (1996) 921–980.

37 Declaration of Continuity by the Republic of Estonia concerning the Convention on Non-fortification and neutralization of the Aaland Islands, signed at Geneva on October zo, 1921. Lithuania made a similar declaration.

the Protocol entered into force on 28 August 1931, 3 June 1931 and 15 June 1933 respectively.[38] Furthermore, at the Secretariat of the UN, Estonia is registered as being member to the *Convention on the Use of Broadcasting in the Promotion of Peace* since August 18, 1938, and to the *Convention on Measures against Counterfeiting* since February 22, 1931.[39] In addition, Estonia and Latvia declared, without encountering protest, their continued membership of a number of ILO conventions to which they were already bound before 1940.[40] Similarly, Latvia continued its pre-war participation in the 1929 *Warsaw Convention on the Unification of Certain Rules relating to International Carriage by Air*.[41]

c *Practice Related to Bilateral Treaties*

States recognizing the State identity claim of the Baltic republics proceeded from the general presumption that pre-World War II treaties with those States continue(d) in force.[42] However, it often appeared necessary to establish precisely which pre-1940 treaties continued to bind their parties.[43] In the case of Estonia, for instance, on December 31, 1939, 199 bilateral agreements had been in force.[44] Half a century having passed, many things in the world had changed so much that in several cases these treaties were terminated *ex nunc* after 1991.[45] There had been several pre-1940 treaties on consular affairs that obviously

38 See the evidence collected by Dörr, *op. cit.*, p. 164.

39 See E. Mattisen, *Searching for a Dignified...*, p. 95.

40 See K. Ipsen, *Völkerrecht*, 4. Auflage, München: C.H. Beck'sche Verlagsbuchhandlung, 1999, p. 60.

41 See R. Szafarz, *op. cit.*, p. 233.

42 See the evidence about France, Germany and Norway, submitted by A. Zimmermann, *Staatennachfolge in völkerrechtliche...*, p. 55.

43 See on Estonia: T. Kerikmäe, H. Vallikivi, 'State Continuity in the Light of Estonian Treaties Concluded before World War II', 5 *Juridica International* (*Tartu University Law Review*) 2000, p. 30.

44 See M. Kaljurand, *Some Aspects of Succession...* 1995, p. 4 *et seq.*

45 See J. Klabbers, M. Koskenniemi, O. Ribbelink and A. Zimmermann (eds.), *State Practice Regarding State Succession and Issues of Recognition: The Pilot Project of the Council of Europe*, The Hague: Kluwer Law International, 1999, p. 96. In some cases, the formulation of new treaties—and the implicit application of the pre-1940 treaties—lasted several years after 1991. For instance, the Agreement on Commerce and Shipping between Estonia and Turkey, concluded on September 16, 1929 (Riigi Teataja 1930, 56, 377) and other agreements on economic matters were terminated by the Agreement on Commercial and Economic Cooperation, concluded between Turkey and Estonia on August 28, 1995 (Riigi Teataja II 1995,42, 188). Article XIII of the 1995 stipulates: *The treaties and protocols and clearing agreements on commercial and economic cooperation concluded between the two States before 1940 shall be terminated upon the entry into force of this agreement.'* In similar vein, the preamble of the Turkish-Estonian Treaty of Friendship and Cooperation of 1993 states that '*...the Parties confirm their commitments to the Treaty of Friendship of I*

fell under the scope of the 1963 Vienna Convention on Consular Relations, and thus lost their relevance with the codification of international law and the Baltic States' accession to the Vienna Convention in 1991.[46] Similarly, most maritime agreements regulated questions of mutual recognition of measurement of vessels. In 1991, the pre-1940 measurement systems were no longer in use and the bilateral agreements of the Baltic States were no longer revived. Instead, multilateral conventions concluded under the auspices of the International Maritime Organization became applicable to the Baltic States, which had become members of the IMO.[47] Due to changes in national legislation and international law, pre-1940 mutual assistance treaties,[48] although temporarily applied after 1991, were replaced by new treaties on mutual assistance.[49]

Nevertheless, a number of bilateral treaties from the pre-World War II period were revived following the restoration of the independence of the Baltic republics. Thus, Great Britain and Estonia renewed their visa-free travel regime, established before the incorporation of Estonia into the Soviet Union but not applied for half a century.[50] Moreover, through an exchange of letters, Finland and Estonia renewed application of the Agreement on cultural co-operation.[51] Austria revived treaties on extradition and legal assistance in criminal matters, negotiated with Estonia in 1928 and Latvia in 1932, and the consular convention with Estonia of 1926.[52] Similar actions were taken by France,[53] Norway[54] and other States.

December 1924…' Cf. 3 Riigi Teataja II (1994) and Treaty on Friendship, December 1, 1924, Estonia-Turkey, 115/116 Riigi Teataja, Art. 77 (1925).

46 Kaljurand, *Some Aspects of Succession…*, p. 30.

47 Kaljurand, *Some Aspects…*, p. 30.

48 Some of these treaties were concluded on a trilateral basis, e.g. the Convention on Assistence in Civil Matters between Estonia, Latvia and Lithuania from December 10, 1935 (The official source in Estonia: 109 Riigi Teataja, Art. 908 (1935)), the Convention on Settlement of Some Matters of International Private Law between Estonia, Latvia and Lithuania from June 26, 1924 (In Estonia: 60 Riigi Teataja, Art. 71 (1923)), the Convention on Mutual Recognition of Court Decisions in Civil Matters between Estonia, Latvia and Lithuania from January 10, 1936 (108 Riigi Teataja, Art. 896 (1935)). See also Kaljurand, *op. cit.*, p. 32 *et seq.*

49 See e.g. Estonian-Latvian-Lithuanian Treaty on Legal Aid and Legal Relations, October 11, 1992, in force from April 3, 1994, 6 Riigi Teataja (1993).

50 See R. Müllerson, 'The Continuity of States by Reference to the Former USSR and Yugoslavia', 42 *ICLQ* 1993, p. 482.

51 Exchange of notes between the Ambassador of the Republic of Finland in Estonia and the Deputy Foreign Minister of the Republic of Estonia, February 5, 1992. See also Agreement on Cultural Cooperation, December 1, 1937, Estonia-Finland, 1 *Riigi Teataja*, Art. 2 (1938).

52 See Tichy, *op. cit.*, p. 127.

53 See *Liste des Traités et Accords de la France* (Status as of October 1992), vol. II, p. 681, 741 and 744.

54 See Klabbers *et al.* (eds.), *The Pilot Project of the Council of Europe*, 1999, p. 96.

For practical purposes, some Soviet bilateral treaties continued to apply temporarily, with the agreement of both parties. Some treaties concluded between the USSR and Finland and in force in Estonia during the Soviet period were applied for a limited time by the governments of Finland and Estonia. It was agreed by an exchange of notes that the rights and obligations stemming from Soviet-Finnish bilateral agreements should be applicable to bilateral relations between Finland and Estonia as far as the nature of certain treaties and political interests would so dictate.[55] The force of the treaties was limited to three years and both governments promised to speed up the process of negotiation to conclude new treaties in the fields concerned.[56] With respect to the delimitation of certain maritime areas, treaties concluded by the USSR were used as a basis for delimiting these zones.[57]

The Hungarian legal scholar Hanna Bokor-Szegö critically referred to the treaty practice of the Baltic States with Italy, namely, that the insistence on State continuity throughout the Soviet occupation did not prevent these States benefiting from certain advantageous Italian-Soviet treaties as well.[58] She concludes that the Baltic republics decided on the future of international treaties in conformity with their current interests—without any distinction as to whether they were concluded before or after 1940.[59] If certain inconsistencies occurred in practice, this may also have been partly due to the scarcity of resources and the only recent acquisition of international legal expertise at the Baltic Foreign Ministries in the beginning of 1990s.

d *Other Consequences of State Identity in Relations with Western States*

Recognition of the identity of the Baltic States also had other consequences in bilateral relations with Western countries. For example, the pre-World War II Estonian embassy building in Berlin's Tiergarten was returned to its owner, and the embassy continues to operate in this building to this today. After the Republic of Estonia re-established its independence, a Berlin court ordered

55 See Kaljurand, *op. cit.*, p. 38. See also M. Lehto, 'Succession of...'. FYBIL, pp. 214–217.

56 The respective questions concerned jurisdiction and the maritime border in the Gulf of Finland and in the north-eastern part of the Baltic Sea, environment, customs, rescue at sea, nuclear plants, and the like. See Kaljurand, *op. cit.*, p. 38 *et seq.* Estonia did not carry on this practice with other States, although some States would, for practical reasons, have preferred to do so.

57 See Klabbers *et al.* (eds.) *The Pilot Project of the Council of Europe*, p. 96.

58 H. Bokor-Szegö, 'Questions of State Identity and State Succession in Eastern and Central Europe', in: M. Mrak (ed.) *Succession of States*, The Hague: Martinus Nijhoff, 1999, p. 95 at 100.

59 *Ibid.* p. 100 *et seq.*

that guardianship be lifted and the property restored to Estonia.[60] Several Western governments had, however, already turned Baltic embassy and consulate buildings over to the USSR during the Soviet annexation period. The Latvian Mission to the League of Nations in Geneva was a curiosity in the sense that it was transferred to the USSR, but listed in the Geneva real estate registry as the property of the Latvian Government.[61] Although Switzerland initially insisted that the issue should be resolved between Latvia and Russia, in June 1994 it decided to pay Latvia an agreed-upon amount for the embassy premises.[62] The Baltic governments reached similar agreements on financial settlement with France during 2001.[63] Some property issues were pending for a while:[64] for its Villa Lituania (Villa Maria Luisa) in Rome, which after 1940 was used by the USSR and then, from 1991, the Russian Federation, Lithuania received compensation from Italy only in February 2013.[65]

With Great Britain and Sweden, settlements were reached regarding Baltic pre-World War II gold deposited in the banks of those countries.[66] On

60 See *Beschluß des Amtsgerichts Berlin Tiergarten,* FRG, Distr. Ct. Berlin (Judge Finck) (Decision of September 23, 1991). See also J. Klabbers *et al.* (eds.), *State Practice Regarding State Succession and Issues of Recognition: The Pilot Project of the Council of Europe*, p. 126.

61 See Ziemele, *op. cit.*, p. 195.

62 See *ibid.* p. 195.

63 See *Postimees,* 07.08.2001.

64 Upon the admission of the Russian Federation to the Council of Europe, the Parliamentary Assembly noted that 'real estate (embassy buildings in third countries), as well as cultural and historical property which was expropriated by the Soviet Union in 1940 and in subsequent years, still has not been returned to the Baltic states. The Assembly should encourage, and where possible, facilitate a rapid settlement of this question.' See Mühlmann, *Explanatory memorandum on Russia's request for membership,* January 2, 1996, the Council of Europe Parliamentary Assembly Doc. 7443, 22, para. 99.

65 On conflicting claims to the former Lithuanian embassy in Rome (Villa Maria Luisa), now used by the Russian Federation, see already Satkauskas, 2000, p. 69.

66 During the 1930s, the Central Banks of Estonia, Latvia and Lithuania built up deposits of gold at the Bank of England. In 1940 Estonia held 4.48 tons, Lithuania 2.96 tons and Latvia 6.58 tons. On the restitution of the Baltic gold, see the statement of the British Foreign and Commonwealth Office on May 26, 1992:
Following the Government's announcement on 22 January 1992 of our proposals for settling with Estonia gold and other claims questions, the Government and the Estonian Government today concluded in Tallinn a final agreement on these matters. HM Ambassador to Estonia, Bob Low, and the Estonian Deputy Foreign Minister, Enn Liimets, exchanged diplomatic notes, which constitutes an agreement under which the Government will transfer to the Bank of Estonia on 31 March 154, 754.859 fine ounces of gold, a sum equal to the Bank of Estonia's pre-1940 deposit with the Bank of England. In addition, the Government and the Estonian Government have dropped all other claims.' The gold was at the time worth about 30.5 million British pounds. See Brit. YBIL 1991, p. 616; 1992, pp. 779–781. A similar agreement with Lithuania was concluded in March 1992. On

February 14, 1992, France transferred Lithuanian gold reserves (worth *ca* 25 million USD) to Lithuania, after rejecting similar requests by the USSR until the end of the 1980s.[67] Similarly, Switzerland returned pre-1940 Baltic gold reserves to the Baltic States.[68]

e Practice as Related to Membership in International Organizations

The world's most important international organization, the United Nations, was created after the Baltic States had already been annexed by the USSR. The League of Nations, its predecessor, of which the Baltic republics had been members, was abolished in 1946. Therefore, on September 17, 1991, Estonia, Latvia and Lithuania were admitted as new members to the United Nations according to Article 4 of the Charter.[69] The President of the UN Security Council, in a brief statement after admission of the Baltic States to the UN, mentioned that those countries had 'regained' their independence.[70] However, at the same time, the UN determined the Baltic States' membership contribution on the basis of data supplied previously by the USSR (and not by the Baltic States).[71] Thus, for certain practical (financial) purposes, the Baltic States were treated as if they were States that had separated from the USSR and not as States which had regained their independence after illegal annexation.[72] It seems, however, that at a time of considerable financial difficulties, the UN's primary—and legitimate—concern was to secure its budget, not to make a definite point about the legal status of the Baltic republics as States.

March 19, 1993, the Foreign and Commonwealth Office of the UK issued a statement in which it was *inter alia* declared: 'FIM Ambassador to Latvia, Mr Richard Samuel, and the Latvian Foreign Minister, Mr Georgs Andrejevs, exchanged diplomatic notes, constituting an agreement under which the Government will transfer on 31 March to the Bank of Latvia /10,719.919 fine ounces of gold, a sum equal to the Bank of Latvia's pre-1940 deposit with the Bank of England.' At the time of the agreement, the value of the Latvian gold was about 48.2 million pounds. See 64 BYBIL (1993), p. 693.

67 See Una Bergmane, "The Uncertainty That Persists': The Bank of France, the Baltic Gold and the Non-Recognition of a Forcible Seizure of Territory during the Cold War', *The International History Review* 2021.

68 See R. Satkauskas, *États baltes: succession ou identité,* Master's thesis at Sorbonne, 2000, p. 67.

69 Estonia: UN GA-Res. 46/4 (1991), September 17, 1991; Latvia: UN GA-Res. 46/ 5 (1991), September 17, 1991; Lithuania: UN GA-Res. 46/6 (1991), September 17, 1991; all Resolutions reprinted in 45 UNYB 97S (1991). See also K. Bühler, *op. cit.*, p. 196.

70 U.N.S.C. Official Records, 46th year, September 12, 1991, in UN Doc. S/INF/47, 1991, 48–9.

71 U.N.G.A. Res. 46/221A states that 'the assessment rates will be deducted from the assessment rate of the [USSR]...' *Report of the Committee on Contributions,* UN Doc. A/49/11, 1994, para. 28.

72 D.A. Loeber, *Consequences of the Molotov-Ribbentrop...*, p. 99.

In a procedure similar to that admitting them to the UN, Estonia, Latvia and Lithuania became new members of numerous other specialized agencies of the UN.[73]

Somewhat oddly, the three Baltic republics became technically new members of the International Labour Organization (ILO) in 1994, although they had been members of this organization from its creation in 1921 until 1940. The procedure of 'admission' rather than 're-admission' was adopted.[74] The legal and policy reasons that determined the admission of the Baltic States as 'new' member States to the ILO are difficult to establish in retrospect.[75] The French international lawyer Brigitte Stern suggests that in the case of restoration of the old memberships, the ILO could then also have been entitled to collect membership fees from the Baltic States for the period of their hibernation.[76] Nevertheless, the decision of the ILO has been criticized by Baltic scholars of international law.[77] However, the Baltic States at least formally reconfirmed their continuity claim, while becoming members of the ILO for the second time.[78] Similarly, Estonia and Latvia also had to accede anew to membership in the Paris Union (Union for the Protection of Industrial Property Rights), although in both cases, in the status lists the following footnote was added: 'Estonia [Latvia] acceded to the Paris Convention (Washington Act, 1911) with effect from February 12, 1924. It lost its independence on August 6 [August 5], 1940, and regained it on August 20, [August 21] 1991.'[79]

---

73 IAEA: see 46 UNYB 1093 (1992) (Estonia), 47 UNYB 1245 (1993) (Lithuania); FAO: see 45 UNYB 941 (1991); UNESCO: see *ibid.*, at 947; WHO, see *ibid.*, at 953 (Latvia, Lithuania), 47 UNYB 1265 (1993) (Estonia); IBRD and IMF: see 46 UNYB 1123, 1140 (1992): ICAO: see *ibid.*, at 1145; UPU: see *ibid.*, at 1149; WMO: see *ibid.*, at 1156; WIPO: see *ibid.*, at 1165 (Lithuania), 47 UNYB 1313 (1993) (Latvia, Estonia); ITU: see 45 UNYB 987 (1991) (Latvia, Lithuania), 46 UNYB 1152 (1992) (Estonia). For this and also for the practice of IMO and UNIDO, see K. Buhler, *op. cit.*, p. 197 fn. 805.

74 The ILO simply noted that the Baltic States were members of the ILO before 1940. See *Official Bulletin*, 1991, vol. LXXV, 23, 25.

75 Symbolically, the Baltic position seems to be recalled by a mighty oak-tree which grows in the backyard of the former ILO (now WTO) building in Geneva, and which was planted by the Latvian delegation when the construction of the building started at the beginning of the 1920s.

76 B. Stern, 'La succession d'États', 262 *RCADI* 1996, The Hague, 2000, p. 222.

77 See e.g. I. Ziemele, *State Continuity and Nationality: The Baltic States and Russia*, Leiden: Martinus Nijhoff, 2005*op. cit.*,, p. 68 *et seq.*

78 Lithuania declared that its application shall in no way affect the legel consequences proceeding from the [original] membership of the Republic of Lithuania.' See ILA, Taipei Conference, *Rapport interimaire sur la succession en matiere de traités constitutifs d'organisations internationales et de traités adoptes au sein des organisations internationales*, (Brigitte Stern), London, 1998, pp. 9 and 625 *et seq.*

79 See K. Bühler, *op. cit.*, p. 197.

f *The Continuity Thesis of the Baltic States and the Russian Federation*

The only State that has emphatically opposed the thesis that the present-day independent Baltic States are identical, as subjects of international law, with the three pre-1940 Baltic republics annexed by the Soviet Union in 1940, is the Russian Federation.[80] Analysis of Russian-Baltic legal relations since 1989 is complicated by the fact that, for a brief time until 1991, the Russian Federation co-existed with the USSR, with both claiming to be sovereign States simultaneously.[81] Furthermore, due to changing policies and attitudes, the Russian position on the legal status of the Baltic States has not always been presented consistently.

On December 24, 1989, the Congress of the People's Deputies of the USSR adopted, not least also due to the participation of and political pressure from the Baltic deputies there, a resolution titled 'On Political and Legal Evaluation of the Soviet-German Non-Aggression Treaty of 1939.'[82] The text of the resolution was drafted by a special 26-member commission chaired by Aleksandr Yakovlev.[83] The Congress noted that before 1939 'the relations of the USSR with Latvia, Lithuania and Estonia were regulated by a system of agreements. According to the peace treaties of 1920 and non-aggression pacts, signed in 1926–1933, the parties thereto undertook to insure mutual respect, in all circumstances, of sovereignty, territorial integrity and inviolability.'[84]

The Congress of the Peoples' deputies of the USSR declared the 'fact of signing 'the secret additional protocols' on 23 August 1939 and other secret protocols legally null and void from the moment of their signing.'[85] The Congress concluded that '[t]he protocols did not create any new legal basis for relations between the Soviet Union and these countries; however they were employed by Stalin and his associates to produce ultimatums and subject other states to force, in violation of legal obligations'[86] However, while the USSR Congress decounced the secret protocols of the Hitler-Stalin Pact, it failed to explicitly point out their consequences for the legal status of the

80 See e.g. Declaration of the Russian Foreign Ministry of July 4, 1994, *Dipl. Vestnik* 1994, No. 13–14, 52.

81 On June 12, 1990, the First Congress of People's Deputies of the Russian Republic adopted a Declaration proclaiming the sovereignty of the Russian Soviet Federative Socialist Republic (RSFSR) over its entire territory. See Bulletin of the RSFSR Congress of People's Deputies and the RSFSR Supreme Council, No. 2, 1990, Art. 22.

82 Files of the Congress of the Peoples' Deputies of the USSR and the Supreme Soviet of the USSR, No. 29, 27 December 1989, Article 579, pp. 833–834.

83 See for the political background to this adoption in an interview with A. Yakovlev, in: Postimees, 09.07.2001.

84 See Files of the Congress, *ibid.* para. 5.

85 See *ibid.* para. 7.

86 See *ibid.* para 7.

Baltic republics, especially in the context of Soviet-Baltic relations in 1940. The Soviet Congress resolution thus failed to pronounce explicitly the illegality of the 1940 annexation.

In 1991, Moscow became a political battleground between two co-existing and rival powers—the Soviet Union, led by General Secretary of the Communist Party, Mikhail Gorbachev, and its major constituent part, the Russian Socialist Federalist Soviet Republic (RSFSR), led by Boris Yeltsin. While Gorbachev was widely held responsible for signs of economic decline and political turmoil in the collapsing USSR, Yeltsin claimed to be the actual representative leader of Russia.

In January 1991, the political situation in the Baltic republics escalated when special units of the Soviet security forces OMON ('black berets') attacked pro-independence demonstrators in Vilnius and Riga with tanks, killing fourteen in Vilnius and four people in Riga. During these events, a political alliance was formed between Yeltsin's Russia and the Baltic States. The Russian Federation, led by Mr. Yeltsin, concluded the so-called *Treaties on the Fundamentals of Interstate Relations* with the Republic of Estonia (January 12, 1991), the Republic of Latvia (January 13, 1991), and the Republic of Lithuania (July 29, 1991). The Supreme Council of the Russian Federation ratified the Fundamentals Treaty with Estonia on December 26, 1991,[87] and the treaty with Lithuania on January 17, 1992. The treaty with Latvia was not ratified, arguably because of different views on the rights of Russian speakers in Latvia.[88]

In each of the three 'Fundamentals' treaties, the parties 'recognize each other as sovereign States and subjects of international law.' The treaties with the republics of Estonia and Latvia declared: '*Taking into consideration the historical experience in mutual relations and intending to establish them on the principle of good neighborship, the parties recognize the obligation not to violate generally recognized norms of international law in their mutual relations…*' The preamble to the Foundation Treaty with the Republic of Lithuania stressed '*that the liquidation of the consequences caused by the USSR to the sovereignty of Lithuania through the annexation of 1940, will create additional conditions for trust between the High Treaty parties and their peoples.*'[89]

Therefore, with this treaty, Yeltsin's Russia essentially recognized the Republic of Lithuania as a subject of international law and a sovereign State under

87 The Russian-Estonian 'Fundamentals Treaty…' entered into force on January 14, 1992. For the Estonian text, see *Riigi Teataja* 1991, 2, 19.

88 Cf. B. Meissner, *Die Russische Politik gegenilber der Baltischen Region als Prüfstein für das Verhältnis Russlands zu Europa*, p. 291.

89 Quoted from Meissner, *Die Russische Politik…*, pp. 292–293.

Lithuania's State status as defined in the fundamental acts of March 11, 1990. The inevitable conclusion here is that in the 'Fundamentals' Treaty, which continues in force between Russia and Lithuania, Russia recognizes that the restoration of the independence of the Republic of Lithuania was based on the principle of State identity.[90] A similar argument can be made on the basis of the Russian-Estonian Fundamentals Treaty, which refers to the decision of the Declaration of the Estonian Supreme Council of March 30, 1990—a document that proclaims the restoration of the Republic of Estonia on the basis of State continuity.[91] It seems that later on conflicting views emerged mainly with respect to the implications of State identity. Nevertheless, Boris Yeltsin, the President of the Russian Federation, later argued that the wording of the 'Fundamentals' treaties ('*the Russian RSFSR and the Republic of Estonia recognize each other as sovereign States*') points to the fact that the Baltic States were nevertheless only recognized as new States.[92]

Yeltsin's Russia had recognized the independence of the Republic of Lithuania on July 29, 1991. The Republics of Estonia and Latvia were recognized by the Russian RSFSR on August 24, 1991. Only on September 6, 1991—after the independence of the Baltic States was recognized by most States throughout the world—did recognition of their independence follow by the Soviet Union, led by its General Secretary, Mikhail Gorbachev. Diplomatic relations between the Soviet Union and the Republics of Estonia and Lithuania were established on October 9, 1991. Latvia and the USSR established diplomatic relations on October 15, 1991. The Soviet government recognized the Baltic States as new States, and consequently considered the independence process as one of secession.

It is interesting to note that at least in one important question, namely the financial legacy of the USSR, the Russian Federation and other former union republics of the USSR have *de facto* accepted the special status of the Baltic States. The Baltic States—by then independent—did not become members of the *Treaty on Succession in Respect of External State Debts and Property of the Former USSR*, signed in Minsk on December 4, 1991. Correspondingly, the Baltic republics neither accepted any part of the foreign debt nor presented claims for the assets of the USSR. Later on, in the *Agreement on the Deferral of Debt of the USSR and its Successors to Foreign Official Creditors*, signed in Paris

90 D. Zhalimas, 'Legal and Political...,' p. 115.

91 See further E. Sarv, *Õiguse vastu ei saa ükski: Eesti taotused ja rahvusvaheline õigus* (No One Can Withstand the Law: Estonia's Efforts and International Law), Tartu, 1997, p. 185.

92 President Yeltsin used this argument in a letter sent to US President Clinton. See a translation published in the Estonian newspaper Postimees, July 11, 1996.

in January 1992, the Russian Federation took responsibility for the whole foreign debt of the former USSR, and was by way of compensation allocated all ex-Soviet foreign assets.[93]

However, when the Soviet Union was finally abolished in December 1991, the Russian Federation in many ways assumed the former Soviet position in its foreign relations. Since then, the official Russian view has not only opposed the Baltic continuity thesis, but also occasionally denied the illegality of the Soviet annexation of 1940.

Some relevant examples can be mentioned. In May, 1992, the Minister of Foreign Affairs of the Russian Federation, Andrei Kozyrev, stated in a memorandum presented to the Council of Europe:

> The events of 1940 and the situation which developed in the succeeding decades in Latvia, Lithuania and Estonia, cannot be interpreted unequivocally. As is known, various political assessments exist in this respect.[94]

The Deputy Foreign Minister of the Russian Federation, Vitali Churkin (later even more widely known as Russia's permanent representative at the UN), used more explicit language when he told the Latvian newspaper *Diena: 'Russia by no means agrees with the point of view held by Latvia and Estonia that the Baltic*

---

93 See e.g. Дипломатическая Академия МИД РФ *et al.* (соз.), *Международое право*, 2nd ed., Москва: Международные отношения, 1998, p. 82. See also J. Klabbers *et al.* (eds.) *The Pilot Project of the Council of Europe*, 1999, p. 130. For a detailed analysis, see A. Reinisch, G. Hafner, *Staatensukzession und Schuldenübernahme beim 'Zerfall' der Sowjetunion*, 1995. See also D. Grashoff, *Staatensukzessionbedingter Schuldnerwechsel. Die Teilung öffentlicher Schulden unter Nachfolgestaaten im Dismembrationsfall*, Frankfurt a.M.: Peter Lang, 1995, p. 186 *et seq* and C.T. Ebenroth and D. Grashoff, *Öffentliche Schulden im Prozeß desintegrierender Staatensukzession—die Zuordnung von Staatsschulden auf Nachfolgestaaten, ZVglRWiss* 92 (1993), pp. 1–28; H. Beemelmans, *Die Staatennachfolge in Staatsvermögen in Drittstaaten, Auslandsschulden, gebietsbezogene rechtliche Regelungen und Staatsangehörigkeit—eine Problemskizze, 41 Osteuropa Recht* 1995, pp. 73–98; D.A. Loeber, ‚Die baltischen Staaten vor völkerrechtlichen Problemen: Kontinuität oder Staatennachfolge in bezug auf Staatsverträge, Staatseigentum und Staatsschulden', in: B. Meissner, D.A. Loeber, E. Levits (eds.), *Die Wirtschaft der baltischen Staaten im Umbruch*, 1993, Köln, p. 29 *et seq;* G. Burdeau, 'Money and State Succession in Eastern Europe', in: B. Stern (ed.) *Dissolution, Continuation and Succession in Eastern Europe*, The Hague, 1998, pp. 35–66 and P. Juillard, 'The Foreign Debt of the Former Soviet Union: Succession or Continuation?', *ibid.*, pp. 67–86. For general considerations, see also V.D. Degan, 'Equity in Matters of State Succession', in: *Essays in Honour of Wang Tieya* (R.St.J. Macdonald ed.), Leiden: M. Nijhoff, 1993, pp. 201–210.

94 B. Meissner, *The Occupation of the Baltic States from a Present-Day Perspective*, p. 473.

States were occupied.'[95] In the view of the Russian Ministry of Foreign Affairs, the Baltic republics ceased to exist as subjects of international law after their incorporation into the Soviet Union in 1940. One high official of the Russian Foreign Ministry has accepted the forcible nature of Soviet incorporation in 1940, but argued that according to international law of the time, such annexation was 'legalized.'[96]

Specifically, Moscow has denied any continuing legal validity to the 1920 peace treaties concluded between Soviet Russia and the republics of Estonia, Latvia and Lithuania. In a note of November 17, 1992 directed to the Latvian Ministry of Foreign Affairs, the Russian Ministry of Foreign Affairs explained:

> Whatever the circumstances of Latvia's entry into the composition of the USSR in 1940 may have been, we cannot deny that factually and juridically, Latvia had for 50 years the status of a [Soviet] union republic. It is known that the incorporation of a State into the composition of another brings about the termination of any bilateral treaties concluded between them as independent States.[97]

With respect to Estonia, Russia's official position was elaborated in a letter from Russian Deputy Foreign Minister Avdeyev to the Russian State Duma on January 8, 1998. According to that letter, the Soviet army was present in 1939 in the territory of the Republic of Estonia in response to Estonia's own 'invitation', and therefore, one cannot speak of the military invasion, occupation and annexation in 1940. The representative bodies of the Baltic republics themselves requested the Supreme Council of the USSR for admission to the USSR. According to the Russian Deputy Foreign Minister, the norm prohibiting threat of military force was unknown in international law before the UN Charter was adopted in 1945.[98]

On February 2, 2000, when the 80th anniversary of the Peace Treaty of Tartu was commemorated in Estonia, the Russian ambassador in Estonia explained that according to the Russian view, the Peace Treaty of 1920 had lost any legal significance in relations between the Russian Federation and the Republic

95 Quoted by B. Meissner, *op. cit.*, 1998, p. 473.

96 Interview with the Deputy Department Chief A. Udaltsov, *Eesti Päevaleht,* February 1, 1996.

97 Meissner, *Die Russische Politik*..p. 303. (Translated from German.)

98 *Postimees*, January 19, 1998. See also V.J. Riismandel, *Nõukogude Liit oli agressor,* (the Soviet Union was an Aggressor) in: Vaba Eesti Sõna (Free Estonian Word), February 26, 1998.

of Estonia. He elaborated further that nowadays, the Russian-Estonian Tartu Peace Treaty could be attributed only 'historical' significance.[99]

This Russian view with respect to the validity of Soviet Russian peace treaties of 1920 had been advanced earlier, in the 1990s. For example, on February 5, 1993, an official of the Russian Ministry of Foreign Affairs stated:

> The representatives of the Russian Federation have repeatedly explained to the Estonian side that the Peace Treaty of Tartu between Soviet Russia and the Republic of Estonia, signed on February 2, 1920, lost its legal validity in connection with the end of the existence of Estonia as an independent subject of international law, independently of the circumstances and reasons bringing this about. Since 1940, the relationship between Estonia and the Soviet Union was based solely on the legislation of the federation state, and not on the treaties and agreements concluded earlier between Estonia and Russia as independent subjects of international law, which have lost their validity.[100]

Finally, on June 9, 2000, the Russian Foreign Ministry, reacting to the bill concerning a reparations claim against Russia, then under discussion in the Lithuanian Seimas (parliament),[101] declared:

> The introduction of the forces of the USSR in 1940 was carried out with the agreement of the supreme leadership of this country, an agreement which was received (*polucheno*) within the framework of international law as practiced at the time. The authoritative functions in the Soviet period here were carried out by the national organs of authority. The decision of the USSR Supreme Soviet of August 3, 1940 concerning the acceptance of Lithuania into the framework of the Soviet Union was preceded by corresponding requests of the highest representative organs of the Baltic states.
>
> In this way, it is legally not correct (*nepravomerno*) to qualify the entrance of Lithuania into the make-up of the USSR as the result of unilateral actions by the latter.[102]

99 See *Postimees*, 2.02.2000 and 3.02.2000.

100 Meissner, *Die Russische Politik...*, p. 304–305. (Translation from German by this author.)

101 See Annex 4 of this book.

102 Quoted from and translated by A.E. Senn, 'What Happened in Lithuania in 1940?', in: *Lithuanian Foreign Policy Review* 2000, pp. 179–195 at 179–180.

As can be seen from the above, the views of the States who or whose predecessor regimes were the actual *dramatis personae* in the relevant historical situation, differ. While the Baltic States claim that their State continuity was preserved throughout the prolonged Soviet occupation, the Russian Federation, which has established its status as the continuator State of the USSR,[103] has not subscribed to the Baltic view.

In practice, most other States have recognized the identity of the Baltic States with the pre-1940 Republics.[104] A Charter of Partnership among the United States of America and the Republic of Estonia, Republic of Latvia, and Republic of Lithuania signed on January 16, 1998 explicitly states that friendly relations between these States 'have been continuously maintained... since 1922' and that the USA regards the statehood of the Baltic States 'as uninterrupted since the establishment of their independence, a policy which the United States has restated continuously for five decades.' However, as far as the remainder of the State practice is concerned, it is not completely free from unanswered questions and inconsistencies. It cannot therefore be *prima facie* established whether the Baltic States continued to exist in terms of international law throughout the Soviet annexation period, or whether they still became extinguished in 1940 or at some point of time afterwards, but their identity was recognized in 1991 along the lines that States can be re-established.

It is not uncommon in international relations for issues related to State continuity and succession to remain pending for a long period.[105] Some issues of State continuity/succession have even entered history as essentially unresolved. But how have legal scholars interpreted State practice pertaining to the legal status of the Baltic States?

3 The Legal Status of the Baltic States: Views in the Legal Literature

The position that the present-day Baltic States are, as subjects of international law identical with the pre-World War II Baltic republics, has generally been

---

103 See among others ILA, Helsinki Conference (1996), *Rapport préliminaire sur la succession d'États en matiere de traités*, London, pp. 13–14 and 18; ILA, Taipei Conference (1998), *Rapport...*, pp. 620–622. See also a similar position held by a Russian scholar, A. Kolodkin, 'Russia and International Law: New Approaches', *RBDI* 1993, No. 2, p. 554.

104 Martti Koskenniemi speaks about 'the overwhelming international acceptance of the continuity thesis invoked by the Baltic states.' See M. Koskenniemi, 'The Wonderful Artificiality of States', in: *The ASIL Proceedings of the 88th Annual Meeting. April 6–9, 1994*, p. 24.

105 See И. Клапсас, 'Правопреемство, и континуитет в международном праве', *Moscow JIL* 1992, No. 4, pp. 22–35 at 33; Б. Клименко, 'Проблемы правопреемсмва на территорий бывшего Союза CCP', in: *Moscow JIL* 1992, No. 1, pp. 3–24 at 24.

confirmed in international law scholarship.[106] This is not too surprising, since State practice by and large seems to dictate this outcome. Many authors, confirming the identity of today's Baltic republics, seem to begin conceptually with the unity of the notions of identity and continuity.[107]

However, upon closer examination of the views presented by scholars, certain differences and nuances become apparent. For instance, Ulrich Fastenrath holds the Baltic claim of State identity to be justified, but categorizes the case of the Baltic States (like the historic cases of Austria and Czechoslovakia) as entailing 're-establishment.'[108] Similarly, Soledad Torrecuadrada argues that the revival of the Baltic States in 1991 is a case of State identity without continuity.[109] Władysław Czapliński[110] and Vladimir-Djuro Degan[111] have recently referred to the concept of *postliminium* when discussing the legal status of the Baltic republics after 1991. Rein Müllerson invokes *inter alia* the concept of

---

106 See e.g. T. Schweisfurth, 'Soviet Union, Dissolution', *EPIL*, Vol. 4, 2000, pp. 529–547 at 541; R. Müllerson, 'The Continuity and Succession...', *ICLQ*, p. 482; A. Peters, *Das Gebietsreferendum im Völkerrecht. Seine Bedeutung im Licht der Staatenpraxis nach 1989*, Baden-Baden: Nomos, 1995, p. 150 *et seq;* M. Silagi, *Staatsuntergang und Staatennachfolge mit besonderer Berücksichtigung des Endes der DDR*, Franfurt a.M.: Peter Lang, 1996, p. 260; S. Talmon, *Recognition of Governments in International Law. With Particular Reference to Governments in Exile*, Oxford: Clarendon Press, 1998, p. 50; I. Ziemele, 'The Application of International Law in the Baltic States', 40 *GYIL* 1997, pp. 243–279 at 243; K. Bühler, *State Succession and Membership in International Organizations. Legal Theories versus Political Pragmatism*, Dissertation, Vienna, 1999, p. 195; G. Hafner and E. Kornfeind, 'The Recent Austrian Practice of State Succession: Does the Clean Slate Rule Still Exist?', 1 *Austrian RIEL* 1996, pp. 1–49 at 11; E. Sciso, 'Dissoluzione di stati e problemi di successione nei trattati', in: 49 *La comunità internazionale* 1994, pp. 83–4; J. Huntzinger, 'La renaissance des États baltes', in: *Colloque de Nancy*, Paris, 1994, p. 51; M. Bothe et C. Schmidt, 'Sur quelques questions de succession posées par la dissolution de l'URSS et celle de la Yougoslavie', 96 *RGDIP* 1992, p. 831.

107 See above and e.g. LA. Shearer (ed.), *Starke's International Law*, 11th ed., London: Butterworths, 1994, p. 88 and H. Beemelmans, 'State Succession in International Law: Remarks on Recent Theory and State Praxis', 15 *Boston UILJ* 1997, p. 81.

108 U. Fastenrath, ‚Das Recht der Staatensukzession', in: *Berichte der Deutschen Gesellschaft für VR*, 1996, p. 15–16 ('*Das heißt nicht unbedingt, daß der zeitweise nicht bestehende Staat als rechtlich vorhanden fingiert werden müßte, wohl aber, daß die völkerrechtlichen Beziehungen fortgesetzt werden können, nachdem das zeitweilige Wirksamkeitshindernis entfallen ist.*) Similarly, Wilfried Fiedler in ‚Der Zeitfaktor im Recht der Staatensukzession', in: *Staat und Recht. Festschrift für Günther Winkler*, Wien: Springer, 1997, p. 232.

109 S. Torrecuadrada, ‚Le rôle du consentement dans la succession d'Etats aux traités', 23 *Polish YBIL*, p. 127 at p. 134.

110 See W. Czaplinski, 'International Legal Aspects of Polish-Lithuanian Relations', 19 *Polish YBIL* 1991–1992, pp. 31 at 41.

111 See V.-D. Degan, *op. cit.* (*RCADI* 1999), p. 295.

'reversion to sovereignty' for an explanation of the Baltic case.[112] Many authors seem to be somewhat hesitant about the claim of the *continued existence* of the Baltic States.[113] Some authors clearly indicate that the Baltic republics *did* become extinct after their annexation in 1940.[114] In the words of Christine Gray: 'Although the Baltic States had a legal claim to statehood during the period of their annexation, they did not in fact qualify as States in international law. Their situation was similar in that respect to that of Palestine today.'[115]

Several international lawyers argue that international politics had a role to play in recognition of the identity of the Baltic republics. According to the Finnish scholars Koskenniemi and Lehto, the continuity of the Baltic States was recognized for reasons of 'political symbolism', and not because of international law.[116] Ronald Rich has highlighted some explicitly political reasons for explaining recognition of the continuity of the Baltic republics. In the view of this Australian scholar, it was important in August 1991 to distinguish the Baltic States legally from other republics of both the USSR and SFRY.[117] Back then, a 'mere' claim for the right of peoples to self-determination could not have legally justified secession, while claims to restore the independence of

---

112 See R. Müllerson, 'New Developments in the Former USSR and Yugoslavia', 33 *Va. JIL.* 1993, 299 at 311.

113 See e.g. A. Reinisch and G. Hafner, *Staatensukzession und Schuldübernahme beim 'Zerfall' der Sowjetunion,* p. 107: *'Nach herrschender Lehre kann bloß eine 'relativ kurze' Unterbrechung der territorialen Souveränität eines Staates die normativen Folgen des Wegfalls der Staatsgewalt, nämlich den Verlust der Staatlichkeit, verhindern. Die Tatsache, daß die illegale Annexion der baltischen Staaten immerhin doppelt so lang währte als deren ursprüngliche Unabhängigkeit, legt dem Schluß nahe, daß bier die 'normative Kraft des Faktischen die ursprüngliche Rechtswidrigkeit 'geheilt' habe.'*

114 Oliver Dörr writes that *'die tatsächliche Staatenpraxis der 'postsowjetischen Zeit'* [*versucht*], *den Untergang der baltischen Staaten zu ignorieren, indem diesen heute zugestanden wird, zum Beispiel in bezug auf völkerrechtliche Vertragsverhältnisse an ihre souveräne Existenz vor 1940 nahtlos anzuknüpfen. Diese politisch motivierte Fiktion ist mit den Regeln des positiven Völkerrechts nicht zu erklären.'* See Dörr, *op. cit.*, p. 355. See also L. Antonowicz, 'The Disintegration of the USSR from the Point of View of International Law', 19 *Polish YBIL* 1991–1992, p. 7 at 14–15: *'The annexation of the Baltic states to the USSR being illegal, the passage of time exceeding twice their existence as independent states combined with the inertion of the international community legalized the original illegality. Such a solution is not rare in international relations.'* Cf. J. Verhoeven, 'La reconnaissance internationale: déclin ou renouveau?', in: 39 *AFDI* 1993, pp. 7–40 at p. 13 and 36 *et seq.*

115 C. Gray, 'Self-Determination and the Breakup of the Soviet Union', 12 *YBEL* 1992, pp. 483–4.

116 Koskenniemi and Lehto, 'La succession...', p. 198.

117 R. Rich, 'Recognition of States: The Collapse of Yugoslavia and the Soviet Union', 4 *EJIL* 1993, p. 38. See also Verhoeven, *Reconnaissance,* p. 13.

illegally occupied and annexed territories were to be treated more favourably.[118] Nevertheless, in December 1991 the dissolution of the remaining Soviet Union happened anyway.

In post-Soviet Russia, the legal literature has tended to deny the continuity of the Baltic States—or the Baltic claim of Soviet occupation until 1991.[119] Some authors have suggested that one of the reasons to raise the claim of State continuity was to discriminate against Russian speakers who had settled in the the Baltic States during the Soviet period.[120] However, there have also been voices in international law literature who at least affirm the illegality of the Soviet occupation and annexation of the Baltic States in 1940.[121]

Altogether, there seems to exist a consensus among legal scholars that the continuity and/or identity of the Baltic States involves a certain legal fiction. Differences among scholars involve attitudes towards this fiction—some endorse it; others are more sceptical. This element of fiction is particularly interesting from the point of view of international law.[122] In philosophy,

118 The hypothesis of Rich seems to be confirmed at least by one letter, titled 'Recognition of the Baltic States', and sent on August 30, 1991, by the Netherlands Minister for Foreign Affairs to the Parliament. In this letter, under the heading 'Precedental effects', it is declared: 'Given the special historical and international legal position of the Baltic States, *recognition of them does not constitute a precedent for recognition of other territories which have declared themselves independent or which do so in future, as far as the Twelve are concerned.* (Italics by this author.) The Baltic States were, after all, fully independent States between 1920 and 1940, were members of the League of Nations and internationally recognized, by the Soviet Union among others. As mentioned earlier, incorporation into the Soviet Union in 1940 took place against the will of the population, and was never recognized *de jure* by most countries. This does not hold true for the other parts of the Soviet Union, which all have their different histories. The 'independence' now foreseen by some of the republics of the Soviet Union is, in many cases, insufficiently defined, and need not necessarily mean that these republics reject all forms of amalgamation in a looser, Union Treaty. (...) If the question whether there should be recognition and diplomatic relations should arise at any time, then this can be answered only on a case-by-case basis, relying on the existing international criteria with respect to the recognition of States.' See *Netherl. YBIL* XXIII (1992), pp. 299–300.

119 See e.g. S.V. Chernichenko, *Teoria mezhdunarodnogo prava*, Vol II, Moscow: NIMP, 1999, pp. 72–79; P.P. Kremnev, *Raspad SSSR: mezhdunarodno-pravovye problemy*, Moscow: Zertsalo-M, 2005, pp. 57, 211.

120 V.I. Kuznetsov, B.R. Tuzmukhamedov (eds.) *Mezhdunarodnoe pravo*, Moscow: Norma, 2007, p. 307.

121 See I.V. Getman-Pavlova, *Mezhdunarodnoe pravo*, Moscow: Yurait, 2013, p. 345; G.M. Melkov (ed.) *Mezhdunarodnoe pravo*, Moscow: RIOR, 2009, p. 81; K.A. Bekiashev (ed.) *Mezhdunarodnoe publichnoe pravo*, 2nd ed., Moscow: Prospekt, 2003, p. 582.

122 See also R. Lewis, *Legal Fictions in International Law*, Cheltenham: Edward Elgar Publishing, 2021.

'fiction' has been understood as a logical or imaginative construction framed by the mind to which nothing corresponds in reality.[123] In law, 'fiction' seems to have several meanings.[124] First, each legal concept contains elements of 'fiction' due to the inevitable need for abstraction. In this sense, 'fictions' are everyday tools of legal life and analysis. When legal fictions are criticized, it is mostly when 'to them nothing corresponds in reality.'

State practice relating to statehood demonstrates that in international relations, different kinds of fictions are conceivable: political fictions, backed by arbitrary decisions, and legal fictions aimed at supporting legally established rights. Legal fictions can be employed to interpret a complex reality '*pour accéder d'une réalité inférieure à une réalité supérieure.*'[125] Certain fundamental principles of international law, such as the principle of the sovereign equality of States, contain strongly fictional elements, as critics have pointed out,[126] in the spirit of Orwell's comment that in reality, 'some animals are more equal than others.' Nevertheless, the element of fiction in the case of Syrian continuity was of a different character than that of Czechoslovakia. What kind of fiction do we then have in the Baltic case?

We need to examine more specifically whether the Baltic States existed continuously between 1940–1991 as subjects of international law or not. As we have observed, some international legal scholars have already expressed doubts in that respect. Some scholars base their doubts upon the facts on the ground, others upon doctrinal views on international law. In order to arrive at definitive conclusions about the legal status of the Baltic republics during the Soviet annexation period, we need to examine both the facts and the doctrine, and apply the latter to the former.

123 From Latin *fictio*, from *fingere*, i.e. to devise or form. See D.D. Runes (ed.) *Dictionary of Philosophy*, Ames, Iowa: Littlefield, Adams & Co., 1958, p. 109.

124 Cansacchi gives the following definition of the legal fiction: '*La fiction juridique, c'est une procédé de droit par lequel on presuppose une certaine situation comme existante, tandis que, dans la réalité des choses, elle s'etait produite différemment; cela pour réaliser des effets juridiques et politiques qui découlent de la situation fictive et qui ne pourraient pas decouler de la situation réellé.*' See Cansacchi, *op. cit.*, p. 40, but also pp. 10 and 47 *et seq.* See also M. Chemillier-Gendreau, 'Origine et rôle de la fiction en droit international public', in: 32 *Archives de Philosophic du Droit* 1987, pp. 153–162 and L.L. Fuller, 'Legal Fictions', 25 *Illinois Law Review* 1930–1931, p. 513.

125 J. Touscoz, *Le principe d'effectivité dans l'ordre international*, 1964, pp. 177–8. "To reach from a lower reality to a higher reality."

126 See e.g. R.W Tucker, *The Inequality of Nations*, New York: Basic Books, 1977. Philip Allott has even criticized the 'dangerous fiction of State responsibility' in: 'State Responsibility and the Unmaking of International Law', 29 *Harvard JIL* 1988, pp. 1–26 at 13 *et seq.*

CHAPTER 3

The Baltic States Between 1940 and 1991: Illegality and/or Prescription

1 Introduction

For some fifty years, the independent Republics of Estonia, Latvia and Lithuania were effectively—it has been argued—incorporated into the USSR. During that period (with the exception of the German occupation from 1941–1944), the Soviet Socialist Republics of Estonia, Latvia and Lithuania operated on the territories of the former independent Baltic States. According to the Soviet view, the independent 'bourgeois' Baltic States had become extinct and the new, Baltic Soviet republics their successor States within the USSR. From the point of view of other States, this claim could be supported, if not by the legitimacy of the socialist revolutions taking place—according to Soviet claims—in the Baltic States in 1940, then at least by the lasting effectiveness of Soviet rule in the Baltics.

Indeed, from the point of view of the pure three-elements theory, the realistic basis of which cannot be denied, it would have seemed peculiar to argue after the end of World War II that the Baltic republics continued to exist as subjects of international law. With Soviet rule in Estonia, Latvia and Lithuania, the independent 'bourgeois' Baltic States clearly no longer existed. Therefore, it is no surprise that several highly respected voices in the legal literature accepted the extinction of the Baltic States as a *fait accompli*.[1] However,

1 See e.g. W. Grewe, ‚Völkerrechtliche Umschau—Europa nach dem Waffenstillstand', in: 7 *Monatshefte für Auswärtige Politik* 1940, p. 686 ('Die baltischen Staaten haben (nach ihrer Eingliederung in die UdSSR) aufgehört zu existieren, als selbständige Subjekte des Völkerrechts zu bestehen. Sie sind Bundesrepubliken der Sowjetunion geworden (die litauische Sowjetrepublik nunmehr mit der Hauptstadt Wilna) und haben als solche keinen internationalen Status mehr.') See also E.J. Castrén, ‚Aspects récents de la succession d'etats', 78 *RCADI* 1951, p. 419; A. Baade, ‚Baltische Staaten', in: K. Strupp and H.-J. Schlochauer (eds.), *Wörterbuch des Völkerrechts*, 2. Ausg., Band I, 1960, p. 148: '*Formell gesehen sind die baltischen Staaten durch Einverleibung in die Sowjetunion als selbständige Völkerrechtssubjekte untergegangen.*'; G. Cansacchi, *op. cit.*, p. 20 ('Si cette independance disparaît parce que l'Etat est annexe par un Etat étranger … sa personnalité internationale cesse d'exister… Ainsi cessèrent d'exister comme sujets internationaux… les Etats baltes dans l'URSS en 1940.') See also R.W.G. De Muralt, *The Problem of State Succession with Regard to Treaties*, The Hague: W.P. van Stockum & Zoon, 1954, p. 40. De Muralt's conclusion 'Insofar as the annexation was

notwithstanding all the *effectivité* of prolonged Soviet rule, far from all States and legal scholars considered the Baltic States extinct as legal subjects.

The Baltic republics have based their claims of State continuity primarily on the illegality of the Soviet annexation. In different forms, this proposition has been contested by Soviet and later Russian diplomacy and doubted by some Western scholars. Therefore, we need to examine carefully the legal aspects of the events that occurred in the Baltic States in 1939/1940. The problem of the (il)legality of the Soviet annexation lies at the heart of the debate over the legal status of the Baltic republics.

2 The Illegality of Soviet Annexation

a *The Soviet Occupation and Annexation of the Baltic States in 1940: Facts*

The story of the annexation of the Baltic republics by the Soviet Union in 1940 has been told repeatedly in various studies of law and history.[2] In particular, later researchers of the legal aspects of the Baltic question have relied on the findings in Krystyna Marek's and Boris Meissner's classic studies.[3] Even earlier, in 1949, a legal scholar from Lithuania, Juozas Repečka, submitted an interesting thesis with a substantive historical part on this matter.[4] It is unnecessary to repeat here in detail the facts and arguments presented in earlier works. However, historians have recently revealed documents that further complement the picture of the policies pursued by the Soviet government in the Baltic States in 1939/1940.

---

legal, the case of the Baltic republics is comparable to that of Texas' at p. 40 was based upon erroneous factual assumptions, namely that the Baltic States had joined the USSR voluntarily. See also D.P. O'Connell, 'Recent Problems of State Succession in Relation to New States', *RCADI* 1971-II, p. 150.

2 See e.g. J.A. Swettenham, *The Tragedy of the Baltic States. A Report compiled from Official Documents and Eyewitnesses' Stories*, London: Holli and Carter, 1952; I.J. Vizulis, *Nations Under Duress. The Baltic States,* Port Washington: Associated Faculty Press, Inc., 1985; B.J. Kaslas, *The USSR-German Aggression against Lithuania,* New York: Robert Speller & Sons, 1973; M. Rosenbusch, H. Schützler, S. Striegnitz (Hg.) *Schauplatz Baltikum: Szenarium einer Okkupation und Angliederung: Dokumente 1939/1940*, Berlin: Dietz Verlag, 1991.

3 See K. Marek, *Identity and Continuity of States in Public International Law,* 1954; B. Meissner, *Die Sowjetunion, die baltischen Staaten und das Völkerrecht,* 1956.

4 J. Repečka, *Der gegenwärtige völkerrechtliche Status der baltischen Staaten, unter besonderer Berücksichtigung der diplomatischen Vorgeschichte der Eingliederung dieser Staaten in die Sowjetunion,* Dissertation, Göttingen, 1950.

The Soviet takeover of the independent Baltic States in 1939/1940 occurred in phases.[5] Politically, the ground was prepared by the secret Nazi-Soviet protocol which was attached to the German-Soviet Non-Aggression Pact (the so-called Molotov-Ribbentrop or Hitler-Stalin Pact) in Moscow on August 23, 1939.[6] According to this agreement, Stalin gave Hitler a free hand to attack Poland without Germany risking simultaneous entanglement with the Western democracies and the Soviet Union. As a *quid pro quo*, in the secret protocol Nazi Germany left Finland, eastern Poland, Bessarabia and the Baltic republics to the Soviet 'sphere of interest.' On 1 September 1939, Nazi Germany attacked Poland and unleashed World War II. On 17 September 1939, when Germany had already crushed the Polish army, the Soviet Union invaded Eastern Poland. Initially, Lithuania had been allocated to the German sphere of interest with the Nazi-Soviet secret protocol. However, in an additional secret protocol, concluded after the conquest of Poland, on September 28, 1939, Germany agreed to exchange Lithuania for certain Polish territories. Moreover, in early 1941, the USSR paid Germany $ 7,500,000 gold US dollars for the portion of Lithuania that had been assigned to the German sphere of influence but that had been occupied and incorporated by the Soviet Union along with the rest of Lithuania.

After Poland's independence had been liquidated by Nazi Germany and the Soviet Union, the diplomatic representatives of the Baltic States and Finland were quickly and separately called to Moscow where the Soviet leaders demanded the stationing of military bases on their territories.[7] Regarding the atmosphere awaiting the Estonian foreign minister in Moscow, the Estonian ambassador A. Rei gave the following testimony: '[The Soviet foreign minister] *Molotov repeatedly used the expressions 'I beg you not to compel the Soviet Government to use other, more radical methods of safeguarding its security' and 'if the Estonian Government fails to accept the Soviet proposal, then the USSR will achieve the aims mentioned in the Security Pact by resorting to different means.' Especially in view of the situation which had been created before that*

5 See J.-B. Duroselle, *Histoire diplomatique de 1919 à nos jours*, 2e édition, Paris, 1993, p. 261 *et seq.*

6 See generally on the diplomatic moves leading to the conclusion of the Nazi-Soviet alliance and the outbreak of World War II in H. Kissinger, *Diplomacy*, p. 332 *et seq.* and p. 350 *et seq.*

7 Eugene A. Korovin must have had *inter alia* these events in mind when he wrote in 1946: '*The sad history of the League of Nations and the grim lessons of the Second World War eloquently show that as long as there are rapacious imperialistic countries, the very existence of small states, let alone the question of equality, depends first and foremost upon the preparedness of the great peace-loving state to come to their defence.*' E. A. Korovin, 'The Second World War and International Law', 60 *AJIL* 1946, p. 746.

conversation, it was impossible to interpret Molotov's expressions as anything but a threat to use military force in order to enforce the Soviet demands.'[8]

In 1939, the governments of the Baltic republics yielded to Soviet demands and concluded Treaties of Mutual Assistance with the USSR.[9] Under the Soviet guarantee that the military bases would be established only for the duration of the war and that the sovereignty of the Baltic States would definitely be respected (Art. V of the Pacts), a Soviet military contingent was dispatched to the territories of the Baltic States (25 000 soldiers in Estonia, 30 000 in Latvia and 20 000 in Lithuania).

The government of Finland rejected similar Soviet demands for military bases. As a consequence, the USSR attacked Finland on December 1, 1939, initiating the so-called Soviet-Finnish Winter War that ended with Finland's loss of a part of its territory, as sealed by the Soviet-Finnish Peace Treaty of March 13, 1940. Nevertheless, at least Finland's independence remained intact. Because of its aggression against Finland, the Soviet Union was expelled from the League of Nations on December 14, 1939.[10]

For half a year, it seemed that the Soviet leadership, having acquired military bases on the territories of the Baltic States for the duration of the war in Europe, had found a certain *modus vivendi* with the independence of those States. The Baltic governments adhered to the rules of neutrality in the Soviet conflict with Finland.

On June 14 and 16, 1940, coinciding with the fall of Paris to German occupation forces, the Soviet government presented the Estonian, Latvian and Lithuanian governments with ultimatums demanding total military occupation of the Baltic States and the creation of new 'Soviet-friendly' governments.[11] The ultimatums were presented together with warnings that military resistance would be supressed. Handing over the ultimatum in Moscow, the Soviet People's Commissar of Foreign Affairs Molotov said to the Lithuanian Foreign Minister Juozas Urbšys: 'Irrespective of your answer, our troops will anyhow enter Lithuania tomorrow.'[12] With the Soviet army already in their territories,

8 A. Rei, *Nazi-Soviet Conspiracy and the Baltic States*. p. 41.

9 The Mutual Assistance Pact with Estonia was concluded on September 28, 1939 (198 LNTS 381), with Latvia on December 5, 1939, and with Lithuania on October 10, 1939.

10 Decision of the Council of the League of the Nations, LNOJ 1939, pp. 505–508. See further A.M. Rifaat, *International Aggression. A Study of the Legal Concept: Its Development and Definition in International Law*, Stockholm, 1979, pp. 98–99.

11 See Repečka, *op. cit.*, pp. 57–63.

12 See for Lithuanian archive sources: V. Vadapalas, V. Žalys, 'Secret Protocols to the Soviet-German Treaties of 1939 and the Problem of Prescription in International Law', in: *Proceedings of the Estonian Academy of Sciences. Social Sciences*, 1990, 39/2, p. 128.

the governments of the Baltic republics capitulated.[13] Approximately ten hours after the Soviet ultimatums were presented to the Baltic governments, the Soviet military invaded those countries. The Baltic States were occupied by the Soviet army on June 15–17, 1940.[14]

Since the Baltic Governments had yielded to Soviet demands, no military conflict occurred when the Baltic republics were occupied by the Soviet army on June 15–17, 1940. However, the Soviet ultimatum to Estonia was preceded by the Red Army's occupation of Naissaar, an island allowing control of sea access to the Estonian capital, Tallinn.[15] Moreover, in order to guarantee acceptance of Moscow's ultimatums, the Soviet navy had established a blockade along the coast of the Baltic Sea on June 14, 1940. (See Appendices)

Probably the first victims of Soviet repression in the Baltic States were crew members working for the President of Estonia who were travelling by sea from Tallinn, the capital of Estonia, to the President's summer residence in Toila on June 15–16, 1940. The crew was arrested by the Soviet navy, transported to Leningrad by the Soviets, and later put on trial for 'betrayal of the homeland.'[16] Moreover, on June 14, 1940, during the Soviet military blockade, a Finnish civil airplane ('Kaleva') flying from Tallinn to the nearby Finnish capital, Helsinki, was shot down by the Soviet army.

Subsequent to the occupation of the Baltic republics by the Soviet army, Stalin sent his emissaries Andrei Zhdanov, Andrei Vyshinski and Vladimir Dekanozov to direct the Soviet takeover in Estonia, Latvia and Lithuania. The lists of new governments were presented by the Soviet embassies in Tallinn, Riga and Kaunas to the Presidents of the Baltic States.[17] Even after the Baltic States were occupied by the Red Army, the Latvian and Estonian Presidents, who now found themselves under house arrest, were assured that the structure of government and the independence of the Baltic States would remain intact.[18] The President of Lithuania, Antanas Smetona, who had wanted the

13 For the deliberations of the Lithuanian government leading to acceptance of Soviet demands, see A. Eidintas, 'The Meeting of the Lithuanian Cabinet, 15 June 1940', in: J. Hiden and T. Lane (eds.), *The Baltic and the Outbreak of the Second World War*, Cambridge, 1992, pp. 165–173.

14 See Repečka, *ibid.*

15 See E. Sarv, *Õiguse vastu ei saa ükski*, 1997, p. 36.

16 Archive documents quoted in a special edition of the Estonian magazine 'Kultuur ja Elu', dealing with the first wave of Soviet deportations in 1940–1941. *Kultuur ja Elu* 3 (453) 1998, p. 2.

17 See for developments in Lithuania: A.E. Senn, 'What Happened in Lithuania in 1940?', p. 184 *et seq.*

18 A similar impression was left on the general public. On July 21, 1940, the newly-sent Soviet emissary in Riga, Andrei Vyshinski, ended his speech from the balcony of the

Lithuanian government to publicly protest against the Soviet occupation, had fled to Germany and was residing in East Prussia at that time. The Estonian and Latvian Presidents were isolated by the Soviet emissaries and, in a climate that was characterized by intimidation, agreed to appoint new, Soviet-friendly governments.

The new Baltic governments immediately announced parliamentary elections for July 1940. The following events were staged not without theatrical flair, and demonstrate how much importance the Soviet leadership attributed to the democratic simulacrum. The 1940 parliamentary elections played a major role in Soviet attempts to legitimize the sovietization of the Baltic republics, since the Soviets insisted upon the will of the people(s). However, initial violations of this will occurred when workers' demonstrations had been organized in the capitals of the Baltic States: the demonstrators were accompanied by Soviet tanks, and many demonstrators were imported from Soviet Russia.

Similar violations of the principle of legality occurred in connection with the parliamentary elections of July 1940. The elections turned out to be a farce, not only because they were meticulously guarded by the Soviet Army: the dates foreseen in the Baltic election laws were ignored, the candidates of the democratic opposition were prohibited from running, while the election results could not be confirmed in any transparent manner. The second chamber of the Estonian parliament was even not convened, and so on.

There was no mention at all of the change of the State system in the election platforms of the officially winning 'lists of the working people.' On the contrary, the official programmes of the 'lists of the working people' confirmed that the lists 'stand for friendly relations between the *independent* Baltic States and the mighty USSR' (italics added).[19] The results of the elections were announced by the official Soviet news agency TASS twelve hours in advance of the closing of the polls.[20] According to Henry Kissinger, not quite 20 percent of the population participated in what he calls Soviet sham elections.[21]

Soviet embassy by stating in the Latvian language: Long live free Latvia! and Long live the friendship between the Republic of Latvia and the Soviet Union!' See *Lettland unter sowjetischer und nationalsozialistischer Herrschaft. Eine Darstellung des lettischen Okkupationsmuseums*, Riga, 1998, p. 23.

19 See Repečka, p. 74 *et seq.*

20 See e.g. *The Baltic States 1940–1992. Documentary Background and Survey of Developments Presented to the European security and Cooperation Conference,* Stockholm: The Baltic Committee in Scandinavia, 1972.

21 See H. Kissinger, *Diplomacy,* p. 355. However, according to official Soviet data, 95.51 % of entitled Lithuanians participated in the elections, and 99.2 % voted for the candidate of the 'list of the working people'. In Latvia, 94.8 % were reported to have voted and 97.6 %

It is hard to disagree with Repečka, who came to the conclusion that 'the Baltic elections in 1940 were not only not *free* elections, but generally speaking, were not *elections* in the usual sense at all.'[22] Red Army soldiers sat among the deputies, some of whom had, it later turned out, been elected against their will.[23] However, the new 'parliaments' immediately proclaimed the Soviet republics of Estonia, Latvia and Lithuania, and petitioned for incorporation into the USSR.[24] According to the Baltic constitutions, the change of the system of government would have required organization of referendums.

Unsurprisingly, the Supreme Council of the Soviet Union promptly satisfied the petitions for incorporation. On August 3, 1940, the Lithuanian SSR was admitted to the Soviet Union. Similar decisions were taken with respect to the Latvian SSR on August 5, 1940, and the Estonian SSR on August 6, 1940. Even before the formal incorporation of the Baltic States into the USSR, the Presidents and Commanders-in-Chief of the Republics of Estonia and Latvia had been deported to Soviet Russia.[25]

In 1940, the three Baltic States—the Republics of Estonia, Latvia, and Lithuania—ceased to exist as independent States. But what role, from the point of view of international law, was played by the manner in which their independence had been erased?

b Soviet Occupation and Annexation of the Baltic States: Applicable Law

The legality of incorporation of the Baltic States into the Soviet Union in 1940 must be assessed on the basis of both international treaties and customary

voted in favour of the official candidates; in Estonia, 92.9 % voted and 96.8 % voted in favour of the official candidates.

22 Repečka, *op. cit.*, p. 160. Soviet elections in the occupied Baltic States in 1940 have even given rise to a special notion in the literature of political science during the Cold War, referring to unfair and orchestrated elections as 'Baltic elections.'

23 See R.A. Vitas, *The United States and Lithuania. The Stimson Doctrine of Nonrecognition*, p. 12.

24 Later, some members of those parliaments testified that Moscow's directive to vote to join the Soviet Union came as a surprise even for them, and was accompanied by threats that a 'no' vote would cost one's life. On the atmosphere created in new Lithuanian parliament, see Repečka, *op. cit.*, p. 78 (quoting the testimonies given by A. Garmus and L. Dovydenas, members of the 1940 Lithuanian parliament.)

25 Thus, for example, Kārlis Ulmanis, the President of the Republic of Latvia, was deported on July 22, 1940 to South Russia. He died presumably in 1942. See Reinhards (ed.) *Letton-ie-Russie*, p. 132. The Estonian President Konstantin Päts was for many years kept in a mental hospital—he died in Russia in 1956.

international law in force in 1939/1940. This is the rule of intertemporal law[26] which was addressed by Max Huber in a classic dictum in the *Island of Palmas* case:

> ...a juridical fact must be appreciated in the light of the law contemporary with it, and not of the law in force when a dispute arises regarding that fact.[27]

It is interesting to note, however, that this principle has sometimes been contested in international jurisprudence and doctrine. Judge Huber himself balanced his dictum in the same award with another one, namely:

> The same principle which subjects the act creative of a right to the law in force at the time the right arises, demands that the existence of the right, in other words its continued manifestations, shall follow the conditions required by the evolution of law.[28]

More recently, jurisprudence regarding problems of intertemporal law has remained quite ambiguous. This was well illustrated by the South West Africa (1966) and Namibia (1971) cases at the ICJ.[29] In the former, the ICJ ruled that

> ...the Court must place itself at the point in time when the mandate system was being instituted... the Court must have regard to the situation as it was that time...[30]

In the Namibia case, however, the ICJ used contrary argumentation to support its new judgment:

> The Court must take into consideration the changes which have occurred in the supervening half-century, and its interpretation cannot remain unaffected by the subsequent development of law.[31]

---

26 See generally W-D. Krause-Ablaß, *Intertemporales Völkerrecht. Der zeitliche Anwendungsbereich von Völkerrechtsnormen*, Hamburg: A. Metzner Verlag, 1970 and T.O. Elias, 'The Doctrine of International Law', 74 *AJIL* 1980 pp. 285–307; G.Y. Barsegov, 'On the Criticism of the 'Inter-Temporal Law' Doctrine', 1985, *Soviet YBIL*, pp. 202–205.

27 *Island of Palmas Case*, II UNRIAA, p. 845.

28 *Ibid.* p. 839.

29 See for discussion M. Koskenniemi, 'The Normative Force of Habit: International Custom and Social Theory', 1 *Finnish YBIL* 1990, pp. 77–153 at 132 *et seq.*

30 South West Africa Case, ICJ Reports 1966, p. 23 (§ 16).

31 Namibia Case, ICJ Reports 1971, p. 31 (§ 53).

In light of the ICJ dictum in the Namibia case, it has been suggested that post-1940 developments in the international prohibition of use (and threat) of force cannot be completely disregarded in legal evaluations of the Baltic case, especially in the period when the situation created in 1940 was consolidated. However, the principle of intertemporal law must be respected at least to the extent that references to the UN Charter must be avoided in the discussion of the legality of the Baltic—or any—events of 1939/1940.

The applicable law, especially the treaties in force between the Baltic States and the Soviet Union, was twofold: of a general and of a particular character. Importantly, in terms of protection the norms prescribed by specific international agreements in force between the respective countries surpassed the generally applicable treaties of the time.

Since the Soviet Union had been expelled from the League of Nations in December 1939, the League of Nations Covenant, especially Article 10, no longer formally bound the Soviet government by 1940.[32] With Article 10 of the Covenant, the League of Nations undertook to respect and preserve as against external aggression the territorial integrity and existing political independence of all Members.[33] However, Article 10 of the League of Nations Covenant still bound the Soviet Union when it concluded the Nazi-Soviet Non-Aggression Pact with its secret protocols.[34] The secret protocols of the Hitler-Stalin Pact of 1939 thus undoubtedly violated the League Covenant.

With adoption of the Kellogg-Briand Pact in 1928 in which States banned war as an instrument of national policy, the prohibition of aggressive wars became a part of general international law.[35] However, it can still be debated whether the *threat* of military force was equally prohibited in general international law before such a prohibition was explicitly expressed in the Charter

32 Cf. Y. Dinstein, *War, Aggression and Self-Defence,* 2nd ed., Cambridge, 1994, p. 80.

33 *League of Nations Covenant,* printed in: W. Schücking, H. Wehberg, *Die Satzung des Völkerbundes,* 2. Aufl., Berlin: Franz Vahlen, 1924. See also related articles 12, 13, 15 and 16. Although the text of Article 10 did not mention non-recognition explicitly, Langer wrote in 1947 that Article 10 implied a duty of non-recognition of the forcible seizure. See R. Langer, *Seizure of Territory. The Stimson Doctrine and Related Principles in Legal Theory and Diplomatic Practice,* 1947, p. 96. See also L. Hannikainen, *Peremptory Norms (Jus Cogens) in International Law. Historical Development, Criteria, Present Status,* Helsinki, 1988, p. 134 *et seq.*

34 See also Repečka, *op. cit.,* p. 98.

35 See N. Maim, *Völkerbund und Staat. Ein Beitrag zur Ausarbeitung eines allgemeinen öffentlichen Rechts,* Tartu: K. Mattiesen, 1932, p. 196 *et seq.* As to the exceptions, see Y. Dinstein, *War, Aggression...* pp. 81–83. See also A.M. Rifaat, *International Aggression,* p. 69 *et seq.*

of the United Nations, adopted in 1945.[36] A conservative view maintains that before the entry into force of the UN Charter, *general* international law, although undoubtedly prohibiting such a use of force itself, did not explicitly prohibit the *threat* of military force.[37] Some contemporary authors therefore suggest that the policy of the USSR against the Baltic States in 1939/1940 did not violate general rules of customary international law.[38] We will need to look at additional legal commitments between the USSR and the Baltic States.

In the first place, relations between the Soviet Union and the Baltic States were legally regulated by bilateral or regional, that is, non-universal treaties. Seldom in the history of international relations have the contracting parties taken upon themselves such comprehensive commitments with regard to a neighbour's sovereign rights and interests. The legal foundation of bilateral relations was provided by the Peace Treaties concluded between Soviet Russia and the Baltic republics in 1920, after successful wars of secession fought by Estonia, Latvia and Lithuania. In those treaties, Russia recognized the secession of the Baltic republics based on the right of peoples to self-determination—a principle proclaimed by Lenin and for the first time introduced to the practice of international law by those very Peace Treaties.[39] This was highly progressive in 1920, and as part of regional international law decades ahead of universal legal developments.[40] For example, Article 2 of the Tartu Peace Treaty between Soviet Russia and the Republic of Estonia reads:

> On the basis of the right of all peoples freely to decide their own destinies, and even to separate themselves completely from the State of which they form a part, a right proclaimed by the Federal Socialist Republic of Soviet Russia, Russia unreservedly recognizes the independence and autonomy of the State of Estonia, and renounces voluntarily and for ever all rights of sovereignty formery held by Russia over the Estonian people and territory by virtue of

---

36 See L. Hannikainen, *Peremptory Norms (Jus Cogens) in International Law*, p. 135 *et seq*. Cf. A. Randelzhofer, 'Commentary to Article 2(4)', in: B. Simma (ed.) *The Charter of the United Nations. A Commentary*, Oxford: University Press, 1994, p. 111.

37 Note, however, that in that case one would also be compelled to conclude that the German takeover of Czechoslovakia and Austria was not unlawful. This outcome, however, contradicts Nuremberg practice.

38 See H. Krieger, *Das Effektivitätsprinzip im Völkerrecht,* 2000, p. 440, O. Dörr, *Inkorporation...*, p. 352.

39 See further L. Mälksoo, 'The Soviet Approach to the Right of Peoples to Self-Determination: Russia's Farewell to *jus publicum europaeum*', 19 *Journal of the History of International Law* 2017, pp. 200–218.

40 See further on the right of peoples to self-determination: C. Tomuschat (ed.), *Modern Law of Self-Determination,* Dordrecht: Martinus Nijhoff Publishers, 1993.

> the former legal situation, and by virtue of international treaties, which, in respect of such rights, shall henceforth lose their force.
>
> No obligation towards Russia devolves upon the Estonian people and territory from the fact that Estonia was formerly part of Russia.[41]

The Soviet peace treaties with Latvia and Lithuania used, *mutatis mutandis*, similar language.[42] Therefore, with the Peace Treaties signed and ratified by Soviet Russia and the Baltic States in 1920, the legally binding force of the principle of self-determination of peoples was recognized in the form of specific international law.[43]

Furthermore, Estonia, Latvia, Poland, Romania and the USSR had on February 9, 1929 signed in Moscow a Protocol, intiated by the Soviet Peoples Comissar of Foreign Affairs Maksim Litvinov, and therefore called the Litvinov Protocol.[44] Under this Protocol, the Kellogg-Briand Pact, renouncing war as an instrument of national policy, was brought into effect between the signatories even before it entered into force for the original contracting parties. Lithuania signed the Litvinov Protocol on April 5, 1929.

The Soviet government had also concluded non-aggression pacts[45] with all three Baltic States—with Lithuania on September 18, 1926,[46] with Latvia on February 8, 1932,[47] and with Estonia on May 4, 1932.[48] Article 1 of the non-aggression pact between the Soviet Union and Latvia stipulated:

---

41 LNTS, Vol. II, p. 29.

42 See the *Riga Peace Treaty*, signed by Russia and Latvia on August 11, 1920, in LNTS, Vol. 2, p. 195 and *Moscow Peace Treaty*, signed by Lithuania and Russia on July 12, 1920, LNTS, Vol. III, p.105. A. Reinhards, *Lettonie-Russie. Traites et documents de base vet* extenso, Lausanne, 1998.

43 Yuri Barsegov evaluates these self-determination provisions in early Soviet treaties very highly: '*The analysis of the treaty relations of the first years of the Soviet state demonstrates that even then many states were formally obliged to honour the right of peoples to self determination. The treaty practice of the USSR prepared the ground for general recognition of the right of self determination as one of the main principles of international law. The principle of self determination obtained final and complete recognition with the victory of the democratic nations, led by the Soviet Union, over the forces of fascism and imperialism in the years of World War II.*' Ю. Г. Барсегов, *Территория в международном праве. Юридическая природа территориального верховенства и правовые основания распоряжения территорией*, Москва: Государсвенное издательство юридической литературы, 1958, p. 73 (Translated from Russian.)

44 LNTS, Vol. 89, p. 369.

45 See generally J.M. Mössner, 'Non-Aggression Pacts', *EPIL* III, 1997, pp. 596–600.

46 LNTS, Vol. 60, p. 146.

47 LNTS, Vol. 148, p. 126.

48 LNTS, Vol. 131, p. 297.

> Each of the High Contracting Parties guarantees to the other Party the inviolability of the existing frontiers between them, as defined by the Peace Treaty signed on August 11, 1920, and undertakes to refrain from any act of aggression or any violent measures directed against the integrity and inviolability of the territory or against the political independence of the other Contracting Party, whether such act of aggression or such violent measures are undertaken separately or in conjunction with other Powers, with or without a declaration of war.

The Soviet non-aggression pacts with Estonia and Lithuania contained identical provisions. The non-aggression pacts with Estonia and Latvia were supplemented by arbitration agreements dated June 16, 1932, and June 18, 1932, respectively.[49] These arbitration agreements supplemented the provisions of the non-aggression treaties (see for example Article 4 of the Soviet-Estonian Treaty of Non-aggression) in which the Parties undertook to submit all disputes between them 'to a procedure of conciliation in a mixed Conciliation Commission.'

There was one more remarkable treaty in force between the Soviet Union and the Baltic States. On the initiative of the USSR, Estonia, Latvia, Poland, Turkey, Iran and Afghanistan and the USSR signed the Convention on the Definition of Aggression[50] in London, on July 3, 1933. The terms of the Convention were later extended to Lithuania under a special treaty between the Soviet Union and Lithuania.[51]

The contracting parties undertook to accept in their relations with each other the definition of aggression that was framed by the Committee on Security Questions of the Conference for the Reduction and Limitation of Armaments, 'following on the Soviet delegation's proposal' (so Article 1 of the Convention).[52]

---

49 LNTS, Vol. 131, p. 309 and Vol. 148, p. 129, respectively.

50 LNTS, Vol. 147, p. 69. See about the background to this convention J.F. Triska, R.M. Slusser, *The Theory, Law, and Policy of Soviet Treaties*, Stanford: Stanford University Press, 1962, p. 262 *et seq.* and C. Rousseau, *Le droit de confits armés*, 1983, p. 581.

51 LNTS, Vol. 148, p. 79.

52 Soviet international legal scholars highlighted the importance of the *Convention on the Definition of Aggression* for the development of public international law. Thus, Eugene A. Korovin, discussing the lessons of World War II, concluded: '*But of really great theoretical and practical significance is the international law experience of the Soviet state in introducing new democratic principles into international usage and in fighting for their recognition. Some of the stages and landmarks in this glorious path are: (...), the Soviet pacts regarding the definition of aggression. (...) Whether it has been the question (...) of the sovereignty and independence of small peoples and states— always and everywhere representatives of the*

Article 2 of the Convention on the Definition of Aggression stated:

Accordingly, the aggressor in an international conflict shall, subject to the agreements in force between the parties to the dispute, be considered to be that State which is the first to commit any of the following actions:

1. Declaration of war upon another State;
2. Invasion by its armed forces, with or without a declaration of war, of the territory of another State;
3. Attack by its land, naval or air forces, with or without a declaration of war, on the territory, vessels or aircraft of another State;
4. Naval blockade of the coasts or ports of another State;
5. Provisions of support to armed bands formed in its territory which have invaded the territory of another State, or refusal, notwithstanding the request of the invaded State, to take in its own territory all the measures in its power to deprive those bands of all assistance or protection.

Moreover, Article 3 of the Convention for the Definition of Aggression provided:

> No political, military, economic or other considerations may serve as an excuse or justification for the aggression referred to in Article 2.

In sum, it can be submitted that the international treaties binding the Soviet Union and the Baltic States prohibited any aggression or violent measures against any of the contracting States. Furthermore, and without precedent for the time under consideration, the definition of aggression was agreed upon in a legally binding manner.

c Legal Evaluation of Soviet Policy against the Baltic States in 1939/1940

Threats of use of force against the Baltic republics were first employed by the Soviet government in autumn 1939, soon after the Hitler-Stalin Pact with its secret protocols was concluded.[53] Acting under duress, the governments of the

---

USSR have been the foremost champions of democracy and international justice, defending the sacred cause of freedom of the peoples and peace among nations (...).' See E.A. Korovin, 'The Second World...', p. 754.

53 It is not necessary to undertake a detailed legal analysis of the Hitler-Stalin Pact's secret protocols here. It may be briefly noted that from a legal point of view, this treaty violated peremptory norms of international law, such as independence of States and prohibition of intervention. The secret protocols were thus legally null and void. See G.-H. Gornig, *Der Hitler-Stalin Pakt: eine völkerrechtliche Studie,* Frankfurt a.M.: Peter Lang, 1990, p. 86 and H. Lindpere, 'Evaluation of the Soviet-German Pacts of August 23 and September 28 1949 from the Standpoint of International Law', 1 *FYBIL* 1990, pp. 415–439. Moreover, the USSR,

Baltic States yielded to Soviet demands, upon which Soviet military bases were established on their territories.[54] Some Baltic authors have argued that those agreements of mutual assistance, as they were arrived at under threat—and even by open demonstration—of military force, must be qualified as legally void. According to these authors, Soviet policy towards the Baltic republics in 1939 must even then be qualified as aggression.

Boris Meissner has opposed this argument. According to him, the mutual assistance treaties between the Baltic States and the Soviet Union, although concluded under duress and even in violation of the Soviet-Baltic Non-aggression Pacts, were not automatically null and void.[55] In any case, it was specifically stressed in those treaties and during negotiations leading to the treaties that the sovereignty of the Baltic republics remained untouched. It seems to the present author that Meissner's argument is legally sound. Notwithstanding duress, the Baltic governments accepted the conditions of the mutual assistance treaties, and those treaties were implemented in practice for more than half a year. Moreover, with an emphasis on practice related to the conclusion of peace treaties in 1919, it was the prevailing legal opinion at the time that coerced treaties were not automatically legally void.[56]

However, the Soviet ultimatums of June 1940 were clearly presented along with threats of military force.[57] It is evident that such threats attacked the very spirit and essence of all major treaties then in force between the Soviet Union and the Baltic States, including the 1939 Soviet-Baltic agreements. By issuing those threats, the Soviet Union violated its obligations under the non-aggression treaties it had concluded with the Baltic republics. We may *gratia*

---

still being a member of the League of Nations at the time of this agreement, undoubtedly violated its obligations under the Statute of League of Nations (e.g. Art. 10). See Repečka, *op. cit.*, p. 98 *et seq.* See also for a late Soviet view: Р.А. *Мюллерсон*, 'Советско-Германские договоренности в аспекте межднародного права', *in:* Советское государство и право но. 9 1989, pp. 105–109.

54 One of the leading Soviet authors, Yuri Barsegov, criticized such a policy in the context of the 'imperialist states': *'Under the pretext of 'spheres of influence', 'longterm rent', 'pre-occupation and administration', the establishment of military bases 'in the mutual defence interest', the imperialist states, with the help of force, make attempts to win for themselves extraterritorial rights within the borders of formally equal and sovereign states.'* See Ю.Г. Барсегов, *Территория в международном праве*, 1958, p. 34. (Translated from Russian).

55 See Meissner, *Die Sowjetunion…*, 1956, pp. 188–9.

56 See e.g. H. Lauterpacht, *Private Law Sources and Analogies*, 1927, sections 73–74 at pp. 161–167.

57 Crawford writes that the Baltic States were 'occupied and illegally annexed by the Soviet Union in 1940 in circumstances involving the use of force and duress.' See J. Crawford, 'State Practice and International Law in Relation to Secession', 69 *BYBIL* 1998, p. 96.

argumentandi accept the somewhat legalistic reading of the treaties in force between the countries concerned, namely that the *threat* of military force was not yet aggression (that is, the invasion by Soviet military forces was not really a classic invasion because the Baltic governments accepted the Soviet ultimatums). At the same time, it is impossible to deny that Soviet policy with respect to the Baltic States in the summer of 1940 was 'directed against the integrity and inviolability of territory or against the political independence' of those States. (See *supra* the wording of the non-aggression treaties.) Therefore, the Soviet occupation of the Baltic republics in June 1940 must be defined as illegal intervention under general international law.[58]

Moreover, even if the issue of the (il)legality of the *threat* of use of force in general international law, as it was in force in 1940, may remain in some aspects disputable, at the same time the Soviet military blockade in June 1940 merits unequivocal legal qualification. As a matter of fact, this qualification can best be undertaken by the method suggested in 1933 by the Soviet People's Commissar of Foreign Affairs, Maksim Litvinov. In connection with the Soviet definition of aggression at the League of Nations, Litvinov presented the Soviet view on how to determine who is an aggressor. To do so, first of all the facts need to be determined, and second, a definition applied to the established facts. The aggressor in an international conflict is the State that first commits any of the five precisely defined actions that the Soviet government suggested for adoption by the League of Nations.[59]

As is known, the States represented at the League of Nations did not conclude any general treaty defining aggression.[60] However, under the Soviet initiative such a legally binding definition of aggression was adopted in London in 1933 between the USSR and the States of the so-called *cordon sanitaire.* According to this treaty (see *supra*), direct military attack, meeting resistance, was but one, although of course the most important form of aggression (See subpoint 3 in the Treaty: aggression as an attack by land, naval and air forces').

Repečka[61] and Meissner[62] have argued that the occupation of Estonia, Latvia and Lithuania by the Red Army in June 1940 violated *inter alia* subpoint 3 of the treaty (aggression as 'invasion by armed forces, with or without a declaration of war, of the territory of another State'), making the

58 Repečka, *op. cit.,* p. 132.

59 Quoted in C.A. Pompe, *Aggressive War—an International Crime,* The Hague: Martinus Nijhoff, 1953, p. 77.

60 See also B.B. Ferencz, 'Aggression', in: R. Bernhardt (ed.) *EPIL*, Vol. 1, pp. 58–65.

61 Repečka, *op. cit.*, pp. 128–129.

62 Meissner, *Die Sowjetunion...*, 1956, pp. 199–200.

invasion of Soviet troops qualify as aggression. Supporting this argument is the article's systematic interpretation, namely its distinction between 'invasion by armed forces' (2) and 'attack by land, naval or air forces' (3). It could indeed be argued that in order to give any logical meaning to this distinction between invasion and attack in the treaty definition, an invasion by armed forces could also take place after 'acceptance of the ultimatum' (by decision not to fight back) of the respective government when this is achieved by the threat of war.

The relevant treaties do not explicitly distinguish between true consent and 'acceptance' achieved by military force (when acceptance of an ultimatum, as in the Baltic case, can be qualified as consent at all[63]).

Among other acts of aggression such as the naval blockade of coasts and ports of other States was listed in the *Convention on the Definition of Aggression*. As shown above and in the Appendices, the evidence is indisputable that precisely such a military blockade was undertaken by the Soviet Union against the Baltic States in June 1940. Without confronting military resistance, the Soviet army had overrun certain parts of some of the Baltic republics, for example the island of Naissaar in Estonia, before Moscow's ultimatums were accepted by the Baltic governments. Therefore, the Soviet occupation of the independent Baltic republics qualifies as an act of aggression.[64]

Moreover, Soviet policy was at variance with the right of the Estonian, Latvian and Lithuanian peoples to self-determination—a right recognized by Soviet Russia in its Peace Treaties with the Baltic States, and therefore constituting part of regional international law.[65]

The decision of the Baltic governments to yield to the Soviet ultimatums in 1940 does not accord legality to the Soviet occupation of those States. However, what has made the waters somewhat murkier is the fact that the governments of the Baltic republics[66] did not protest in public against Soviet

63 Nikolai Kaasik, an international legal scholar from Estonia, has rejected the argument that through acceptance of the Soviet ultimatum, it could have acquired a legal quality: '*Devant une menace d'ouverture immédiate des hostilités, le gouvernement estonien dut céder. Toutefois, la soumission à un ultimatum ne signifie pas son acceptation, elle ne constitue pas la reconnaissance des accusations y formulées, elle ne le rend pas légal. Accepté ou repoussé, l'ultimatum reste illegal en vertu du droit conventionnel en vigueur entre les parties, il reste un acte contraire au droit, il constitue une infraction ou un délit...*' N. Kaasik, 'L'Ultimatum Soviétique à l'Estonie', 1946, p. 17.

64 Repečka , p. 130 *et seq.* and 142 *et seq.*

65 See B. Meissner, *The Occupation of the Baltic States from a Present-Day Perspective*, p. 480.

66 As already mentioned, the President of Lithuania, A. Smetona, fled the country on June 15, 1940. Therefore, the following Soviet acts lacked legality in Lithuania even from the

aggression, and, while their countries were already occupied, their presidents even formally approved the new 'Soviet-friendly' governments. The Estonian historian Magnus Ilmjärv has characterized this as silent submission.[67]

Even leaving *gratia argumentandi* aside, the aspect of the intimidating conditions in which the Soviet ultimatums in June 1940 were presented, even the formal acquiescence of the individual Baltic leaders (or absence of public protest) could not have accorded legality to the abrupt political changes undertaken during the first two months of Soviet occupation. The authority of the Baltic presidents was constitutionally limited, and even their own genuine approval of political changes under Soviet rule could not have legalized gradual handing over of sovereignty.[68]

Moreover, the genuineness of the presidents' acquiescence must be seriously doubted. In Estonia, for instance, President Päts initially refused to nominate the new cabinet selected by the Soviet embassy. He yielded to the demands only when a demonstration of Soviet-friendly workers (partly from Estonia, partly 'imported' from the USSR), supported by the Soviet military, encircled the Presidential Palace in Tallinn on June 21, 1940.[69] It is clear that, once the Baltic States were subjugated under Soviet occupation, nothing comparable to what was actually undertaken could—whether from the constitutional or the international law point of view—accord legality to the steps already undertaken under the guidance of the Soviet authorities.[70]

In terms of international law concerning State responsibility, there are no grounds in the Baltic case for speaking of valid consent or any other circumstance precluding wrongfulness. Consent must be valid; consent given under the threat of invasion is ineffective to preclude the wrongfulness of the military

---

most formalistic point of view, even not taking into account the fact of aggression or physical intimidation. See Repečka, p. *66 et seq.*

67 M. Ilmjärv, *Silent Submission. Formation of Foreign Policy of Estonia, Latvia and Lithuania. Period from Mid-1920-s to Annexation in 1940*, Acta Universitatis Stockholmiensis, Studia Baltica Stockholmiensia 24, Stockholm, 2004.

68 See also Repečka, pp. 141–143. Meissner opposes this argument in *Die Sowjetunion...*, 1956, p. 221.

69 See e.g. Repečka, p. 72.

70 There are also indications that the Baltic leaders, while trying to save the independent statehood of their respective republics, considered their countries as being under occupation. When the Commander-in-Chief of the Estonian Army Johan Laidoner drove to Narva, in order to sign the accord about the entry of the 'unlimited Red Army contingent' into Estonian territory, he met advancing Soviet troops even before he could reach Narva. He has been reported to have said: '*We are in an occupied country.*'

occupation of a State's territory.[71] Nor can the wrongfulness of Soviet acts be precluded by the defence of necessity.[72]

A certain legitimizer of the changes undertaken by the Soviet government would have been genuine communist revolutions in the Baltic States. In Riga, Kaunas and Tallinn, demonstrations by workers were organized under the protection and direct participation of the Red Army. Historical research, especially the memoirs of the participants, confirm that these demonstrations—in Marek's characterization a typical 'fake revolution'[73]—were orchestrated by Moscow. There was hardly any evidence of a 'revolutionary situation' in the Baltic States. The underground Communist Party of Estonia, for instance, numbered 133 members in 1940 (Estonia's population being 1.5 million). In Lithuania, according to the official Soviet data, the Communist Party numbered 1500 members (0.05 % of the Lithuanian population) on February 25, 1941 (or roughly half a year after the beginning of the Soviet occupation and annexation).[74]

Nevertheless, the Soviet occupation of the Baltic republics in June 1940 has not always been qualified as an 'act of aggression' in Western legal scholarship.[75] Sometimes, cautious and ambiguos euphemisms such as 'incorporation' or 'absorption' are used to refer to the Soviet 'takeover.' This may partly be due to the mistaken belief that the Baltic leaders formally 'consented' to occupation and to the nomination of new governments, as dictated by Moscow. When the Baltic States had been annexed, there were initially no governments in exile left to protest Soviet policy, so that the remark by Krylov about the 1933 *Convention on the Definition of Aggression* ('none of these conventions were invoked during the events leading up to World War II')[76] was technically speaking almost as true as it was cynical.

---

71 See UK, *Judgement of the International Military Tribunal for the Trial of German Major War Criminals*, Cmd. 6964, (1946), p. 17 at pp. 18–19. The Tribunal denied that Austrian consent had been given, and noted that the *Anschluß* was illegal. See *ibid.* p. 17. See also J. Crawford (ed.) *Commentaries on the ILC Draft Articles on State Responsibility*, Article 20.

72 Meissner, *Die Sowjetunion*, 1956, p. 205 *et seq.*

73 See Marek, *op. cit.*, p. 64 *et seq.*

74 72 Repečka, *op. cit.*, p. 155.

75 However, note the finding of the Kersten Committee of the US House of Representatives in 1954: '(...) *the Soviet Union, without provocation, did in June 1940 invade and take military and political control over Lithuania, Latvia, and Estonia, thus committing an act of unprovoked aggression.*' See *Report of the Select Committee to Investigate Communist Aggression and the Forced Incorporation of the Baltic States into the USSR*, Third Interim Report, Washington, DC, 1954, p. 7.

76 С.В. Крылов, 'Борьба СССР за мир' (The Fight of the USSR for the Peace), in: В.Н. Дурденевски, С.Б. Крылов, *Международное право*, Институт права Академий Наук СССР, Москва: Юридическое издательство,, 1947, para. 122, pp. 578–79.

In international comparison, another compelling argument for characterizing the Soviet takeover of the Baltic States in 1940 as aggression is analogy. The view that the USSR committed aggression against the Baltic republics finds further confirmation in an analysis of the practice of the Nuremberg International Military Tribunal, by analogy. It was the task of the Nuremberg tribunal to find sound legal qualification for Nazi Germany's leaders' aggressive acts before and during World War II. Among the crimes under the jurisdiction of the Nuremberg Tribunal were war crimes, crimes against humanity, and most importantly in our context, crimes against peace, which were defined as '[the] *planning preparation, initiation or waging of a war of aggression, or a war in violation of international treaties, agreements or assurances, or participation in a common plan or conspiracy for the accomplishment of any of the foregoing.*'

While it was unproblematic to define most of Germany's conquests—for example against Poland or against the Soviet Union—as crimes against peace at Nuremberg, other borderline cases proved to be legally more challenging. Germany had seized some independent States—Austria, Czechoslovakia, and Denmark—without the outbreak of hostilities by using the threat of military force. Thus, Czechoslovakia's President Emil Hácha finally yielded to German demands to let the *Wehrmacht* march in after Hermann Göring threatened to have the German *Luftwaffe* bomb Prague. Before Czechoslovakia was seized, Austria was annexed by Germany in March 1938 without a military conflict, after Austrian Chancellor Kurt von Schuschnigg had yielded to German threats and nominated the local Nazi leader as prime minister. The case of Denmark's occupation again reveals slight differences—Denmark surrendered without military resistance (although some Danish units offered resistance during the first hours of the German invasion.) However, the Danish King Christian forbade resistance to the German army's invasion only after it had already started.[77]

According to the classic understanding of international law, Germany's seizure of Austria, Czechoslovakia, and Denmark did not amount to 'war.' There was neither 'military conflict', nor a 'state of war'[78] in those cases. In terms of the classic dichotomy of belligerent versus pacific occupation, those actions should technically have been qualified as pacific occupations.[79]

---

77 See further A. Ross, 'Denmark's Legal Status during the Occupation', 1 *Jus Gentium* 1949, p. 3 *et seq.*

78 But see the critique of the concept of state of war in C.A. Pompe, *op. cit.*, p. 3 and 34 *et seq.*

79 Pompe, *op. cit.*, p. 24.

The absence of war and the formal approval of invasion (lack of public protest) in these cases was no reason for the Nuremberg Tribunal to handle them differently from Nazi aggression involving outright war. However, the cases of Austria and Czechoslovakia, on the one hand, and Denmark on the other hand, were distinguished from each other in the judgment rendered by the Nuremberg Tribunal. The case of Denmark was construed as a case of aggressive war (Danish accession to German demands came only after the German invasion had already started).[80] According to the Judgment of the Nuremberg Tribunal, Germany committed 'aggressive acts' against Austria and Czechoslovakia.[81] While not deemed aggressive wars, these invasions were still held to amount to aggression. It follows that some peacetime occupations may still be viewed as crimes against peace, threats to peace or even acts of war.[82]

The rationale for such legal findings is easily understandable: in all these cases, a war would have been waged against these countries if their cooperation had not been assured by threats and intimidation.[83] An armed reaction would have been unavoidabe for the attacked State if its independence or the integrity of its territory were to be preserved against the aggressor.[84] Therefore, as C.A. Pompe has explained, for the Nuremberg Tribunal this intimidation had the same effect as a war or use of force on a war footing.[85] To conclude, the practice of Nuremberg demonstrated that during World War II crimes against peace could be committed without the outbreak of actual hostilities.[86]

The Nuremberg analogy is only of auxiliary importance for a legal evaluation of the Baltic case. As shown above, Soviet acts against the Baltic States fall under the definition of aggression as crystallized in the Convention on the Definition of Aggression. However, the Nuremberg judgment still provides important evidence concerning standards of international law in the context of World War II. By analogy to the Nuremberg precedents, the Soviet invasion of the Baltic republics in June 1940 would have to be qualified as aggression as well—even if a legally binding definition of aggression together with

80 See I. Brownlie, *International Law and the Use of Force by States*, Oxford: Clarendon Press, 1963, p. 211.

81 See Judgment, p. 17, 19, 93, 106. See also Brownlie, *Use of Force*, p. 211.

82 Roberts, *What Is a Military Occupation?* BYBIL 1984, p. 273. See also the judgment of the US Military Tribunal of April 14, 1949, in *US v. Weizsäcker and Others*, Annual Digest, 16 (1949), Case No. 118, p. 347.

83 Pompe, *op. cit.*, p. 22.

84 Pompe, *op. cit.* p. 50.

85 Pompe, *op. cit.*, p. 120.

86 See for a critique of the Nuremberg Tribunal's judgment with respect to Czechoslovakia: Marek, *op. cit.*, p. 302 *et seq.*

non-aggression pacts had not been in force between the Soviet Union and the Baltic States. It is hard to disagree with the logic of Dainius Žalimas:

> There are no reasons to treat the analogous actions of the Soviet Union in 1940 in a different way. If we took an opposite view, we would deny the legal nature of international law. Under any system of law it is impossible to qualify analogous acts made under the same circumstances differently, i.e. we can not treat an action made by one state as an international crime and the same action made by another state as a legitimate act.[87]

In light of the foregoing, the following conclusions can be drawn. In June 1940, the Soviet Union committed acts of aggression against the Baltic States. Air and naval blockades were established by the Soviet army but hostilities with the Baltic armies did not break out. Thus, technically, no state of war was established between the USSR and the Baltic republics. However, in essence, the occupation of the Baltic republics by the Red Army was closer to military than to peaceful occupation. It represents a borderline case between the two, which the Austrian international lawyer Alfred Verdross might have called quasi-belligerent occupation (*occupatio quasi-bellica*), and which still legally bound the occupier to the 1907 Hague Regulations.[88]

The special feature of the Soviet occupation of the Baltic States is that at no time did the occupying power publicly recognize that it was merely an occupying power. Instead, the government of the USSR persistently argued that the (already Sovietized) Baltic republics joined the Soviet Union in August 1940 of their own will. As demonstrated above, and in many other works preceding the present study, this statement was simply false. The incorporation of Estonia, Latvia and Lithuania into the Soviet Union in August 1940, after the occupation of these States in June 1940, was not a voluntary act, but has been correctly qualified as forcible seizure of territory, in other words annexation. Moreover, as we will see next and beyond the specific Baltic case, the legal views expressed in Soviet literature speak strongly against the legality of forcible annexation *per se*.

d *The Illegality of Annexation in International Law: Soviet Views*

The Soviet legal position on the legality of annexations should not be neglected in the discussion, since it is the fairest way to establish what is legally allowed and what is prohibited when applying the legal rules, as perceived by the

87 D. Zhalimas, 'Legal and Political Issues…', p. 110.

88 See A. Verdross, ‚Völkerrechtliche Identität von Staaten…', p. 20.

relevant State itself. Part of the complexity with legally assessing Soviet actions in the Baltic States in 1939–1940 is that during the interwar period, first Soviet Russia and then the Soviet Union was far from agreeing with everything that was considered as settled in the Western or 'bourgeois' doctrine of international law. Soviet legal scholars, following the views of Vladimir Lenin, determined the legality of territorial acquisitions on the basis of the principle of self-determination of peoples rather than on the right of States to sovereignty.[89] According to Lenin, annexation qualifies as '*a violation of the right of peoples to self determination, an establishment of the State boundaries against the will of the population*.'[90] On November 8, 1917, the II Russian General Congress of the Soviets proclaimed the Decree on Peace, formulated by Lenin. Annexation was defined in the following complex passage:

> Under the annexation or forcible seizure of foreign countries the government understands, according to the legal consciousness of democracy generally and of the working class especially, every unification of a small and weak people with a large and strong State, without the exact, clear and voluntarily expressed wish or consent of this people, regardless of how developed or backward the nation might be that is unified violently or held within the boundaries of the existing State, and notwithstanding whether the nation is situated in Europe or in distant transoceanic countries.[91]

The logical consequence of the Soviet concept of annexation was that the decisive criterion for the legality of territorial change was the will of the affected people. In a way, this concept enabled according legality to annexations undertaken against a State (government) but were supported by the affected population.[92] The assumption of Marxist-Leninist doctrine was that as the majority of the population was always made up of the working people, they would, based on their own class interests, eventually support the Soviet system of government. Maybe they only needed a push or 'awakening' from outside, especially considering that the bourgeois class would be suppressing the workers and the expression of their free will.

---

89 See further P. Morré, *Die Änderung der staatlichen Gebietshoheit nach sowjetischer Völkerrechtslehre und Völkerrechtspraxis, mit besonderer Berilcksichtigung des Annexionsverbots*, Dissertation, Münster, 1967, p. 147 *et seq.*

90 See V. Lenin, *Collected Works*, Vol. XIX, p. 304. Quoted in Morré, p. 147.

91 See e.g. *Документы внешней политики СССР*, том. I, Москва,, 1957, p. 12.

92 See Morré, *op. cit.*, pp. 156, 165 and 176.

The available Soviet sources of legal opinion confirm the view that even with respect to the World War II era, forcible seizure was considered to be illegal by the Soviet government and Soviet scholars, at least when forcible seizure violated the right of peoples to self-determination.[93] Paradoxically, this legal position appears *inter alia* from the treatment of the Baltic case in Soviet legal literature. The Soviet argument has never been that annexations as such were legal (in 1940), but that the Baltic nations voluntarily asked to join the USSR by exercising their right to self-determination. Therefore, from the legal point of view, the Soviet argument was mainly based on an alternative factual narrative, namely that the socialist revolutions overturned the Baltic 'bourgeois' governments, and the new 'people's governments' organized elections, as a result of which the Baltic parliaments asked Moscow to let them join the USSR. The requests by the Baltic parliaments were then satisfied.[94]

If the Soviet handling of the facts in the Baltic case is rejected (and it was rejected above), the Soviet view of the legal status of the annexations as such emphasizes the illegality of Soviet practice itself. In the words of the international lawyer Yuri Barsegov:

> Conquest and enslavement run completely counter to the norms of contemporary international law. The basis of conquest, such as the basis of subjugation, is the use of naked force. It follows that conquest and subjugation are not compatible with the free self-determination of the population. Also, they are incompatible with the principles of the territorial integrity and inviolability of state territory... In the whole range of official international acts (...) legal force is denied to territorial conquest achieved under the threat of war or as a consequence of subjugation by armed force. In particular, the peace treaties of the year 1947 that ended World War II, annulled the territorial changes accomplished by the Axis powers.[95]

---

93 See also the concept of the 'ethnic principle' (Barsegov), according to which nations establish their 'national territories', as a consequence of which their borders can only be changed according to the principles of the right of peoples to self-determination. See Ю.Г. Барсегов, *Территория в международном праве*, p. 128 *et seq.*

94 See e.g. Ю.г. Барсегов, *Территория* ...., p. 88 *et seq.* The gap between Soviet legal doctrine and practice is highlighted by E. Kordt, ‚Ungleicher Vertrag und Annektion im sozialistischen Völkerrecht und in der Staatenpraxis sozialistischer Länder', *FS Hermann Jahrreiss*, Köln: Carl Heymanns Verlag, 1964, pp. 201–220.

95 Ю.Г. Барсегов, *Территория...*, p. 94. (Translated from Russian.)

In the case of the Baltic States, however, the territorial changes were not accomplished by Germany or other Axis powers, but by one of the victors of World War II. While this reality did not make any difference from the legal viewpoint, it had important consequences from the practical perspective of power politics.

e *The Illegality of Soviet Annexation: General Conclusions*

On the basis of the analysis conducted above, this author concludes that the Soviet annexation of the Baltic States in 1940 was an illegal act under international law. It violated at least two fundamental international legal norms that bound the USSR and the Baltic States in their inter-State relations: prohibition of the use of force and the right of peoples to self-determination. Illegality of the use of force does implies the illegality of the annexations.

However, in the case of the Baltic republics, the situation created by illegal acts lasted for half a century. It must therefore be asked whether the illegality of the annexation was by some means cured during this long period.

3 Prescription and Soviet Rule in the Illegally Annexed Baltic States

a *The Concept of Prescription in International Law*

It has been widely disputed in the international legal literature whether the institute of prescription—found in virtually all domestic legal systems—exists in the field of the law of nations. To what extent can a lapse of time cure an initially illegal act, for example create title to a territory acquired by use of force? At what point in time does international law recognize *die normative Kraft des Faktischen* (the normative force of the factual)[96] and legalize a *fait accompli?*[97]

Early writers on international law, for example Hugo Grotius,[98] Christian Wolff, and Emer de Vattel,[99] but also early Anglo-Saxon doctrine, recognized the institute of prescription under certain preconditions.[100] However, Johan Jacob Moser regretted that although a legal docrine of prescription would be vital for peace and security, international law offered no guidance regarding

96 See for the beginnings of this doctrine: G. Jellinek, *Allgemeine Staatslehre*, 1914, p. 340 *et seq*.

97 See for discussion C. Bilfinger, Vollendete Tatsachen und Völkerrecht—Eine Studie', 15 *ZaöRV* 1953/54, pp. 453–481.

98 H. Grotius, *De iure belli ac pads*, lib ii., Cap. 4, §§ 1,7,9.

99 E. Vattel, *Le droit des gens ou principes de la loi naturel*, liv. ii, chap. XI, § 147.

100 See further for references in B. Wiewióra, *Uznanie nabytków...* (The Recognition of the Territorial Acquisitions in International Law) 1961, p. 163.

claims made by States to lands occupied by others.[101] Similarly, Georg von Martens pointed out that the European powers urged prescription inconsistently and that there was no agreed time limit.[102] Nevertheless, the institute of prescription has been recognized and applied in a number of international arbitration cases in the 20th century.[103] Therefore, although always a controversial subject, prescription has at least been a part of classic international law.[104] Prescription has been a crucial institution in international law for taking into account the demands of effectiveness. Without the institute of prescription, the danger would exist that the long-term correspondence of law to realities would render international law non-effective and irrelevant.

Nevertheless, after the entry into force of the UN Charter and its clear prohibition of the threat and use of force in 1945, voices rejecting the institute of acquisitive prescription have increased.[105] A part of legal doctrine still upholds the view that acquisitive prescription is a general legal principle still recognized by the international legal system.[106] It has, however, become extremely doubtful whether prescription of an illegally seized territory still can take place under the UN Charter regime once *droit de conquête* (right of conquest) had been abolished in international law.[107] However, it is fair to proceed from the proposition that since the Baltic States were annexed in 1940, that is, some years before the entry into force of the UN Charter, the institute of prescription could in principle have played a certain role in the process of judging the Baltic situation.

---

101 See J.J. Moser, *Versuch des neuesten Europäischen Völkerrechts in Friedens- und Kriegszeiten*, Book I, Chapter 1, 1777, pp. 24–25.

102 G. von Martens, *Précis du droit des gens moderne de l'Europe, fondé sur les traités et l'usage*, 2e ed., Göttingen: Henri Dietrich, 1801, pp. 64–67.

103 See *Chamizal*, RIAA XI, 1911, p. 328; *Grisbadarna* (1909) in Scott, *The Hague Court Reports* 1916, p. 487 *et seq.* See also *Island of Palmas*, RIAA II, p. 839. ('the continuous and peaceful display of territorial sovereignty (peaceful in relation to other States) is as good as a title.') and *Minquiers and Ecrehos*, ICJ Reports 1953, p. 47 *et seq.*

104 See for a good overview and critique of the doctrinal views: G. Zimmer, *Gewaltsame territoriale Veränderungen und ihre völkerrechtliche Legitimation*, Berlin, 1971, pp. 46–67; E.A. Belgrad, *The Theory and Practice of Prescriptive Acquisition in International Law*, Dissertation, Johns Hopkins U., Baltimore, 1967.

105 See e.g. Langer, *Forcible Seizure…* and Verdross-Simma, *Universelles Völkerrecht*, p. 759, § 1163. See also the negative views of Polish international legal scholars in Wiewióra, *Uznanie…*, 1961, p. 147 *et seq.* ('Prescription must be *permanent, undisturbed and undisputed.*')

106 See e.g. Dahm/Delbrück/Wolfrum, *Völkerrecht*, Bd. I/1, p. 365; Seidl-Hohenveldern, *Völkerrecht*, 1997, Rdnr. 1157; D.H.N. Johnson, 'Acquisitive Prescription in International Law', 27 *BYIL* 1950, p. 353; Doehring, 'Effectiveness', in: *EPIL* 7, 1984, p. 73.

107 But see C.A. Fleischhauer, 'Prescription', *EPIL* 10, 1987, p. 330.

i The Time Factor as an Objective Element in Prescription Analysis?

It has been debated in the legal literature whether a lapse of time has an independent motive force in favour of prescription.[108] When a hundred years have passed, does the situation consolidate objectively due to the long period involved, or only because of the weight the States attribute to the time factor? In the annexed Baltic States, Soviet rule lasted almost fifty years, in itself a quite long time.

Joe Verhoeven points out an important difference between the case of the Iraqi occupation of Kuwait in 1990 and that of the Baltic States (1940–1991), namely the time factor. Kuwait was occupied for six months, the Baltic States for fifty years.[109] For Charles de Visscher, the lapse of time itself was a factor pointing in favour of prescription.[110] Several other authors have included the time factor in discussion, arguing that the extinction of a given State takes place when there is no reasonable chance of the independence of the State being restored.[111] By *inter alia* using that argument, Doehring explained the continued existence of the German State after World War II and the case of Austria, annexed by Germany.[112] Another German international law scholar, Georg Dahm argued that protests and formal non-recognition could not prevent prescription from taking place; rather the source of the prescription was the *normative Kraft des Faktischen* itself.[113]

It is true that historically—when universal prohibition of the threat and use of force was not yet a legal norm or, even further, a peremptory norm—the time factor played a more important role in the question of State extinction/continuity.[114] However, even during the 1930s the time factor was given a contextual interpretation due to the emerging aspect of illegality. For instance,

---

108 See generally M. Kohen, *Le droit international et le temps,* in: Societé française pour le droit international, Colloque de Paris, Paris: Pedone, 2001, pp. 129–157 and in the context of State succession: W. Fiedler, 'Der Zeitfaktor im Recht der Staatensukzession', in: *Staat und Recht. Festschrift für Günther Winkler*, Wien: Springer, 1997, pp. 217–235.

109 J. Verhoeven, *La reconnaissance...*, p. 37.

110 See C. de Visscher, *Theories et realtites en droit international public,* 1967, p. 256 («Le temps est un facteur de consolidation juridique.»).

111 K. Doehring, *Völkerrecht,* p. 71. 'Der Untergang eines Staates wegen Wegfalls seiner Staatsgewalt (...)—erst dann angenommen wird, wenn keine vernünftige Aussicht mehr besteht, einen solchen wieder herzustellen.'

112 *Ibid.*

113 See G. Dahm, *Völkerrecht,* Stuttgart, 1958, 1 Band, pp. 593–595. Cf. J. Charpentier, *La reconnaissance internationale et l'evolution du droit des gens,* Dissertation, Paris, 1956, p. 158.

114 See for an elaboration of the aspect of the 'time factor' in the case of the annexed Baltic States in a judgment of a German civil court, LG Göttingen of 25.5.1948, MDR 1948, p. 361 *et seq.*

Maxim Litvinov, the Soviet People's Commissar for Foreign Affairs until 1939, declared in connection with the occupation of Austria and Czechoslovakia:

> We have to reckon not only with the question of whether any struggle between the aggressor and his victim has come to an end, but also—should that have occurred for the time being—whether there are any chances of the struggle being renewed, and likewise we have to reckon with other circumstances which may bring about a chance in the situation created by aggressive acts of violence.[115]

It is highly doubtful whether the time factor can be attributed an independent objective role in modern international law when deciding about State extinction or continuity in cases of illegal annexation. The body of contemporary international law includes a norm prohibiting recognition of illegal annexations; the time factor would make the legal personality of illegally annexed States dependent on whether liberation can succeed quickly and efficiently or not. Although based on the effectiveness principle, this would be an arbitrary criterion and raise the question what kind of law international law is. In this sense, the illegality of occupation may hardly be overturned by the lapse of time.

ii Criteria for Prescription Analysis

The British international law scholar Sir Hersch Lauterpacht's concept of prescription can here serve as a further basis for analysis. Lauterpacht defined prescription as *the acquisition of sovereignty over a territory through continuous and undisturbed exercise of sovereignty over it during such a period as is necessary to create under the influence of historical development the general conviction that the present condition of things is in conformity with international order.*[116] Lauterpacht supported the institution of prescription in international law, and saw its rational basis—just as in domestic law—in considerations of stability and order.[117] He stressed that no general rule can be fixed as regards the length of time and other circumstances which are necessary to create a title by prescription: everything depends upon the individual case.[118] However, he took the view that '[*a*]*s long as other States keep up protests and claims, the actual exercise of sovereignty is not undisturbed, nor is there the required general*

115 19 LNOJ at 341 (1938).

116 H. Lauterpacht (ed.) *International Law. A Treatise*, 8th ed., 1955, p. 576.

117 *Ibid.* p. 576.

118 *Ibid.* p. 576.

conviction that the present condition of things is in conformity with international order. But after such protests and claims, if any, cease to be repeated, the actual possession ceases to be disturbed and thus in certain circumstances matters may gradually ripen into that condition which is in conformity with international order.'[119]

As repeatedly highlighted in legal doctrine, there is no established time limit for prescription.[120] In the legal literature, prescription with respect to conquered territory has been denied for even longer periods than half a century. For instance, the Polish scholar Piotr Laski has argued that no prescription took place in Poland under partition (1795–1919), *inter alia* due to the numerous Polish uprisings.[121] Therefore, even fifty years over the 20th century cannot by themselves serve as a conclusive argument in favour of prescription.

Laski seems to summarize the arguments presented in legal doctrine when he contends that prescription can be confirmed only when the situation has stabilized with finality. The stability necessary for prescripton can be disturbed by either a previous sovereign, by the international community acting in solidarity, and, last but not least, by the population of the territory concerned, '*whose resistance brings on the use of power, to mean at the same time, that the exercising of sovereign rights ceased to be peaceful.*'[122]

We may, therefore, distinguish three important elements in prescription analysis: the position of the ousted sovereign (government in exile), the views held by third States, and the attitudes of the subjugated people. It therefore becomes necessary to analyze whether these elements support the legal continuity or extinction of the Baltic republics during the period of Soviet annexation. Of these, one of the most visible roles, from the standpoint of international law, was played by the opinion of third States in the framework of non-recognition policy.

b *Non-Recognition of the Soviet Annexation of the Baltic States: Law and Politics*

i Non-recognition in History

Non-recognition is a doctrine that has historically been employed for achieving primarily political purposes. European monarchies and the USA, for

---

119 *Ibid.* p. 576–577.

120 See for many: D. Blumenwitz, 'Ex factis ius oritur'—'ex injuria ius non oritur', in: B. Meissner, G. Ziegler (Hg.) *Staatliche und nationale Einheit Deutschlands—ihre Effektivität*, Köln: Verlag Wissenschaft und Politik, 1984, p. 55 and Zimmer, *op. cit.*, p. 52.

121 P. Laski, 'The Prescription in International Law—Some Remarks', 23 *Polish YBIL* 1997–1998, p. 225 *et seq.*

122 Laski, *op. cit.*, p. 225.

partly different reasons and in different regions, insisted in the 19th century on non-recognition of the changes in government brought about by revolutions or *coups d'état*. In the 19th and early 20th centuries, non-recognition was occasionally employed in the implementation of imperialistic policies.[123] The ultimate purpose of non-recognition has been reversal of the undesired situation or at least signalling a considerable challenge to it. Non-recognition has been accompanied by denial of the realities on the ground for normative or ideological reasons—for example the refusal of the USA to recognize the Soviet government in Russia until 1933. Non-recognition can be controversial. It has been criticized that non-recognition may initially even be well-meant, but since it cannot really serve as an effective sanction, 'will only create further instability.'[124] Talking at the American Society of International Law in 1941, Herbert W. Briggs demonstrated the lawyers' age-old need to decide either in favour of facts or normative expectations, and advocated against non-recognition: 'There is quite definitely something to be said for dealing with facts.'[125]

ii The Stimson Doctrine

The doctrine of non-recognition of annexation following the illegal use of force was first time employed quite soon after adoption of the Kellogg-Briand Pact in 1928.[126] However, its application in State practice was not initially uniform and consistent.[127] The annexation of the Baltic States initiated one of the very first cases in which—notwithstanding all the facts and realities—the legality of annexation was continuously denied by an influential part of the international community, the political West.

The doctrine of non-recognition of the fruits of aggression was formulated by the US Secretary of State, Henry L. Stimson, on the occasion of Japanese aggression in Manchuria in 1932.[128] The last sentence of the US diplomatic note served as the basis of the Stimson doctrine:

> and that it (i.e. the US government) does not intend to recognize any situation, treaty or agreement which may be brought about by means

---

123 See with respect to US policies in Latin America in Anonymus, 'Non-recognition: A Reconsideration', 22 *The University of Chicago Law Review* 1954–1955, p. 261 at 271 *et seq.*

124 H.W. Briggs, 'Non-recognition of Title by Conquest and Limitations of the Doctrine', 34 *Am. Soc'y Intl L. Proc.* 1940, p. 72 at 81–82.

125 *Ibid*, at 82.

126 See Langer, *Seizure of Territory*, 1947, p. 46 *et seq.*

127 See *ibid.* p. 123 *et seq.*

128 See Langer, *op. cit.*, p. 50 *et seq.* See also P.C. Jessup, *The Birth of Nations*, 1974, p. 305 *et seq.*

> contrary to the covenants and obligations of the Pact of Paris of August 27, 1928, to which treaty both China and Japan, as well as the United States, are parties.[129]

The doctrine immediately found positive resonance among other States, most notably on the American continent.[130] Also, on March 11, 1932, with the Manchurian situation in mind, the League of Nations Assembly passed a resolution, pursuant to which:

> ...it is incumbent upon the Members of the League of Nations not to recognize any situation, treaty or agreement which may be brought about by means contrary to the Covenant of the League of Nations or to the Pact of Paris.[131]

It has been discussed in the literature whether the League of Nations Assembly Resolution of March 11, 1932—together with Article 10 of the League Covenant—already created a legal duty of non-recognition.[132] While some scholars have argued that it did, at least for those States that voted for the resolution—others have denied those legal effects to that resolution, that is, technically a legally non-binding instrument, not a treaty. Especially problematic is the legal evaluation of State practice in the late-1930s—almost all States, including the

129 See the text in 26 *AJIL* 1932, p. 342.

130 See the Chaco Declaration of August 3, 1932, in which the nineteen American republics declared: '*The American nations further declare that they will not recognize any territorial arrangement of this controversy which has not been obtained by peaceful means nor the validity of territorial acquisitions which may be obtained through occupation or conquest by force of arms?* See also the Saavedra Lamas Anti-War Treaty of October 10, 1933, in which twenty-one American republics and eleven European States declared '*that as between the high contracting parties territorial questions must not be settled by violence, and that they will not recognize any territorial arrangement which is not obtained by pacific means, nor the validity of the occupation or acquisition of territories that may be brought about by force of arms?* See LNTS 163 (1935–6), p. 393. Finally, Article 11 of the Montevideo Convention on the Rights and Duties of States of December 26, 1933, stipulated that: '*The contracting States definitely establish as the rule of their conduct the precise obligation not to recognize territorial acquisitions or special advantages which have been obtained by force... The territory of a State is inviolable and may not be the object of military occupation nor of other measures of force imposed by another State directly or indirectly or for any motive whatever even temporarily?* See LNTS 165 (1936), p. 19.

131 See further Repečka, *op. cit.*, p. 216 *et seq.*

132 See the discussion in Langer, *op. cit.*, p. 9 5 et seq.

Baltic republics,[133] finally recognized the annexation of Ethiopia and Austria. International lawyers have been reluctant to argue that those States violated their own legally binding standards.

Robert Langer concludes that the issue remains somewhat doubtful.[134] However, even though non-recognition did not become a legally binding rule or duty in 1932, the positions of the States played a significant role in the consolidation and later conversion of the political doctrine into a legally binding one, up to the point of *opinio iuris.*

Of special interest for the study of the Baltic case is the Soviet view, as expressed in a note of March 7, 1933 dealing with the case of Manchuria. In this note, the Soviet position on the Japanese conquest and annexation was expressed as follows:

> Since the origins of the Soviet State, it has proclaimed as an essential principle of its policy the right of all peoples to self determination in conditions of freedom to manifest their desires and in the absence of all external pressure; it has pronounced in the most decisive fashion against annexations and exactions as a result of military conquest or occupation by violence. These principles logically lead to absolute respect for the territorial integrity and for the political, social, economic and administrative independence of all States, to the inadmissibility of the settlement of international conflicts by any non-pacific means, and in the clearest possible manner to the obligation to respect strictly the international agreements which embody these principles...'[135]

iii Non-Recognition of the Soviet Annexation in the Baltic Case

State practice was not completely uniform in the case of the annexation of the Baltic States.[136] Since thorough studies on the diplomatic history of

133 For Estonian and to some extent also to the other two Baltic states' policies at the League of Nations, see V. Made, *Külalisena maailmapoliitikas: Rahvasteliit ja Eesti 1919–1946* (As Guest in World Politics: the League of Nations and Estonia 1919–1946), Tartu: Tartu Ülikooli Kirjastus, 1999.

134 Langer, *op. cit.*, p. 98.

135 Quoted by Repečka, *op. cit.,* p. 217. According to Repečka, this declaration gives evidence that already in 1933, the USSR officially rejected annexation as a ground for legal title. See pp. 217–218.

136 Writing in 1941, Makarov even came tentatively to the conclusion that in the turmoil of World War II, the annexation of the Baltic States had been recognized, except by Portugal.

non-recognition of the annexation of the Baltic States have been completed earlier,[137] repetition of all interesting facts is neither necessary nor possible here. Historians keep coming up with new realist interpretations on how the USA and the UK related to Soviet annexation of the Baltic States in 1943–1944 and discuss whether President Roosevelt and Prime Minister Chruchill at least tacitly acquiesced in Soviet annexation plans regarding the Baltic States while the USSR was an ally in World War II, during the Teheran and Yalta conferences.[138] Nevertheless, when the Cold War broke out, the USA in particular, following the 1940 acting Secretary of State Sumner Welles declaration on non-recognition of the Soviet takeover of the Baltic States, remained consistently faithful to the initial non-recognition doctrine.

In terms of their position on the annexation of the Baltic republics, States can be divided into four groups. The basis for this classification is the distinction between recognitions *de facto* and *de iure*. Although such a distinction has been held by some authors as 'inadmissible in international law,'[139] it was indeed employed by several influential States in the Baltic case.

As for the first group, some Western countries, most influentially the USA, accorded neither *de iure* nor *de facto* recognition to the Soviet annexation of the Baltic States.[140] As a corollary of US non-recognition policies, the Baltic legations in the USA continued to work and function during the five decades of Soviet rule. Throughout the years of Soviet rule in the Baltic republics, the USA

See N. Makarov, ‚Die Eingliederung der baltischen Staaten in die Sowjet-Union', *ZaöRV* 1941, pp. 705–706.

137 See W.J.H. Hough, III, 'The Annexation of the Baltic States and its effect on the Development of Law Prohibiting Forcible Seizure of Territory', 6 *New York L.S.J.Int'l. L.*, 1985, p. 391 *et seq*. See also V.J. Riismandel, 'The Continued Legal Existence of the Baltic States', 12 *The Baltic Review* 1957, p. 48 *et seq.*; Repečka, *op. cit.*, p. 282 *et seq.*

138 See K. Piirimäe, *Roosevelt, Chruchill, and the Baltic Question. Allied Relations during the Second World War*, London: Palgrave Macmillan, 2014.

139 Michael C. van Walt van Praag asserts that a State cannot exist in fact (…) without existing in a juridical sense. (…) The terms *de facto* and *de jure* serve in the process of recognition only when conflicting claims to sovereignty over territory remain unresolved and the recognizing State is anxious not to commit itself in favour of either claimant.' See *The Status of Tibet. History, Rights, and Prospects in International Law*, Boulder: Westview Press, 1987, p. 99.

140 Of the earlier cases in the US Courts, see *The Maret*, A.D. Case No. 9 (1943/45); *A/S Merilaid*, A.D. Case No. 6 (1947). See also M. Whiteman, *Digest of International Law*, Vol. 5, US Department of State, 1965, p. 942, H.W Briggs, 'Non-recognition in the Courts: The Ships of the Baltic Republics', 37 AJIL 1943, pp. 585–596 and L. Juda, 'United States' Non-recognition of the Soviet Union's Annexation of the Baltic States: Politics and Law', 6 JBS 1975, pp. 272–290.

continued to issue reaffirmations of its non-recognition policy on the national holidays of the three States. The US Government considered its treaties concluded with the Baltic States to be contining in force.[141] The US Government's lists of countries of the world continued to include the three independent Baltic republics, with a note to the effect that the USA did not recognize their inclusion in the USSR.[142]

Non-recognition of Soviet conquest was particularly emphasized by the Reagan administration at the height of the Cold War, when Baltic Freedom Day was officially introduced in the USA in 1982. June 14, the anniversary of the first Soviet mass deportation in the Baltic States and other Soviet-annexed eastern European territories in 1941, was chosen for Baltic Freedom Day. On July 26, 1983, on the occasion of the 61st anniversary of the *de iure* recognition of the three Baltic republics, the US ambassador to the UN, Jeane J. Kirkpatrick, presented the UN General Secretary with a declaration of continued non-recognition of Soviet rule in the Baltic republics.[143]

The Vatican and Ireland also never recognized the incorporation of Estonia, Latvia and Lithuania into the Soviet Union either *de iure* or *de facto*.

The second, and probably numerically the biggest group of States, never accorded *de iure* recognition to Soviet annexation while recognizing it *de facto*. This group of States included Australia, Belgium, Brasil, Canada,[144] Chile, China, Colombia, Costa Rica, Denmark, Ecuador, France,[145] the Federal Republic of

---

141 Cf. *Treaties in Force—A List of Treaties and Other International Agreements of the United States in Force on January 1, 1983*, Washington, Department of State, 1983, p. 102.

142 See R.J. Misiunas, 'Sovereignty Without Government: Baltic Diplomatic and Consular Representation, 1940–1990', in: Y. Shain (ed.) *Governments-in-Exile in Contemporary World Politics*, New York: Routledge, p. 137.

143 E. Jaakson, *Eestile* (To Estonia), Tallinn: SE & JS, 1995, p. 312.

144 See *Estonian State Cargo and Passenger S.S. Line v. Laane and Boutser* (*The Elise*), A.D. Case No. 50 (1948). See also House of Commons Debates, May 19, 1987, p. 6229, printed in 26 *CanYBIL* 1988, p. 336 et seq. ('These measures prove that Canada continues to reject the legality of Soviet control over the Baltic countries, a fact which the Soviet authorities have duly noted.')

145 See *Gebraud v. Meden,* France, Cour de Cassation, January 10, 1951 which held: 'No act of international scope has cancelled the disappearance of the State of Latvia. No Treaty has confirmed its extinction as a subject of legal rights and obligations. Accordingly, the lower Court held correctly that 'as long as the Treaty of Peace has not decided the future of Latvia, it is not possible to say that Latvians have become stateless'.' 18 ILR 1951, pp. 288–289. See also the statement by the Foreign Minister Roland Dumas in *Le Monde,* 12.3.1990 and for an overview of the French positions in J. Huntzinger, 'La renaissance des États baltes', 1994, p. 48 *et seq.*

Germany,[146] Greece, Guatemala, Luxemburg, Malta, Mexico, Norway, Paraguay, Portugal, Switzerland, Turkey, Venezuela, the UK,[147] Uruguay and Yugoslavia. For instance, the British Embassy in Moscow did not engage in official communication with the State organs in the Soviet Baltic republics.[148] Until his death in 1971, the pre-World War II diplomat August Torma continued to represent the Republic of Estonia as Minister in London.[149] During the 1980s, it became clear in many instances that the rhetoric of the leaders of these countries made it—at least politically speaking—increasingly less relevant to distinguish between *de iure* and *de facto* recognition of Soviet annexation. Thus, the French Foreign Minister Claude Cheysson declared in the French Senate on December 16, 1981:

> France has not recognized the annexation of the states of Latvia, Estonia and Lithuania by the USSR in 1940. Since then, it has not extended any recognition, either expressly or tacitly. This attitude was confirmed in 1975, at the time of the signing of the Helsinki Final Act by the President of the Republic, when he indicated that 'in the view of France, the texts signed [at the time] do not imply the recognition of situations, which it would not have recognized otherwise.[150]

Non-recognition on European soil was also expressed by a few collective declarations, most notably those adopted by the Consultative Assembly of the Council of Europe. Resolution 189 (1960) on the situation in the Baltic States on

146 See e.g. the position of the Federal Government on 8.11.1985, in: *Verhandlungen des Deutschen Bundest ages, Stenographische Berichte,* 172. Sitzung, Bd. 134, p. 12959 in which State minister Möllemann, in answer to a question from deputy Dr. Hupka, replied: 'The Federal Government has not recognized the annexation of the Baltic States by the USSR. This position has been maintained in various declarations of the Federal Government, and also in the *Bundestag*.' (Transl.) For a review of German court decisions in the British and American occupation zones, confirming the continued legal existence of the nationality of the Baltic States, see H. Jellinek, *Der automatische Erwerb und Verlust...* 1951, p. 172 *et seq*.

147 See, for instance, the communication of the Foreign Office to the court in *A/S Tallinna Laevaühisus and others v. Tallinna Shipping Company, Ltd., and Estonian State Steamship Line*, (1946) 79 Ll.LR 245 at p. 251: 'I. His Majesty's Government recognize the Government of the Estonian-Soviet Socialist Republic to be the *de facto* Government of Estonia...'

148 See HC Debs., vol. 82, WA, col. 273: 5.7.1985, printed in: 56 BYBIL 1985, p. 390.

149 See further T. Tamman, *The Last Ambassador. August Torma, Soldier, Diplomat, Spy*, Leiden Brill, 2011.

150 *Journal officiel de la République Française,* 3 mai 1982.

the twentieth anniversary of their forcible incorporation into the Soviet Union, adopted by the Assembly on September 29, 1960 (20th sitting), declared:

1. The Assembly,
2. On the twentieth anniversary of the occupation and forcible incorporation into the Soviet Union of the three European States of Estonia, Latvia and Lithuania,
3. Notes that this illegal annexation took place without any genuine reference to the wishes of the people;
4. Expresses sympathy with the sufferings of the Baltic peoples and assures them that they are not forgotten by their fellow Europeans;
5. Is confident that Communist oppression will not succeed in crushing their spirit and faith in freedom and democracy;
6. Notes that the independent existence of the Baltic States is still recognized *de jure* by a great majority of the Governments of the nations of the free world;
7. Urges member Governments to support appropriate efforts of Baltic refugees to maintain their natural culture traditions and languages, in anticipation of the time when Estonia, Latvia and Lithuania will be able to play their part as free nations in our democratic international institutions.[151]

A third group of States recognized the Baltic republics as part of the Soviet Union. Nearby Sweden, although it showed much generosity by accepting many Baltic refugees in 1944, was one of the first Western countries to extend its *de iure* recognition to Soviet rule in Estonia, Latvia and Lithuania. During World War II, the Netherlands established diplomatic relations with the Soviet Union, and as they did not make any reservations about the Soviet western border, this arguably also amounted to a *de iure* recognition of the incorporation of the Baltic States. Some European nations changed their policies over time. Under General Franco, Spain did not recognize the annexation of the Baltic States either *de jure* or *de facto* and allowed the Baltic legations to be maintained in Madrid. For example, the Estonian diplomat Kaarel Robert Pusta, who had for a time before 1940 been the Estonian Minister of Foreign Affairs and permanent representative at the League of Nations, represented his country until his death in 1964, mainly living in Madrid but covering both Spain and France as a diplomat.[152] However, soon after the death of Franco, Spain implicitly recognized the annexation of the Baltic States in 1977 when

151 Reprinted in: *The Baltic States and the Soviet Union. Reprinted from a Report of the Council of Europe, with a Preface and Supplementary Comments*, Stockholm, 1962.

152 See also Pusta's extensive personal archive at Stanford University's Hoover Institute in Palo Alto, California.

it established diplomatic relations with the USSR without reservations on this issue.[153] New Zealand also extended *de iure* recognition of the Baltic republics as constituents of the USSR.[154]

The fourth group of States was eloquently silent on the matter. Thus, for example, one of the closest neighbours of the Baltic States, Finland, managed never to make any formal pronouncement on the issue during Soviet rule in the Baltic States. This enabled Finland to formally restore diplomatic relations with the Baltic States rather than recognize these States anew in 1991. Nevertheless, for most practical purposes, Finnish recognition of Soviet incorporation of the Baltic States, if not explicit, can be said to have been implicit. The visit by Finnish President Urho Kaleva Kekkonen to Soviet Estonia in March 1964, can be understood as tacit Finnish recognition of Soviet rule in Estonia—even though Finland emphasized that Kekkonen's visit was 'unofficial.' Recognition of the Soviet annexation was also implied by the Shah of Iran's visit in 1974, and by that of India's prime minister in 1981 to the Estonian SSR[155] during their State visits to the USSR.

Of the UN member States, many were born after World War II and especially in the process of decolonization. States created after Soviet annexation of the Baltic States in 1940, and therefore never having had relations with the pre-World War II Baltic States, usually did not have to take an explicit position on this matter.

iv The Legal Duty of Non-Recognition of Illegal Annexations since 1970

Coinciding with the prolonged Soviet annexation of the Baltic States were several important developments in international law, partly also inspired by the experience of the international community in the Baltic case. What started as the Stimson doctrine in the USA in 1932 was soon to develop into a general policy of non-recognition of illegal territorial changes in international law and became accepted by many States both as politically inevitable and legally binding. Article 11 of the UN draft resolution on the rights and duties of States, as adopted by the ILC in 1949, stated the duty of non-recognition: 'Every State has the duty to refrain from recognizing any territorial acquisition by another State acting in violation of [Art. 9 prohibiting aggression]'[156] However, due to

153 See 1 *Spanish YBIL* 1991, p. 48 *et seq.*

154 See R.J. Misiunas, 'Sovereignty Without Government...,' p. 136.

155 See http://www.okupatsioon.ee/1940/1940.html, information submitted by historian Eero Medijainen.

156 *Draft Declaration of Rights and Duties of States* of December 6, 1949 (Res. 375 (IV) UNGA). See YB of the ILC, 1949, p. 288.

disagreements on the definition of aggression, the draft declaration was not adopted by the General Assembly.

The UN General Assembly emphasized the duty of non-recognition in 1970. The UN Declaration on Principles of International Law concerning Friendly Relations and Co-operation among States in accordance with the Charter of the United Nations of October 24, 1970,[157] establishes: '*The territory of a State shall not be the object of acquisition by another State resulting from the threat or use of force. No territorial acquisition resulting from the threat or use of force shall be recognized as legal.*'[158] It follows that the principle of non-recognition of illegal acts—during the 1930s sometimes dismissed as primarily a political tool—has subsequently become a part of positive international law,[159] a legal duty.

In 2001, the UN's International Law Commission adopted Draft Articles on State Responsibility which addresses in its Chapter III serious breaches of obligations under peremptory norms of general international law. Article 41 of the Draft Articles deals with particular consequences of a serious breach of an obligation of a peremptory norm and paragraph 2 states explicitly:

'No State shall recognize as lawful a situation created by a serious breach (…), nor render aid or assistance in maintaining that situation.'[160]

V The Helsinki Final Act: A Western Recognition of the *de facto* Situation?

The Soviets sometimes argued that in the Helsinki Final Act of 1975 the Western States finally recognized the territorial integrity of the Soviet Union, including the Baltic republics.[161] Article III of the Helsinki Final Act stipulated that: '*The participating States regard as inviolable all one another's frontiers as well*

157 On this influential declaration, see J. Viñuales (ed.) *The UN Friendly Relations Declaration at 50*, Cambridge: Cambridge University Press, 2020.

158 U.N.G.A. Res. 2625 (XXV), October 24, 1970.

159 See e.g. J. Crawford, *Fourth report on State responsibility*, ILC, 2 April 2001, A/ CN.4/517, p. 20 (para. 52.)

160 See ILC, *Draft Articles on Responsibility of States for Internationallly Wrongful Acts*, 2001.

161 See Visek, 'Creating the Ethnic…', p. 326. At the same time, the legally binding character of the Helsinki Final Act was denied. For instance, I.A. Smirnov observed that the states had no intention of giving the Conference acts the force of an international law source. The obligations assumed within the CSCE framework are a package of political arrangements fully in accordance with current international law, while remaining outside its system.' LA. Smirnov, 'The Legal Qualification of the Documents on Security and Cooperation in Europe', *Soviet Journal of International Law*, No. 2, 1991, pp. 111–120.

as the frontiers of all States in Europe....'[162] However, major Western countries delivered declarations expressing reservations with respect to the Baltic States. Prior to the signing, US President Gerald Ford stated:

> Specifically addressing the understandable concern about the effect of the Helsinki declarations on the Baltic Nations, I can assure you...that the United States has never recognized the Soviet incorporation of Lithuania, Latvia, and Estonia and is not doing so now. Our official policy of non-recognition is not affected by the results of the European Security Conference. There is included in the declaration of principles on territorial integrity the provision that no occupation or acquisition of territory in violation of international law will be recognized as legal.[163]

Moreover, after the signing of the Helsinki accords, the US House of Representatives adopted a resolution declaring that US non-recognition policy with respect to the illegally annexed Baltic States was not changed by the Helsinki accords.[164] Thus, it can be inferred that the signatories to the Helsinki Final Act disagreed on the Baltic issue,[165] even if the plain language of the Final Act seems to support the Soviet interpretation that the West had acquiesced in Soviet rule in the Baltic States.[166] Moreover, during the subsequent so-called Helsinki process, the US representatives sometimes addressed the Soviet presence in the Baltic States as a situation violating the Helsinki principles.[167]

Overall, there was also a certain disagreement between the Soviet Union and the Western States on the legal nature of the Helsinki Final Act. Soviet international jurists asserted that this was a legally binding document whereas the Western governments and international lawyers considered it merely politically binding.

---

162 Conference on Security and Co-operation in Europe, Final Act (Helsinki Accords), 14 I.L.M. 1292, 1294 (1975).

163 US Department of State, Department of State Bulletin, 73, 1885, 11 August 1975, pp. 204–206.

164 HR 864, US Congress, *Congressional Record*, 2 December 1975, p. H 11587.

165 Cf. also with the diplomatic statement of the French President in connection with the signing of the Helsinki Final Act: '[I]n the view of France, the texts signed here do not imply the recognition of situations which it would not have recognized otherwise...' Quoted in Hough, *op. cit.*, p. 430. See also a statement by the British Prime Minister Margaret Thatcher in a parliamentary debate of April 3, 1990: 'I have indicated that this country never recognized the legality of the annexation of Lithuania, Latvia and Estonia into the Soviet Union. (...) The Helsinki accord recognized the boundaries in fact but not in law.' See 61 *BYBIL* 1990 p. 497.

166 See also F. Lange, ‚Die baltischen Staaten und die KSZE', in: 44 *Osteuropa*, Marz 1994, p. 233.

167 See for evidence in Vitas, *op. cit.*, pp. 99–100.

vi The Legal Relevance of Inconsistencies and Controversial Aspects of Non-Recognition Policy in the Baltic Case

What conclusions can be drawn from the reaction of the State community to the Soviet annexation of the Baltic States? It is clear that non-recognition of Soviet annexation by so many States over such a long period was an unprecedented phenomenon in the history of international relations. However, this practice was never unanimous, and sometimes took peculiar forms. Many things in that respect are open for different interpretations, and much depends on whether one regards the glass to be half-full or half-empty.[168] For example, in 1974 the Australian Labour government of Gough Whitlam extended *de iure* recognition to the incorporation of the Baltic States in the USSR,[169] but the following Liberal government of Malcolm Fraser annulled that recognition.[170] In international legal doctrine, *de iure* recognition, once given, is generally considered irrevocable.[171] In any case, it is important to note that to speak of non-recognition of the Soviet annexation by *the* Western States—as has been popular in the Baltic States—is an over-statement and an over-simplification. The attitude of *the* Western countries was always fragmented. However, one can speak almost without reservation of the non-recognition policy of the USA.

Reception of non-recognition policy (and doctrine) in the legal literature has been correspondingly mixed. At some points during the Cold War, it must have felt that non-recognition itself would not lead anywhere or 'save' the annexed Baltic States. Belgian international law scholar Joe Verhoeven wrote in 1975 that the non-recognition policy in the case of the Baltic States

---

168 For instance, Helmut Tichy, while confirming that the claim [of the Baltic States] to be legally identical with the three States annexed by the Soviet Union in 1940 was accepted by the international community', estimates that: '*Until August 1991, there were only a few States which had never recognized these annexations either explicitly or implicitly. The overwhelming majority of States had taken the position, at least implicitly, that the Baltic States were part of the Soviet Union. This was also the case for Austria...*' See H. Tichy, 'Two Recent Cases of State Succession...', *Aust. JPIL* 1992, p. 127. See also J. Salmon, 24 *RBDI* 1991, 'Pays baltes', p. 265 ('*L'affirmation de la non-reconnaissence de l'annexion par les Occidentaux cachait mal l'acceptation du fait accompli de 1944.*') and P. M. Eisemann, 'Bilan de recherches...', in: *State Succession* (Hague), 1996, p. 53.

169 See 6 *Austr. YIL* 1974/5, p. 230.

170 See 7 *AYIL* 1976/7, p. 432. See also E. Dunsdorfs, *The Baltic Dilemma. The Case of the de jure Recognition by Australia of the incorporation of the Baltic States into the Soviet Union*, 1975.

171 See Article 6 of the 1933 Montevideo Convention: '(...) Recognition is unconditional and irrevocable.' See for the adoption in literature e.g. J.L. Kunz, 'Identity of States Under International Law', 49 *AJIL* 1955, p. 75.

'reste aujourd'hui la satisfaction ultime accordée à un personnel diplomatique et à un groupe de réfugiés dans l'attente de leur disparition après celle de leurs États, qui estompera un scandal parmi tant d'autres dont sont faites les relations internationales.'[172]

For Soviet legal doctrine, non-recognition policy was a purely political undertaking—an exercise in anti-Soviet propaganda and ideological struggle.[173] Even Western scholars who agreed that the Soviet annexation of the Baltic States had been illegal pointed out that from a certain point onward, non-recognition could equally have become a manifestation of Cold War politics rather than of noble normative convictions.[174] Non-recognition of the annexation of the Baltic States seemed increasingly a curiosity, so that one approach adopted by Western legal scholars was to ignore the issue altogether, even in contexts where it should have been substantively relevant, and remain silent on the Baltic case.[175]

Another view has celebrated non-recognition of Soviet annexation as a triumph of legality over the illegal exercise of power, a victory of international law and morality over unprincipled pragmatism.[176] W.J.H. Hough emphasized this more idealistic aspect in 1985: *'In contrast to the purely political motivation vis-à-vis the doctrine of non-recognition in the 1930s, it is difficult to see what immediate political interest the world community had in a restoration of the Baltic States in the 1940's and afterwards.'*[177] It is obvious, of course, that questioning the legality of Soviet territorial conquest did not in the least contradict the political interest of the USA and other Western democracies in undermining the adversary Soviet empire, especially after the Cold War broke out in 1946. The political dimension of recognition of the virtual Baltic States by the USA became apparent during 1987–1991 when the political attitude of the USA with respect to the immediate restoration of the Baltic States became somewhat

172 J. Verhoeven, *La reconnaissance internationale dans la pratique contemporaine,* 1975, pp. 307–308. "remains today the ultimate satisfaction accorded to diplomatic personnel and a group of refugees awaiting their disappearance after that of their States, which will cast a blur over one scandal among so many others that international relations are made of."

173 See Misiunas, *op. cit.* p. 138 and A. Liivak, 'Soviet Responses to Western Nonrecognition of Baltic Annexation', in: Loeber/Vardys/ Kitching (eds.) *Regional Identity Under Soviet Rule,* 1990, pp. 375–394.

174 As suggested by J. Crawford, *The Creation of States in International Law,* 1979, p. 219.

175 For instance, the Swedish diplomat Hans Blix lays out the history of non-recognition policies since the Stimson doctrine without mentioning the Baltic case. See H. Blix, 'Contemporary Aspects of Recognition', *RCADI* 1970-II, pp. 567–703.

176 See e.g. Hough, *op. cit.,* 1985.

177 Hough, *op. cit.,* p. 467.

more reserved. In April 1991, the US-sponsored Radio Free Europe presented to the Baltic chief editors a draft, according to which Baltic journalists were urged to propagate an alternative association with the USSR instead of full independence.[178] Paradoxically, when the Baltic nations finally saw a realistic chance for restoration of their independence, the rhetoric of some Western leaders *vis-à-vis* the independence of the Baltic States became more reserved than it had been during the Cold War.[179] It was said that the Baltic peoples should not to rock the boat that was the Soviet Union.

In order to realistically estimate the context and value of non-recognition in the Baltic case, one has to look not only at the words pronounced by certain governments, but also what was *not* said, or even more, what else happened in international relations. While non-recognition policy was adopted as a formal legal position, then in terms of political reality, there stood the *de facto* new world order established at the Yalta Conference in February 1945.[180]

Non-recognition was a half-hearted undertaking. It appears a less courageous and principled deed when one takes into account that the Baltic States were the only ones to lose their independence as victims of aggression during World War II. While the independence of the victims of Nazi aggression was restored at the end of the war, the Soviet Union, which herself had conspired with Nazi Germany between 1939–1941, and thus contributed to the outbreak of the war, could annex the Baltic States that it had seized by pursuing policies that it had earlier condemned as 'aggression' in treaties concluded with those States. While other Eastern European countries also fell under Soviet domination, the Soviet satellites of Poland, Hungary, and so on, although not free in terms of choosing their form of government, they at least preserved their formal independence as sovereign States.

While the USA and the UK never recognized the absorption of the Baltic States in terms of law, they occasionally had to accept it in terms of political reality. In the Atlantic Charter of August 14, 1941, President Roosevelt and Prime Minister Churchill had promised to stand for the freedom of all illegally

---

178 TH. Ilves, *Eesti välispoliitika peegelmaastikul,* (Estonian Foreign Policy on the Mirror Landscape), Postimees, 07.08.2001.

179 See for evidence: R. Kherad, *La reconnaissance internationale des États Baltes,* 96 *RGDIP* 1992, p. 858 *et seq.*

180 See for a severe critique: K. Skubiszewski, 'The End of Yalta', in: K. Wellens (ed.) *International Law: Theory and Practice. Essays in Honour of Eric Suy*, The Hague: Nijhoff, 1998, pp. 107–119.

subjugated peoples.[181] However, during the conferences at Teheran,[182] Yalta[183] and Potsdam,[184] they tacitly accepted Stalin's control over the Baltic States as a

---

181 In the Atlantic Charter, the leaders of the USA and Great Britain declared:
'...*Second, they desire to see no territorial changes that do not accord with the freely expressed wishes of the peoples concerned.*
Third, they respect the right of all peopes to choose the form of government under which they will live; and they wish to see sovereign rights and self-government restored to those who have been forcibly deprived of them.
...*Sixth, after the final destruction of the Nazi tyranny, they hope to see established a peace which will afford to all nations the means in dwelling in safety within their own boundaries, and which will afford assurance that all the men in all the lands may live out their lives in freedom from fear and want.*
The representative of the USSR declared his country's adherence to the principles of the Atlantic Charter on September 24, 1941 in London. However, the Soviet commitment was accompanied by another declaration, the ambiguous wording of which indicated that the USSR considered the Baltic republics as a legitimate part of its territory. See Meissner, *Die Sowjetunion, die baltischen Staaten...*, p. 119 *et seq.*

182 President Roosevelt is quoted as saying at Teheran: 'He [Roosevelt] said that he fully realized the three Baltic Republics had in history and again more recently been part of Russia and added jokingly that when the Soviet armies re-occupied these areas, he did not intend to go to war with the Soviet Union on this point.' However, Roosevelt was concerned 'that the world opinion would want some expression of the people, perhaps not immediately after their re-occupation by Soviet forces, but some day, and that he personally was confident that the people would vote to join the Soviet Union.' Stalin agreed, with the reservation that such a 'vote would not be carried out under international control' whereas in the US records, no answer or objection by Roosevelt is registered and according to the Soviet records, Roosevelt replied: 'Of course not.' See *Foreign Relations of the United States. Diplomatic Papers, The Conferences at Cairo and Teheran*, 1943, 1961, pp. 594–596. Cf. A. Fischer, *Teheran, Jalta, Potsdam. Die sowjetische Protokolle von den Kriegskonferenzen der 'Großen Drei'*, Köln, 1973, p. 139. See also U. Bollow, *Die baltische Frage in der internationalen Politik nach 1943*, Berlin: FU Politikwissenschaft, 1993, p. 4.

183 For a recent American view on the Yalta Conference, see H. Kissinger, *Diplomacy*, 1994, p. 394 *et seq.* According to Kissinger, 'Roosevelt agreed to Stalin's plan to move the frontiers of Poland westward and indicated that he would not press Stalin on the question of the Baltics. If Soviet armies occupied the Baltic States, he said, neither the United States nor Great Britain would 'turn her out'—though he also recommended holding a plebiscite.' However, Kissinger adds, 'Roosevelt was... reluctant to undertake discussion of the postwar world... [and] put forward his comments on Stalin's postwar plans for eastern Europe so tentatively as to sound almost apologetic.' See at p. 411. It must be for these reasons that Benvenisti comes to the conclusion that '[t]he international community acquiesced to the Soviet resurrection of the 1940 international borders, although formal recognition of the incorporation was generally withheld.' See Benvenisti, *The International Law of Occupation*, 1993, p. 68.

184 On the other hand, at the Potsdam Conference the US official position was more straightforwardly based upon non-recognition of the Soviet conquest. See FRUS, The Conference at Berlin/Potsdam 1945 (1960), p. 799.

fact of life. During World War II, Great Britain was inclined to accept the Soviet claim to the Baltic republics as a *quid pro quo* for Moscow's war effort;[185] the respective agreement with Moscow was mainly prevented by US opposition. The question whether the Western statesmen who co-drafted the new world order in 1943/45 were left with any realistic alternatives to swallowing a violation of the principles of the Atlantic Charter in the Baltic case should be asked in a study of history or political science rather than of international law.[186]

The annexed Baltic States, which by now were already Soviet republics within the USSR, became pawns on the chessboard of Cold War diplomatic battles. Stalin's request in 1945 to give full UN membership at least to the Lithuanian SSR—along with the Ukrainian SSR and Belorussian SSR—was rejected by the Western States.[187]

Next, the Nuremberg trials revealed 'a level of hypocricy rarely achieved in even this imperfect world.'[188] In Nuremberg, the victorious Western allies condemned horrendous Nazi crimes, in the first place Germany's aggressive wars—'supreme crimes under international law'—in a shared effort with Soviet judges and prosecutors.[189] While Soviet policy continued to assert that the Baltic

185 The British Foreign Office laid out the policy considerations, commenting at the time that '*it was doubtful whether American opinion understood the complexity of the political and geographical problems involved in the question of 'self determination in Europe'... If for instance, the USSR decided, after the war, to absorb the Baltic States, we might be compelled to recognize the facts, and, for the sake of the peace of Europe and our own wider interests, to maintain friendly relations with Russia. The United States would also tolerate the facts, but might refuse to give them formal recognition on moral grounds while accusing us of a selfish surrender of principle* See L. Woodward, *British Foreign Policy in the Second World War*, London: Her Majesty's Stationery Office, 1970–6, p. 205. Another British Foreign Office memorandum of December 1941 stated: 'I do not feel that the independence of the Baltic States is a European necessity.' Quoted from Bollow, p. 12.

186 For one possible answer by a political scientist, see R.A. Vitas, *op. cit.*, p. 67. For a critical view on the application of the Atlantic Charter in practice, see also S. Korman, *The Right of Conquest. The Acquisition of Territory by Force in International Law and Practice*, Oxford: Clarendon Press, 1996, p. 163: '*Thus, despite the avowed commitment of the Allies to principles which entailed the renunciation of the right of conquest, an examination of their practice would suggest a continued acceptance of the rule whereby the right to dispose of territory could be gained by means of military victory or conquest.*'

187 See e.g. Misiunas, *op. cit.*, p. 136. See also AJ. Kochavi, *Prelude to Nuremberg. Allied War Crimes Policy and the Question of Punishment*, Chapel Hill, 1998, p. 47 *et seq.* Note that at the UN General Assembly the Baltic issue as such was not taken up by States until 1991, and was mentioned only in other, 'related' contexts— colonialism, Hungary 1956, Afghanistan 1979. See e.g. the statement by Varela Quiros (Costa Rica) at UN-Doc. 6th Emergency Special Session, A/PV.4, UN GA Official Records, January 12, 1980.

188 A.P. Rubin, *Ethics and Authority in International Law*, Cambridge UP, 1997, p. xiii.

189 See generally G. Ginsburgs, *Moscow's Road to Nuremberg, the Soviet Background to the Trial*, The Hague: Martinus Nijhoff, 1996 and, more recently, F. Hirsch, *Soviet Judgment at*

nations had joined the USSR voluntarily, the non-belligerent Nazi invasions of Austria, Czechoslovakia and Denmark were condemned together with Nazi aggressive wars as crimes against peace in Nuremberg. The similarities with the Soviet takeover of the Baltic States must have been difficult to overlook, even though the Nuremberg trial was set up solely to prosecute Nazi crimes.

Sometimes, the 'right' balance between power, law and politics was difficult to maintain at the Nuremberg trials. The presentation by the defence counsel of Rudolf Hess, Dr. Alfred Seidl, who was trying to raise the issue of the Nazi-Soviet secret protocols of August 23, 1939, was interrupted by the Soviet general prosecutor, Major Rudenko.[190] Nevertheless, US prosecutor Robert H. Jackson filed a reservation to the Nuremberg judgment with respect to the Baltic States.[191] Moreover, soldiers from the Baltic States who had been conscripted into the German army, and other Baltic nationals, were generally not treated like Soviet citizens, who were usually forcibly sent back to the Soviet Union.

A delayed but important political attempt at a legal evaluation of the Soviet takeover of the Baltic States was made in 1954 when the US House of Representatives established a special committee for the study of the incorporation of the Baltic States into the USSR (*House Select Committee to Investigate Communist Aggression and the Forced Incorporation of the Baltic States into the USSR*), chaired by Representative Charles Kersten. Having collected the available evidence, testimonies and so on, the Kersten Committee came to the following final conclusions:

> I. The evidence is overwhelming and conclusive that Estonia, Latvia, and Lithuania were forcibly occupied and illegally annexed by the USSR Any claims by the USSR that the elections conducted by them in July 1940 were free and voluntary or that the resolutions adopted

---

Nuremberg. A New History of the International Military Tribunal after World War II, Oxford: Oxford University Press, 2020.

190 See Internationaler Militargerichtshof (Hrsg.) *Der Prozeß gegen die Hauptkriegsverbrecher vor dem Internationalen Militargerichtshof*, Bd. X, S. 14 *et seq.*, Bd. XIV, S. 315 *et seq.* See also Bd. XIX, S. 390 *et seq.*

191 The reservation of the US Prosecutor Jackson contained the following wording:
'*In the indictment of German war criminals signed today reference is made to Estonia, Latvia, Lithuania and certain other territories as being within the area of the USSR This language is proposed by Russia and is accepted to avoid delay on an alteration in the text. The indictment is signed subject to this reservation and understanding.*
I have no authority either to admit or to challenge, on behalf of the United States, the Soviet claims to sovereignty over such territories. Nothing, therefore, in this indictment is to be construed as a recognition by the United States of such sovereignty or as indicating any attitude, either on the part of the United States or on the part of the undersigned, toward any claim to redisposition of such sovereignty.' Quoted in E. Jaakson, *Eestile*, Tallinn: SE & JS, 1995, p. 136.

by the resulting parliaments petitioning for recognition as a Soviet Republic were legal are false and without foundation in fact.

II. That the continued military and political occupation of Lithuania, Latvia, and Estonia by the USSR is a major cause of the dangerous world tensions which now beset mankind and therefore constitutes a serious threat to peace.[192]

Although the Kersten Committee had parliamentary—and thus political—legitimation, its comprehensive investigation and final report penetrated the realm of the juridical. The work of the Kersten Committee is an interesting example of how, given the absence of central government in the international community, big powers are capable of pronouncing (and, on some other occasions, even enforcing)[193] international law.

Another form of the interplay between law and politics is illustrated by the entire concept and application of the doctrine of *de facto* recognition of annexation. Occasionally, *de facto* recognition of annexation left the respective government *de facto* a free hand to pursue its policies, and achieve its desired goals. Although Great Britain never recognized the Soviet annexation of the Baltic States *de iure*, Her Majesty's Government handed over the gold reserves of Estonia and Latvia to the Soviet government in a deal concluded in 1968.[194] The gold deposit of the Baltic States was used to cover all claims by British citizens against the Baltic States, while the Soviet Union renounced all its claims on the UK However, the UK agreed to transfer to the Soviet Union half a million pounds of Baltic gold deposits.[195]

The British position with regard to the Baltic question was sometimes ambiguous. In 1979, the British Under Secretary of State was asked by a member of

192 Report of the Select Committee to Investigate Communist Aggression and the Forced Incorporation of the Baltic States into the USSR Third interim report: *Baltic States—a Study of their Origin and national Development; their seizure and incorporation into the USSR*, Washington: United States Government Printing Office, 1954, p. 8. See also V. Riismandel, 'Kersteni komisjoni töötulemusi' (Work Results of the Kersten Committee), in: *Võitlev Eesti* (Fighting Estonia), Nr. 6, 1956, p. 35.

193 For more recent and sometimes controversial US practices, see L.F. Damrosch, 'Enforcing International Law Through Non-Forcible Measures', 269 *RCADI* 1997, p. 41 *et seq.*

194 This, on the other hand, did not prevent the Government of the United Kingdom, which had recognized the continuity of the Baltic States, from returning the respective amounts of gold to the Baltic governments after the independence of the Baltic States was restored. See *infra*. For the U.K-Soviet deal, see *Agreement between the United Kingdom and the USSR concerning the Settlements of Mutual Financial and Property Claims* of 5 January, 1968, UKTS 12 (1968), Cmnd. 3517.

195 See also E. Jaakson, *Eestile*, p. 193.

parliament whether acceptance by the United Kingdom of a Soviet invitation to observe a Soviet military manoeuvre in Lithuania was not an implied recognition of the Soviet annexation. The Under Secretary replied: '*In accordance with the provisions of the Helsinki Final Act the Soviet Government notified us of the military maneuvre 'NEMAN', which will be held in Lithuania from 23–27 July. Under a further voluntary provision, the Soviet Government invited the United Kingdom and others to send observers. The United Kingdom has accepted, in common with a number of other Western countries and in accordance with our wish to take full advantage of the Final Act. This has no implications for our position on the recognition of the incorporation of the Baltic States into the Soviet Union in 1940: we recognize this incorporation* de facto *but withhold full recognition.*'[196] Especially the *de facto* (but not *de iure*) recognition of the Soviet incorporation offered a comfortable solution for satisfying various and sometimes divergent interests.

Non-recognition of the annexation of the Baltic States demonstrates that formal non-recognition of territorial seizure is an incomplete means of reacting against aggression unless supported by effective sanctions.[197] Non-recognition, while preventing the consolidation of illegal situations, is as such not a method of enforcement or, in any real way, a sanction.[198] Instead, it is a precondition for other enforcement action. Due to political hardships and/or lack of interest, no such real enforcement action took place following the Soviet annexation of the Baltic States.

The Swiss international lawyer Rudolf Bindschedler has highlighted this inconsistency in State practice:

> The doctrine of non-recognition is of somewhat doubtful value as it permits States to salve their consciences with platonic declarations and exonerates them from taking positive measures and imposing sanctions which would put real pressure on the offending States. This has been shown clearly in practice; in the cases of Ethiopia, Austria and Czechoslovakia, the principle was not followed at all consistently, but most States have not recognized the annexation of the Baltic States.[199]

---

196 970 Parl. Deb., H.C. (5th ser.) 849 (1979). See also *BYBIL* 1979, p. 293.

197 For an earlier and more optimistic look at non-recognition politics, see W. Schätzel, 'Die Annexion im Völkerrecht', *AVR* 1950, p. 28.

198 Crawford, *The Creation...*, p. 122 and 128.

199 R.L. Bindschedler,'Annexation', in: R. Bernhardt (ed.) *EPIL*, Inst. I, 1992, p. 172. See for similar critique in P. de Visscher, *Théories et réalites en Droit international public,* Paris: Editions A. Pedone, 4ème éd., 1970, p. 261.

In the Baltic States, the mainly symbolic non-recognition has been occasionally criticized even more harshly. One Estonian author even asked: how many Balts did the non-recognition doctrine help to save from Soviet deportations to Siberia?[200]

This is the Janus-faced nature of the non-recognition doctrine, as applied in the case of the Baltic States.[201] Do inconsistencies in non-recognition render this policy legally insignificant? Some scholars have distinguished between 'effective protests' and 'paper protests.'[202] Was non-recognition of Soviet annexation tantamount to a passive and ineffective 'paper protest'? The Belgian scholar and practitioner of international law, Charles de Visscher, has argued that the legal effects of non-recognition and protests depend on their impact on the real consolidation of the situation. As long as such acts are not supported by effective countermeasures, they cannot prevent consolidation of the situation in the long term.[203] These doctrinal views have, however, never represented the majority view in modern legal literature.[204] It is doubtful whether, in the UN Charter era, one can speak of true acceptance of an illegal situation when third States still regularly file notes registering their non-recognition, even though such unilateral acts may be largely symbolic.

vii Non-recognition and Prescription in the Baltic Case: Conclusions

For the purposes of the present study, the fact remains that a significant number of Western States formally refused to recognize the Soviet incorporation of the Baltic States, right up the restoration of their independence in 1991. According to one estimate, by the end of the 1980s, some fifty States had not recognized the incorporation of the Baltic States into the Soviet Union.[205] This number may be exaggerated and depends on how one interprets State practice. In terms of legal effects, the question whether this was done solely for 'noble'

---

200 K. Tarand, 'Kasvuraskused' (Difficulties of Growing), in: *EÜSi Album* XVIII, Tartu, 2000, p. 58.

201 See also R.C. Visek, 'Creating the Ethnic Electorate through Legal Restorationism: Citizenship Rights in Estonia', 38 *Harvard JIL* 1997, p. 326: '*In retrospect, the West's refusal to recognize the Soviet annexation was a relatively low-risk act. It did not entail military confrontation, nor by itself did it jeopardize continued relations with the USSR.*' See also the criticism expressed by M. *Silagi, Staatsuntergang und Staatennachfolge mit besonderer Berücksichtigung des Endes der DDR, pp.* 259–260.

202 See E. Suy, *Les actes juridiques unilateraux en droit international public*, Diss. Paris, 1962, p. 71 et seq.

203 P. de Visscher, *Les éffectivités du droit international public*, Paris, 3me ed., 1967, pp. 25 and 108.

204 See Jennings, *Acquisition of Title…*, p. 25 and Zimmer, *Gewaltsame territoriale…*, pp. 45–46.

205 Reinhards, *Lettonie-Russie…*, p. 158.

reasons, and whether enough was done, remains of secondary importance. It is therefore not 'hypocritical'[206] to argue that there existed a continuous non-recognition policy, even if there were signs of what may be called hypocrisy in some States' attitude *vis-à-vis* non-recognition. Nevertheless, in the context of the survival or extinction of the Baltic States, the very fact of non-recognition of their annexation by a number of States speaks against prescription.[207] Similarly, Ti-Chiang Chen doubted whether the conditions for prescription would ever be fulfilled if protests and claims are being filed by the conquered State (if its government still exists) and other States.[208] Therefore, the attitude of third States in the Baltic case speaks against prescription, even though many States at least acquiesced in the Soviet seizure.[209]

viii The Status of the Baltic Soviet Socialist Republics from the Viewpoint of International Law

Part of the problematics of non-recognition is connected to the legal status of the Baltic Soviet Republics. In 1940, the USSR transformed the three Baltic republics into Soviet Socialist Republics. According to the Soviet view, crystallized for example in the Constitution of 1977, the Baltic republics continued to be 'independent and sovereign States,'[210] just like all other Union Republics of the USSR, and as such 'subjects of international law.'[211] Thus, from the Soviet point of view, the question of State identity had been solved by transforming

---

206 As argued by H. Ruiz Fabri, 'État (création, succession, compétences)...', *AFDI* 1992, p. 162.

207 See for a similar conclusion: V.J. Riismandel, 'The Continued Legal Existence of the Baltic States', 12 *Baltic Review* (7 November 1957), p. 49.

208 T.-C. Chen, *The International Law of Recognition. With Special Reference to Practice in Great Britain and the United States*, London: Stevens & Sons, 1951, p. 431.

209 See on the distinction between recognition and acquiescence in R.Y. Jennings, *The Acquisition of Territory in International Law*, Manchester: Manchester University Press, 1963, p. 36: '*Whereas recognition, even though it be tacit, is the adoption of the positive acknowledgment on the part of a State, acquiescence may arise from a mere omission to protest against a situation where a right to protest existed and its exercise was called for.*'

210 See Article 78 of the Soviet Constitution, adopted on October 7, 1977: 'Soviet republic—sovereign Soviet socialist State which has joined with other Soviet republics into the Union of the Soviet Socialist Republics. In the limits foreseen in Article 73 of the Constitution of the USSR, the Soviet republic independently carries out state power on its territory.'

211 See J.N. Hazard, 'Soviet Republics in International Law', in: *EPIL*, 1987, pp. 527–8 (see also for further references) and L. Schulz, 'The Relationship of the Union to the Republics in Soviet Constitutional Law', in: D.A. Loeber, S.V. Vardys, L.P.A. Kitching (eds.) *Regional Identity under Soviet Rule—the Case of the Baltic States*, 1990, pp. 351–354. For a Soviet exposition, see Д.И. Фельдман (соз.), *Международная правосубьектность* (*некоторые вопросы теории*), Москва: Юридическая литература, 1971, p. 37 *et seq.*

the bourgeois Baltic States into socialist States, while at the same time formally continuing their legal personality but now *within* the USSR. In earlier legal theory, it has often been argued that a State continues to exist when it enters into a federal State or is incorporated by another State, so that it preserves certain capacities of an international law subject.[212]

The text of the last (1977) Soviet Constitution contained provisions that could indeed indicate the sovereignty of the Soviet republics. For instance, Article 80[213] outlined the right of the Soviet republics to pursue foreign affairs:

> A union republic shall have the right to enter into relations with foreign states, conclude treaties with them, and exchange diplomatic and consular representatives, and to participate in the activity of international organizations.

However, the reality of the Soviet Constitution[214] was much more determined by Article 81:

> The sovereign rights of the Soviet republics are preserved by the Union of the SSR.

Thus, Soviet claims to have accorded independent 'subject of international law' status to its constituent parts were unanimously rejected by the international community, except in the anomalous case of agreeing to the Ukrainian and Byelorussian SSR s becoming original members of the UN, beside the USSR itself.

In the Baltic situation, the aspect of non-recognition of illegal occupation and annexation must be included in any evaluation of the legal status of the Baltic Soviet Republics. It is then understandable why Soviet attempts to present the Baltic SSR foreign ministries as legitimate representatives of independent States were unsuccessful. Only twelve people in 1952 and four in 1962 were employed in the so-called Foreign Ministry of the Estonian SSR. Among

---

212 See e.g. G. Jellinek, *Allgemeine Staatslehre,* 3. Aufl., Berlin, 1914, p. 283. For a more recent adoption, see D. Rauschning, *Das Schicksal völkerrechtlicher Verträge bei der Änderung des Status ihrer Partner,* Hamburg: Hansischer Gildenverlag, 1963, p. 44.

213 Article 80, the Constitution of the USSR, adopted on October 7, 1977.

214 For a detailed analysis, see H.-J. Uibopuu, *Die Völkerrechtssubjektivität der Unionsrepubliken der UdSSR,* Vienna, New York: Springer, 1975 and 'International Legal Personality of Union Republics of the USSR', in: *ICLQ*, Oct. 1975, p. 811. See also the discussion in B. Meissner, ‚Die Souveränität der baltischen Nationen' (1980), reprinted in: B. Meissner, *Die baltischen Staaten im weltpolitischen und völkerrechtlichen Wandel,* 1995, p. 174 *et seq.*

the evident goals of the foreign ministries of the Baltic Soviet republics was to discredit the pre-World War II independence period. Occasionally, the USSR succeeded in presenting the Baltic Soviet viewpoint even at the UN.[215]

215 Thus, Mrs. Leokadia Pilyushenko was identified at the 1967 fall session of the UN as the Foreign Minister of the Lithuanian SSR. The US representative to the Third Committee, Mrs. Patricia Roberts Harris, replied that Pilyushenko had no right to speak on behalf of Lithuania.
Similarly, Mr. Arnold Green from Estonia, being registered as the 'Minister for Foreign Affairs of the Estonian SSR', represented the USSR in the 17. General Assembly of the UN when colonisation was the main political issue on the agenda. Between him and the representative of the UK, the following exchange of comments developed. Sir Patrick Dean (UK): 'The Soviet representative in this debate, who bears the title of Foreign Minister of Estonia, spoke with feeling against the creation of federations or other unions contrary to the wishes of the populations concerned. Could it be that he is recalling the unhappy fate of his own country of Estonia, which was a free and independent State and a member of the League of Nations until 1940, when it was forcibly incorporated into the Soviet Union?' Mr. A. Green (USSR): '.In his statement [1175th meeting] Sir Patrick Dean said that the Soviet representative bore the title of Foreign Minister of Estonia. I can inform him that not only do I bear that title but that I am in fact the Foreign Minister of the Estonian Soviet Socialist Republic and that I represent the interests of its people. In the present instance, however, I represent first and foremost the interests of all the peoples of the great Soviet Union. As for the assertion that I ought to know the history of my own country, I may say categorically that I do know it and I will ask you, in this connexion, to allow me to present some typical facts drawn from it. The whole world must know that the hard-working Estonian people took an active part in the Great October Revolution at the side of the workers and peasants of Russia (...) Sir Patrick Dean mentioned in his statement that the 'bourgeois' Estonian Republic, which was the creation of the imperialists (this last clarification is mine), was independent and was even a member of the League of Nations. Yes, it was indeed a member of the League of Nations; but the sort of independence it enjoyed is best known to the Estonian people itself. (...) The result of Estonia's so-called independence was that it had the lowest standard of living of any nation in Europe, not to speak of such evils as permanent unemployment, the paucity of secondary schools, and so on. In 1940, when the pro-fascist Estonian Government stood alone and could no longer count on help from its imperialist patrons, the workers of Estonia drove it out and replaced it with the Soviet power, which opened up for them vast prospects of economic and cultural development (...) With the fraternal help of the Russian people, many small nations and peoples have been able, in two or three decades, to attain to development which in other circumstances they would have taken centuries to reach. (...) The Soviet Union is the only country in the world which has saved many nationalities from extinction. (...) On this subject let me make it clear once more that the Soviet peoples, including the Estonian people, do not need any self-appointed advocates such as the delegates of certain Western countries who have spoken here endeavour to constitute themselves. We would say to these gentlemen: the facts of history are against you. Indeed, history should clearly instruct you that, if it has proved impossible to make the dreams of the imperialists come true by armed intervention, there is absolutely no help to be derived from the malicious and slanderous attacks to which, in this Assem-

International legal personality was thus never attributed to the Estonian, Latvian and Lithuanian SSRs.[216] For example, in December 1987 the US ambassador in Moscow, Jack Matlock, refused to receive a delegation from the Supreme Soviet of the Latvian SSR which was protesting a US House Representatives resolution on Latvia's independence day.[217] Although the administration of the Soviet Socialist Republics included certain elements of autonomy and self-government for the population of the annexed Baltic States, the Soviet Baltic republics were internationally not recognized as successor States to the annexed Baltic States.

At the same time, it would of course be too simplistic to *prima facie* classify everything done under the aegis of the Baltic Soviet Republics as the work of the occupation regime. In that context, Ulrich Fastenrath has argued that:

> ...the Balts were incorporated against their will into the Soviet State, but then—in contrast to the colonial population—had a share in its Government. What happened during that time under the co-responsibility of the Estonians, Latvians and Lithuanians, cannot simpy be declared to be a consequence of earlier injustice.[218]

This point raises the important issue of the specific circumstances of Soviet rule in the Baltic States, especially its long duration. The Nazi occupations in European countries, including the Baltic republics, demonstrated that a certain segment of population is always—for various reasons—willing to collaborate with the occupier. It is even more obvious that during fifty years, most people adopt some form of collaboration or at least 'cooperation' instead of open 'struggle'—to allude to the Soviet international lawyer Grigory Tunkin[219]—with the ruling regime. Not everyone may be unhappy in a territory illegally seized.

---

bly, the representatives of the colonial Powers resort.' See A/PV.1172–1202 *Official Records of the General Assembly Seventeenth Session*, Plenary Meetings, Volume III, Verbatim Records of Meetings, 21 November-20 December 1962, United Nations, New York, 1964, p. 934–5.

216 We therefore disagree on this matter with Obiora Chinedu Okafor who sees 'legitimacy that was for a long time accorded to the Soviet states of the Baltic region.' See *Redefining Legitimate Statehood. International Law and State Fragmentation in Africa*, The Hague: Nijhoff, 2000, p. 66.

217 See R.A. Vitas, *op. cit.*, p. 83.

218 U. Fastenrath, ‚Das Recht der Staatensukzession', in: *BDGV*, Heidelberg, pp. 9–48 at p. 16. (Transl. from German.)

219 See G. Tunkin, 'International Law in the International System', 147 *RCADI* 1975, pp. 41–44.

c *Survival of State Organs of the Baltic Republics in Exile*

Beside the attitudes of third States, the second aspect in the prescription analysis is the possible continued existence of the government of the annexed State. As indicated above, the main difficulty in the case of a full annexation of an independent State is that no effective and independent State government can continue to exist within the country in such circumstances. In some cases (for example Austria 1938–1945), there are no traces of remaining State power at all. The Austrian case demonstrates that the existence of a government in exile is not a *conditio sine qua non* for eventual later recognition of State identity. However, thanks to US non-recognition policy, one parcel of the Baltic State organs remained continuously functioning in American exile, and one can include the discussion of the preserved State organs in the study of prescription/State continuity.

Once the Soviet army had successfully managed to establish a military blockade in June 1940, the governments of Estonia, Latvia and Lithuania did not succeed in taking refuge in exile. However, it is interesting to note that throughout Soviet rule in Estonia, Latvia and Lithuania, some legations of the pre-World War II independence period continued to exist and function in the Western world. According to the Baltic claim, these legations symbolized the continued existence of the illegally occupied and annexed republics. In addition to that, although no genuine governments in exile were initially created, the Estonian government in exile was later proclaimed in 1949 in Oslo. In the following, a more detailed account of these developments is given.

i The Functioning of the Baltic Legations in 1940–1991

On May 17, 1940, a secret decision was reached by the Latvian Government in order to assure the legal continuity of the Republic of Latvia. In the event of an emergency, the powers of the government were to be conferred on Kārlis Zarinš, Latvian Minister in London. Zarinš was *inter alia* authorized to appoint and recall the diplomatic and consular representatives of Latvia should connections with Latvia be interrupted because of war.[220] Alfred Bilmanis, Latvian Ambassador to Washington, was designated as Zarinš' substitute.[221] The diplomatic representatives of Latvia were called on to inform the foreign offices in the countries of their residence about this decision.[222] These special emergency powers of the Latvian Minister were recognized by the USA, the Holy See, and Spain.

---

220 See Repečka, *op. cit.*, p. 47.

221 See *The Baltic States 1940–1972...*, p. 20.

222 See Repečka, *op. cit.*, p. 47.

Similar developments occurred in Lithuania. On June 2, 1940, the Lithuanian government designated a senior diplomat, former Minister of Foreign Affairs Stasys Lozoraitis, then Minister to Italy, as head of the Lithuanian diplomatic service with the right to appoint replacements in case that government was no longer able to function.[223]

Although no analogous move is known to have been made by the Estonian government,[224] the diplomatic representations of all three Baltic republics assumed a similarly active role following the Soviet occupation and annexation of their countries.

Thus Johannes Kaiv, the Estonian Acting Consul General in charge of the Legation in New York, declared in his note of July 23, 1940, to the US Secretary of State:

> 'Being appointed by the former constitutional Government as senior representative in this country, I regard the above-mentioned elections as null and void, as well as all acts passed by this unconstitutionally elected Chamber of Deputies, in particular the decision about the union with the USSR.[225]

The Estonian Minister in London, August Torma, also filed a protest with the British Foreign Office in which he *inter alia*, stated:

> The decision to surrender the independence of the country has, therefore, quite obviously been arrived at under duress and it cannot be considered to be a free and genuine expression of the will of the overwhelming majority of the Estonian people.[226]

Similar protests against the overthrow of the constitutional governments at the beginning of the Soviet occupation were filed by other Baltic diplomatic representatives—for example by the Lithuanian ambassador in Berlin, Škirpa, on July 22, and by the Lithuanian ambassador in London, Balutis, on July 25, 1940.[227]

Immediately after the occupation of the Baltic States, Soviet officials tried to force diplomatic representatives of those States to turn over their missions

---

223 Misiunas, *op. cit.*, p. 135 and Vitas, *op. cit.*, p. 39.
224 Misiunas, *op. cit.*, p. 135.
225 Quoted in *The Baltic States 1940–1972...*, p. 14.
226 Quoted in *The Baltic States 1940–1972...* p. 14.
227 Repečka, *op. cit.*, p. 83.

to the Soviet government, and return home. It is known that only one diplomat, the recently appointed Estonian consul-general in Istanbul, followed those orders.[228] In order to force diplomatic representatives to return home, draconic penal laws were adopted by the Soviet authorities. For instance, a Law on the Punishment of Traitors, published in the Estonian State Gazette on August 5, 1940, declared as outlaws those diplomats who refused to return homel. Individuals convicted of this crime were to be shot dead within twenty-four hours of their capture. However, this unprecedented penal law failed to convince key Estonian diplomatic representatives to return to their occupied capitals.[229] In Lithuania, however, a different method was used: on August 14, 1940, a decision was publicized which stripped the Lithuanian minister in the USA, Zadeikis, of his Lithuanian citizenship, confiscated his property, and forbade him to return to Lithuania.[230]

Thanks to the determined non-recognition policy and the quite powerful position of the host country in international relations, the centre of gravity of the foreign representations was in the USA. The Estonian, Latvian and Lithuanian legations continued to exist and function in the USA during the 51 years of Soviet annexation. When the independence of the Baltic States was restored in August 1991, three Lithuanian legations (in Washington, London, and the Vatican), one Latvian legation (in Washington)[231] and one Estonian legation (in New York) had survived the normative pressure of the facts, and handed over a living piece of the pre-1940 State organs to the newly established Baltic republics.

Throughout the Soviet period, the Baltic legations faced three main difficulties: convincing their host countries of the importance of their continued functioning; the aging and eventual death of their staff; and the struggle to ensure their funding, As they represented occupied and annexed States, there was understandably no financing by their central governments (which had ceased to exist). Over time, 'natural causes' (in other words, death of diplomats) meant cessation of activities for most Baltic legations, as only the USA and the Vatican allowed replacement of personnel to functioning diplomatic missions.[232]

Thus, for instance, the Estonian Ambassador to the UK since 1934, August Torma, died in 1971. After Torma's death, Anna Vageström-Taru, who had been

228 Misiunas, *op. cit.*, p. 139.

229 See E. Jaakson, *Eestile* (To Estonia), p. 96.

230 R.A. Vitas, *op. cit.*, p. 42.

231 Cf. Misiunas, *op. cit.*, p. 140.

232 Misiunas, *op. cit.*, p. 140.

in the service of the legation since 1948, did not receive accreditation from the British Foreign Office. Although the UK continued to refuse recognition of Soviet rule in Estonia *de iure*, it held the position that since 1940, no government of the Republic of Estonia existed which would have been entitled to appoint new representatives to Her Majesty's Government.[233] Similarly, Uruguay refused to accept replacements for the Lithuanian legation, nominated by the head of the Lithuanian diplomatic service.[234]

The Lithuanian legation in Argentina was closed in connection with that country's establishment of diplomatic relations with the USSR. The Estonian consulate in São Paolo, Brazil, the only surviving Estonian representation in South America, ceased to function with the death of the consul Ferdinand Saukas on December 29, 1976.[235] Later, the Brazilian government closed the Lithuanian and Latvian legations in its territory, recognizing the Soviet incorporation *de facto*.[236] Similarly, the Estonian representation in Spain ceased to function soon after the death of Kaarel Robert Pusta on May 4, 1964.[237] Former Foreign Minister Karl Selter served as diplomatic agent of Estonia in the Federal Republic of Germany and Switzerland, but Estonia's representation came to an end with his death.[238]

As replacements were allowed by the US government, the Baltic legations in the USA continued to operate without interruption throughout the whole period of Soviet annexation. For instance, when the Acting Consul General of Estonia in charge of Legation,[239] Johannes Kaiv, died on November 20, 1965, he was replaced by fellow Consul Ernst Jaakson, who was added to the US Diplomatic List on December 15, 1965,[240] and continued to hold the position of Consul General until Estonia's independence was restored.

---

233 See the certificate of the Foreign and Commonwealth Office in *Re an Application by Ernst Jaakson and Aarand Roos*, 85 *ILR* 53 at p. 57. See also HL Debs., vol. 440, col. 1449: 28.3.1983, printed in: 54 *BYBIL* 1983, p. 3384.

234 Misiunas, *op. cit.*, p. 139.

235 Jaakson, *op. cit.*, pp. 207–208.

236 Misiunas, *op. cit.*, p. 139.

237 Jaakson, *op. cit.*, p. 214. For the contribution of K.-R. Pusta to international law scholarship, see e.g. K.-R. Pusta, 'Le statut juridique de la mer Baltique à partir du XIXe siècle', 52 *RCADI* 1935, pp. 105–190.

238 Misiunas, *op. cit.*, p. 140.

239 This was the nonconventional name of this Legation. In the strict terms of international diplomatic law, such a name was a curiosity, yet the US Government recognized it as such, and it was included in the Diplomatic List in Washington, DC See E. Jaakson, *op. cit.*, p. 65.

240 Jaakson, *op. cit.*, p. 174. See also A. Velliste, *Ernst Jaaksonile*, Tallinn: Eesti Entsüklopeediakirjastus, 2000.

Ernst Jaakson and his life story personifies in many ways the continuity claim of the Republic of Estonia.[241] Jaakson, born in the year of the first Russian revolution in 1905, started to serve in the Estonian diplomatic representation in Riga, Latvia, in 1919, when he was only fourteen (*sic*) years old. In April 1932, he was appointed to the Estonian consulate general in New York City.[242] As already indicated, Jaakson became Acting Consul General in charge of the Legation in 1965, served in this position until the restoration of the power of the constitutional authorities in Estonia in 1991/1992, and continued to work in the diplomatic service as the first Estonian ambassador at the UN until his death in 1998. With his 75 years in service, Jaakson was considered the longest-serving diplomate in the world.[243]

The US State Department also allowed the Baltic Legations to appoint new consuls[244]—with the sole precondition that individuals nominated would hold the respective Baltic citizenship. Under the Estonian General Consul E. Jaakson, Aksel Linkhorst was nominated by the US State Department as Consul in 1967. After Linkhorst's death in 1981, Evald Uustalu was accepted as the new Estonian Consul by the US State Department. Uustalu himelf died in 1982, and subsequently a linguist from Lund University, Aarand Roos, was accredited by the US State Department as new Estonian Consul in New York City on April 4, 1982.[245]

Similarly, the Chief of the Latvian Mission in Washington, DC, Alfred Bilmanis, was replaced upon his death by Jules Feldmans. After the death of Feldmans, work was continued by Arnolds Spekke. With restoration of the independence of Latvia in August 1991, the Latvian Legation was headed by chargé d'affaires Anatol Dinbergs.[246]

The Lithuanian ambassador in Washington, DC in 1940, Povilas Zadeikis, died in 1957 and was replaced by Juozas Kajeckas. In 1977, Kajeckas was succeeded by his assistant Stasys Backis. The Lithuanian Consul General in New York City, Jonas Budrys, was replaced after his death by Vytautas Stasinskas, and later by Stasys Backis.[247] The last Soviet era Lithuanian minister in

241 See also E. Medijainen, *Saadiku saatus. Välisministeerium ja saatkonnad 1918–1940*, (The Fate of the Ambassador: The Foreign Ministry and the Legations in 1918–1940), Tallinn: Eesti Entsüklopeediakirjastus, 1997, p. 258. (Summary in English.)

242 See Jaakson, *op. cit.*, p. 19 *et seq.*

243 See 'Ernst Jaakson, Estonian Envoy, Dies at 93', *International Herald Tribune* 26–27 September 1998.

244 See *Digest of United States Practice in International Law* 1979, p. 111.

245 See Jaakson, *op. cit.*, pp. 216–217.

246 See Jaakson, *op. cit.*, p. 113.

247 Jaakson, *op. cit.*, p. 113. Cf. Vitas, *op. cit.*, pp. 43, 110 and 112.

Washington, DC, beginning in 1987, was Stasys Lozoraitis, Jr., son of the former head of the Lithuanian Diplomatic Service. He was recognized in 1970 by the Vatican as *chargé d'affaires*, and divided his tasks between the Vatican and Washington, DC[248] Until the end of the Soviet period, the Lithuanian legation in London was headed by a prewar appointee, Vincas Balickas, who had arrived in Great Britain in 1938 as commercial counsellor and was 84 years old when Lithuania regained its independence in 1991.[249]

One of the most crucial questions from the point of view of the survival of the Baltic diplomatic representations was of a practical nature: financing in a situation where ties to the annexed countries had been severed. For instance, only $ 4,525.15 remained at the disposal of the Estonian consulate general in New York on July 1, 1940. This sum would not have enabled the functioning of the consulate general for more than a few months.[250] Fortunately for the Baltic legations, in 1941 the US State Department authorized limited use of the previously blocked deposits of the Baltic republics in the USA.[251] The USA had rejected the order forwarded by the Soviet Central Bank, Gosbank, to transfer the Baltic assets to it. The US State Department also authorized the use of these deposits for the activities of the Baltic representatives in South America (such as the Estonian consulate in Sao Paolo, Brazil).[252] Beginning in 1951, the expenses of the Estonian legation in London were financed from gold reserves deposited in the USA.[253] Additionally, in all three cases, voluntary contributions from Baltic exiles played a role in the maintenance and renovation of the legation premises, for example.[254] In financial need, the Baltic legations helped one another. At one point, Latvian *chargé d'affaires* Dinbergs authorized a loan of $ 185,000 to his Estonian colleague Consul General Jaakson for maintenance of the Estonian legations.[255]

The main function of the Baltic legations was of a symbolic nature: to represent the sovereignty of the three occupied and annexed States. Throughout the period of Soviet annexation, Baltic diplomats were listed in the State Department's Diplomatic List, and were therefore invited to participate in diplomatic

248 Misiunas, *op. cit.*, p. 140. As the head of Lithuania's mission, Lozoraitis Jr. played a prominent role in the restoration of Lithuania's independence, acting as the adviser to Supreme Council Chairman Landsbergis. See Lieven, *op. cit.*, pp. 235 and 71.

249 Misiunas, *op. cit.*, p. 140.

250 See Jaakson, *op. cit.*, p. 95.

251 See also *Digest of United States Practice in International Law* 1979, p. 173.

252 See Jaakson, *op. cit.*, pp. 111 and 115.

253 Jaakson, *op. cit.*, p. 115.

254 Misiunas, *op. cit.*, p. 141.

255 Jaakson, *op. cit.*, p. 202. Cf. Vitas, *op. cit.*, p. 111.

ceremonies and receptions organized by the US State Department. The Baltic consuls also had standing (*locus standi*) in the US courts. The first US case confirming this rule was *Buxhoeveden v. Estonian State Bank*.[256] In the matter of *Luks' Estates*[257] the New York Surrogates Court granted standing to the Consuls General of Latvia and Estonia. Apart from this, the Baltic legations continued to issue passports to those who could prove Estonian, Latvian, or Lithuanian citizenship and to their offspring.[258]

Baltic passports and seamen's IDs continued to be honoured by States which did not recognize the Soviet incorporation of the Baltic States. Moreover, some countries such as Sweden, which otherwise recognized the Soviet incorporation of the Baltic republics, still also accepted these passports as travel or residence documents.[259]

Besides issuing passports, the Baltic legations served the exiled citizens of their respective countries with the various usual consular activities, such as exercising notarial functions—providing translations of official documents, issuing certificates, and legalizing documents issued in the pre-1940 Baltic States.[260]

Another interesting aspect about the Baltic legations in Western countries during the Soviet annexation period was that their leading minds – for example Kaarel Robert Pusta who was Estonia's diplomatic representative in Spain and member of the Institut de Droit International – were actively interested in arguments in international law scholarship such as the books of Marek and Meissner.[261] There was a constant interaction between arguments in legal practice and those in scholarship.[262]

ii A Particular Estonian Development: The Government(s) in Exile

A certain amount of confusion reigns in the legal literature about the Baltic governments in exile. Some authors have claimed that the annexed Baltic

---

256 The New York Supreme Court, Special Term, Queens County, April 21, 1943; 41 N.Y.S. (2d) 752–757; *Ibid.*, Part I, October 8, 1948; 84 N.Y.S. (2d)2. (the Estonian consul general's status was affirmed on the basis of general international law and US-Estonian treaties.)

257 *In re Luks' estates*, 256 N.Y.S. 2d 194, also reported at 59 *AJIL* 1965, p. 642 *et seq.*

258 Misiunas, *op. cit.*, p. 141.

259 Misiunas, *op. cit.*, p. 141–142.

260 See E. Roosaare, 'Consular Relations between the United States and the Baltic States', 27 *Baltic Review* (June 1964), pp. 23–32. Cf. Jaakson, *op. cit.*, p. 98.

261 See Kaarel Robert Pusta's archive, Hoover Institute at Stanford University.

262 See e.g. A. Warma, 'Pensées, sur l'identité et la continuité de l'Etat. (Situation juridique de la République d'Estonie.), in: J.G. Poska (ed.) *Pro Baltica. Mélanges dédiés á Kaarel R. Pusta*, Stockholm: Comité des Amis de K.R. Pusta, 1965, pp. 219–228 (referring repeatedly to Marek).

States did not have governments in exile who could have claimed to represent legitimate State power in their countries.[263] Other authors have mistakenly suggested that (all) three Baltic States had governments in exile during the Soviet period.[264] In reality, only one of them—Estonia—did so,[265] and the confusion in the literature demonstrates how fragile the role and status of that government was.

The origins of the Estonian government in exile are closely connected with the name of the last pre-Soviet occupation era prime minister of Estonia, Professor Jüri Uluots.[266] Uluots managed to survive the first year of the Soviet occupation in Estonia in hiding, and came to be regarded as the bearer of State continuity under the 1938 Constitution of Estonia, occupied by Germany (1941–1944) at that time. As President of the Republic, Konstantin Päts, had been deported to Soviet Russia, the five-member Election Assembly, established under the 1938 Estonian Constitution, decided at a secret meeting held on April 20, 1944, that the duties of the President of the Republic were to be transferred to the last pre-Soviet occupation Prime Minister, Jüri Uluots.

Legally, Uluots' title remained controversial, as in June, 1940, notwithstanding the Soviet occupation, the Uluots government had been relieved of office by President Päts in a way formally compatible with the Estonian constitution. On the other hand, this point has been rejected by the argument that Estonian President Päts acted under extreme duress in an already occupied country when he appointed a new pro-Soviet government in June 1940; the change of the government was thus unconstitutional.[267]

On September 18, 1944, Uluots appointed a new Government of the Republic of Estonia, led by Otto Tief. The German army was retreating and the Estonians hoped to restore their independence before the Soviet Army could establish control over the country. The Tief Government was active for a week, controlled the capital Tallinn for about a day and tried to organize military resistance against the advancing Soviet Army. However, the Soviets occupied Tallinn on September 22, 1944, and soon, meeting only sporadic resistance from the sporadically formed Estonian troops, reached the coast of Western Estonia. Most members of the Tief Government—including Tief himself—were

---

263 See e.g. H. Krieger, *Das Effektivitätsprinzip im Völkerrecht*, p. 443.

264 A. Peters speaks of 'im Exil befindlichen Exilregierungen', see *op. cit.*, p. 151.

265 For related attempts in Lithuania and Latvia, see *The Baltic States 1940–1972…*, pp. 63–69.

266 See also L. Mälksoo, 'Professor Uluots, the Estonian Government-in-Exile and the Continuity of the Republic of Estonia', 69 *Nordic JIL* 2000, pp. 289–316.

267 As put by Marek: The Estonian Constitution obviously did not provide for the nomination of national governments according to lists drawn up by organs of a foreign State. See Marek, *op. cit.* p. 384.

arrested by the Soviets; only a few managed to escape across the Baltic Sea to Sweden. The Tief Government had ceased to exist and Estonia was again under Soviet occupation.

Uluots, who made claims for the continuity of Estonian State power, died in Sweden on January 9, 1945. A day before his death, the surviving four members of the Tief government decided in Stockholm that under the 1938 Estonian Constitution, the tasks of the President of the Republic should be transferred to the oldest member of the Tief government, August Rei, who had been Estonia's Minister of Foreign Affairs and was the Estonian Minister in Moscow in 1939/1940.

However, the Estonian Constitution allowed a different interpretation for such a situation of constitutional crisis, namely that the new President of the Republic must again (as had been the case in 1944 with Uluots) be elected by the special Election Committee. These two interpretations of the 1938 Estonian Constitution brought about the creation of two competing Estonian governments in exile.

More than eight years after the end of the Tief Government in September 1944, its oldest member, August Rei, proclaimed his Estonian government in exile in Oslo on January 12, 1953. The government in exile established by Rei became known as the 'exiled government in Oslo.' The surviving members of the former Election Committee felt their ambitions hurt by Rei's move, and gathered near Detmold in Germany. The Election Committee elected one of its members, Alfred Maurer, the former Second Assistant Chairman of the second chamber of the pre-1940 Estonian parliament, as acting President of Estonia in exile. Maurer appointed Johan Holberg prime minister of his own Estonian government in exile on March 2, 1953.

Thus, two Estonian governments in exile had come into existence simultaneously. Since Estonia continued to be ruled by the Soviets, and the Election Committee was unable to renew itself as the basis for the government in exile, Maurer's alternative government in exile was extinguished with the death of its members.

The exiled government in Oslo, proclaimed by Rei, continued to exist until the restoration of constitutional power in Estonia through elections in 1992.[268] This government in exile was based on an interpretation of the 1938 Constitution according to which, in the case of the death of a President (or, respectively, an acting President), the oldest member of the existing government would

268 See M. Orav, E. Nõu (eds.) *Tõotan ustavaks jääda...: Eesti Vabariigi Valitsus 1940–1992* (I Swear to Remain Faithful...: Government of the Republic of Estonia 1940–1992), Tallinn: Eesti Kirjanduse Selts, 2004.

automatically continue as the next acting President. It could thus be rejuvenated each time its acting President died. Theoretically, this method could have guaranteed the existence of the Estonian government in exile *ad aeternum*. After the death of August Rei, Aleksander Warma became the new Acting President in exile in 1964. Warma was succeeded by Tõnis Kint in 1971 and Kint by Heinrich Mark in 1990. Throughout the Soviet period, the Estonian government in exile continued to exist, being symbolically composed of all pre-World War II governmental portfolios from foreign affairs to transport and agriculture.

As with the Baltic legations, the main *raison d'être* of the Estonian government in exile was to keep alive the issue of the illegal annexation of Estonia on the international agenda and represent the idea that the Republic of Estonia continued to exist in terms of international law.[269] Its members actively voiced Estonian views at conferences and during political events, and awarded orders in the name of the Republic of Estonia to outstanding individuals, and the like. However, partly due to constitutional complexities and questions concerning its birth, the Estonian government in exile was not recognized by any foreign government.[270] Moreover, even the Estonian legations in New York and London refused to accept the Estonian government in exile's authority over their functioning, political and practical matters.[271]

The Estonian government in exile thus had no international status throughout its existence (1953–1992). Lack of international recognition severely diminished its effectiveness as a government in exile. Nevertheless, at the end of the day the Estonian government in exile came to enjoy recognition from the Estonian constitutional perspective. On the official website of the Estonian President, the Acting Presidents of the Republic of Estonia in exile have been listed as the predecessors of post-1992 Presidents, bearers of State continuity during the time of Soviet annexation. The interpretation of the present-day Estonian constitutional organs in favour of the legitimacy of the Estonian government in exile must be accorded due respect, as it indicates 'the way a State concerned sees itself.'[272]

---

269 For an early account of these endeavors, see *We Demand Freedom for Estonia. Memoranda Presented to the Delegations at the Paris Conference* (1946), London: Boreas, 1947.

270 On positions of the US and UK, see Jaakson, *op. cit.*, p. 170 and 195.

271 See the meeting of the Estonian diplomatic representatives from the legations in New York and London with the Acting President of the government in exile, A. Warma, in London on April 27, 1966. See Jaakson, *op. cit.*, p. 171.

272 See Fiedler, 'Continuity', p. 808.

Thus, the ultimate reward that erased all previous humiliations for the Estonian government in exile was when, on October 7, 1992, on the day the first post-Soviet era Estonian parliament, the 7th *Riigikogu,* was convened, the Acting President in exile, Heinrich Mark, gave a speech at the *Riigikogu* which represented the ceremonial 'handing over' of State power to the newly elected constitutional organs. On the same day, the *Riigikogu* elected Lennart Meri as the first post-Soviet era President of the restored Republic of Estonia. The government in exile thus ended its activities, whereas the newly elected President of the Republic of Estonia, Lennart Meri, expressed his 'deep gratitude' to Heinrich Mark and all the other members of the government in exile 'for preserving the continuity of the Republic of Estonia.'[273] This constitutional policy of 'restorationism' was further highlighted by the fact that President Meri avoided taking over power ceremonially from the last Chairman of the Supreme Council of the Republic of Estonia, Arnold Rüütel. It remains one of the ironies of history (and, maybe, of Estonia's continuity claim) that in September 2001, President Meri had to hand over the Estonian President's power to the ex-Chairman of the Supreme Council, Mr. Rüütel, who had been elected President by the Election Assembly.

iii The Baltic Legations and the Estonian Government in Exile: Evaluation from the Point of View of State Continuity and Prescription

As no governments in exile of Latvia or Lithuania existed—and the Estonian legations did not recognize the Estonian government in exile which was established in 1953—the Baltic legations in the USA and other Western countries were not bound to any higher State authority during the Soviet annexation of the Baltic republics. Indeed, they were the only continuously surviving State organs of the Soviet-annexed Baltic republics. The view has been widespread in the literature that the continuity of the Baltic States was vested in their legations.[274] The legations in the USA functioned *de facto* as *quasi*-governments in exile and thus symbolized the continued existence of the third constitutive element of the State: State power.

273 See H. Mark, Vabariigi President ja Vabariigi Valitsus Eksiilis 1988–1992 (President of the Republic and the Government of the Republic in Exile in 1988–1992), *Akadeemia* 1997 No. 7, p. 1443 *et seq.*

274 See Marek, *op. cit.*, p. 410; Misiunas, *op. cit.*; Silagi, *op. cit.*, p. 257; Meissner, *Sowjetunion, die baltischen Staaten...* p. 200; Yakemtchouk, *op. cit.*, p. 273.

Although the USA did not recognize the Baltic legations formally as 'governments in exile,'[275] its representatives insisted that the role of the Baltic envoys was 'to uphold the ideal of a free Estonia, Latvia, and Lithuania.'[276] Although some authors have therefore explicitly rejected qualification of the Baltic legations as *quasi*-governments in exile during the Soviet annexation period,[277] the legal significance of these legations in light of the continuity claim of the Baltic States should not be neglected. The symbolic preservation and functioning of the legations throughout the entire period of illegal annexation guaranteed the uninterrupted existence of at least one symbolic 'piece' of the legal order of the occupied and annexed States, and thus is an important argument in favour of the Baltic States' continuity claims. Whether the legations should be qualified as '*quasi*-governments in exile' or not can remain undecided in the last resort, as this qualification is not determinative for either affirmation or rejection of State continuity as such. As noted earlier, in cases of illegal annexation, State continuity could be preserved—true, in previous precedents for shorter periods than in the Baltic case—even notwithstanding the absence of any government in exile, legations or other State organs.

From the academic point of view, it is debatable whether the Estonian government in exile was indeed a governmente in the international legal sense. Due to its lack of international recognition, its existence had little influence on the decision by Western States to recognize the identity of the restored Baltic States with pre-World War II republics in 1991. Moreover, the State identity of all three Baltic republics was recognized, although only Estonia had a (as some have argued: self-proclaimed) government in exile.

Nevertheless, the existence of the Estonian government in exile had a strong influence on constitutional decisions taken in Estonia in 1990–1992. Even if the Estonian government in exile did not 'preserve' the legal personality of the Republic of Estonia, many citizens believed (or wanted to believe) it had indeed done so.

In retrospect, it may be concluded that although the Estonian legations did not recognize the Estonian government in exile, these institutions did not contradict each other either as parallel bearers of State continuity and representatives of the claim to Estonia's independence. Both spoke out against

275 Cf. R.A. Vitas, *op. cit.*, p. 41.

276 US Department of State, Statement by Robert L. Barry, Assistant Secretary for European Affairs, before the Subcommittee on International Organizations of the House Committee on Foreign Affairs, June 26, 1979, pp. 4–5.

277 See e.g. W. Schaumann, ‚Exilregierung', in: K. Strupp and H.-J. Schlochauer (eds.) *Wörterbuch des Völkerrechts*, 2. Aufl, Band I, Berlin: Springer, 1960, p. 498.

acquisitive and extinctive prescription in the case of the annexed Baltic States; it is recognized in the doctrine that the continued existence of a government in exile is a fact that speaks against consolidation of seizure.[278]

At the same time, it is clear that neither the Baltic legations nor the government in exile (in the Estonian case) could effectively fulfill government functions in exile.

d *The Baltic Peoples and Prescription*

Finally, for the purposes of prescription analysis, we should turn to the study of the role of the peoples of the Baltic States themselves. During the second half of the 20th century the principle of democratic legitimation assumed greater weight in terms of the legal analysis of statehood.[279] The increasing importance of the right of peoples to self-determination and of human rights generally caused a departure from a static and formalistic concept of statehood. In the early 1990s, some prominent Western international lawyers even argued for an emerging right to democratic governance in international law.[280]

Hence, it is unsurprising that the attitude of the affected population toward the State exercising authority over it has become increasingly important. At the same time, 'the people' seems to be the most challenging element for the legal inquiry of statehood. 'The people's will' has figured among the most powerful—and therefore most misused—arguments used in political rhetoric and legal legitimation.

An illegally occupied State can change into something else when its population accepts the new regime and State identity, when it no longer stands for its own independent State. Due to the primacy of individuals' interest over State interest in contemporary international law, acquiescence of the population in conquest may be a factor in favour of accepting prescription.[281] In other words, without the true consent of the affected population, no prescription can take place.[282] Philip Marshall Brown postulated during World War II that:

> Military occupation by itself does not confer title or extinguish a nation. Nor does a proclamation of annexation so long as the claims of the occupying Power are effectively challenged and remain unrecognized. (...)

278 See K. Doehring, 'State', in: *EPIL* 10, 1987, p. 427.

279 Cf. J. Crawford, *The Criteria for Statehood...*, p. 144 *et seq.*

280 See T. Franck, 'The Emerging Right to Democratic Governance', 89 *AJIL* 1992, pp. 46–91; J. Crawford, 'Democracy and International Law', 64 *BYBIL* 1993, p. 113.

281 Bowett, *Case Concerning Territorial Dispute (Libya-Chad)*, I.CJ., Public Sitting, CR 93/28, p. 19.

282 See e.g. A. Verdross, *Völkerrecht* I, Wien, 1964, 5. Aufl., pp. 288–289 and H. Krieger, *Das Effektivitätsprinzip im Völkerrecht*, p. 455.

> There is no automatic extinction of nations. (…) A nation is much more than an outward form of territory and government. It consists of the men and women in whom sovereignty resides. So long as they cherish sovereignty in their hearts their nation is not dead.[283]

The second element of the three-elements-theory, State people, may thus influence analyses of statehood to a certain extent.

In non-democratic countries, the people's true will is hard to find out. Non-democratic regimes are in a position to a certain extent to manipulate the will of the people, combining a monopoly over information and education with lies or half-truths provided by a propaganda apparatus. Even if not as pervasively as in George Orwell's fiction 'Nineteen Eighty-Four,'[284] such regimes are capable of at least partly confusing the people about what they want, just as they would try to confuse the outer world about what the people under the regime's control wants.[285] In annexed territories, they can force or entice people to collaborate in order for them to survive. Certain individuals from the seized territories are recruited and trained as the new representatives of the population.

Although such camouflage can presumably be revealed relatively easily—especially since the 20th century has given us a profound experience and insight into the functioning, methods and possibilities of totalitarian regimes[286]—the problem remains: how to establish the true will of the people? For instance, it is quite likely that Western decision makers asked themselves at some point during the Cold War: does non-recognition of the Soviet annexation of the Baltic States serve the interests of the Estonian, Latvian or Latvian peoples or not? The question was, pragmatically speaking, also: which is more important, continuing cultural and economic relations—which would have proved beneficial for all participating peoples and individuals—or refusing, for principled ideological reasons, all cooperation with the annexed country? Finland, for instance, chose the first path during the presidency of Urho Kaleva Kekkonen, and paying lipservice to the Soviet regime, re-established active cultural ties with Estonia, to the extent this was endorsed by the Soviet government. Soviet

---

283 J.S. Brown, 'Sovereignty in Exile', 35 *AJIL* 1941, pp. 667–668.

284 See G. Orwell, *Nineteen eighty-four*, London: Secker & Warburg, 1997.

285 Cf. also with respect to totalitarian States G. Arangio-Ruiz, 'L'État dans le sens du Droit des Gens…', p. 292.

286 See esp. H. Arendt, *The Origins of Totalitarianism,* London: André Deutsch, 1986. With respect to Soviet totalitarianism see especially p. 303 *et seq.*

occupation or not, such ties and information helped Estonians considerably during the transition period from Soviet *perestroika* to restored statehood.

Whatever the difficulties of finding out a people's will, recent developments have shown that whenever people are free in determining their choices, and care enough to manifest their preferences strongly, such manifestations are not ignored in international legal practice. Ultimately, it is those people that are most affected by a decision on State personality.

In that light, it becomes apparent that special importance in the case of the annexed Baltic States must be attributed to their peoples' claims and manifestations of self-determination. Equally as much as the Baltic legations (or, as in the Estonian case, the government in exile,), preservation of the Baltic republics as subjects of international law could be attributed to claims by the Baltic peoples and their representatives to independent statehood, based on the principle of State continuity.

But could such claims for independent statehood really have existed during the decades of Soviet rule? During the independence process of 1988–1991, the Baltic peoples and politicians raised quite powerfully their claim for restoration of the independence of their pre-war republics. By this demand they demonstrated that they perceived the bond of State continuity with their independent pre-World War II republics—older generations still alive had been citizens of those republics in their youth—rather than with the then still existing Soviet State.

Thus, when representatives of the Lithuanians, Latvians and Estonians insisted in 1990/91 on restoration of the pre-World War II independent republics, and not on 'secession' from the USSR (Russia), this must not have been surprising to those analysts who had observed developments in the Baltic republics after Soviet control was established there in 1940, and again in 1944.

The animosity towards—and resistance by the Baltic peoples against—the Soviet regime was expressed in many ways. The particular reasons for this animosity against foreign rule, especially towards State crimes committed during the Stalin era, are addressed below in a later part of this study. However, at this point a brief historical sketch is nevertheless appropriate. In the summer of 1941, the Baltic guerillas, having formed themselves following Soviet mass deportations of June 14, 1941, took advantage of the context of Nazi Germany's military attack against the USSR, and in some regions even managed to make Soviet occupation forces withdraw before the *Wehrmacht* in turn occupied the Baltic States for Nazi Germany. After it became obvious in 1944 that Stalin's Soviet Union would again seize possession of the Baltic republics, hundreds of thousands of Lithuanians, Latvians and Estonians voted against the Soviet State with their feet—by escaping as refugees to the West.

From 1944–1956, the USSR was confronted with a serious guerilla movement in the Baltic States. The guerillas, called 'forest brethren' by the local population and 'bandits' by the Soviet authorities, were especially active in Lithuania, and usually enjoyed the support and sympathy of the local population. They occasionally controlled rural regions where Soviet rule could be re-established only at the cost of casualties.[287] Although military resistance by the Baltic guerillas ceased during the 1950s, the last men were caught much later. In Estonia, for instance, one of the last active forest brothers, August Sabe, was killed when he tried to escape from two KGB men in a southern Estonian forest in 1978.[288] Since the restoration of the Baltic States, Soviet actions against the Baltic guerillas have produced interesting case law in the courts of the Baltic States as well as in the European Court of Human Rights in Strasbourg.[289]

The USSR confronted armed and other resistance in the Baltic republics with mass deportations and liquidations. These can be qualified as State crimes—crimes against humanity, and possibly even genocide.[290] The German international law scholar Heike Krieger, who in her recent monograph otherwise quite strongly emphasizes the importance of effectiveness in international law, also insists that when a State has annexed a territory illegally, and combines this violation with mass deportations or genocide, 'prescription is under no conditions possible.'[291]

When, at the end of the 1940s, the majority of Estonians, Latvians and Lithuanians realized that continuing the military struggle against Stalin's USSR led to further repression, they adopted more passive forms of resistance.[292] For

287 In Estonia, up to 30 000 Estonian 'forest brethren' fought against the Soviet army and functionaries in 1944–1956. See M. Laar, *War in the Woods. Estonia's Struggle for Survival 1944–1976*, Washington, DC: The Compass Press, 1992. See also Lieven, *op. cit.*, pp. 87–92.

288 The last known Estonian forest brother, Johannes Lillenurm, died at liberty in 1980.

289 See also L. Mälksoo, 'The European Court of Human Rights and the Qualification of Soviet Crimes in the Baltic States', 39 *Human Rights Law Journal* 2019, pp. 19–22.

290 See for discussion L. Mälksoo, *Soviet Genocide? The Communist Mass Deportations in the Baltic States and International Law,* 14 Leiden JIL 2001, pp. 757–787.

291 H. Krieger, *Das Effektivitätsprinzip im Völkerrecht,* 2000, p. 426.

292 See e.g. D. Bungs, 'Joint Political Initiatives by Estonians, Latvians, and Lithuanians as Reflected in Samizdat Materials 1967–1987', in: Loeber/Vardys/Kitching (eds.) *Regional Identity...*, 1990, pp. 429–462. For the resistance movement in Estonia, see the articles by Viktor Niitsoo in the monthly *Akadeemia* (with summaries in English): *Rahvuslik vastupanuliikumine aastail 1977–1962* (National Resistance Movement 1955–1962) No. 12, 1994, pp. 2513–2539 and No. 1, 1995, pp. 58–71; *Eesti rahvuslik vastupanuliikumine aastail 1968–1977,* No. 9–10, 1993, pp. 1819–1833 and 2905–2110.); *Avalik vastupanuliikumine aastail 1977–1984,* No. 9–10, 1992, pp. 1917–1933 and 2180–2194. For a tragic individual act of resistance in Soviet Estonia, see R. Taagepera, *Softening without Liberation in the Soviet Union: the Case Jüri Kukk,* University Press of America, Inc., 1984.

example, on national holidays, the flags of independent Estonia, Latvia and Lithauania, prohibited and criminalized by the Soviet authorities, were occasionally raised in various places as signs of protest: this was a harshly punished offence in the USSR. Since the 1950s, the majority of the population was left with no choice but to cooperate with the Soviet authorities, and most people tried to find refuge in cultural identity rather than active resistance. The Soviet decades were thus definitely not only a period of heroism and resistance, but also collaboration. Kazimiera Prunskiene, former prime minister of Lithuania, writes about this experience of the Balts:

> ...freedom then only makes sense when the people that should enjoy it survive. Is there anything more important than freedom? I think that it is the very life of the people who have sometimes also to wait a bit, until God or historical fate offers a new chance for a life in freedom.[293]

Opposition by the majority of Estonians, Latvians and Lithuanians to the Soviet regime thus found its expression in an ironic and nonchalant attitude towards the Soviet State. Baltic freedom fighters and resistance groups never ceased to protest the illegal occupation and annexation of the independent Baltic republics by the USSR.[294] Occasionally, student and worker protests erupted in the Baltic States—for instance in Kaunas, Lithuania, in 1972 thousands of youths rioted for several days and some 500 were arrested after a nineteen-year old student, Romas Kalanta, burnt himself to death in protest against Soviet occupation.

The historical details of Baltic resistance to Soviet rule will not be further elaborated here. It is essential that notwithstanding the often violently repressive Soviet efforts to do away with Baltic identity and differences from the rest of the USSR, the Baltic peoples preserved their separate identities, and the ideal of pre-1940 independent statehood.

In the years of Soviet annexation, the voices of the Baltic peoples were also expressed by Baltic refugees who had fled from Lithuania, Latvia and Estonia to the West. The Baltic refugee communities lobbied actively in Western power corridors, and by keeping the question of the Baltic States on the agenda of the Western States, prevented ultimate acquiescence in Soviet rule. To a certain

---

293 K. Prunskiene, ‚Unabhängigkeit als Option...', in: K. Ludwig (ed.) *Perspektiven für Tibet*, 2000, p. 94. (Translated from German.)

294 See further Lieven, *op. cit.*, pp. 103–108.

extent, the non-recognition policy of the Western States was also the result of the Baltic refugees' activism.[295]

In international law, one of the few ways—and in Krystyna Marek's view the only way[296]—to legitimate an illegal act is validation by the injured party.[297] Such validation must inevitably be genuine, as no legally relevant validation can result from fake circumstances such as a puppet government or a sham plebiscite.[298] Apart from the fact that no such genuine expression of will could be expressed by the Baltic peoples under the Soviet regime the Baltic peoples refused to validate the Soviet occupation on their own initiative either. Non-acquiescence of the population in territory seized by force and suppressed by non-democratic regimes must be assumed so long as the people have not accepted the new constellation of power in a *genuine expression of self-determination.* As the Baltic peoples never had the chance to express their free will almost until the end of the Soviet regime, one cannot speak of genuine acquiescence by the affected population.

4 Prescription? Conclusions

The preceding analysis leads to the conclusion that the USSR did not acquire legal title to the Baltic States by prescription.[299] This position finds strong support in the views expressed by Soviet legal doctrine on prescription in international law as well. Soviet international law doctrine strongly supported the view that there cannot be such a thing as prescription for territorial seizure in contemporary international law.[300] For example, according to Yuri Barsegov,

---

295 For instance, in 1967, the World Organization of Free Latvians (PBLA) presented the French President Charles de Gaulle with a memorandum in which it discouraged the President from visiting the Latvian capital Riga during his official visit to the USSR. The Kremlin had insisted upon such a visit, but the PBLA argued that it would imply recognition of Latvia's incorporation into the USSR. Finally, President de Gaulle did not go to Latvia during his visit to the USSR. Protests by Baltic exiles also played a crucial role in the unprecedented reversal of Australia's decision to recognize the incorporation of the Baltic States into the USSR. See *Lettland unter sowjetischer und nationalsozialistischer Herrschaft*, 1998, p. 172.

296 Marek, *op. cit.*, p. 579.

297 See H. Lauterpacht, *Recognition in International Law*, pp. 427–430. See also Marek, *op. cit.*, pp. 577–578.

298 See Marek, *op. cit.*, p. 578.

299 For a similar conclusion, see F. Frhr. Waitz von Eschen, ‚Zur internationalen Lage der baltischen Republiken nach Erlangung der Unabhängigkeit', in: 42 *Osteuropa* 1992, p. 321.

300 See e.g. A.A. Эсаян, *Некоторые вопросы теории и истории международного права*, Ереван: Издательство Ереванского Университета, 1977, p. 163 *et seq*. See also for an overview B. Meissner, ‚Die sowjetische Stellung zur Annexion und zur Ersitzung', in: *Int. Recht und Dipl.* 1964, pp. 96–100.

an illegal annexation might even last several centuries, without creating legal title,[301] since:

> 'In order to break the prescription and to avoid acquisition of legal title for a territory, any act that would be appropriate to the situation, and that would bear witness to non-recognition of the legitimacy of the existing factual situation, would suffice. Evidently for this purpose e.g. the usual diplomatic protest by a State would suffice, even if it not empowered by the use of force. It is respected that a break of prescription can occur not only as a consequence of an act by a State, but also as a result of acts by the inhabitants of a governed territory, in the form of protests or other activities that express the will of a nation.'[302]

A logical consequence of denial of acquisitive prescription (the illegality of Soviet rule) would be denial of extinctive prescription, in other words that, from the standpoint of international law, the Baltic States continued to exist and remained under illegal occupation throughout half a century. But what is meant by occupation in international law? Is the concept of illegal occupation suitable to qualify the legal status of the Baltic States from 1940–1991?

301 Ю.Г. Барсегов, *Территория в международном праве*, 1958, p. 141.

302 Ю.Г. Барсегов, *op. cit.*. Cf. also Wiewióra, *op. cit.*, p. 168.

CHAPTER 4

The 'Occupation' of the Baltic States (1940–1991)?

1 The Baltic Thesis of Soviet Occupation (1940–1941, 1944–1991)

Today's Baltic States have claimed they were *occupied* by the USSR from 1940–1941, by Germany from 1941–1944, and again by the USSR from 1944–1990/1991. For instance, on March 30, 1990, the Supreme Soviet of the Estonian SSR in its *Resolution on the State Status of Estonia* declared:

> The Supreme Soviet of the Estonian SSR asserts that the occupation of the Republic of Estonia by the Soviet Union on June 17, 1940 has not suspended the existence of the Republic of Estonia *de jure*. *The territory of the Republic of Estonia is occupied to this day.*[1]

In 1994, the Estonian Parliament, the *Riigikogu*, adopted a declaration calling on the States of the world to pressure the government of the Russian Federation to change its view according to which the Republic of Estonia was not occupied by the USSR and the Republic of Estonia was created by secession from the USSR in 1991.[2]

In a decision rendered on December 21, 1994, the Supreme Court of Estonia decided that the occupation of the Republic of Estonia in 1940 had been illegal and that hence the military forces of the USSR had never acquired property rights to Estonian soil and buildings.[3]

On August 22, 1996, the Latvian Parliament, or *Saeima,* adopted a 'Declaration on the Occupation of Latvia'[4] in which it expressed Latvia's concern over Russia's continued refusal to recognize that the Soviet Union had occupied Latvia ('the occupation that lasted half a century'). At the end of the declaration,

1 Italics added by this author. Text reprinted in A. Kiris, *Restoration of the Independence of the Republic of Estonia. Selection of Legal Acts (1988–1991)*, Tallinn 1991, p. 22.

2 See *Riigi Teataja* I (State Gazette) 1994, 13, 235.

3 The decision of the Estonian Supreme Court (which also serves as the Constitutional Court of the country) held as constitutional a law which declared void all contracts of sale with the Soviet army. See Riigi Teataja (State Gazette) I 1995,2,34.

4 For the text, see *Latvijas Vestnesis,* August 27, 1996, p. 1.

the Latvian Parliament requested the community of States, as well as international organizations, to recognize the fact that Latvia was occupied.[5]

2 Reception of the Baltic Thesis of Soviet 'Occupation'

During the Cold War, the USA repeatedly referred to the notion of occupation in the Baltic case. For example, the Kersten Committee of the US House of Representatives spoke in 1954 of 'the continued military and political occupation of Lithuania, Latvia and Estonia.'[6] On July 26, 1983, on the sixty-first anniversary of the first declaration of US non-recognition policy (the Stimson declaration), President Reagan declared that by the continued *occupation* of the Baltic States, the USSR was violating international law.[7] US Ambassador Jeane J. Kirkpatrick delivered to UN Secretary-General Javier Pérez de Cuellar the text of the Reagan statement at the UN.[8] Pursuant to the US Defense Department's authorization for 1983, the funds appropriated could not be used 'to prepare, purchase or produce any map 'showing the USSR which would not include the designation 'Soviet Occupied' under Estonia, Latvia, and Lithuania.'[9]

Support for the 'occupation' thesis was reconfirmed by the USA subsequent to restoration of the independence of the Baltic States. The US Congress declared in a Resolution of October 10, 1998 that 'this illegal and forcible occupation was never recognized by the US.'[10]

Similar language was used by European institutions. On September 29, 1960 the Assembly of the Council of Europe adopted a Resolution on the Baltic republics in which the latter were considered to be under military occupation.[11] Similar concepts were used in the *Resolution On the Situation*

5 See *ibid.* For a French translation, see A. Reinhards, *Lettonie-Russie...*, p. 284. See also B. Meissner, *The Occupation of the Baltic States from a Present-Day Perspective*, Riga 1998, p. 483 *et seq* and *Letter from the Saeima of Latvia to the UN Secretary General His excellency Kofi Annan*, October 22, 1998, available at http;//www.bafl.com/saeimaletter.html.

6 Report of the Select Committee, 1954, p. 8.

7 President Reagan's Statement on the Baltic States, Press Release. Cf. also with the US House of Representatives, House Concurrent Resolution 57, 4 February 1981, pp. 2–3.

8 US Mission to the United Nations, *The United States Reaffirms Recognition of Independence of Estonia, Latvia and Lithuania*, press release, 29 July 1983, pp. 1–3.

9 Public Law 97–252, Department of Defence Authorization Act, 1983, 8 September 1982, section 1134.

10 Quoted from www.usislib.ee/congress.html.

11 See also the report of Mr. Lowzow for the consultative Assembly of the Council of Europe of 14.9.1960 (Doc. 1173), p. 6, 23, 27 *et seq.*

in the Baltic States, adopted by the European Parliament on January 13, 1983.[12] Furthermore, a non-governmental tribunal of international jurists that called itself *The Baltic Tribunal in Copenhagen* declared on July 26, 1985, *inter alia* that Estonia, Latvia and Lithuania were occupied.'[13] Generally, the Western States which did not recognize Soviet annexation of the Baltic States refused to call it simply an annexation, but used qualifying terms such as 'illegal annexation.' The Estonian lawyer Enn Sarv suggests that the very non-recognition of Soviet annexation by Western governments automatically implies that (at least for non-recognizing countries), the Soviet presence in the Baltics can only be characterized as a continuing occupation.[14] Thus, it has been argued that many Western countries shared the view that the Baltic republics continued to be 'occupied' territories because of the illegality of annexation in 1940.[15]

At the same time, until restoration of the independence of the Baltic republics in 1991, the main international governmental organization, the UN, did not adopt resolutions condemning the 'occupation' of the (annexed) Baltic States, in contrast to resolutions, regularly adopted regarding the territories occupied by Israel, in Northern Cyprus, and so on. The Security Council would not have expressed a view on this topic, not least because of the veto power of the Soviet Union.

Consequently, reception of the thesis that the Baltic States were under military occupation from 1940–1991 has been somewhat cautious in the legal literature. It is not uncommon for authors discussing the legal status of the Baltic States during the Soviet period to distance themselves from the occupation theory, by qualifying the reference to occupation theory in quotation marks (the Soviet 'occupation.')[16] Furthermore, a number of Russian authors

---

12 'Condemning the fact that after the conclusion of the Molotov Ribbentrop Pact these independent and neutral States were in 1940 occupied by the Soviet Union *and that this occupation lasts* (emphasis added).' See the Resolution on the Situation in Estonia, Latvia and Lithuania, European Parliament, January 13, 1983. Doc. 1-777/80. However, the later Resolutions of the Council of Europe ('Resolution on the Baltics', Strasbourg, January 28, 1987) and of the European Parliament ('Resolution on the Independence of the Baltic States', Doc. B2-1247/88), while strongly supportive of the Baltic pursuit of independence, avoid using the concept 'occupation.' For the texts, see Looming 1989, No. 3, pp. 429–430.

13 The members of the Baltic Tribunal were Theodor Veiter (Chairman), Per Ahlmark, Jean-Marie Daillet, Michael Bourdeaux and Sir James Fawcett. For an Estonian translation of the Copenhagen Manifesto, see *Looming* 1989, No. 3, p. 428.

14 E. Sarv, *Õiguse vastu ei saa ükski*, p. 60.

15 See e.g. U.W. Saxer, 'The Transformation of the Soviet Union: From a Socialist Federation to a Commonwealth of Independent States', in: 14 *Loy. L.A. Int'l & Comp. L.J.* 1992, p. 633.

16 See e.g. Lieven, *The Baltic Revolution;* Hafner/Reinisch, *op. cit.*, 1996, p. 107; M. Koskenniemi, in: *State Succession: Codification Tested Against the Facts,* Hague Academy of IL, 1996, p. 126.

emphatically rejected the Baltic occupation theory. The international lawyer Stanislav Chernichenko emphasized: '*The term 'occupation', however, cannot be applied to the situation that took shape in the Baltic states after their accession to the USSR, even if one acknowledges that they were forcibly joined to the USSR (annexed by it). The exception is only the period of German occupation.*'[17]

The difference between occupation and no occupation is not a terminological nicety. It is a crucial element in the legal appraisal of Soviet rule in Estonia, Latvia and Lithuania. Take, for instance, the Soviet mass deportations of 1949. Was it a violation of international law or not? We are curious to find out, knowing that the French political thinker Raymond Aron argued in 1966: '(...) nothing the Soviet Union does on the territories that, in 1939, were subject to the Estonian or Lithuanian sovereignty any longer relates to international law (...)'[18]

Is the use of the concept 'occupation' for legal qualification of the Soviet period in the Baltic States correct or not? What would it mean to say that the Baltic States were *occupied* in 1940–1991, especially in light of the fact that they were annexed by the Soviet Union in August 1940? In the first place, the question arises: does annexation, however illegal, indeed terminate the legal regime of occupation?

3 Development of the Concept of Occupation in International Law

The concept of occupation, in the words of Adam Roberts, itself a 'triumph of legal thinking'[19] as opposed to the more 'reality-based' view of international relations employed by political science, introduces a distinction between factual and the legal possession of a territory, between *de facto* control and legal title. As the occupation of a *terra nullius* no longer plays a practical role in the present world, the concept of occupation is nowadays used to signify the exercise of control and power over another State's territory.

The law of occupation has been subject of important developments during the last century. Initially designed strictly for cases of occupation of enemy territory *durante bello,* it later became applicable in a much broader set of cases of foreign control.[20] However, legal developments in the international law of occupation have been overshadowed by the fact that—probably more than in

17 S. Chernichenko, 'Ethnic Russians in the Baltics', in: 44 *International Affairs* (Moscow) 1998, pp. 118–123 at 119–120.

18 R. Aron, *Peace and War; A Theory of International Relations,* NY: Doubleday, 1966, p. 108.

19 A. Roberts, 'Prolonged Military Occupation: The Israeli-Occupied Territories Since 1967', 84 *AJIL* 1990, p. 45.

20 See Roberts, 'What Is Military Occupation?', p. 299.

any other field of public international law—the law has often been violated by States.[21]

The *locus classicus* of international law on occupation is the Convention with Respect to the Laws and Customs of War on Land, first adopted in The Hague at the International Peace Conference of 1899 and slightly revised at the Second International Peace Conference of 1907 (The IV Hague Convention.)[22] The bulk of the law of occupation, still largely applicable today, is contained in the annex to the IV Hague Convention, entitled Regulations respecting the laws and customs of war on land, adopted on October 18, 1907. The Hague law of occupation was applicable during both World Wars and thus serves as the most important source for analysis of the Baltic situation, whose origins lay in 1940.

Under The Hague Regulations of 1907, an international legal regime of occupation was originally envisaged for cases of belligerent occupation (*occupatio bellica*), namely when control over a foreign territory was gained through military force in the context of war.[23] Belligerent occupation consisted of direct control of one hostile State's territory by the enemy's armed forces.[24] With the establishment of belligerent occupation, 'the authority of the legitimate power' passed into the hands of the occupier.[25] This, however, did not imply a transfer of sovereignty to the occupying State, which remained bound by the considerable restrictions envisaged in Section III of the 1907 Hague Regulations.[26] The

21 See E. Benvenisti, *The International Law of Occupation,* 1993, p. 5: 'Modern occupants came to prefer, from a variety of reasons, not to establish such a direct administration. Instead, they would purport to annex or establish puppet states or governments, make use of existing structures of government, or simply refrain from establishing any form of administration. In these cases, the occupants would tend not to acknowledge the applicability of the law of occpation to their own or their surrogates' activities, and when using surrogates' institutions, would deny any international responsibility for the latter's actions.' '[M]ost contemporary occupants ignored their status and their duties under the law of occupation. [...] This practice of occupants poses [a] decisive challenge that the law of occupation has to face in order to maintain its relevance.' *Ibid.* p. 6. See also A. Roberts, *Prolonged Military Occupation: The Israeli-Occupied Territories Since 1967,* 84 AJIL 1990, pp. 44–71.

22 For the records of these Hague conferences, see J. B. Scott, *The Proceedings of The Hague Conferences,* 5 volumes incl. index, New York: Oxford University Press, 1920.

23 See M. Bothe, 'Occupation, Belligerent', in: *EPIL*, Inst. III, p. 64.

24 See Article 42 of The Hague Regulations: 'Territory is considered occupied when it is actually placed under the authority of the hostile army. The occupation extends only to the territory where such authority has been established and can be exercised.'

25 See Article 43 of The Hague Regulations.

26 See G. v. Glahn, *The Occupation of Enemy Territory,* 1957, p. 31 *et seq.*

legitimate government of the territory retained its sovereignty, which was suspended during a period of belligerent occupation.[27]

Linking a regime of occupation to a state of war and military conduct implied that, conceptually, military occupation was conceived as a provisional state of affairs. Military occupation ended either by a change in the fortunes of war (reconquest by the sovereign of the occupied territory), permanent and voluntary withdrawal by military forces, transformation of the legal status of the territories as a result of negotiations (for example *qua* peace treaty), or through subjugation and annexation of territories by an occupying power.[28]

a *Were/Are the 1907 Hague Rules Applicable beyond War?*

The practice of World War II demonstrated that a restricted concept of belligerent occupation had become insuficcient from several points of view. First, the presumption of the neat distinction between belligerent and pacific occupation, or occupation when the sovereign to which the territory belongs 'agrees' to occupation, proved artificial and unsatisfactory. Situations like the German occupations of Czechoslovakia (1939) and Denmark (1940) did not, strictly speaking, match the grammatical threshold of the 1907 Hague Regulations due to the lack of military hostilities and state of war. However, as discussed in the first part of this study, the intrinsic analogy of such cases of *occupatio quasi-bellica* with classic cases of belligerent occupation meant that the rules of The Hague Regulations were applied to those situations as well.

It can be presumed that equating legal regimes of classic military occupations with Czechoslovakian-type occupations which Adam Roberts has called 'forcible peacetime occupations,'[29] had become a part of international customary law for the period of World War II. Considerable support for this view can be found in both the legal literature and in State practice. As early as 1920, Walter Schätzel argued that '[e]*s entspricht nur der Logik, auch die friedliche*

---

27 See Glahn, *ibid.*, p. 31. For the historical development of this rule, see C. Rousseau, *Le droit des conflits...*, p. 134 *et seq.*

28 See A. Roberts, *Prolonged Military Occupation...*, 84 *AJIL* 1990, p. 47 *et seq.* Cf. Glahn, *The Occupation...*, p. 30. The transfer of sovereignty of an occupied territory under a peace treaty is a legitimate way of ending the occupation. See M. Sassòli and A. Bouvier, *How Does Law Protect in war? Cases, Documents and Teaching Materials on Contemporary Practice in International Humanitarian Law*, Geneva: ICRC, 1999, p. 155.

29 Cf. A. Roberts, 'What Is a Military Occupation?', *BYBIL* 1984, p. 261 and 274 *et seq.* Roberts defines forcible peacetime occupations as occupations 'of all or part of the territory of a State without the previous consent of the government, but also without causing the outbreak of an armed conflict with that State. Usually it is because the invader has made an implicit or explicit threat to use force, and military resistance against invasion appears hopeless, that this kind of invasion is militarily unopposed.' See *ibid.* at p. 274.

Annexion eines ganzen Staates genau so zu behandeln wie die Eroberung. Ein juristischer Unterschied läßt sich auf keine Weise konstruieren.'[30] In 1924, it had been suggested that in cases of peacetime occupation, the rights of the occupant were even more curtailed than in cases of classic belligerent occupations.[31] The Hague Regulations were regarded as already applicable in the case of the invasion of Bulgaria by the Romanian army, a military operation without fighting.

The Hague Regulations were regarded as applicable in the classic cases of Czechoslovakia and Denmark.[32] The writings of eminent jurists have subsequently reasserted this position. Alf Ross, analyzing Denmark's legal status during World War II, came to following conclusions:

> The point of departure must be the provisions in The Hague Regulations concerning military occupation (Art. 42–56), with the *modifications indicated by the fact that there is no state of war between the two sides.*
>
> The occupied state must, of course, at least enjoy all the rights which would be granted if the Regulations would be used directly.
>
> On the other hand the rights of the occupant must be limited, in accordance with the peaceful character of the occupation. Here the leading idea must be that the territory is occupied merely in order to assist the occupant's warfare, without there being any intent to supersede the state apparatus or to take over the occupied state's means of coercion.[33]

Arnold McNair and Arthur Watts suggest somewhat cautiously that 'there seems to have been a tendency to act upon a basis broadly analogous to that of a belligerent occupation during a war.'[34] Kelly also asserts that during the period of interest to us, non-belligerent occupations unregulated by treaty shared much in common with belligerent occupation.[35] Kelly defines the legal

30 W Schätzel, *Die Annexion im Völkerrecht,* 1920, reprinted in 1959, p. 199. "It is only logical to treat the peaceful annexation of an entire state in the same way as conquest. A legal difference cannot be construed in any way."

31 F. Llwellyn Jones, 'Military Occupation of Alien Territory in Time of Peace', *Transactions of the Grotius Society*, Vol. 9, 1923, p. 159 *et seq.*

32 See A. Roberts, *What Is a...*, p. 276. Regarding the German occupation of Bohemia and Moravia, see also *Anglo-Czechoslovak and Prague Credit Bank v. Janssen* [1943–1945] AD Case no. 11, at 47 (Australia, Supreme Court of Victoria.)

33 See A. Ross, 'Denmark's Legal Status During the Occupation', 1 *Jus Gentium* 1949, p. 10.

34 A. McNair, A. Watts, *The Legal Effects of War* (4th edn., 1966), p. 423.

35 M.J. Kelly, 'Non-Belligerent Occupation', 28 *Israel YB on Human Rights* (1998), p. 30. Kelly, citing the occupation of the Ruhr by French and Belgian forces in 1923, which was opposed by the German government, defines non-belligerent as opposed to pacific

particularities that restricted the power of the occupier even further than in cases of classic belligerent occupation:

> The maximum deference had to be given to local institutions which could only be interfered with on grounds of necessity related to the need to maintain order and the security of the force. The difference in non-belligerent occupations was that the inhabitants of the territory were not an 'enemy population' and the relationship between the force and the inhabitants was to be governed as far as the security situation permitted by peacetime legal regimes.[36]

For contemporary purposes, the situation is legally clarified by adoption of the four Geneva Conventions of August 12, 1949, the common Article 2 of which provides:

> In addition to the provisions which shall be implemented in peacetime, the present Convention shall apply to all cases of declared war or of any other armed conflict which may arise between two or more of the High Contracting Parties, even if the state of war is not recognized by them.
>
> The Convention shall also apply to all cases of partial or total occupation of the territory of a High Contracting Party, even if the said occupation meets with no armed resistance.
>
> Although one of the Powers in conflict may not be a party to the present Convention, the Powers who are parties thereto shall remain bound by it in their mutual relations. They shall furthermore be bound by the Convention in relation to the said Power, if the latter accepts and applies the provisions thereof.

According to the Pictet' commentaries on the 1949 Geneva Conventions, this Article is one of the most important in the Convention, as it notably extends its applicability.[37] It can be inferred that since the 1949 Geneva Conventions, the legal regime of quasi-belligerent occupations (or: pacific coercive occupations) coincides with the law of military occupations, and indeed, special

---

occupations—'while no state of war existed, there was nevertheless a lack of consent.' See *ibid.* p. 4.

36 Kelly, *op. cit.*, p. 30.

37 J,S. Pictet, *Commentary to the I Geneva Convention,* Geneva: ICRC, 1952, p. 28. See also *Commentary to the III Geneva Convention,* Geneva: ICRC, 1951, p. 19 *et seq.*

legal considerations in the case of the former have lost practical significance.[38] Occupation is no longer necessarily the outcome of actual fighting, but can be the result of a threat to use force that prompted the threatened government to concede effective control over its territory to a foreign power.[39]

b *Occupation Versus Annexation*

The second major issue raised in the context of World War II occupations was the question of illegal annexations, the crucial question being once again which annexations were to be considered illegal. According to the general understanding developed in the 19th century, incorporation of occupied territory (subjugation or conquest) had been a legal way of bringing occupation to an end.[40] Three consequent stages: invasion by armed forces, occupation of territory, and annexation were clearly distinguished in both practice and legal doctrine.[41]

However, not every annexation could legally terminate a regime of occupation. Pursuant to the underlying concept of The Hague Regulations, premature annexations, or annexations carried out *durante bello,* were considered illegal and without the desired international legal effects. For instance, in the Italo-Turkish war the Italian annexation of Tripolitania and Cyrenaica by an Italian royal decree of November 5, 1911 was considered illegal, since at the time of the act of annexation only some coastal towns had been occupied by the Italian army.[42] In the context of World War II, Germany's annexation of parts of Poland in 1939 and 1940, of Belgian districts Eupen and Malmédy on May 18, 1940, and of the French regions Alsace and Lorraine on August 7, 1940, were illegal under international law, since they were carried out while the legitimate sovereign or its war allies were continuing the fight.[43]

---

38 M. Bothe, 'Occupation, Belligerent', *EPIL*, vol. 4, p. 68.

39 See E. Benvenisti, *The International Law of Occupation,* 1993, p. 3 *et seq.*

40 See D. A. Graber, *The Development of the Law of Belligerent Occupation 1863–1914,* New York: Columbia University Press, 1949, especially chapter 2. See also N. Ando, *Surrender, Occupation and Private Property in International Law. An Evaluation of US Practice in Japan,* 1991, p. 35.

41 For a distinction between the phases of invasion and occupation, see *US v. List and Others,* Judgment of February 19, 1948, Annual Digest, 1948, case no. 215, pp. 637–640. See also G. von Glahn, *the Occupation of Enemy Territory. A Commentary on the Law and Practice of Belligerent Occupation,* 1957, p. 28; Roberts, *What Is a Military Occupation?* p. 256 and C. Rousseau, *Le droit des conflits armés,* Paris, 1983, p. 134 *et seq.*

42 G. von Glahn, *ibid.*, p. 33.

43 In the Krupp Trial, the US Military Tribunal condemned the confiscations of private property in Alsace during World War II and held: 'This confiscation was based on the assumption of the incorporation of Alsace into the Reich and that property in Alsace owned by Frenchmen living outside of Alsace could be treated in such a manner as to

However, when war itself becomes outlawed the whole logic of accepting subjugation or annexation as modes of ending an occupation regime and transferring territory becomes counterintuitive. As discussed earlier, there can be no legal transfer of sovereignty to an aggressor in modern international law.[44] However, World War II and even post-World War II practice have sometimes given ambiguous signals in situations where an illegal annexation was carried out and the situation stabilized to an extent. This is a clash between normativity—unsupported by an adequate system of sanctions—and reality. Would annexation of occupied territory, although illegal at first, eventually still bring about certain modifications in the legal regime of the territory concerned? Do restrictions imposed by the occupation regime as envisaged in The Hague Regulation still continue to apply during a longer period of illegal yet to an extent already effective annexation? Oxford professor Adam Roberts has observed that '*not all aspects of the law of occupations were designed for a situation such as this; and in partcicular that the prohibitions of making extensive legal and political changes may sometimes be of limited relevance where the desire (...) of the occupants (...) is precisely to make certain changes.*'[45]

An early classic case is the incorporation of Austria into the German Reich on March 13, 1938, after Germany's occupation of the country a day ealier. In the words of Roberts, the annexation of Austria by Germany complicates evaluation of the legal status of Austria.[46] As discussed above, several theories have been developed to characterize Austria's legal status between 1938 and 1945. Most Austrian scholars and most jurisprudence have advanced the theory that Austria was under (quasi-)belligerent occupation.[47]

---

totally disregard the obligations owned by a belligerent occupant. The attempted incorporation of Alsace into the German Reich was a nullity under international law and consequently this interference with the rights of private property was a violation of Article 46 of The Hague Regulations.' *US v. Alfred Krupp, et al.*, Case No. 68, US Military Tribunal at Nuremberg, in: The United Nations War Crimes Commission, Law Reports of Trials of War Criminals, vol. X, 1949, p. 130–159.

See also *US v. Greifelt and Others*, Annual Digest, 1948, case no. 216, p. 655. For a good overview of the cases handled in Belgian municipal courts, see C. Rousseau, *Le droit des conflits armés*, p. 141. See also Glahn, *ibid.*, p. 33. For Poland, see also A. Randelzhofer, O. Dörr, *Entschädigung für Zwangsarbeit? Zum Problem individueller Entschädigungsansprüche von ausländischen Zwangsarbeitern während des Zweiten Weltkrieges gegen die Bundesrepublik Deutschland*, Berlin, 1994, p. 18.

44 See also Roberts, 'What Is Military...?', BYBIL, p. 259.

45 Roberts, 'What Is a Military...?', p. 287.

46 Roberts, 'What Is a Military Occupation?', p. 275.

47 See especially with respect to the annexation/occupation dilemma in S. Verosta, *Die internationale Stellung Österreichs 1938 bis 1947*, 1947, p. 7 *et seq.* For a critique of Verosta's views, see H. Jellinek, *Der automatische Erwerb und Verlust...*, 1951, p. 148.

However, Adam Roberts points out some reluctance, in post-war decisions, to view Austria as having been under occupation and to apply The Hague Regulations.[48] The International Military Tribunal at Nuremberg did not render a direct ruling on the applicablity of The Hague Regulations in the Austrian case. The later practice of the post-war United States Military Tribunals was somewhat ambiguous. In *US v. Krauch and Others*, the US Military Tribunal ruled that The Hague Regulations were not applicable to Austria 1938–1945, but appended:

> In so ruling, we do not ignore the force of the argument that property situated in a weak nation which falls a victim to the aggressor because of incapacity to resist should receive a degree of protection equal to that in cases of belligerent occupation when actual warfare has existed.[49]

However, in another judgment, *US v. Weizsäcker and Others*, it was held that the German invasions of Austria and Czechoslovakia 'were tantamount to, and may be treated as "a declaration of war."'[50] Such fluctuating viewpoints expressed by US Military Courts may inter alia be attributed to the fact that the United States had recognized the incorporation of Austria into Germany.[51] Therefore, most inconsistencies in treatment of the Austrian case may be ascribed to the particular features of the case. Generally, however, the Austrian occupation theory was accepted and even propagated by the Allied Powers, finding final confirmation in the 1955 Austrian State Treaty.[52]

Altogether, the experience of World War II led the community of States to adopt the four Geneva Conventions of August 12, 1949 under the auspices of the International Committee of the Red Cross. The fourth Geneva Convention Relative to the Protection of Civilian Persons in Time of War contains an important provision that throws some light on the occupation *versus* annexation controversy:

> Protected persons who are in occupied territory shall not be deprived, in any case or in any manner whatsoever, of the benefits of the present Convention by any change introduced, as the result of the occupation of

48 Roberts, 'What Is a Military...,' p. 276.

49 *US v. Krauch and Others*, judgment of 29 July 1948, Annual Digest, 15 (1948), Case no. 218, p. 672.

50 *US v. Weizsäcker and Others*, Annual Digest, 16 (1949), Case No. 118, p. 347.

51 See *US v. Uhl*, Annual Digest, 12 (1943–1945), Case No.8, p. 23 *et seq.*

52 See Oberhammer/Reinisch, 'Restitution of Jewish Property...', *ZaöRV* 2000, p. 742 *et seq.*

> the territory, into the institutions or government of the said territory, nor by any agreement concluded between the authorities of the occupied territories and the Occupying Power, *nor by any annexation of the latter by the whole or part of the occupied territory* (italics added).[53]

Thus, Marco Sassòli and Antoine A. Bouvier cautiously note: 'Unilateral annexation of the occupied territory by the occupying power—whether lawful or unlawful under *ius ad bellum*—(...) can not deprive persons from the protection offered by IHL.'[54] This formulation confirms the continued application of humanitarian rules on unilaterally annexed territories, but leaves open whether such annexation might still be legal under certain circumstances.[55]

To support the latter view, a decision by the Indian Supreme Court rendered on March 29, 1969, with reference to India's annexation of Goa, may be quoted.[56] India occupied the Portuguese colonies of Goa, Damao and Diu on December 19, 1961, following a brief military action that was qualified by the Indian Supreme Court as a war of liberation. Goa was annexed by India on March 27, 1962. The Apellant, Rev. Father Monteiro, argued that an end to occupation could not be brought about unilaterally—'the contention is that occupation does not come to an end by annexation and, therefore, the protection continues till there is either cession of the territory or withdrawal of the Occupying Power from the territory, both of which events have not taken place.'[57] The contention on behalf of the State of Goa was that 'by occupation is meant occupation by armed forces or belligerent occupation and occupation comes to an end by seizure followed by subjugation.'[58] The Indian Supreme Court was determined to decide between these two submissions:

> Military occupation is a temporary *de facto* situation which does not deprive the Occupied Power of its sovereignty nor does it take away its statehood. [...] Annexation, on the other hand, occurs when the

53 Geneva Convention Relative to the Protection of Civilian Persons in Time of War of August 12, 1949, Art. 47 ('Inviolability of Rights').

54 See Sassòli and Bouvier, *op. cit.*, p. 155. IHL = international humanitarian law.

55 For the view that it can, see O. Debbasch, *L'Occupation militaire. Pouvoirs reconnus aux forces armées hors de leur territoire national*, Paris: R. Pichon et R. Durand-Auzias, 1962, pp. 333–6.

56 *Rev. Mons. Sebastiao Francisco Xavier Dos Remedios Monteiro v. State of Goa*, March 26, 1969, India, Supreme Court Reports, pp. 87–102. (Also printed in M. Sassòli and A.A. Bouvier, *op. cit.* p. 752 *et seq.*)

57 See *ibid.* Quoted from Sassòli and Bouvier, p. 754.

58 See *ibid.* p. 754.

> Occupying Power acquires and makes the occupied territory as its own. Annexation gives a *de jure* right to administer the territory. Annexation means that there is not only possession but uncontested sovereignty over the territory. [...] [Military occupation must be distinguished from subjugation, where a territory is not only conquered, but annexed by the conqueror.
>
> There is, however, a difference between true annexation on the one hand and premature annexation, or as it is sometimes called anticipated annexation, on the other. [...] The [1949 Geneva] Conventions rightly lay down that annexation has no effect on the protection. But they speak of premature or anticipated annnexation. Premature or anticipated annexation has no effect. [...] In fact, when the Convention itself was being drafted the experts were half-inclined to add the word 'alleged' before 'annexation' in Art. 47 to distinguish between annexation following conquest and subjugation and annexation made while hostilities are going on. [...] In subjugation, which is recognised as one of the modes of acquiring title, not only the *de facto* but also the *de jure* title passes to the conqueror. After subjugation the inhabitants must obey the laws such as are made and not resist them. [...] [W]hen the conflict is over and there is no hostile army in the field, annexation has the effect of creating a title to the territory. *[A]lthough the United Nations Charter includes the obligation that force would not be used against the territorial integrity of other States (Art. 2 para. 4), events after the Second World War have shown that transfer of title to territory by conquest is still recognised.* [...] If cession after defeat can create title, occupation combined with absence of opposition must lead to the same kind of title.
>
> In the present case the facts are that the military engagement was only a few hours' duration and then there was no resistance at all. [...] The occupation on December 20, 1961 was neither belligerent occupation nor anticipated occupation, but true annexation by conquest and subjugation.[59]

However, the value of analogy of this interpretation of international law by the Indian Supreme Court's decision seems limited.[60] First, in its argumentation, the Court fails to specify which post-World War II practice overturns the illegal status of annexations that stems from the prohibition contained in the UN

59 See *ibid.*, quoted in Sassòli and Bouvier, *op. cit.* at 756 *et seq.* (Italics added.)

60 See also PCIJ, Recueil des Avis Consultatifs, Serié B No. 12: '...nul ne peut être juge dans sa propre cause.'

Charter of the threat or use of military force. Moreover, the specific features of the annexation of Goa, which was described as a colonial enclave, were quite unique, pertaining to decolonization. Although most of the UN Security Council members took the view that the Indian action was illegal,[61] the right of the Indian people to self-determination influenced accommodation of the illegality of use of force through the processes of recognition and prescription.[62] Tacitly, the international community accepted the Indian justification of the occupation of Goa as a war of liberation, and thus accepted annexation by force in the particular postcolonial situation. Colonization in India had to come to an end.

The texts of the 1949 Geneva Conventions and subsequent UN Security Council practice clearly indicate that an illegal occupier cannot legally annex occupied territories.[63] The British international lawyer Christopher Greenwood is therefore correct to note that under modern international law, a purported annexation of occupied territory by the occupying power is ineffective to alter the status of the territory or its inhabitants, who remain subject to the law on belligerent occupation.[64] However, the issue is more doubtful regarding the years immediately following World War II. At least some earlier voices in the literature presumed that annexation of an occupied territory either terminates the regime of occupation or causes a change in sovereignty, or both.[65]

---

61 *S/5033* SC Official Records, 988th mtg., 18 Dec. 1961, pp. 26–27. The draft resolution of the SC, although supported by seven out of eleven States, failed to be adopted due to the negative vote of the USSR. See also M. M. Whiteman, *Digest of International Law,* Vol. 2, Washington, DC, 1963, p. 1140 *et seq* and Q. Wright, 'The Goa Incident', 56 *AJIL* 1962 p. 617 *et seq.*

62 See Crawford, 'The Criteria of Statehood', p. 169.

63 See e.g. SC Res. 252, SCOR, 23rd Session, Resolutions and Decisions, p. 9, UN Doc. S/INF/23/Rev.I (1968)—in the context of Israel's legislative measures affecting occupied East Jerusalem, the resolution states that a belligerent occupant may not annex occupied territory.

64 C. Greenwood, 'The Administration of Occupied Territory in International Law', in: E. Playfair (ed.) *International Law and the Administration of Occupied Territories. Two Decades of Israeli Occupation of the West Bank and Gaza Strip*, Oxford: Clarendon Press, 1992, p. 245. For conflicting views, see also O.Y. Elagab, 'The Law of Belligerent Occupation Versus the Law of Annexation of Territories: A Case Study of the Golan Heights', 6 *Development of Peace* 1985, pp. 118–128, M. Chemillier-Gendreau, 'Le droit international et la protection d'un peuple contre l'annexion', in: *Revue d'études Palestiniennes* No. 34, 1990, pp. 63–73 and R. Lapidoth, 'The Expulsion of Civilians from Areas which came under Israeli control in 1967: Some Legal Issues', 2 *EJIL* 1990, pp. 97–109.

65 See e.g. O.M. Uhler, *Der völkerrechtliche Schutz der Bevölkerung eines besetzten Gebiets gegen Maßnahmen der Okkupationsmacht (unter besonderer Berücksichtigung der Genfer*

c The Main Requirements of the 1907 Hague Regulations for the Occupying Power and Practice in World War II

This is not the place for a thorough analysis of the rules of occupation as crystallized in the 1907 Hague Regulations. These rules have been analyzed in detail in the legal literature.[66] However, citation of certain basic norms highly relevant to the Baltic situation is still a must.

The gist of the law of occupation is contained in Article 43 of the 1907 Hague Regulations, which states:

> The authority of the legitimate power having in fact passed into the hands of the occupant, the latter shall take all the measures in his power to restore and ensure, as far as possible, public order and safety,[67] while respecting, unless absolutely prevented, the laws in force in the country.

The civilian population in the occupied territory is *inter alia* protected by Articles 46 and 50 of the 1907 Hague Regulations. Article 46 reads:

> Family honour and rights, the lives of persons, and private property, as well as religious convictions and practice, must be respected.
>
> Private property cannot be confiscated.

These prescriptions for the occupant are complemented by Article 50:

> No general penalty, pecuniary or otherwise, shall be inflicted upon the population on accounts of the acts of individuals for which they cannot be regarded as jointly and severally responsible.

All these fundamental rules protecting ousted governments and the civilians living in the occupied territory were massively violated during World War II. On a regular basis, occupied territories were annexed, no proper occupation administrations were established, private property was expropriated, civilians were massacred and deported.[68] From the standpoint of the validity of

---

Zivilkonvention vom 12. August 1949), Zürich: Polygraphischer Verlag, 1950, pp. 34–5; A. F. Schnitzer, *Staat und Gebietshoheit,* Zürich: Verlag für Recht und Gesellschaft, 1935, p. 86.

66 See e.g. R.A. Picciotti, 'Legal Problems of Occupied Nations after the Termination of Occupation', 33 *Military Law Review* 1966, pp. 25–57.

67 Instead of 'safety', the expression 'civil life' has been suggested by writers as more adequately reflecting the original French text of the 1907 Hague Regulations. See E. Benvenisti, *op. cit.*, p. 7.

68 For a thorough account of the practices, see Benvenisti, *op. cit.* p. 59 *et seq.*

legal norms, this enormous gap between the letter of law and the cruel reality has been very difficult to explain. Most writers have in a way ignored the problem, by finding some satisfaction in the fact that as far as Axis illegal acts[69] were concerned, the validity of the Hague law of occupation was reconfirmed at Nuremberg. Nevertheless, Eyal Benvenisti has suggested that World War II practices led to a 'decline' of the 1907 Hague rules of occupation.[70] He argues that

> there is sufficient ground to claim that in light of the recurring disregard of the law of occupation, the Hague Regulations had lost their legal authority by the end of the war.'[71] 'At the same time that the International Military Tribunal in Nuremberg described these rules as being declaratory of customary international law, they effectively lost their normative value.[72]

This view is in contradiction with statements by the Nuremberg and Far East Military Tribunals, according to which the Hague rules were applicable as customary international law during World War II.[73] Benvenisti's view is not shared by all writers on laws of occupation.[74] However, Benvenisti points to an important problem: when a legal rule is often violated and the perpetrators cannot be held accountable, what value does it have to argue stoically that the validity of the rule remains unaffected? This question is also relevant for analysis of

---

69 See the seminal work of R. Lemkin, *Axis Rule in Occupied Europe. Laws of Occupation. Analysis of Government. Proposals for Redress*, Washington: Carnegie Endowment for International Peace, 1944.

70 Benvenisti, *op. cit.*, p. 30 *et seq.*

71 Benvenisti, *op. cit.*, p. 59.

72 Benvenisti, *op. cit.*, p. 98. See also at p. 97.

73 See International Military Tribunal in Nuremberg, *The Trial of the Major War Criminals* 65 (1947) and the International Military Tribunal for the Far East, *In re Hirohita*, 1948, AD Case no. 118, at 366 (1907 Hague Regulations as 'good evidence' of customary international law.)

74 Somewhat contradictorily, Benvenisti argues elsewhere that the pains taken by the occupants to demonstrate the indigenous endorsement of their measures, or at times even indigenous consent to formal annexation 'do not discharge occupants from their international obligations.' Benvenisti, *op. cit.*, p. 58. It is inconceivable why this should have been—legally—different during World War II, leading to the acceptance of an extralegal 'black hole.' However, uneasiness about international legal rules in World War II has been expressed by other authors as well. Adam Roberts writes that many cases of prolonged occupation since World War II 'have raised complex questions about the applicability and utility of international rules.' See Roberts, 'Prolonged Military Occupation', *AJIL* 1990, p. 47.

the Soviet occupations in World War II, which questioned the validity of the international law of occupation, due to the specific ideological foundations of Soviet policies.

4 An Evaluation of the Baltic Case: Fiction and Reality in Occupation Theory

a *The Soviet Union and the Hague Regulations*

There is some controversy in legal practice and literature about whether and/or since when the USSR was formally bound by the 1907 Hague Regulations.[75] While Tsarist Russia was one of the initiators and original contracting States to The Hague Regulations, the Bolsheviks who came to power in 1917 initially refused to formally accept this 'bourgeois' legal instrument.[76] It has been argued that formally the USSR became bound to The Hague Regulations only after a declaration of intent issued by Vyacheslav Molotov, People's Commissar of Foreign Affairs, on November 25, 1941.[77] However, as The Hague Regulations had—according to the dictum of the Nuremberg trials—acquired the status of customary international law, both Nazi Germany as well as the USSR were materially bound by its rules since the very beginning of World War II.[78]

Although The Hague Regulations had become customary international law, both the Nazi and the Soviet States in the 1930s-1940s largely ignored their provisions in practice. Krystyna Marek traces this to a 'break in the homogeneity of European civilization':

> It was in complete harmony with the inner logic of that Revolution [of 1917], that, in the initial period and before embarking on an era of an apparently normalized international collaboration, Soviet Russia claimed her freedom from the limitations of the Hague Regulations. The wars of the Soviet Union lacked any common denominator between her and her

75 For a thorough treatment of the problem, see J. Toman, *L'Union Soviétique et le droit des conflits armés,* Genève, 1997, p. 109 *et seq.* Practically speaking, the problem was first of all that the Germans, referring to the requirement of reciprocity, refused to apply international treaty standards to Soviet prisoners of war.

76 See B. Meissner, *Sowjetunion und Haager LKO. Gutachten und Dokumentenzusammenstellung,* Hamburg: Universität Hamburg, 1950, p. 7 *et seq.* and *Die Sowjetunion, die baltischen Staaten*... 1956, p. 231 *et seq.*

77 See discussion in Meissner, *Sowjetunion und Haager LKO,* p. 6 *et seq.* and in *Die Sowjetunion*..., p. 233.

78 See J. Toman, *L'Union Soviétique*..., p. 115.

> opponents, such as may have existed between the France of Napoleon III and the Prussia of Bismarck. Where the Soviet armied would come, they would naturally enough come not to respect the existing capitalist institutions of the occupied State or territory; their purpose would be to change them.[79]

This applied to World War II and its aftermath to the extent that the Soviet occupations in Eastern and Central Europe were characterized by disrespect for the basic demands of the Hague law of occupation.[80] Instead of respecting the sovereignty of the States occupied following the conclusion of the Nazi-Soviet Non-Aggression Pact, complete control over the occupied territories and Sovietization were sought.[81] In 1939, Nazi Germany and the Soviet Union wanted to overturn the order established at Versailles in 1919 regarding new countries geographically located between them and which had historically been subjugated either by Germany or Russia. In 1939, the two countries even held a common military parade in Brest-Litovsk (then Eastern Poland, now Belarus), the same city in which in March 1918 they had concluded an earlier Peace Treaty.[82] In 1939, the two countries literally went back to where they made their previous attempt at delimitation of territories in 1918.

In 1940, there was also the important aspect that, according to Marxist-Leninist teachings, the dictatorship of the proletariat was a State of a new type. It was not a simple change of personnel in the Government, 'not a change of the cabinet… that left the old economic and social relations untouched', but a new State…, 'a State of the proletariat that has come into being on the ruins of

79 K. Marek, *Identity and Continuity of States in Public International Law*, 1954, p. 124.

80 See e.g. Benvenisti, *The International Law of Occupation*, pp. 59 and 67 *et seq.*

81 Benvenisti, *op. cit.*, p. 68. For similar Soviet practices in Rumania, Bulgaria and Hungary after 1945 see N. Ando, *Surrender, Occupation, and Private Property…* (1991), p. 53 *et seq.* ('… throughout the period of occupation, the Soviet Union intervened in the domestic affairs of the occupied states, mainly for the purpose of putting pro-Moscow groups into power.' p. 56.) See also C. Rousseau, *Le droit des conflits armés*, Paris: A. Pedone, p. 141 ('*Dans les pays que l'U.R.S.S. a contrôlés pendant et après la deuxième guerre mondiale (Pologne, Etats baltes, Allemagne orientale, Hongrie, Roumanie, Tchecoslovaquie, Bulgarie) ce n'est pas seulement un occupant qui est arrivé avec elle, mais la révolution. Par le biais de la lutte antifasciste, des procès, de l'épuration, des réformes industrielles et agricoles, des transferts de population, elle a détruit systématiquement les vestiges de l'ancienne société.*')

82 See further L. Mälksoo, 'The Treaties of Brest-Litovsk, Versailles and Moscow: Contesting Sovereignty and Hegemony in Eastern Europe in 1918–1939', 62 *German Yearbook of International Law* 2019, pp 189–209.

the old State, of the State of the bourgeoisie.'[83] Such a dictatorship can only 'come into being as a consequence of the destruction of the bourgeois State machine, of the bourgeois army, of the bourgeois bureaucratic apparatus, of the bourgeois police.'[84]

Practice followed theory and in the end result one has to agree with the judgment of Eyal Benvenisti:

> These [Soviet] occupations were...illegal on two grounds: first, illegality predicated on the aggression that led to the occupation, and second, the illegal mode of governance chosen by the occupying army upon assuming control.[85]

Therefore, the Soviet military occupations of 1940, just as other occupations of that time, even though they were quickly turned into annexations, must still be measured by the yardstick of the 1907 Hague Regulations.[86]

b *Which Rules of Occupation Were Legally Applicable in the Case of the Baltic states?*

The occupation of the Baltic States by the USSR in 1940 can be characterized as a quasi-belligerent occupation,[87] forcible peacetime occupation,[88] *occupation militaire pacifique de fait ou sans titre juridique*,[89] 'intervention occupation' (*occupatio interveniens*)[90] and/or coercive occupation.[91] As no belligerent confrontations occurred in 1940, a state of war between the Baltic States and the

83 J. Stalin, *Über die Grundlagen des Leninismus,* in: Zu den Fragen des Leninismus, 1926, p. 42 *et seq.* See also V. I. Lenin, *Staat und Revolution* (1917), especially pp. 180 and 185.

84 J. Stalin, *ibid.*, p. 45.

85 Benvenisti, *op. cit.*, p. 68.

86 Ando concludes that in the case of post-surrender occupations in World War II, '[t]he Hague Regulations were applicable to the occupation of the East European states.' See Ando, *op. cit.*, p. 72.

87 About this concept, see A. Verdross, 'Die völkerrechtliche Identität der Staaten', *FS Klein*, 1950.

88 About this concept, see A. Roberts, 'What Is a Military Occupation?', p. 274 *et seq.*

89 See J. Repečka, *op. cit.*, p. 145, referring to Frangulis (ed.) *Dictionnaire diplomatique,* 3 tomes, Paris, 1933, p. 246. "peaceful military occupation de facto or without legal title".

90 See B. Meissner, *Die Sowjetunion, die baltischen Staaten und das Völkerrecht,* p. 224. Acording to Meissner, *occupatio interveniens* is a mixed form between *occupatio bellica* and *occupatio pacifica.* See *ibid.*

91 See e.g. O. Uhler, *Der völkerrechtliche Schutz...*, 1950, p. 34.

USSR never came into existence. Rather than outright war, the Soviet military advance can be characterized as (illegal) 'intervention.'[92]

As noted above, in the context of World War II the applicability of the 1907 Hague Regulations to forcible peacetime occupations has been affirmed in both legal practice and literature.[93] It is then correct to conclude that the standards of the 1907 Hague rules were legally applicable in the occupied Baltic States.[94]

A further, somewhat more complicated question is whether the provisions of the Fourth Geneva Convention of 1949[95] were applicable as a legal standard in Soviet-ruled Estonia, Latvia and Lithuania. At the end of the 1980s, a non-governmental organization called Geneva 49 (Genf-49) became active in the Baltics, protesting against the conscription of Baltic men into the Soviet 'occupation army', and referring to the relevant stipulations in the 1949 Geneva Conventions prohibiting drafting in occupied territories.[96]

As we shall see, the issue of the applicability of the Geneva Convention became especially controversial later, with respect to the settlement of Soviet immigrants in the Baltic Soviet Republics, especially in Latvia and Estonia.[97] The following stipulation of the fourth Geneva Convention was often invoked in these countries (the last passage of Art. 49):

> The Occupying Power shall not deport or transfer parts of its own civilian population into the territory it occupies.

Yet the view that the IV Geneva Convention became formally applicable in the Baltic States may also be challenged. First, the Baltic States had already been occupied and annexed for ten years when the Geneva Conventions became binding on the USSR. The *travaux préparatories* of the Geneva Conference

92 See B. Meissner, *Die Sowjetunion, die baltischen Staaten und das Völkerrecht*, p. 223 *et seq.*

93 For an overview, see B. Meissner, *op. cit.*, p. 226 *et seq.* See also R. Laun, *Haager LKO*, p. 104 *et seq.*

94 See B. Meissner, *op. cit.*, p. 226 *et seq.*

95 See Geneva Convention Relative to the Protection of Civilian Persons in Time of War of August 12, 1949, especially Section III ('Occupied territories').

96 See the first passage of the Article 51 of the Fourth Geneva Convention ('The Occupying Power may not compel protected persons to serve in its armed or auxiliary forces. No pressure or propaganda which aims at securing voluntary enlistment is permitted.')

97 Several politicians in the early 1990s argued that as the Geneva Convention forbids the settling of colonists in occupied territory, the Baltic States have the right to use social and economic pressure to make them leave. See Lieven, *The Baltic Revolution...*, p. xxvii.

do not indicate that the Geneva Conventions were to be formally applied to *ex post facto* situations. In addition, it remains open whether certain Geneva rules relating to foreign occupation were still legally applicable before 1949. In practice, however, the 1949 Geneva rules of occupation only specified and developed the fundamental rules already applicable under the 1907 Hague Convention. For instance, the 1949 Soviet mass deportations of civilians from the annexed Baltic States to Soviet Russia would be illegal under both the 1907 and 1949 rules.

c Conclusions: International Legal Rules Binding the USSR during Its Occupation (Illegal Annexation) of the Baltic States

Regarding several World War II and post-World War II occupation situations, it has been a debated question whether certain international laws of occupation, such as the 1907 Hague Regulations and/or the IV Geneva Convention of 1949, were applicable. For instance, in post-surrender occupations at the end of World War II, such as those of Germany and Japan, the Western Allies denied the applicability of the 1907 Hague Regulations for legal and political reasons.[98] Even if legal opinion in the occupied countries insisted on the applicability of the protecting Hague Regulations,[99] and different legal theories on the legal nature of the occupation regime were presented,[100] the more fact-based theory—that the denazification policies of the occupation powers did not violate international law—was enforced.

Yet the Allied occupation of Germany after 1945 was the occupation of an aggressor State after the unconditional surrender of its military forces,[101] while the Baltic republics were themselves victims of aggression. If the prolonged application of The Hague or Geneva law of occupation were challenged in the Baltic case, this would be so for other reasons—such as the very fact of the annexation (as opposed to mere occupation without the *animus* to annex), or the long duration of illegal rule—than in the German case.

It is diffcult to establish with authoritative precision and persuasiveness which rules of occupation, directly or by analogy, continued to bind the USSR in the Baltic States until the end of the former's *de facto* rule in 1991. Because of lack of authoritative judicial settlement, these questions are likely to remain

98 In those cases, the occupation policy went far beyond the provisions for military occupation contained in the 1907 Hague Regulations.

99 See e.g. R. Laun, *Die Haager Landkriegsordnung. (Das Übereinkommen über die Gesetze und Gebräuche des Landkrieges.)*, 4. Aufl., Wolfenblüttel: Wolfenblütteler Verlagsanstalt G.m.b.H, 1949.

100 See e.g. T. Schweisfurth, 'Germany, Occupation After World War II', in: *EPIL*, p. 196 *et seq.*

101 See the 'Act of Military Surrender' of May 7/8, 1945.

open to differing legal-political arguments. This is connected to the more systemic defect of international (humanitarian) law, namely the problem of its authoritative determination. In the words of Georges Abi-Saab:

> (...) what is most problematic in the implementation of international law in general and international humanitarian law in particular is not so much the ultimate and extreme stage of 'enforcement', but the intermediate one of 'determination.'
>
> As long as we remain with general rules or principles that each subject interprets from his own vantage point and as a function of his own values and interests, we do not have objective determination. The role of law is thus reduced to rhetorical advocacy or justification and the legal character of these rules and principles remains hypothetical or subject to doubt.[102]

The US critical international law scholar David Kennedy has pointed out the indeterminate nature of international law in even harsher words by arguing that 'international law discourse is a conversation without content—a ritualized exchange which avoids confronting the very question it purports to address. (...) no one is persuaded.'[103]

Two issues must be distinguished: the question whether the legal status of the USSR in the Baltic States was that of an occupier; and the question which international standard should be used to assess Soviet policies. The first question is easier to answer than the second. Since the Soviet annexation of the Baltic States in 1940 lacked any ground in international law, and a significant segment of the international community refused to grant formal approval of Soviet seizure, the ultimate failure of the USSR to acquire legal title over the Baltic States implies that the regime of occupation was, as a matter of international law, not terminated until the independence of Estonia, Latvia and Lithuania was re-established in 1991.[104] Notwithstanding the annexation of the Baltic republics by the USSR in 1940, it is therefore simultaneously correct

---

102 G. Abi-Saab, *Conclusions. les Nations Unies et le Droit International Humanitaire. Actes du Colloque International de l'Université de Genève,* Paris: A. Pedone, 1996, p. 309. Abi-Saab thus advocates monitors and other mechanisms of scrutiny to overcome the problem of indeterminacy in international humanitarian law.

103 D. Kennedy, 'Theses about International Law Discourse', 23 *GYBIL* 1980, p. 353 at 376.

104 See for a similar conclusion: D.A. Loeber, 'Forced Incorporation: International Law Aspects of the Soviet Takeover of Latvia in 1940', in: R. Clark F. Feldbrugge, S. Pomorski (eds.) *International and National Law in Russia and Eastern Europe*, The Hague: M. Nijhoff, 2001, pp. 225–259, p. 259.

in the legal sense to speak of their (continued) 'occupation.'[105] The prolonged Soviet occupation of the Baltic States was an unorthodox occupation *sui generis*, an *Annexionsbesetzung*[106] ('annexation occupation'). Until 1991, the Baltic situation was in important ways the classic situation of occupation: external control by a force whose presence emerged in violation of norms of international law, and related to it, the conflict of interest between the people and the government exercising *de facto* power over them.[107]

However, in certain aspects the situation in the Baltic States was different from a classic situation of occupation. Both the fact of the Soviet annexation and the long duration[108] of Soviet rule in the Baltic republics are a factor here. The Soviets made a genuine attempt to integrate the Baltic States back into old imperial Russian territory, now transformed into the USSR. 'But actually after 1940 the USSR did not install occupation regimes in the Baltic States...'[109] Again, this is a tension between international legal doctrines and the reality established on the ground.[110]

For instance, by imposing the Soviet economic system on the Baltic States, the USSR of course violated the 1907 Hague rules of occupation. However, the principle *ex factis ius oritur* compels acceptance as historical facts of certain aspects of the foreign-imposed Soviet economic system in the decades following the illegal annexation. After 1991, the whole Soviet occupation/annexation period could not, in all the effects that it produced, be regarded as a legal nullity. However, Moscow also imposed the State socialist economic system in East European countries in which socialist governments were established even though those countries formally maintained their sovereignty. It can be argued—but would be artificial to maintain—that this economic system continued to violate the 1907 Hague Regulations. As the Danish international lawyer and legal realist Alf Ross warned with reference to the Danish context:

105 See already M. Brakas, 'Lithuania's International Status: Some Legal Aspects', 38 *Baltic Review* (August 1971), p. 14.

106 See for this concept: S. Cybichowski, 'Das völkerrechtliche Okkupationsrecht', *Z. für VR* 1934, p. 318.

107 Cf. A. Roberts, 'Prolonged Military Occupation', p. 44.

108 For special considerations in the cases of 'prolonged occupation', see A. Roberts, 'Prolonged Military Occupation...', *AJIL* 1990, p. 44 *et seq.*

109 T. Schweisfurth, 'Soviet Union, Dissolution', in: *EPIL*, Vol. 4, 2000, pp. 529–547 at 540.

110 Cf. P. Guggenheim, *op. cit.*, t. I, p. 443: '*Le droit des gens, qui est un droit primitif, ne dispose pas d'une technique assez évoluée pour pouvoir contester tout validité juridique à un pouvoir politique créé en violation du droit, mais durable et effectif.*'

> It would be naive to believe that the aggressor is punished by being denied all legal rights. To take up the categorical attitude, that whatever the occupying power does in the occupied territory, is unlawful, as being the mere consequence of the original unlawful act of invasion, does in practice amount to giving up any attempt at defining a legal *modus vivendi*.[111]

This observation is by analogy also true in the Baltic case.

The absolutely minimal standard that the USSR, not having acquired sovereign title, was bound to respect in the illegally annexed Baltic States and with regard to their populations, was the obligation to respect the rules of international law protecting civilian populations. Crimes against humanity are crimes under international criminal law but an occupying power, too, should not commit them.[112] Moreover, developing international human rights standards, applicable in domestic situations, were equally binding on the USSR in the illegally annexed Baltic States.[113]

5 Conclusion: The Baltic States 1940–1991, Continuity or Extinction?

The conclusions in the previous chapters—that prescription did not take place in the annexed Baltic States and that the three republics, even though annexed, remained occupied by the USSR in the sense of international law—point inevitably to the result that the State identity of the Baltic States was maintained. The legal concept of State identity seems to imply the continuity of these States as well. However, that conclusion is an existentially important turning point for this study, and here is the last opportunity to take into account all the considerations that might still point in a different direction. At this juncture, it is relevant to reflect upon how determinate, to what extent, can observations about international law and legal status be at all.

This seems the appropriate moment to recall an analysis of the methodology of international law, an analysis that much provoked the field of international law. In a much-celebrated and -debated treatise initially published in 1989, the distinguished Finnish international lawyer Martti Koskenniemi

111 A. Ross, 'Denmark's Legal Status', p. 7.

112 Cf. the legal opinion of the US Department of the Army of December 10, 1946, JIR. Vol. 6, 1956, 300. See also T. Schweisfurth, 'Germany, Occupation After World War II', *EPIL*, p. 196 *et seq.*

113 Cf. Roberts, 'Prolonged Military Occupation', pp. 49, 52 and 70 *et seq.*

deconstructed the international legal argument as being condemned to oscillate between apology and utopia.[114] The first kind of argument proceeds from the presumption *ex factis oritur ius,* the second from the maxim *ex injuria ius non oritur.*

As we can see, over time both types of argument have been presented on the question of the Soviet annexation period and the status of the Baltic States. The 'utopians' suggest the applicability of the rules of military occupation and the uninterrupted legal existence of the Baltic States; the 'apologists', however, point to the eventual effectiveness of prolonged Soviet rule in the Baltic States. But both positions can be reversed as well—for example the Baltic insistence on Soviet occupation and illegality can be a form of realism when seen from alternative angles. Moreover, the Soviet and later Russian insistence on on the legality or at least a certain legitimacy of the Soviet period can be seen as expression of utopianism and a certain type of universalism.

The Estonian legal scholar Enn Sarv takes the Baltic argument to the extreme when he argues that the USSR in the Baltic States continued to be bound by the 1949 Geneva rules of occupation until 1991. In his interpretation, Soviet settlement policies during the 1950s–1980s, aiming at irreversible changes in the ethnic composition of the Baltic republics, must be qualified as a war crime and a violation of Article 49 of the IV Geneva Convention.[115] According to this position, the conscription of Baltic men into the Soviet army in the 1980s was also a war crime, for example. At the other end of the scale is the argument of Russian diplomacy: '*The fact that the Baltic States had been forcibly incorporated into the Soviet Union did not imply a subsequent occupation in any legal sense, any more than Texas or New Mexico could be regarded as territories 'occupied' by the United States.*'[116]

---

114 See M. Koskenniemi, *From Apology to Utopia. The Structure of International Legal Argument,* 1989. See also M. Koskenniemi, 'The Politics of International Law', 1 *EJIL* 1989, pp. 4–32 at 9.

115 See E. Sarv, *Õiguse vastu ei saa ükski...,* p. 193 and 227. (The 'ethnic cleansing' pursued by the Soviets in Estonia as a 'war crime'; the 'settlement of Soviet citizens in occupied Estonia' as 'a blatant violation of Article 49 of the IV Geneva Convention.') For Sarv's elaboration of the Soviet 'civil occupation', see *ibid.,* p. 47 *et seq.*

116 See representative of Russia, S. Chernychenko during deliberations at the UN Economic and Social Council, Commission on Human Rights. Sub-Commission on Prevention of Discrimination and Protection of Minorities, 33rd Meeting, Geneva, 26 August 1992, E/CN.4/Sub.2/1992/SR.33, p. 16. Interestingly, this view carries continuity with the Soviet *tu quoque*-rhetoric. See e.g. V.P. Karpov, 'The Soviet Concept of Peaceful Coexistence and Its Implications for International Law', in: H.W. Baade (ed.) *The Soviet Impact on International Law,* Dobbs Ferry, NY: Oceana, 1965, p. 20 (criticizing 'some resolutions' of the US Congress from the point of view of the principle of the inviolability of borders: 'I

Such controversial positions were expressed in the context of evaluating the effects of non-recognition[117] of the Soviet annexation. Koskenniemi himself together with Marja Lehto presented a cautious argument when he suggested that '*On peut douter qu'il faille recourir à la fiction de la continuité pour parvenir aux conséquences juridiques découlant déjà de la reconnaissance de l'illegalité de l'occupation.*[118] At the other end of the scale, however, a contrary argument was presented by Juozas Repečka in 1949: the Baltic States continue to exist as subjects of international law as long as there exists a single third State that still refuses to recognize the legality of Soviet annexation. A qualified 'middle position' was taken by Boris Meissner,[119] who concluded in 1980 that, notwithstanding illegal Soviet annexation, Estonia, Latvia and Lithuania continue to exist as subjects of international law for those States (such as the USA and other Western nations) that did not recognize Soviet annexation *de iure.*[120] For those States, however, which recognized Soviet annexation *de iure,* the Baltic States lost their sovereign existence.[121] From these divergencies, it becomes apparent that it is uncertain whether the present legal status of the Baltic States—having maintained State continuity or not—would possess an *erga omnes* character.

Similarly, the 'utopian'-'apologist' dilemma came into play in assessments of the Baltic situation in the light of the Montevideo criteria of statehood. Looking at the matter from the persepective of the Baltic argumentation, the Utopians suggest the existence of a State, in the case of illegal annexation, when on the ground it does not exist (according to the 'three elements

---

would say this is roughly the same as if the parliament of Mexico, for example, would have passed a resolution demanding that Texas, Arizona, and California be 'liberated from American slavery.')

117 See generally on the effects of recognition: J. Verhoeven, *La reconnaissance…, 1975,* p. 665 *et seq.*

118 See Koskenniemi and Lehto, *AFDI* 1992, p. 198. "It is doubtful whether the fiction of continuity is necessary to achieve the legal consequences already arising from recognition of the illegality of occupation."

119 See B. Meissner, 'Die Souveränität der baltischen Nationen' (1980), in: B. Meissner, *Die baltischen Staaten im weltpolitischen und völkerrechdichen Wandel. Beiträge 1954–1994,* Hamburg: Bibliotheca Baltica, 1995, pp. 174–195.

120 *Ibid.* p. 181.

121 '*…haben die baltischen Nationen ihre staatliche Selbständigkeit im vollen Umfange eingebüßt.*' See Meissner, *ibid.*, p. 182. Professor Meissner goes on to elaborate on this: '*Auch die meisten Staaten, die erst nach dem Zweiten Weltkrieg diplomatische Beziehungen mit der Sowjetunion aufgenommen haben, dürften von dem bestehenden Gebietsstand der Sowjetunion ausgehen, ohne zu seiner völkerrechtlichen Problematik Stellung bezogen zu haben. Diese Staaten werden daher auch nicht die sowjetische Behauptung in Zweifel ziehen, daß die baltischen Unionsrepubliken Gliedstaaten der Sowjetunion darstellen.*' *Ibid.* p. 182.

theory.') On the other hand, the apologists, emphasizing effectiveness, would take the world more 'as is', regardless of whether it came about by legal or illegal means. Thus, they would see the reality of the Soviet Baltic republics within the USSR rather than the 'continued existence of the Baltic States, notwithstanding their annexation.' The German international law scholar Heike Krieger suggests that the principle of effectiveness played a role in the Baltic case, to the extent that the initially illegal situation consolidated and the USSR acquired territorial sovereignty over the Baltic States.[122] Joe Verhoeven, one of the most persistent defenders of *l'effectivité*, maintains that '*l'interdiction du recours à la force et la nullité du titre qui prétendrait s'y appuyer sont une chose, l'existence ou la disparition de l'Etat qui en est la victime en est une autre.*'[123] He warns that the acceptance of State continuity in cases such as that of the Baltic States may '*bouleverse[r] la conception traditionelle de l'Etat*', since '*a l'ordinaire, celui-ci naît ou meurt de la présence ou de l'absence d'éléments de pur fait: un territoire, une population, un gouvernement independent.*'[124] From this perspective, Verhoeven raises an important question: '*Doit-il aller jusqu'à nier que l'Etat est né ou qu'il est mort au motif qu'il l'a été illégalement?*'—and gives a cautious answer: '*On ne peut qu'hésiter à l'admettre*'[125] Therefore: '*Mieux vaut dès lors—au moins dans l'etat actuel des choses—laisser l'effectivite décider seule de la naissance ou de la mort de l'Etat. C'est probablement plus réaliste et peut-être plus prudent.*'[126] Joe Verhoeven thus intends to save the relevance of the three elements theory for determining statehood, emphasizing effectiveness, and maybe even: the relevance of international law when corresponding to the realities in international relations.

However, the paradox of the utopian-apologetic dilemma is also that accepting Professor Verhoeven's apologetic proposition returns like a boomerang to question the very possibility and relevance of international law as a normative system at all. Joe Verhoeven's call for realism attempts to save international

---

122 H. Krieger, *Das Effektivitätsprinzip im Völkerrecht*, p. 455.

123 See J. Verhoeven, 'La reconnaissance internationale: déclin ou renouveau?', 39 *AFDI* 1993, pp. 7–40 at 36. "Prohibition of the use of force and nullity of a title that would claim to be based on it are one thing, the existence or disappearance of the victim State is another."

124 See *ibid.* p. 37. "Upsets the traditional conception of the State… ordinarily, it arises or dies from the presence or absence of elements of pure fact: a territory, a population, an independent government."

125 See *ibid.* p. 38. "Is it needful to go so far as to deny that the state was born or died on the grounds that it was born illegally?"; "One can only hesitate to admit it…"

126 See *ibid.* p. 39. "It is better then—at least in the present state of affairs—to let effectivity alone decide the birth or death of the state. It is probably more realistic and perhaps more cautious."

law from irrelevancy—and yet paradoxically also makes it irrelevant. It is well known that due to its decentralized character, international law is a primitive legal system when compared to a well-functioning domestic legal order.[127] Hence, there always exists the danger that international law mandates a certain behaviour—act or omission— and yet the legal norm is violated, but nonetheless, the violation of such legal norms may in practice have no serious consequences. The fewer answers international law offers for confronting such situations, the less relevant it becomes in international relations.[128] This consideration applies most urgently in cases where the most fundamental international norms, such as the prohibition of aggression, are violated.

Paradoxically, a capitulation of law to facts delivers a further argument to the realists, to the effect that international law does not matter. Their dismissiveness about international law makes even more sense when international law ceases to protect what it has been designed to protect, and when it is needed most. Hedley Bull suggests that international law condemns aggression but once aggression has been successful it ceases to be condemned.[129] Hans Morgenthau, one of the fathers of modern realism, posed a critical question for international lawyers:

> ...problems arise with respect to the Briand-Kellogg Pact and the Peace Treaties of 1919, as well as to other political treaties, such as the (...) alliance treaties, the concepts of aggression, independence, intervention, and so forth. They are embodied in written documents which were duly ratified and never invalidated. Have they ever been valid law from the beginning, and what has become of them in the years of their violation? Are they still valid? If they are not, what destroyed their validity?[130]

127 Few lawyers, however, would today—due to the undeniable developments towards the strengthening of the international legal order after World War II—formulate it as strongly as Hans Kelsen did when in 1932 he expressed the view that '... (das) Völkerrecht seiner technischen Struktur nach den Typus einer primitive n Rechtsordnung darstellt und daß es, wenn überhaupt als Recht, so nur als primitives Recht gedeutet werden kann.' See H. Kelsen, 'Unrecht und Unrechtsfolge im Vökerrecht', XII *ZöR* 1932, pp. 481–606 at 481.

128 We agree with the analysis of James Crawford: '... international law risks being ineffective precisely if it does not challenge effective but illegal situations. (...) the argument that international law cannot regulate or control effective territorial entities is an expression of the view that international law cannot regulate power politics at all.' See Crawford, 'The Criteria of Statehood...', p. 145.

129 H. Bull, *The Anarchical Society, A Study of Order in World Politics*, 2nd ed., New York: Columbia Up, 1995, p. 88 (quoting Mazrui.)

130 H. Morgenthau, 'Positivism, Functionalism and International Law', 34 *AJIL* 1940, p. 267.

The principle of effectivity alone cannot be at the very centre of international law, for effectivity taken to the extreme is the right of might, of the stronger—a world order which is the reality according to the realist school of thought, but would then not deserve to be called 'international law', since it would be a very apologetic order indeed. If the world was ruled solely by naked power, and the rules were made by and would support merely the powerful, it would be a misuse of legitimacy to call such a world order by the misleading term 'law.' If this would appear to be so, there would be reasons to join those scholars who, like the US TWAIL scholar Makau Mutua, have argued that 'the regime of international law is illegitimate.'[131]

That the international legal system may appear to be incapable of convincingly answering violations of one of its most fundamental norms—the prohibition of aggression—should be a bigger problem for lawyers who worry about the relevance of the rule of law in international relations, than the fear that international law would become 'unrrealistic' when supporting legal fictions where fundamental legal norms have been violated. In any case, the so-called *normative Kraft des Faktischen* cannot have a legal significance of its own. In the words of the German legal thinker Gustav Radbruch: '*Normative Kraft des Faktischen ist ein Paradoxon, aus einem Sein allein kann nie ein Sollen entspringen, ein Faktum wie die Anschauung einer bestimmten Zeitepoche kann nur normativ werden, wenn eine Norm ihm diese Normativität beigelegt hat.*'[132]

For that reason, at no point during the illegal annexation of the Baltic States did all outstanding legal scholars agree that the Baltic States had lost their statehood for the purposes of international law. On the basis of non-recognition policy, Krystyna Marek concluded in 1968 'that there can still be a relation of identity and continuity between the independent Baltic States of 1940 and such Baltic States as will recover their effective freedom before an overwhelming normative pressure of facts will have brought about their final

131 See M. Mutua, 'What is TWAIL?', in: ASIL *Proceedings of the 94th Annual Meeting*, April 5–8, 2000, p. 31.

132 G. Radbruch, *Rechtsphilosophie*, 4. Aufl., herausg. von Erik Wolf, p. 288. "The normative force of the factual is a paradox, from 'being' alone a 'should' can never arise, a fact such as the view of a certain epoch in time can only become normative if a norm has enclosed this normativity with it." See almost identically Karl Doehring: 'Effectiveness is only legally relevant insofar as the legal system permits it. Effectiveness alone as a consequence of a mere factual event does not create rights.' K. Doehring, 'Effectiveness', *EPIL*, Vol 7, p. 70. And surprisingly, even Kelsen argued in this context that 'Legal consequences cannot simply be deduced from facts, but only from legal rules which confer upon facts the effect of creating new law.' See H. Kelsen, *Principles of International Law*, 2nd. ed., ed. by R. Tucker, 1966, pp. 721–722.

extinction.'[133] Therefore, as anomalous as the length of the illegal occupation and annexation by the USSR may have been, the prolonged period does not imply extinction of these States as subjects of international law.

In the Baltic case, however, the main answer to Professor Verhoeven's question: '*Doit-il alter jusquà nier que l'Etat est né ou qu'il est mort au motif qu'il la été illégalement?*' is given by State practice itself. A considerable portion of State practice indeed *went* as far as denying the extinction of the illegally annexed Baltic States. Diplomatic practice, especially non-recognition policy and the recognition of State identity in 1991, suggests that—as seen from the Baltic perspective—Utopia was preferred over Apologia and the continuity of the Baltic States was upheld.

Of course, there is an element of legal fiction in the claim that the Baltic States continued to exist as subjects of international law between 1940 and 1991. Some States, while refusing to give *de iure* recognition to the Soviet seizure of the Baltic States, were not terribly consequential in their non-recognition either.

Yet recent State practice does not generally indicate that the States which recognized the identity of the Baltic States have kept in mind the controversial and politically motivated constellation of 'identity without continuity.' The Baltic claim has always been one of State *continuity*, and third States, while accepting the identity of the Baltic States, seem to have accepted the Baltic thesis of State continuity as well.

The illegality of the Soviet occupation and annexation, the non-recognition of the Soviet annexation by most Western States, resistance by the Baltic peoples to the Soviet regime, and the uninterrupted functioning of certain State organs in exile compel us to draw the final conclusion in favour of the continuity of the Baltic States throughout Soviet annexation. Non-recognition by Western States only reconfirmed the illegality of the annexation which was the main reason for maintenance of State continuity as a legal-political solution in the Baltic case.

---

133 K. Marek, *Idenity and Continuity* ... 2nd ed., 1968, p. 581. In 1956 Boris Meissner came to similar conclusions: '*Somit haben die baltischen Staaten ihre Völkerrechtssubjektivität nicht eingebuß. Da sie im Rechtssinne nicht untergegangen sind, besteht mit ihrer Staatsangehörigkeit und ihrer Rechtsverfassung grundsätzlich auch ihr materielles Recht nach dem Stand von 1940 weiter.*' Meissner, *op. cit.*, p. 309.

PART 2

Ex Factis Oritur Ius

1 Introduction

The first part of this study ended with conclusions about the triumph of legality over effectiveness in the case of the illegal annexation of the Baltic States. Due to the illegality of the Soviet annexation and the State continuity claim, presented persistently and to an extent skilfully by the Baltic States, in 1991 the State community recognized the identity and continuity of the Baltic States with the pre-World War II Baltic republics. It would be convenient to rest the case here.

However, we are warned by Canadian scholar Obiora Chinedu Okafor that

> ... it is (...) still too early to declare an absolute victory for the principle of legitimacy over the strict version of the doctrine of effectiveness. While effectiveness no longer automatically confers legitimacy, the doctrine is still an important element of international law and practice. The pendulum of international law may yet swing back to the side of the effectiveness principle, especially if the costs of de-legitimising effective but illegal situations become too heavy for the system to bear. (...) the last word has not been said on this subject.[1]

The second part of the present study examines the costs issue, and asks in particular whether the costs of the solution adopted in the Baltic case might have been too heavy to bear. In this context, it is suggested that costs become excessive when engaging in Utopia becomes too uncritical and international law doctrine can no longer fulfil the promises it offers to States affected. Establishing an unrealizable level of expectation may jeopardize consequential enforcement of international law. This has happened before: for example, many post-World War II realist lawyers had felt, as explained by Martti Koskenniemi, that the:

> ...preceding generation had failed because it had engaged in speculative abstraction with insufficient regard for the changed conditions of power and political fact. A notorious example was the collapse of the impressive legal-conceptual framework on neutrality. The law had failed because it carried outdated ideas about legitimacy and order, because it was based on speculative hypotheses with no grasp of the reality of power. It was, in a word, too Utopian.[2]

1 See Okafor, *op. cit.*, p. 69.
2 See M. Koskenniemi (ed.), *International Law*, Aldershot et al: Dartmouth, 1992, p. xvii.

To suggest the existence of a high-minded fiction or rule in international law is one thing; to guarantee its observance and consequential implementation is another, far more complicated task.[3] International legal doctrine has generally taken it for granted that it cannot set its normative expectations as high as a domestic legal system.[4] Some authors explicitly warn that, in international law, there is no space for radical normativity.[5] In the following, we will examine the reverse side of the solution given by State practice in the Baltic case, in particular whether practice and theory have been compatible here.

3 See also S.Yu. Marochkin, 'Questions of Effectiveness of International Law Rules', *Soviet YBIL* 1988, pp. 12–22.

4 See H. Krüger, 'Das Prinzip der Ejfektivität, oder: Über die besondere Wirklichkeitsnähe des Völkerrechts', in: D.S. Constantopoulous *et al* (eds.) *Grundprobleme des internationalen Rechts, Festschrift für Jean Spiropoulous*, Bonn 1957, pp. 265–284 at 266.

5 See H. Krieger, *Das Effektivitätsprinzip im Völkerrecht,* pp. 177 and 202. See also R. Bindschedler, 'Die Anerkennung im Völkerrecht', in: *Berichte der DGV*, Band 4, 1961, pp. 1–27 at 20 ('as long as the decentralized nature of international law exists, it cannot give up the principle of effectiveness and must recognize the *normative Kraft des Faktischen.*' Transl.)

CHAPTER 5

Controversial Claims for Restoration of Legal Rights in the Baltic Case

1 The Prevailing Understanding of State Continuity in Doctrine

In her influential study on State continuity, Krystyna Marek, following an aspect of the Kelsenian concept of the State, tied the concepts of State identity and continuity to the rights and duties of each State: from status follow rights. According to her position, restoration of a State on the basis of continuity means, as a matter of principle, restoration of the state of affairs existing before commission of the illegal act of seizure (*restitutio in integrum*).[1] However, reflections upon State practice during the World War II era compelled Marek to qualify her normatively radical or utopian basic rule with a reservation based on realism: in practice, *normative Kraft des Faktischen* cannot be ignored and *restitutio in integrum* will often become impossible:

> (…)it must be open to the gravest doubt whether in practice the principle of a truly integral restitution stands any chance of implementation or whether, in fact, it does not merely represent a maximum postulate from which important concessions will have to be made. For it is submitted that the actual effectiveness of illegal foreign domination cannot be disregarded and that it will leave its lasting traces even in the most favourable case of its elimination.[2]

Marek went on to refer to the 'plain impossibility of treating an executed illegal act as non-existent,'[3] and pointed out that 'life goes on in the annexed or occupied territory, or under a puppet authority, some sort of a legal order is maintained and acts take place which are not illegal in themselves.'[4]

---

1 Cf. Marek, *op. cit.,* p. 582.

2 Marek, *op. cit.*, p. 582. This idea has been extended to the case of the Baltic States by Rein Müllerson, who argues that '*restitutio ad integrum* after more than fifty years is more often a legal fiction than a realistic option.' See R. Mullerson, 'New Developments in the Former USSR and Yugoslavia', 33 *Va. J. Int'l L.* 1993, pp. 310–311. See also Kaljurand, *Some Aspects of…* 1995, p. 8.

3 Marek, *op. cit.,* p. 582.

4 *Ibid. op. cit.,* p. 582.

© LAURI MÄLKSOO, 2022 | DOI:10.1163/9789004464896_007

As a solution, Marek suggested that it is imperative to distinguish between an original illegal act and subsequent acts in the occupied territory.[5] The legality of subsequent acts on the illegally controlled territory has to be considered on their own merits, which in turn have to be tested 'by the criteria of what is allowed to a belligerent occupant under the Hague regime':[6]

> This criterion fully and absolutely excludes any alteration of the international status of the victim State which—if the principle of its unbroken continuity is to have any meaning at all—must precisely emerge from the period of foreign domination with all its international rights and duties unimpaired, and with the continuing international delimitation of all its spheres of validity under international law. This is why neither changes in the nationality of the population, nor territorial changes, can be accorded even a provisional validity by the restored State or by third States.[7]

Marek concluded that '*the restoration of an illegally suppressed State combines the basic principle of its continuity with necessary and unavoidable limitations, in exactly the same way as a restoration of a State after belligerent occupation. In neither cases does it—or can it—mean a legal earthquake.*'[8]

Although the last formulation elegantly leaves space for manoeuvring, it is clear that even in cases of illegally suppressed States, Marek sees the very continuity of a State—'if the principle of its unbroken continuity is to have any meaning at all'—as the continuity of its international rights and obligations. In any case, in the fundamental issues of nationality, territorial changes and the like, the legal presumption is in favour of the illegally suppressed State, its legal rights and interests. From the emphases of Marek's analysis, it can be presumed that her basic understanding of the concepts of State continuity and identity as a presumption in favour of the continuity of international legal rights and obligations, is formed with a special view toward States restored following illegal suppression.

Although Marek's normative concept of State continuity has to some extent been criticized by Crawford, it still 'haunts legal imagination', as Martti Koskenniemi has argued.[9] In turn, Koskenniemi criticizes the way '*(m)uch of the recent*

5 Marek, *op. cit.*, p. 584.
6 *Ibid.p.* 584.
7 Marek, *op. cit.*, pp. 584–585.
8 Marek, *op. cit.*, p. 586.
9 Koskenniemi, 'The Present State of Research', in: *State Succession* (Hague Academy), 1996, p. 153.

debate on the legal aspects of political transformation in Europe is based on the assumption that the first problem to resolve is whether an entity has become altogether 'new' or whether it continues the existence of an 'old' State and that the determination of its status in this respect is determinative of its rights and obligations.'[10] Marek's normative schema may therefore become quite divisive and maximalistic: when the legal status is x, then y. Marek's concept implies that it is simply crucial to preserve State continuity; once this status has been accomplished, then the restoration of fundamental rights should follow.

But can international law uphold Krystyna Marek's normative promise, the claim of the continuity of rights and duties? At the State level, writes Jean Touscoz, it is only the effectivity of State power that legitimizes employment of fictions.[11] On an international level, there is no comparable effective power. Ulrich Fastenrath is therefore much more doubtful than Marek when suggesting 'it is not clear... what legal concequences can be derived from the restoration of identity, considering the fundamental intervening change in circumstances.'[12] Similarly, the British international law scholar Ian Brownlie warned against the 'tyranny of concepts' in cases of State succession and continuity.[13] The presumption is thus that even the legal world is not black and white, but may contain grey shades. This may be seen in the case of the Baltic States, where the time factor made their continuity with the pre-1940 republics in practice a qualified continuity.

Upon the restoration of their independence in 1991, the Baltic States invoked their legal status as true disciples of Krystyna Marek's normative concept of State continuity. They began from the presumption that, at least with respect to fundamental aspects of statehood (territory, nationality, legal status as occupied countries) they were legally entitled to invoke their (former) rights. Their national leaders seemed to assume that the Baltic States had won back their rightful legal status and as long as this had been recognized, other normative consequences in international relations would have to follow. However, as we shall see in the following, this approach has been only partly successful since it appears that, as the Belgian international law scholar Jean Salmon

10 See ibid. p. 153.

11 J. Touscoz, *Le principe d'effectivité dans l'ordre international*, 1964, p. 179.

12 U. Fastenrath, 'States, Extinction', in: *EPIL* 10,1987, p. 465.

13 See Brownlie, *Principles*... p. 82. However, Professor Brownlie's dissatisfaction with theories seems to go further than the cases of State succession and continuity. See e.g. I. Brownlie, 'Recognition in Theory and Practice', in: 53 *BYBIL* 1982, pp. 197–211 at 197 ('There is no doubt room for a whole treatise on the harm caused to the business of legal investigation by theory.')

argued in August 1991, *'l'hypothése de l'illégalité est un véritable nid de guêpes par ces conséquences.'*[14]

2 Special Circumstances in the Baltic Case

The post-1991 treaty practice of the Baltic States has already been summarized in the second chapter of this study. There are numerous facts in diplomatic practice that demonstrate the restoration of former legal rights and obligations after 1991. Some of the diplomatic steps taken were of a primarily symbolic nature. Nevertheless, contrary evidence also exists. In several cases, third States recognized the identity of the Baltic States as such, but insisted that the pre-1940 treaties could not be applied any longer in the new circumstances.[15] In the case of Estonia, for instance, among those States rejecting the validity of treaties concluded before 1940 are those that in principle recognized claims to State continuity (Germany, Italy), as well as those that did not (Russia, Japan).[16] In many of these cases—with the exception of the Baltic peace treaties with Russia—the treaties concerned are of marginal importance in the modern world, and their continued application would indeed have been a largely empty gesture.

On the other hand—some implications of invoking claims for the identity of the Baltic States with the pre-World War II republics have been accepted even by neighbouring States that had recognized the Soviet annexation in earlier decades, but traditionally had close relations with the Baltic States—for example Sweden.[17]

However, in one interesting sense (leaving aside the obvious time factor), the case of restoration of the Baltic States differs from the other cases of recognized State continuity discussed above (for example Austria 1938–1945 or

14 J. Salmon, 'Pays baltes', 24 *RBDI* 1991, p. 267. "the hypothesis of illegality is a real wasps' nest by these consequences."

15 See e.g. the Protocol between the Republic of Lithuania and the Kingdom of Norway on the agreements governing bilateral Lithuanian-Norwegian relations, signed in Vilnius on April 20, 1994 (as referred to in Satkauskas, *op. cit.*, p. 63).

16 See Kerikmäe/Vallikivi, 'State Continuity in the Light of…', V *Juridica International* 2000, p. 35.

17 Erik Franckx studied the recent maritime agreements between Estonia and Sweden and came to the conclusion that Sweden has at least 'paid lip service' to the Estonian position that no Soviet agreements bind Estonia automatically. See E. Franckx, 'The 1998 Estonia-Sweden Maritime Boundary Agreement: Lessons to be Learned in the Area of Continuity and/or Succession of States', 31 *Ocean Development & International Law* 2000, pp. 271 and 275.

Czechoslovakia 1939–1945). In these cases, the continuity of Nazi victim States was *quasi*-imposed by the victorious allies. The aggressor State, Nazi Germany, had been forced to accept unconditional surrender, and an occupied Germany, undergoing the process of denazification, was neither willing nor able to question legal restoration of the pre-occupation *status quo*.[18]

This differs from the Baltic case, where restoration of independence occurred some months before the collapse of the USSR, with no international judicial or political body giving politically authoritative answers—*à la* 1943 Moscow declaration in the case of Austria—upon termination of the illegal situation. Indeed, in 1991 the Russian Federation demonstrated a fair amount of goodwill in ending the illegal situation created by the USSR, and (of course also due to international pressure) did not impose upon the Baltic States its conditions of separation. Only in 1994, when the last Russian troops had left the Baltic States, were some tradeoffs negotiated in the respective treaties, for example concerning retired members of the Soviet and Russian army still living in the Baltic States.

Understandably, the most important issues concerning restoration of former rights and duties are connected with the State whose predecessor regime was responsible for the illegal situation (as Germany was in the cases of Austria or Czechoslovakia). In short, the result has been a situation in which the Western States (which never recognized the incorporation of the Baltic States into the USSR) have been favourable to the Baltic continuity claim, while the continuator State of the USSR,[19] the Russian Federation, has chosen not to do so.

In practice, it remains an underlying question with respect to restoration of the independence of the Baltic States in 1991: was restoration due at all to international law, whose concepts resulted in the denial of sovereign title to the USSR? Was restoration primarily an extra-legal act? The non-recognition doctrine brought no tangible results in fifty years; is it then realistic to imply that it played a decisive role in the restoration of independence in 1991? Should the Baltic States more than anything be thankful to the Russian Federation for the (almost) peaceful[20] restoration of their independence? This point of

18 Reservations were, however, expressed in the German court practice and literature (particularly with respect to nationality questions). See e.g. H. Jellinek, *Der automatische Erwerb und Verlust der Staatsangehörigkeit durch völkerrechtliche Vorgänge, zugleich ein Beitrag zur Lehre von der Staatensukzession*, Berlin: Carl Heymann, 1951, p. 142 *et seq.*

19 On the question whether the Russian Federation is successor, continuator or, paradoxically although impossibly from the viewpoint of international legal theory, both, see L. Mälksoo, 'International Law and the 2020 Amendments to the Russian Constitution', 115 *AJIL* 2021, pp 78–93 at 83–84.

20 There were Soviet victims in Vilnius and Riga in January 1991.

view was expressed by the former Russian Ambassador in Tallinn, who argued in an interview that the Baltic States should thank Russia and not wait for an apology.[21] If this view—namely, that the restoration of Baltic independence occurred realistically, thanks to Russian benevolence (and especially the goodwill of Russian democrats) rather than due to international law—proves to be true, it cannot be without consequences for the legal concepts involved, especially the concept of 'State continuity.' It would not be nice to harrass a benefactor with claims relating to State responsibility and restoration of rights.

This author has chosen three controversial issues where Baltic and Russian views on the legal status of the Baltic States have clashed. A more detailed understanding of these issues says much about the relevance of the doctrine of State continuity, of the relationship between legal status and its normative consequences. These issues are: first, the controversy about the citizenship rights of the mostly Russian-speaking Soviet era immigrants in Latvia and Estonia; second, the debate about the legal validity of the Latvian-Russian and Estonian-Russian Peace Treaties, particularly the issue of State boundaries; and third, the question of Russia's responsibility for the illegal Soviet annexation of the Baltic States.

3 The Controversy about the Principle of Continuity of Citizenship and the Political Rights of Soviet Era Immigrants

a *Introduction*

In one important respect, today's Baltic States inevitably have a strong *de facto* link or continuity with the Soviet era—the composition of their populations was altered significantly during fifty years of illegal annexation. Consequently, upon re-establishment of their independence, Latvia and Estonia, where the demographic changes of the Soviet era had been most drastic, refused to extend citizenship rights automatically to the mostly Russian-speaking immigrants of the Soviet era. Thus, in the early 1990s, the Soviet-era immigrants became legally speaking aliens in those countries—when they wish(ed) to

21 See A. Ammas, Gluhhov: 'Eesti peab Venemaad tänama, mine ootama vabandamist', *Eesti Päevaleht*, 15.11.2000 ('Russia gave to you freedom, the opportunity to develop freely as you wish yourself! And that already the second time during the last century. (...) You received a great present from history. During the 1980s you could only dream about independence, and suddenly you became independent, thanks to yourself and to your politicians. But agree that you should also thank Russia.')

acquire citizenship in either Estonia or Latvia, they had/have to go through a naturalization process.

The issue of the political rights of the Russian-speaking Soviet era immigrants in the Baltic States has thus become linked with the issue of the legal status of the Baltic republics. More than that, it became one of the most disputed and controversial legal and political questions in the Baltic States after restoration of their independence. In the following, we investigate particularly what impact domestic and international arguments concerning the legal status of the Baltic States have had upon citizenship policy in Latvia and Estonia.[22] However, no analysis of the minorities issue would be complete without first discussing the historical background.

b *The Migration Policies of the Soviet Authorities*

In 1918, the self-determination claims of ethnic Estonians, Latvians and Lithuanians delivered a raison d'être for the creation of these new independent States. However, the declarations of independence already referred to the peoples, in the plural, living there. The titular ethnicities lived together with relatively small but historically significant German, Russian, Jewish, Swedish and other minorities. In 1922–1923, the young Baltic republics delivered declarations extending 'the protection of the League of Nations' to their minorities.[23] As a consequence, the Baltic republics adopted laws of so-called cultural autonomy, which gave their national minorities widespread autonomy in cultural, linguistic, educational, and other matters.[24] Protection of minority rights in the pre-1940s Baltic States, especially in Estonia, has been praised as

22 See generally for the issues of State succession and nationality in: C. Kreuzer, *Staatsangehörigkeit and Staatensukzession. Die Bedeutung der staatensukzession für die staatsangehörigkeitsrechtlichen Regelungen in de Staaten der ehemaligen Sowjetunion, Jugoslawiens and der Tschechoslowakei*, Berlin: Duncker & Humblot, 1998; A. Liebich et al (eds.) *Citizenship East and West*, London: Kegan Paul Int'l, 1995; P. Cumper and S. Wheatley (eds.) *Minority Rights in the 'New' Europe*, The Hague: Nijhoff, 1999; I.M. Cuthbertson and J. Leibowitz (ed.) *Minorities: The New Europe's Old Issue*, Prague etc: OSI, 1993; G. Smith, A. Aasland, R. Mole, 'Statehood, Ethnic Relations and Citizenship', in: G. Smith (ed.) *The Baltic States. The National Self-Determination of Estonia, Latvia and Lithuania*, London: Macmillan, 1994, pp. 181–205.

23 See Lithuania, May 12, 1922, in: J.O. Juni 1922, p. 586 et seq., Latvia, July 7 , 1923, in: J.O. August 1923, p. 933 et seq., Estonia, September 17, 1923, in: J.O. November 1 923, p. 1311 et seq. See also H. Kraus, *Das Recht der Minderheiten*, Berlin: Stake, 1927, pp. 121–126.

24 See M. Laserson, 'Das Minoritätenrecht der baltischen Staaten', *ZaöRV* 1931, p. 401 et seq. For a more recent account, see C. Thiele, *Selbstbestimmung und Minderheitenschutz in Estland*, Berlin: Springer, 1999, p. 79 et seq.

'exemplary' by legal authors.[25] In Estonia, where in 1934 88.2 of the nation's 1,126,413 inhabitants were ethnic Estonians,[26] the MPs of non-Estonian ethnic origin had the right to address the Parliament in their native languages (for example German). During the 1930s, when political developments were marked by the rise of right-wing authoritarianism, the rights of the ethnic minorities became more restricted, particularly in Lithuania (especially the rights of the Jewish minority.)

Repressions by the Soviet occupying power had an immediate effect on the Baltic populations. First, according to the plan of *Umsiedlung* undertaken by Nazi Germany after Estonia and Latvia in the German-Soviet Non-Aggression Pact were left in the Soviet sphere of influence, in 1939–1940 most of the ethnic Germans were (formally voluntarily) transferred to territories that Germany had seized from Poland. Those Germans who refused to leave in 1940 left the Baltic republics in the course of the *Nachumsiedlung* in early 1941, after experiencing the first repressive year of Soviet occupation. That first Soviet year of occupation was marked by the murder of large numbers of the Estonian, Latvian and Lithuanian political and military elite, and the deportation of nearly one hundred thousand Balts to Siberia on June 14, 1941. Death rates in the Siberian camps were very high, and those few deportees who later managed to return to their homelands, were often morally or physically broken.

Fears of continuing Stalinist repression forced several hundred thousand Balts to flee into exile in 1944, when the Soviet army was wresting the Baltic States from the retreating Germans. The Baltic nations lost some 20 % of their populations as a consequence of World War II; beside Poland and Byelorussia, these are among the highest proportional losses in Europe. By 1945, the Estonian population had dropped to 845,000 people, 97.3 per cent of whom were ethnic Estonians. Besides several smaller mass deportations, more than a hundred thousand Baltic citizens were deported to Siberia in another mass deportation of March 25, 1949.[27]

---

25 See e.g. R. v. Laun, *Staat and Volk. Eine völkerrechtliche and staatsrechtliche Untersuchung auf philosophischer Grundlage*, 2. Aufl., Aalen Scientia Verlag, 1971, p. 310 et seq. and D.A. Loeber, 'Language Rights in Independent Estonia, Latvia and Lithuania, 1918–1940', in: S. Vilfan (ed.) *Ethnic Groups and Language Rights*, Vol. 3, 1990.

26 By that time, ethnic Russians constituted 8.2 % of the population.

27 See generally for a qualification of mass deportations under the 1949 Geneva Convention in: O.M. Uhler, *op. cit.*, p. 170 *et seq.* and J.-M. Henckaerts, *Mass Expulsion in Modem International Law and Practice,* 1995, p. 143 *et seq.*

The demographic policies of the USSR in the Baltic States have been described as 'Russification'[28] and sometimes even as colonization[29]—although use of the latter term would be unconventional in the context of international law. It is clear, however, that the USSR attempted to create facts in its favour, including demographically. For instance, at the end of World War II, the Soviet authorities prohibited evacuated ethnic Estonians from returning to their homes in the Estonian city of Narva near the Russian border. Instead, apartments in Narva were made available to Soviet Russian citizens moving in from neighbouring areas. The following decades witnessed a steady influx of mostly Russian immigrants from the USSR, encouraged by Sovietization of the economy of the Baltic States and a massive concentration of the Soviet army in the Baltics, which had now become a *de facto* border region of the USSR. The Baltic States and especially Latvia became a favourite place for retired Soviet army officers and their families. In Latvia, the migration policies of the Soviet annexation period caused the recession

---

28 See e.g. for views in literature: S. Bychkov Green, 'Language of Lullabies: The Russification and De-Russification of the Baltic States', 19 *Mich. JIL* 1997, p. 217; H.-J. Uibopuu, 'Dealing with the Minorities—a Baltic Perspective', in: 48 *The World Today* 1992 (June), pp. 108–112 at 109; T. Ansbach, 'Der Rechtsstatus der nicht-estnischen Bevblkerung in Estland', in: *Recht in Ost und West*, September 1996 No. 7, p. 218.

29 See e.g. the resolutions of the European Parliament adopted in 1983, 1985 and 1987, e.g. in the resolution adopted on January 13, 1983, the Parliament called on the foreign ministers of the EEC States to submit the question of the Baltic States to the UN Committee of Decolonization. The representatives of the US Congress argued in 1975 that US non-recognition policy would 'discourage a great many Soviet citizens from settling in the Baltic countries. Thus it reduces the flow of colonists and considerably hinders Soviet genocidal policies of colonization, ethnic dilution, Russification and effective absorption of Baltic nations into the Soviet Union.' See US House of Representatives, Subcommittee on International Political and Military Affairs, Committee on International Relations, *Conference on Security and Cooperation in Europe*, Washington, DC: US Government Printing Office, 1975, p. 27. Note also that during the UN General Assembly discussions on colonialism, the British Minister of State David Ormsby-Gore, replying to the Soviet demand that the General Assembly call for independence 'forthwith' for all colonies and trust territories, said on November 28, 1960: '...Since 1939, some 500 million people, formerly under British rule, have achieved freedom and independence, and their representatives sit here. In that same period, the whole or part of six countries, with a population of 22 million, have been forcibly incorporated into the Soviet Union; they include the world's newest colonies: Lithuania, Estonia and Latvia...' UN Gen. Ass. Off. Rec 15th Sess., Plenary, 925th Meeting, Nov. 28, 1960, A/PV.925, p. 982. Similar points were made by the US ambassadors to the UN, Adlai Stevenson and Arthur Goldberg during the 1960s. See Vitas, *op. cit.*, p. 81. Irina Busygina, an author from Russia, has also called the Sovied policies a 'gradual colonisation.' See I. Busygina, *Russia, the Baltic states and the European Union,* in: T. Jundzis (ed.) The Baltic States at Historical Crossroads, Riga 1998, p. 505.

of ethnic Latvians in the population from 75.7 % (the census of 1935) to 52 % (1989) and an increase of Russians, Ukrainians and Byelorussians from 12.1 % to 42 %.

In Estonia, developments are indicated by the declining share of the ethnic Estonians in the composition of the population of Estonia:[30]

TABLE 1 Share of ethnic Estonians in the composition of Estonia's population

	Total population	% Ethnic estonians
1945	845,000	97.3
1959	1,196,791	74.6
1979	1,464,476	64.7
1989	1,565,662	61,5
1995	1,491,583	64.2

Migration into Lithuania from the USSR was less drastic, arguably since the local Communist Party included more Lithuanian nationalist members who managed to resist settlements plans proposed by Moscow.[31] In Latvia and Estonia, where the titular ethnic groups were in the minority in the local communist parties, the local population had no means of exercising control over Soviet settlement policies.

Moscow's policy of Russification also included overall promotion of the Russian language, creating a situation in which the majority of the Russian-speaking immigrants felt no need to study local languages—essential elements in the identities of the Baltic titular nationalities. The integration promoted by the Soviet authorities in the Baltic States was in reality a policy aiming at assimilation of the native non-Russian population. On the one hand, Russian culture and the Russian language were extensively introduced in the Baltic States; on the other hand, the USSR did not encourage Russian immigrants to study the Baltic languages, considered too difficult (or, at least, different) and insignificant. According to the 1989 census in the USSR, only 13.7 % of Russians

30 Data from P. Järve, 'Ethnic Democracy and Estonia: Application of Smooha's Model', *ECMI Working Paper* No. 7, Flensburg, 2000, p. 39.

31 The friendship between the Soviet CP General Secretary Khruschev and the Lithuanian CP leader Sniečkus has sometimes been quoted as the reason why Lithuania was able to avoid russification. See H.-J. Uibopuu, 'Minorities and their Rights in the Baltic States', in: 35 *AWR-Bulletin* 1997, pp. 189–197 at 190.

in Estonia, 21.1 % in Latvia and 33.4 % in Lithuania had a command of the local languages.[32]

When the independence movement started in the Baltic States in 1988, and a portion of the Soviet-era immigrants manifested their opposition to the prospect of separation from Russia, the result was the formation of the Citizens' Congresses in Estonia and in Latvia.

c *The Citizens' Congresses in Estonia and Latvia in 1990*

When the independence claim was vocally opposed by some Soviet-era settlers, the political leaders representing the citizens of the (pre-war) republics of Estonia and Latvia and their descendants born during the Soviet annexation period claimed that the settlers' 'no' to restoration of independence could not be measured with the same yardstick as the 'yes' of the citizens of the legally still-existing Republics of Estonia and Latvia.[33] Thus was born the Citizens' Congresses movement.

The very idea of forming the Estonian and Latvian Citizens' Committees began at the grassroots level;[34] the organization for registration of citizens and elections to the Congresses was carried out by volunteers. The election of both bodies thus manifested the desire of the citizens of Estonia and Latvia to reconstitute themselves politically. In winter/spring 1990, the citizens of the republics of Latvia and Estonia elected their own representative assemblies, the Estonian and Latvian Citizens' Congresses. Elections took place without interference by the Soviet authorities and were marked by high levels of participation.[35] The Congresses met for the first time in March and May 1990 in Estonia and Latvia respectively.

Soviet-era immigrants who supported the independence process were encouraged to register as candidates for future citizenship; upon restoration of independence, they were promised naturalization in a simplified process by the movement leaders. A number of people used this opportunity; their

---

32 See Natsionalny sostav naselenia SSSR, 'Finansy i Statistika', Moscow, 199. Quoted in M. Kahn, 'Les Russes dans les ex-républiques soviétiques', in: *Le courrier des pays de l'Est* No. 376 1993, pp. 3–20 at 10.

33 The Soviet authorities in Moscow advanced a Law of Secession in spring 1990 which suggested that in a referendum about secession, only a vote of more than 2/3 of the population in favour of secession would legitimate it. This margin could have nullified the Latvian and Estonian desires for independence.

34 In Estonia, the idea of the Citizens' Congress was not initiated by professional politicians, but initially suggested in a newspaper article written by a pensioner, Harald Tillemann.

35 It is presumed that in Estonia, approxiamately 90 % of the citizens of voting age voted for the Estonian Citizens' Congress. See E. Sarv, *Õiguse vastu ei saa ükski…*, p. 219.

representatives received observer status at the Estonian and Latvian Citizens' Congresses.

The Estonian and Latvian Citizens' Congresses played an important role in the decisions and processes leading to the restoration of independence in 1991. Both served as watchdogs of sorts when legitimate State power had not yet been restored, and put political pressure on the Supreme Councils so that the latter bodies—elected both by citizens and Soviet era immigrants—would not depart from the idea of *restoring* the independence lost in 1940. In Estonia, the new Constitution, adopted in a referendum on June 28, 1992, was drafted by the Constitutional Assembly, to which both the Supreme Council and the Estonian Citizens' Congress elected 50 % of the members.

Most importantly from the point of view of this section in our study, the rationale of the Latvian and Estonian citizenship laws was born in the Estonian and Latvian Congresses. Authors advocating more liberal citizenship rights in the Baltic States have therefore offered a somewhat critical assessment of the Estonian and Latvian Congresses.[36]

d *Baltic Debates about the Political Rights of Russian-Speaking Settlers in the Early 1990s*

As already indicated, the Baltic independence movements in the late 1980s began with the proposition that the Baltic States, being illegally annexed in 1940, did not become extinct as subjects of international law and remained occupied territories from the point of view of international law. Earlier, the author of the present thesis came to the conclusion that Soviet rule, even though annexation was a fact, can be called occupation, although it is debatable whether the 1949 Geneva Conventions became formally applicable in the Baltic States.

The Baltic independence movements invoked the argument that State-sponsored mass immigration from the Soviet Union violated international legal rules on occupation, particularly the 1949 Geneva Conventions.[37] A more radical segment of the political leaders in Latvia and in Estonia argued that, according to international law, the Baltic republics would now, upon termination of occupation, be entitled to demand that the Soviet settlers leave.

---

36 See e.g. Lieven, *op. cit.*, p. 274 *et seq.* and p. 307. Critically also G. Smith, 'When nations challenge and nations rule: Estonia and Latvia as ethnic democracies', in: 33 *International Politics*, March 1996, p. 31.

37 See Convention relative to the Treatment of Civilian Persons in Time of War, Art. 49, 12 August 1949, UNTS, vol. 75, p.

However, radical political proposals and legal interpretations did not correspond with the perceptions of people who had moved to live in the Baltic republics during the Soviet period. The USSR was a totalitarian State and had not told its citizens the truth about how the Baltic republics 'became' members of the USSR in 1940. In this sense, most Soviet immigrants entered the Baltic States in a different psychological and political climate than, for instance, Israeli settlers in the occupied territories. At the point of restoration of independence, many Soviet-era immigrants had lived in the Baltic States for several decades, many were born there, and had started to perceive the Baltic countries as their new home.

For these reasons, the initial sporadic calls in the early 1990s demanding that the mainly Russian-speaking immirgants should return to their countries of origin were unrealistic at the outset. However, there remained concerns about the political loyalty of especially those Soviet-era immigrants who had not learned the Baltic languages, and thus had little access to the political life of the re-emerging Baltic communities.[38] Therefore, in citizenship matters, automatic conferral of citizenship on everybody living in Estonia and Latvia by 1991 was rejected.

As a consequence, Soviet settlers in Estonia and Latvia were not granted automatic citizenship rights. They could choose Russian (or Ukrainian, etc) citizenship and if they did not wish to obtain this, they remained alien residents who could subsequently apply for Estonian or Latvian citizenship through naturalization.[39] At the same time, those ethnic Russians whose ancestors had been, or who themselves had been citizens in 1940, regained their citizenship automatically.

e *Baltic Nationality and Naturalization Laws*

i Estonia

After restoring independence, Estonia highlighted the principle of continuity of citizenship and on February 26, 1992, reintroduced the *1938* Law on Citizenship, as amended in 1940. Estonian citizens were defined as those persons who

38 According to information provided by Teimuraz Ramishvili from the Foreign Ministry of Russia, independence was supported by '20 to 40 percent of Russian speakers' in Estonia. One is surprised that Ramishvili argues in this context that 'It would not be amiss to recall today that Latvia and Estonia in no small measure owe their independence to the vote of their Russian speakers.' See T. Ramishvili, 'Latvia and Estonia: Human Rights Violations in the Center of Europe', 44 *International Affairs* 1998, p. 117.

39 See J. Bojars, 'The Citizenship and Human Rights Regulation in the Republic of Latvia', 39 *Osteuropa Recht* 1993, No. 2, pp. 132–145.

had been Estonian citizens before June 16, 1940, and their direct descendants. All persons who had moved to Estonia after the inception of the Soviet occupation or who were born in Estonia to parents who were not Estonian citizens, could apply for citizenship. Naturalization procedures entailed three main requirements: (1) knowledge of the Estonian language, (2) two years of permanent residence prior to application, beginning on March 30, 1990 at the latest, and one year afterwards, and (3) an age minimum of 18 years or, if younger, permission from parents or guardians.

The new Estonian Law on Citizenship was adopted on January 19, 1995 and took force on April 1, 1995. It stipulated that aliens could apply for Estonian citizenship through naturalization. The naturalization requirements were as follows (Art. 6): the applicant must (1) show five years of permanent residence in Estonia plus one year after registering an application; (2) be at least fifteen years of age; (3) know the Estonian language in accordance with the requirements provided for by law; (4) know the Estonian Constitution and the Law on Citizenship; (5) have a permanent legal income; (6) demonstrate loyalty to the Estonian State; and (7) take the loyalty oath.

According to the 1995 *Law on Citizenship*, the following groups could not apply for Estonian citizenship: (1) foreign military personnel in active service; (2) persons who had been employed by the USSR security and intelligence organizations; (3) persons convicted of a serious criminal offence and imprisoned for over one year, if not rehabilitated, or with a record of repeated sentencing; and (4) persons without permanent income.

The 1993 Estonian *Law on Aliens* introduces the category of permanent residents which includes both Estonian citizens and aliens residing in Estonia who possess a permanent residence permit (Art. 4(1)). The latter persons—usually stateless persons who are permanent residents—may be entitled to a so-called 'aliens' passport.' Thus, subject to more detailed requirements, Estonia agreed to grant Soviet-era immigrants work and residence permits and issue alien passports to those individuals who had become stateless.

ii Latvia

On October 15, 1991, the Supreme Council of the Republic of Latvia adopted the Resolution on the Renewal of Republic of Latvia Citizens Rights and Fundamental Principles of Naturalization, the preamble of which states:

> The premise according to which the citizenship question is dealt with [is] that the aggregate body of the citizens of the Republic of Latvia, as identified by the 1919 Law on Citizenship, continues to exist, irrespective

> of the loss of the State's sovereign power in consequence of the 1940 occupation.

Moreover, the 1991 Latvian Resolution declared that the September 7, 1940 USSR Decree on the Order in which the Lithuanian, Latvian and Estonian SSR Citizens are Granted USSR Citizenship was null and void *ab initio,* and that the rights of Latvian citizens were to be restored. Only those residents who were citizens on June 17, 1940 and their descendants could thus take part in the elections to the Latvian Parliament (the Fifth *Saeima*) in 1993.

The underlying principle of Latvia's citizenship regulation was crystallized in the 1994 Law on Citizenship. Article 12 of this Law stipulated that all permanent residents of Latvia, regardless of ethnic, religious or social background, could apply for citizenship. The naturalization requirements are (1) residence in Latvia for a minimum of five years counting from May 4, 1990, (2) knowledge of the Latvian language, Constitution and history, (3) a loyalty oath to the Republic, and (4) a legitimate source of income.

Certain categories of individuals were not entitled to apply for Latvian citizenship (Art. 11). These were (1) individuals who acted anti-constitutionally after January 13, 1991, if established by a court decree, (2) who are or have been members of foreign security or armed forces, if that fact is established according to procedures set by law, (3) or who have served criminal sentences of more than one year.

The Law on the Status of Former USSR Citizens Who are not Citizens of Latvia or any other State determined that citizens of the former USSR who lived in Latvia on July 1, 1992, and were not citizens of Latvia or any other State, were permanent residents. The Law guarantees human rights, including the right to free movement, to permanent residents in Latvia (Art. 2).

In both Latvia and Estonia, diplomatic protection was extended to stateless persons who were permanent residents of those countries.

iii Lithuania

In 1989, Lithuania adopted the Law on Citizenship, later superseded by the 1991 Law on Citizenship. The 1989 Law stipulated that permanent residents of Lithuania who were not citizens could automatically—through the principle of continuity of Lithuanian citizenship—opt for Lithuanian citizenship within a period of two years. They had to prove permanent residence and take an oath. Thus, Soviet-era immigrants were enitled to opt for Lithuanian citizenship through a simplified naturalization procedure, although they were considered not having it *ipso facto.* Lithuania thus avoided the problem of statelessness for some of its Soviet-era immigrants, although its underlying logic of citizenship was the same as in Estonia and Latvia, namely State continuity with pre-1940 Lithuania.[40]

f *Acceptance by the International Community of Continuity of the Nationality Principle in Estonian and Latvian Citizenship Laws*

Restoration of nationality in Estonia and Latvia, by which a sizable number of Soviet-era immigrants became stateless residents, has elicited mixed reactions from among the international community.[41] Most international actors and analysts recognize that the issue was a difficult one of conflicting interests and legal principles. A UN report on Estonia and Latvia stated that:

> the specific factual situation of annexation accompanied by the influx of very large numbers of persons into a small State with a different ethnic origin, followed by 50 years of settlement and multi-ethnic coexistence, followed by the re-emergence of the original State as an independent entity, does not seem to have been envisaged by drafters of the relevant [human rights] instruments.[42]

The fact that Estonia and Latvia did not accord automatic citizenship to the immigrants of the Soviet period has been criticized by the Russian Federation as discriminatory. The international law scholar Stanislav Chernichenko seems to sum up the Russian critique when he writes that '[*t*]*he authorities of Latvia and Estonia continue to use the events that happened in the Baltic area in 1940 as a pretext for limiting the rights of the Russian-speaking population which lives in their territory*.[43] Russia has invoked the 1991 Fundamental Treaties with Estonia and Latvia which in Articles 2 and 3 envisage for residents the right to choose their citizenship in accordance with the laws of the respective States. Russia and the two Baltic States have interpreted this stipulation differently: while Russia laid emphasis at the 'right to choose citizenship', Estonia

40 For policy-oriented overviews, see V. Popovski, 'Citizenship and Ethno-politics in Lithuania', 33 *International Politics*, March 1996, pp. 45–55 and L.W. Barrington, 'Nations, States, and Citizens: An Explanation of the Citizenship Policies in Estonia and Lithuania', in: 21 *Review of Central and East European Law* 1995 No. 2, pp. 103–148.

41 For policy-oriented overviews, see V. Popovski, 'Citizenship and Ethno-politics in Lithuania', 33 *International Politics*, March 1996, pp. 45–55 and L.W. Barrington, 'Nations, States, and Citizens: An Explanation of the Citizenship Policies in Estonia and Lithuania', in: 21 *Review of Central and East European Law* 1995 No. 2, pp. 103–148.

42 Report of the Secretary-General: Situation of Human Rights in Estonia and Latvia, October 26, 1993, UN Doc. A/48/511, at p. 7.

43 S. Chernichenko, 'Ethnic Russians in the Baltics', in: 44 *International Affairs* 1998, p. 118.

and Latvia have insisted that the qualification 'in accordance with the laws of the respective State' only includes the right to apply for citizenship, subject to naturalization conditions.[44] According to this interpretation, Estonia and Latvia only committed themselves to not refusing naturalization to those settlers who wished to become citizens of Estonia or Latvia.

The Russian critique was shared by some Western human rights NGO s and scholars who were troubled by the fact that as the result of application of the continuity of nationality principle in Latvia and Estonia, a considerable segment of the population—mostly Russian speakers—became stateless.[45] For this reason, some authors have questioned the legitimacy of the State continuity principle in matters of citizenship: '*On the whole this seems a harmless legal fiction, except when the States resurrect laws such as Estonia's 1938 Citizenship law which discriminates against the forty per cent of its population that are Russian settlers from after that date*.[46]

However, this kind of accentuation of the legal status of and human rights situation in Latvia and in Estonia represented a minority view. Generally, the international community seems to have recognized that the principle of continuity of the Baltic nationalities was acceptable under international law.[47] This is not so surprising in light of the fact that a majority of the members of the international community had recognized the restoration of the Baltic States in 1991.

There is an observable tendency in some human rights analyses to be blind with respect to other fudamental principles of international law[48] and to see

44 See the remarks of H.-J. Uibopuu, in: 'Das Recht der Staatensukzession', *BDGV*, Bd. 35, p. 557.

45 See e.g. F. de Varennes, 'Non-Citizens and Minorities in Estonia and Their Economic and Social Opportunities', in: S. Trifunovska (ed.) *Minorities in Europe. Croatia, Estonia and Slovakia*, The Hague: Asser Press, 1999, pp. 123–139; J. L. Blackman, 'State Successions and Statelessness: The Emerging Right to an Effective Nationality Under International Law', 19 *Michigan JIL* 1998, pp. 1141–1194 at 1193 and G. Ginsburgs, *From Soviet to Russian International Law. Studies in Continuity and Change*, The Hague: Nijhoff, 1998, p. 218 *et seq.*; R. C. Visek, 'Creating the Ethnic Electorate through Legal Restorationism: Citizenhip Rights in Estonia', 38 *Harvard JIL* 1997, pp. 315–376.

46 C. Gray, *Self-determination and the Breakup of the Soviet Union*, in: 12 YBEL 1992, p. 483. See for similar arguments: R.C. Visek, *Creating the Ethnic Electorate... in Estonia*, 38 Harvard ILJ 1997, pp. 315 *et seq.*

47 See e.g. Jan De Mayer and Christos Rozakis, *Report on Human Rights in the Republic of Latvia*, the Council of Europe Parliamentary Assembly Doc. AS/Ad hoc.-Bur-EE (43) 4, 20 January 1992, 246, para 4; UN Secretary-General Report, *Situation of Human Rights in Estonia and Latvia*, A/48/511, 26 October 1993, paras. 28–30.

48 For a general critique of exaggerations in some human rights advocacy, see: A. Pellet: *Human Rightism and International Law*, Memorial Lecture in honour of Gilberto Amado on 18 July 2000 at the ILC's International Law Seminar.

human rights as above anything else. Thus, some human rights advocates who condemned Estonian or Latvian citizenship policies persistently ignored the question concerning the legal status of the Baltic republics, and concentrate solely upon the fact that a significant minority of the population became stateless, as if the Baltic case was one of classic secession.

The main troublesome question has been why the language requirements—the legitimacy of which as such has been confirmed by pertinent international institutions and observers[49]—have proven an obstacle for some members of the Russian speaking immigrant population of the Soviet era.[50] The conflict has also been interpreted as one between collective and individual human rights, a dilemma that has traditionally been resolved in favour of individual human rights in Western scholarship.[51] The defence of Estonia and Latvia for their statehood, language and culture through their citizenship laws of the 1990s did not therefore fit smoothly into the predominant discourse of human rights in the West.[52]

For humanitarian and political considerations, the international community took the view that demographic changes in Latvia and Estonia during the Soviet annexation period could not just be wiped out by the Baltic State continuity argument. The populations of Estonia and Latvia had become ethnically much more heterogeneous during the Soviet annexation period, and the majority of Russophone settlers wished to stay in the restored Baltic States. Besides human rights considerations, it was also clear that the long-term socio-political exclusion of an important segment of the population could

49 See e.g. the above quoted Report of the Secretary-General of the UN: 'Since the national identity of Estonians is intimately linked to their language, which is not spoken anywhere else in the world, it is important and legitimate for Estonians to give a high priority to the active use of the Estonian language in all spheres of activity in Estonia.' See *Situation...*, *ibid.* See also J.-M. Henckaerts, *Mass Expulsion in Modern International Law and Practice*, 1995, pp. 93, 96.

50 Georg Brunner even highlights among the reasons the 'linguistic resistance' (*Sprachresistenz*) of some Baltic Russians. See G. Brunner, 'Die rechtliche Lage der Minderheiten in Mittel-, Ost- and Südosteuropa', in: 40 *Osteuroparecht*, September 1994, pp. 157–177 at 166.

51 See e.g. P. Juviler, 'Are Collective Rights Anti-Human? Theories on self-Determination and Practice in Soviet Successor States', in: *Netherlands Quarterly of Human Rights* 1993, pp. 267–282 and also L. Mälksoo, 'Language Rights in International Law: Why the Phoenix Is Still in the Ashes', 12 *Florida JIL* 2000, pp. 431–465 at 443.

52 See for an excellent polemic: T.M. Franck, 'Are Human Rights Universal?', in: *Foreign Affairs* Jan/Feb 2001, pp. 191–204 who summarizes the ongoing struggle 'between the forces of Lockian individual liberty and those championing communitarian values' (p. 195), and argues for individuals' liberation 'from predetermined definitions of racial, religious, and national identities.' (p. 201.)

potentially have destabilizing effects upon the peace and security in the Baltic Sea region.[53]

Changed social and political circumstances influence the perception of law, which is why the principle *ex factis oritur ius* was accorded significance by the international community, and—following some international pressure—by the respective States themselves. The position of the international community was that whatever the legal status of the Baltic States during Soviet-era immigration, there is still a need to begin from existing facts (*normative Kraft des Faktischen!*) when sustainable solutions concerning human beings are sought. For example, the OSCE High Commissioner on National Minorities, Max van der Stoel, accepted the principle that the Soviet settlers could not be considered nationals automatically, but argued that there was a presumption to the effect that the long-term residents had the right to acquire nationality.[54] The UN Human Rights Committee expressed '*its concern that a significantly large segment of the population, particularly members of the Russian-speaking minority, are unable to enjoy Estonian citizenship due to the plethora of criteria established by law, and the stringency of the language criterion...*'[55]

Estonia and Latvia were entitled, in the opinion of the international legal community, to base their nationality laws on the State continuity principle. However, in many ways international institutions took the view that these two States would do wisely to extend nationality to persons who had settled in their territories during the Soviet period and who now had no other citizenship in sight.[56] The requirement introduced in Estonia and Latvia that Soviet-era immigrants would have to learn the respective State languages to be eligible for citizenship, has been accepted as reasonable. At the same time, Estonia was pressured to relax its initial language requirement somewhat and Latvia to remove its initial annual quota (citizenship windows).[57]

---

53 See Lieven, *op. cit.*, p. 174. Anatol Lieven quite frankly presents the pragmatic point of view of many Western observers when he writes that '[*i*]*n my discussions with Balts over the guaranteed rights for the Russian minority, the argument has usually been at cross purposes. They have argued in terms of international law, historical justice, and specific Baltic interests. I have replied on the basis of pragmatism, practical risks, and the interests of Europe and of the former Soviet region as a whole.*' See *ibid.* pp. 174–5.

54 See 'Recommendations by the CSCE High Commissioner on National Minorities, Mr Max van der Stoel, upon his visits to Estonia, Latvia and Lithuania', 14 *Human Rights Law Journal* 1993, p. 216 at 217.

55 UN Doc. CCPR/C/79/Add.59 of 3.11.1995, para. 12.

56 So J. Quigley, 'Mass Displacement and the Individual Right of Return', in: 68 *BYBIL* 1997, p. 103.

57 See Quigley, *ibid.*

Estonia and Latvia, although restored States under international law, have thus not been accorded complete liberty in regulating citizenship policies after 1991. A fundamentalist and exclusivist approach to the continuity of nationality principle has been rejected. The normative expectation of the international and European institutions is that the problem of individuals without citizenship will not remain but will be solved. For example, in 2022, the debate has intensified at least in Estonia again whether to solve the problem of 'gray passports' for good by offering to the people concerned the opportunity of Estonian citizenship, without the usual naturalization requirements such as the language test.

g *Conclusion: No Unrestricted Restoration of Nationality in the Baltic Case*

In a recent article,[58] the US legal scholar John Quigley compared the Austrian (1938–1945) and Alsace-Lorraine (1871–1919) cases with those of Estonia and Latvia (1940–1991). The Versailles Peace Treaty allowed France to refuse to naturalize its post-1871 German settlers, with the exception of persons in Alsace-Lorraine who held citizenship in 1871, or their descendants.[59] Similarly, Austria did not offer Austrian nationality to Germans who had settled in Austria between 1938 and 1945, but extended it only to persons who had held it in 1938, plus their descendants.[60] Quigley traces both cases back to the rule that 'if a State occupies foreign territory, whether by aggresion or not, it may not bring its nationals to settle in the territory while it remains an occupant.' Regarding pressure from European institutions such as the CSCE (now OSCE) on Estonia and Latvia to extend nationality to Soviet settlers, Quigley concludes:

> Other States apparently considered Estonia and Latvia to be States formed as a result of the dissolution of the USSR, rather than as States whose sovereignty continued during a period of belligerent occupation and unlawful annexation. Had the latter analysis, urged by Latvia and Estonia, been accepted, the principle reflected in the law of the belligerent occupation would prevail.[61]

---

58 J. Quigley, *ibid.*, p. 99 *et seq.*

59 Treaty of Peace with Germany (Versailles), Art. 79, Annexes 1, 2, 3 (28 June 1919).

60 See Gesetz vom 10. Juli 1945 über die Überleitung in die österreichische Staatsbürgerschaft (Staatsbürgerschaft-Überleitungsgesetz-St-ÜG) § 1, *Staatsgesetzblatt für die Republik Österreich*, 1945, p. 81 (no. 59).

61 Quigley, *ibid.* p. 104.

Nevertheless, it is questionable to use Germany's annexation of Alsace-Lorraine (1870–1919) as an example of an illegal occupation and annexation, opposing it to the Soviet occupation of the Baltic States as an accepted case of incorporation. In terms of international law, rather the contrary is the case. France's exclusion in 1919 of German settlers in Alsace-Lorraine from citizenship rights was 'victor's justice' rather than an instance of application of international laws prohibiting the use of force—which did not prohibit annexation upon a successful war (which was formally initiated by France) in 1871.[62] Germany did have sovereignty over Alsace and Lorraine between 1870 and 1918.[63] Moreover, Quigley's comparison of the Austrian and the Baltic cases leaves out of consideration not only the differences of scale of the settlement policies during the illegal annexation period, and differences of duration, but also important developments in human rights law (which Quigley otherwise advocates in his article) which suggests that scaling in citizenship matters had to be done differently after 1991, compared to the post-World War I era.

International organizations and other actors accepted the approach taken by the Baltic States in citizenship matters, if with certain political and legal reservations. The legal status of the Baltic States as illegally annexed States did not deliver a comprehensive solution to the legal status of the Soviet-era immigrants. Soviet demographic policies were not be regarded as a nullity. Acceptance of the principle of the continuity of nationality by the international community was supplemented by developments in human rights law such as the the nondiscrimination rule,[64] and the principle of reduction of statelessness.[65] These standards in human rights law do not suggest automatic citizenship for immigrants under the period of illegal annexation; however, they have played a role in the formation of the legal framework of Baltic naturalization laws. Although Latvia and Estonia have generally implemented the recommendations of international organizations such as the OSCE, and elicited praise for their pragmatism,[66] they still had to step back from their initial, more restrictive approach to the nationality problem. According to some authors, this even proves that in the field of citizenship rights, there has

62 But see Quigley p. 100 (*'In the cases of Alsace-Lorraine and Austria, the view of the international community was that the annexations by Germany, in 1871 and 1938 respectively, were unlawful.'*)

63 See also W. Schätzel, *Die Annexion im Völkerrecht* (1920), reprinted in 1959, p. 151.

64 See already E.W. Vierdag, *The Concept of Discrimination in International Law*, The Hague: Nijhoff, 1973.

65 See further Ziemele, *op. cit.*, p. 229 *et seq.*

66 See e.g. P. van Krieken, 'Estonia's Minorities and Aliens: Time for a 'Yes-Campaign', in: S. Trifunovska (ed.) *Minorities in Europe. Croatia, Estonia and Slovakia*, 1999, pp. 105–122 at no.

been a tendency in international legal practice to handle the case of the Baltic States *de facto* as one of succession.[67] Certain human rights obligations contained in the UN GA Resolution on Nationality of natural persons in relation to the succession of States[68] were thus deemed relevant in the Baltic context. Nevertheless, in the end it is also worth emphasizing that the core idea of Baltic citizenship policies since the 1990s supported the State continuity thesis. Illegal annexation and State continuity had created *sui generis* circumstances which made citizenship policies – and the fact that in Estonia and Latvia there was no automatic citizenship for Soviet era immigrants – acceptable in the international practice.

4 Changes with Respect to State Territories: Border Disputes since Restoration of the Independence of the Baltic States

During the first half of the 1990s, through diplomatic negotiations with the Russian Federation, Estonia and Latvia sought to restore the pre-1940 State borders with Russia, or at least to achieve what one author called a 'dignified compromise.'[69] Their efforts have not been successful, partly because the Baltic States have failed to consolidate viable international support for their position. A closer look at the Russian-Baltic boundaries disputes follows.

This analysis concentrates on the issue of State boundaries, although the general issue at stake, from the legal point of view, is the continued validity or non-validity of the 1920 Peace Treaties. For instance, among the issues having their sources in conflicting views about the validity of the Peace Treaties (and not to be discussed here in detail), are Baltic claims that Russia should return certain items of cultural property to their legitimate owners in the Baltic States.[70]

67 See e.g. M.T. Kamminga, 'State Succession in Respect of Human Rights Treaties', 7 *EJIL* 1996, pp. 469–484, pp. 479–80. Cf. Koskenniemi, 'The Present State of Research…', 1996, p. 142.

68 UN GA Res. 55/153, Annex, December 12, 2000.

69 E. Mattisen, *Searching for a Dignified Compromise. The Estonian-Russian Border 1000 Years,* Tallinn: ILO, 1996.

70 Estonia, for instance, has claimed rights to a museological collection that belonged to the University of Dorpat (Tartu), and was evacuated to the University of Voronezh in Russia during World War I. In the Tartu Peace Treaty, concluded on February 2, 1920, Soviet Russia accepted the obligation to return these collections to Estonia. However, the USSR had not fulfilled this obligation when Estonia was occupied and annexed in 1940. After restoration of Estonia's independence, the return of these collections to Tartu has been

a *Estonia*

i Unilateral Corrections of the State Border by the USSR

The border between the Republic of Estonia and Soviet Russia was established in the Tartu Peace Treaty of February 2, 1920. It was a result of the war of secession (War of Independence) of 1918–1920 in which the Estonian army managed to repulse attempts by the Red Army to (re-)establish control over Estonia. The border established by the Tartu Peace Treaty was the subject of long discussions at the Tartu Peace Conference. Although the established border was finally a compromise between the initial Russian and Estonian proposals, the agreed compromise left some villages and townships with predominantly ethnic Russian population within the borders of the Republic of Estonia. The Estonian-Russian border, as established in the Tartu Peace Treaty, was respected by the Soviet government until the occupation of Estonia in 1940. The Russian-Estonian Pact of Mutual Assistence, concluded on September 28, 1939, referred explicitly to the inviolability of the Tartu Peace Treaty, and thus to the borders established by it.

After the annexation of Estonia and the creation of the Estonian SSR, that border was changed by a unilateral decision of the Soviet authorities in August 1944. With the Decree of the Presidium of the Supreme Soviet of the Soviet Union 'On Formation of the Pskov Oblast within the structure of the RSFSR' of August 23, 1944, 1,135 square kilometers of the territory of the Estonian SSR were annexed to the Russian RSFSR.[71] The Decree was grounded by the 'repetitious requests of the people' in the respective territory and by the

---

the object of until now inconclusive interstate negotiations. Recently, a catalogue of the collections was published through collaboration of historians from Voronezh and Tartu. Similarly, Russia has neglected the Estonian demands for the return of the official regalia of the pre-1940 Estonian President. After the occupation and annexation of Estonia in 1940, the President's official medal was taken to Moscow's State Archives where it remains. In October 1996, the individual in charge of the Baltic desk at the Russian Foreign Ministry, Aleksandr Udaltsov, argued that '[w]e do not have any legal ground to give this costly and precious work of art to Estonia.' See T. Mattson, T. Sildam, 'Venemaa välisministeerium peab Eesti presidendi ametitunnuse tagastamise küsimust praegu lahendamatuks' (In the View of the Russian Foreign Ministry, the Question of the Restitution of the Official Regalia of the Estonian President is Currently Unsolvable), *Postimees*, 06.10.1996. In November 2000, the Russian ambassador to Estonia, Aleksei Glukhov, noted that the return of 'some of your symbolic regalia' is 'practically decided.' However, the ambassador referred to the 'situation of ethnic Russians in Estonia', and noted that for the return of the regalia 'a different kind of attitude was necessary.' See A. Ammar, Gluhhov: 'Eesti peab tänama, mitte ootama vabandamist', (Glukhov: Estonia should thank, not wait for an apology), *Eesti Päevaleht*, November 15, 2000.

71 Decree of the Presidium of the Supreme Soviet of the Soviet Union 'On Formation of the Pskov Oblast within the Structure of the RSFSR', in: *Collected Laws of the USSR and Decrees*

appeal of the Presidium of the Supreme Soviet of the Estonian SSR, filed a day before, on August 22, 1944.[72]

The timing of this 'self-contracting' transfer of territory has been pointed out by historians.[73] In August 1944, the Soviet army was advancing in the German-occupied Baltic States. However, patriotic forces in the Baltic States were organizing military resistance against the advancing Soviet forces, and planned to reproclaim and re-establish independence. Moreover, the general outcome of World War II was still open to question. The Western allies still had the option of concluding a separate peace treaty with Germany. The Soviet leadership might have been afraid that its allies would demand application of the principles of the Atlantic Charter with respect to the Baltic States. Therefore, Moscow was eager, at a minimum, to correct the border, and present the international community with a *fait accompli.*

The new Soviet-imposed border between the Estonian SSR and the Russian RSFSR did not correspond to the ethnic composition of the affected territories. For instance, of the 4965 people living in the township of Vilo, entirely incorporated in the Pskov Oblast, 66.3 per cent of the population was Estonian and 33.7 per cent was Russian. Of the 69 villages in this county, 49 had a majority of Estonian inhabitants, and in 30 of them, the population was entirely Estonian.[74] Similar dismissal of ethnic considerations occurred elsewhere during the border correction.

Another piece of Estonian territory, as established in the Tartu Peace Treaty, was cut off from the Estonian SSR with the Decree of the Presidium of the Supreme Soviet of the USSR of November 24, 1944, 'On the allocation of settlements on the east bank of the Narva river to the territory of the Leningrad oblast.' On January 18, 1945, this decision was formally reconfirmed by the Presidium of the Supreme Soviet of the Estonian SSR.[75]

This way of amending the border between the Soviet republics, as carried out by the Presidiums of the Supreme Soviets, did not correspond to the requirements of Soviet constitutional law. Neither the Constitution of the USSR nor the Constitution of the ESSR authorized the Presidiums of the

---

of the Presidium of the Supreme Soviet of the USSR, 1938–1975, Moscow, 1 975' p. 93–94. Reprinted in Mattisen, *op. cit.*, p. 141.

72 See *ibid.* See also Mattisen, p. 73.

73 Mattisen, *op. cit.*, p. 72–73.

74 Mattisen, *op. cit.*, p. 74.

75 See Decree of the Presidium of the Supreme Soviet of the Estonian SSR, regarding the establishment of borders between Viru County and Leningrad Oblast, Tallinn, January 18, 1945, Eesti NSV Teataja, 10.02.1945, art. 59, p. 58.

Supreme Soviets to change the territories of the Soviet republics.[76] This could have been done only by the highest legislative power—the Supreme Soviet.[77] At the demand of Moscow, the border between the Russian SFSR and the Estonian SSR was altered for a third time in favour of the former on September 9, 1957.[78] Although this degree allocated 'in exchange' some Estonian settlements back to the territory of the Estonian SSR, it marked altogether a further diminishing of the territory of the Estonian SSR.

Thus, when the independence of the Republic of Estonia was restored in August, 1991, approximately 5 % of the pre-1940 territory (2,334 square kilometers) had meanwhile been transferred to the Russian Federation.

ii The Rocky Road to Conclusion of the Estonian-Russian border treaties of 2014

As early as 1990, before its independence was restored, Estonia raised a claim for restoration of the State border as established in the February 2, 1920 Estonian-Russian Peace Treaty of Tartu. On September 1991, the Supreme Council of the Republic of Estonia declared null and void all decrees and resolutions of the Presidium of the Supreme Soviet of the Estonian SSR regarding the alteration of the border in 1944–1957, as violating the Tartu Peace Treaty and thus international law.[79] The issue of the State border was to be settled by diplomatic negotiations between the Russian Federation and the Republic of Estonia.

Estonian-Russian border consultations started in November 1991. Initially, as noted by the Estonian historian Edgar Mattisen, the Russian side 'did not even want to hear about the border issue,'[80] and tried to limit discussion to questions related to the border regime. Later, Russia still took a legal stand on the Estonian border claim. According to the Russian view, the Tartu Peace Treaty of 1920 had lost its validity in 1940, when Estonia 'entered into' the USSR. The reliance of Estonia (and Latvia) on the 1920 Peace Treaties upset the Russian legislators to the extent that in the summer of 1993 they were preparing for

---

76 See also for the peculiarities of the practice: G. Shinkaretskaya, 'Succession and the Borders of the Russian Federation', in: 1 *Moscow JIL* 1995, No. 4, pp. 50–62 at 52 ('... the central authorities had free rein to carve up the republics the way the ruling party wanted.')

77 Cf. Mattisen, *op. cit.*, p. 75.

78 See Decree of the Presidium of the Supreme Soviet of the Estonian SSR of September 9, 1957, 'On partial alteration of the border between the Estonian SSR and the RSFSR', referred in Mattisen, *op. cit.*, p. 76.

79 See Mattisen, *op. cit.*, p. 87.

80 Mattisen, *op. cit.*, p. 92.

denunciation of the respective peace treaties. On July 12, 1993, the Presidium of the Supreme Soviet of Russia even approved a draft law proposing to the President and the government that the issue of annulment of the 1920 Estonian-Russian and Latvian-Russian Peace Treaties be presented to the parliament for consideration.[81] Ultimately, no act of formal annulment was taken by the Russian Federation.

The Constitution of the Russian Federation, adopted on December 23, 1993 by referendum, establishes the Russian State border upon the principle of the *status quo* (Article 67). Following adoption of the Constitution, President Yeltsin signed a decree on June 21, 1994, on delimitation of the Russian State border in the Estonian sector.'[82] The Russian-Estonian border was thus unilaterally delimited by Russia before the end of 1994.

Initially, the Foreign Ministry of the Republic of Estonia filed protests. The Estonian Foreign Ministry declared on August 12, 1994 that the only legally binding document which stipulates the border between Estonia and Russia remains the Tartu Peace Treaty, since 'the 1940 Soviet occupation of Estonia did not affect the validity of this treaty.'[83] The Estonian side also pointed out that 'Estonia has repeatedly proposed to Russia that the question be taken to the International Court of Justice at The Hague. Estonia has always been willing to use mediation by a third nation or international organization.'[84]

In particular, Estonia wished Russia to return some predominantly Estonian (Seto) villages in the Pskov Oblast (RSFSR) that were under the jurisdiction of the Republic of Estonia before 1940. The border drawn by the Soviets in 1944/1945 had divided into halves the tiny Setu people, ethnic Estonians with a specific identity and culture. Due to the Soviet unilateral drawing of the border, 8000–9000 Seto people remained under the jurisdiction of the Estonian SSR, while over 6000 belonged to Russia. In the 1990s, around 4000 ethnic Estonians (Setos) remained on the Russian side of the border.[85]

At the end of 1994, a compromise course was taken. The Estonian government declared its readiness to agree to a new Russian-Estonian border that would differ from the border as envisaged by the Peace Treaty of 1920. This stepping back by Estonia from the initial position (which demanded restoration of the

81 Mattisen, *op. cit.*, p. 94. Cf. also with Loeber, *op. cit.*, p. 544.

82 Ukas of the president of the Russian Federation of June 21, 1994, on Demarcation of the Land Border between Estonia and Russia. Sobranie Zakonodatelstva Rossiskoi Federatsi, No. 9, Item 930 (1994).

83 See the Press Release of the Foreign Ministry of the Republic of Estonia, dated August 12, 1994, reprinted in Mattisen, *op. cit.*, p. 162.

84 See ibid, at p. 162.

85 See Mattisen, *op. cit.*, p. 101.

Tartu Peace Treaty border) presented some problems from the point of view of Estonian constitutional law. Article 122 of the Estonian Constitution, adopted by referendum on June 28, 1992, stipulates that the land border of Estonia shall be determined by the Tartu Peace Treaty of February 2, 1920, and other international border treaties. A constitutional debate evolved about whether a retreat from this demand would require amending the Estonian Constitution. Some scholars and politicians argued pragmatically that even if only one metre of the Estonian-Russian border Treaty of 1920 was re-established, with the rest of the border determined by *other* treatie(s), the formal requirement of constitutionality would have been fulfilled. Although several other scholars were sceptical about this interpretation of the Constitution, the general consensus that emerged in Estonia was that the new government policy of accepting the *de facto* border with Russia had become irrevocable both from the legal and political points of view.

When the Russians showed no change in their position, and settlement of all border disputes was a *de facto* condition for Estonia's accession to the EU and NATO, Estonia accepted the existing control border as final and dropped all demands for changes as amended in favour of Russia by the Soviet decrees in 1944, 1945 and 1957. Initially, Estonia conditioned this concession on the demand that in the new border treaty, Russia would explicidy recognize the continuity of the Republic of Estonia, and thus the continued legal application of the 1920 Tartu Peace Treaty *as such* (that is, notwithstanding the changed borders). When Russia persistently refused to do so, the Republic of Estonia took the position that conclusion of the new Estonian-Russian border treaty—which would establish the current 'control border' as the final State border—would not damage claims by Estonia that the Estonian-Russian Peace Treaty of 1920 would not lose its force under international law, even should the border provisions outlined in the 1920 Peace Treaty be changed by the new border treaty.[86]

On March 5, 1998, Estonia and Russia initialled a border agreement, the former formally acknowledging the disputed territory as part of Russia. The two border treaties (one for the land border and the other for the sea border in the Gulf of Finland) were signed in Moscow on 18 May 2005. However, when the Estonian parliament ratified the treaties, it added a preamble to the ratification bill which stipulated that the Peace Treaty of Tartu of 1920 has remained in force: only the course of the border had therewith been amended. Upon this, the Russian government announced that it would revoke its signature and

86 See information provided by the Estonian Foreign Ministry: Eesti-Vene piiriläbirääkimised (Estonian-Russian border negotiations), 4.03.1999, http:// www.vm.ee/eesti/valispol/Bilateraalsed/03piir.htm. See also Mattisen, *op. cit.*, p. 98 et seq.

the process of conclusion of the border treaties must start anew.[87] The process came to a halt for a while. The Estonian-Russian border treaties were signed again in Moscow on 18 February 2014, with certain amendments on general provisions, reflecting the priorities of both parties. As of 2022, the treaties have not been ratified by either of the two States.

b *Latvia*

i Unilateral Changes of the State Border by the USSR

The story of the Latvian-Russian border dispute was similar to the Estonian-Russian controversy. The border between the Republic of Latvia and the Russian RSFSR was established in the Latvian-Soviet Peace Treaty, concluded in Riga on August 11, 1920. However, in 1944 the USSR annexed a tract of Latvian territory, known as the district of Abrene (in Russian: Pytalovo), into the Russian RSFSR. The district has an area of about 2,000 square kilometers, about 3 % of the total area of pre-1940 Republic of Latvia. By the early 1990s, the Pytalovo district had a population of approximately 50,000 people, around 85 % of whom were ethnic Russians.[88]

Technically, the transfer of the Abrene district was initiated by decree of August 22, 1944, in which the Presidium of the Supreme Soviet of the Latvian SSR 'petitioned' at the federal level for transfer of Abrene region to the RSFSR.[89] The Presidium of the USSR Supreme Soviet satisfied the Soviet Latvian petition on the following day.[90] The rationale given in the edict was the desire to satisfy 'repeated requests' by the population in the Abrene region.[91] The Soviet Latvian border with the RSFSR was officially established by legal acts of the Latvian SSR[92] and the USSR[93] in October 1946.

---

87 See further L. Mälksoo, 'Which Continuity: The Tartu Peace Treaty of 2 February 1920, the Estonian-Russian Border Treaties of 18 May 2005, and the Legal Debate About Estonia's Legal Status in International Law', 10 *Juridica International* 2005, pp 144–149.

88 See D.A. Loeber, 'The Russian-Latvian Territorial Dispute Over Abrene. A Legacy from the Times of Soviet Rule', *The Parker School Journal of East European Law* 1995/Vol. 2 Nos. 4–5, pp. 537–538. See also A. Krassilnikow, ‚Die Staatsgrenzen der Republik Lettland nach dem Stand vom Sommer 1993', 39 *Osteuropa Recht* 1993, No. 4, pp. 281–286.

89 See the text and materials reprinted in A. Reinhards, *Lettonie-Russie...*, p. 287 *et seq.*

90 Об образований Псковской Области в составе СССР [On Founding the Pskov Oblast of the RSFSR], August 23, 1944, in Sbornik zakonov SSSR i ukazov Prezidiuma Verkhovnogo Soveta SSSR (1938–1975) at 93.

91 *Ibid.*

92 Decree of the Presidium of the Supreme Soviet of the Latvian SSR On Establishing the Border between the Latvian SSR and RSFSR, October 5, 1946.

93 Указ Президиума Верховного Совета СССР об утверждений изменений границей между Латвиской ССР и РСФСР [Edict of the Presidium of the Supreme Soviet of the USSR On Confirming the Changes to the Border between the Latvian SSR and the RSFSR], October 19, 1946.

ii The Latvian-Russian Border Dispute Since 1991

On January 22, 1992, the Latvian Parliament passed a law which asserted a claim to Abrene, declaring the Soviet decrees of 1944 on the transfer of the Abrene district to be without effect from the moment of their adoption (*ex tunc*), due to the illegal occupation and annexation of Latvia at the time.[94] The Latvian Law on State Frontiers of 1994[95] distinguished between State boundaries and a 'temporary demarcation line', referring thus to Abrene district.[96] In Latvia maps were being produced showing the disputed district as Latvian territory.[97]

Just as in the case of Estonia, the Russian Federation denied the further applicability of the 1920 Latvian-Russian Peace Treaty. However, in December 1994, Russia and Latvia concluded an agreement establishing 'border representatives' with the task of regulating all questions related to the common frontier.[98] The Latvian-Russian border treaty was concluded on March 27, 2007. The treaty recognizes the Abrene district as part of the Russian Federation and was also ratified by the parliaments in both States. Upon ratification of the border treaty, the Constitutional Court of Latvia strongly emphasized Latvia's adherence to the State continuity principle, notwithstanding Latvia having accepted the Abrene district as being part of Russia.[99]

c *The Boundaries of Lithuania*

The question of Lithuanian borders is connected to the debate about the borders of the Baltic States related to the legal status of those States. Paradoxically, Lithuania *de facto* gained territory as a consequence of the 1939 rapprochement with the USSR. By the July 1920 Moscow treaty, Lithuania gained legal title to the territory of Vilnius. However, Poland had occupied the territory of Vilnius (in Polish 'Wilno') and controlled it until the fourth Polish partitition was completed in September 1939. As compensation for Lithuania's acceptance of the Mutual Assistance Treaty in 1939, the USSR assigned the newly 'liberated' Vilnius and Suwałki regions to Lithuania.[100] The Polish government

94 Decree On the Nonrecognition of the Annexation of the Town of Abrene and the Six Communities of the Abrene District, January 22, 1992, Zinotajs, Issue Nos. 6–7, Item No. 69 (1992).

95 Zinotajs, Issue No. 23, Item No. 495 (1994).

96 Loeber, *op. cit.*, p. 543.

97 See J.B. Allcock et al. (ed.) *Border and Territorial Disputes*, 3rd edition, Longman Current Affairs, 1992, p. 35.

98 Loeber, *op. cit.*, p. 543.

99 See further I. Ziemele, 'The State Border Between Latvia and Russia and the Doctrine of the Continuity of the Republic of Latvia', 9 *Baltic YBIL* 2009, pp. 95–132.

100 Allcock et al. (ed.), p. 32.

in exile protested against the transfer of Vilnius to Lithuania, maintaining that this act lacked validity under international law.

At the end of World War II, the Lithuanian SSR created within the USSR recovered Klaipeda/Memel region in May 1950 and retained Vilnius, but the Suwałki region was restored to Poland and some territory south-east of Vilnius was allocated to the Belorussian SSR.[101] Furthermore, the newly created Kaliningrad region as a component part of the Russian RSFSR allegedly gained a sliver of territory that legally, it was sometimes argued, should have been granted to the Republic of Lithuania.[102]

After Lithuanian independence was restored, its government argued for the preservation of the *status quo* as far as the State borders were concerned.[103] However, the question of Vilnius was sometimes raised by Russian politicians, especially in connection with Estonian and Latvian territorial claims. Some Lithuanian radical nationalist politicians responded that the Russian Federation should return to Lithuania the territory awarded for Kaliningrad Oblast.[104]

However, neither Lithuania nor Russia have ever officially presented one another with territorial claims.[105] In February 2001, the Lithuanian Ambassador to the Russian Federation explained in an interview to the newspaper Izvestija: *'I declare officially: Lithuania never had neither does have any territorial claims to Kaliningrad Oblast. Even if it would be proposed to us, we would hardly take it.'*[106]

Lithuania and Byelorussia validated the Soviet administrative border with an agreement of February 6, 1995. Poland, which could have challenged Lithuania's title to Vilnius territory, has considered Lithuania to be the successor State in respect of the Polish-Soviet Agreement concerning the

101 Allcock er al. (ed.), p. 33. See also A. Gureckas, 'Lithuania's Boundaries and Territorial Claims Between Lithuania and Neighboring States', 12 *N.Y.L. Sch. J. Int'l & Comp.L.*, 1991, p. 107 *et seq.* and C. Whomerslay, 'The International Legal Status of Gdansk, Klaipeda and the Former East Prussia', 42 *ICLQ* 1993, p. 919 *et seq.*

102 Allcock *et al., op. cit.*, p. 33.

103 See the Proclamation on the Reestablishment of the Republic of Lithuania, March 11, 1990 which *inter alia* stated: 'The Lithuanian State (...) recognizes the inviolability of borders as codified in the Final Act of the Helsinki Conference on Security and Cooperation in Europe, adopted in 1975 (...).' Note that the USSR also relied on the argument of the very same Helsinki Final Act, in order to defend *its* territorial integrity, i.e. prevent the Baltic States from establishing independence.

104 Allcock et al.(eds.), *op. cit.*, p. 36.

105 Cf. G. Biger, *The Encyclopedia of International Boundaries*, Jerusalem, 1995, p. 365.

106 'Посёл Литвы Зенонас Намавичюс: Российской военной угрозы не существует', *Izvestia*, 20.02. 2001 (No. 30), p. 9.

Polish-Soviet Boundary of August 16, 1945.[107] Both Lithuania and Poland are member States of the European Union since 2004 and they no longer have a territorial dispute over Vilnius even though the two countries have sometimes argued over minority rights.

On October 24, 1997, Presidents Brazauskas and Yeltsin signed the new Russian-Lithuanian border treaty, based on the *status quo.*[108] The Lithuanian parliament ratified the treaty in March 1999 but it took longer for the Russian State Duma to ratify it. The Lithuanian-Russian border treaty finally entered into force in 2003.

d *The Border Debate: Legal Issues*

After restoration of independence, the border claims of Estonia and Latvia were based on the position that the territorial 'amputation' of the Soviet republics of Estonia and Latvia by Moscow had no more legal validity under international law than the annexation of the independent Baltic States themselves. Estonia and Latvia argued that the peace treaties of 1920, which established the Estonian-Russian and Latvian-Russian borders, had not lost their validity under international law.

From the very beginning, the Russian Federation opposed this thesis. In 1994, notwithstanding official protests by Estonia and Latvia, Russia marked the administrative borders (or demarcation lines) with Estonia and Latvia as definitive State borders. Russia also rejected the occasional Estonian and Latvian proposals to present the issue to the International Court of Justice.

From the point of view of the illegality of Soviet annexation in 1940 and recognition of the restoration of statehood by the international community, Estonia and Latvia had strong cases for reinstating their pre-World War II frontiers with Russia. According to Estonia and Latvia, Russia was not entitled to invoke change of circumstances (*clausula rebus sic stantibus*) with respect to the peace treaties of 1920. Under Article 62 para 2 of the 1969 Vienna Convention on the Law of Treaties, a fundamental change of circumstances may not be invoked as a ground for terminating or withdrawing from a treaty if the treaty establishes a boundary or if the fundamental change is the result of breach by the party invoking it either of an obligation under the treaty or of any

107 See R. Szafarz, *op. cit.*, pp. 223–4.

108 See further E. Franckx and A. Pauwels, 'Lithuanian-Russian Boundary Agreement of October 1997: To Be or Not To Be?', in: *Liber Amicorum Jaenicke*, Berlin: Springer, 1998, pp. 63–95.

other international obligation under the treaty or of any other international obligation owed to any other party to the treaty.[109]

Lawyers analyzing the boundar issues have also examined the relevance of the legal principle of *uti possidetis iuris* in the Baltic-Russian boundaries dispute.[110] However, in the *Burkina Faso and the Republic of Mali Frontier Dispute Case* in 1986, the ICJ decided that legal title is accorded preeminence over effective possession.[111] In legal terms, it is therefore difficult to see why the principle *ex injuria ius non oritur* must, as Müllerson seems to argue in the Baltic case, be balanced with the principle *uti possidetis*: '*...we have a situation which is not rare in international law: two conflicting principles, both of which express real values, pointing toward different, even opposite, solutions.*'[112] However, during the post-Soviet decades, Russia has itself started to take distance from the uti possidetis principle in post-Soviet space, especially when it wanted to prevent former Soviet republics such as Georgia in 2008 and Ukraine in 2014 from joining NATO in the future.[113]

In the view of Vladimir Lenin, the Tartu Peace Treaty between Soviet Russia and the Republic of Estonia of February 2, 1920 had a 'global-historical significance.'[114] The importance of this treaty was highlighted by Soviet international law scholars for whom the peace treaty with Estonia was the beginning of the end of the 'bourgeois' blockade erected against the young Soviet State.[115] Upon the collapse of the USSR in 1991, the Russian Federation insisted that the peace treaties came to and end in 1940. However, the Baltic position was that the 1920 Peace Treaties with Russia had not lost their legal force, at least in their core part of giving first recognition to the independent Baltic

---

109 For an analysis of Soviet doctrine on the principle *clausula rebus sic stantibus*, see T. Schweisfurth, *Der internationale Vertrag in der modernen sowjetischen Völkerrechtstheorie*, Köln, 1968, p. 309 *et seq.*

110 Müllerson, 'New Developments in the Former USSR and Yugoslavia', *VJIL* 1993, p. 313 *et seq;* Loeber, *The Russian-Latvian...*, p. 548 *et seq.*

111 I.C.J. Rep. 1986, 544 at 566.

112 Müllerson, 'New Developments...', p. 315. Cf. similar views by M. Shaw, 'The Heritage States: The Principle of Uti Possidetis Juris Today', 67 *BYBIL* 1996, p. 131: 'Thus, there appears to be a conflict of uti possidetis lines, those internationally accepted prior to the annexations and those consequential upon restoration of independence.'

113 See further L. Mälksoo, 'Post-Soviet Eurasia, uti possidetis and the Clash Between Universal and Russian-led Regional Understandings of International Law', 53 *NYU Journ. Int'l L. and Pol.* 2021, pp. 787–822.

114 V.L Lenin, *Collected works* (Сочинения)), t. 30, Moscow, 1959, p. 293.

115 See e.g. S. Olenev, *Mezhdunarodnoye priznanie SSSR,* Moscow: Izdatel'stvo sotsial'no-ekonomitcheskoi literatury, 1962, p. 47.

States. Yet in reality, today's Baltic States have accepted that during World War II, their borders were changed since first being established in 1920.

e *The Border Debate: Conclusions*

Two things are especially interesting from the standpoint of analysis of the border treaties. First, the international community was quite reserved with respect to the initial territorial claims by Estonia and Latvia *vis-à-vis* Russia, and in any case did not accord them significant diplomatic support.[116] This is the importance of power in international relations: even if strong legal arguments are on your side, try to get territories back from a powerful country! Second, as a consequence of the first aspect, both Estonia and Latvia, while not giving up their State continuity claims, decided to step back from their initial territorial claims in the mid-1990s. It appears that as far as the State borders with the Russian Federation are concerned, Estonia and Latvia have not been successful in claiming *restitutio in integrum.*

5 The Issue of State Responsibility for Injuries Caused During Illegal Soviet Annexation

a *Introduction*

The third main issue which has been raised with respect to the continuity claim of the Baltic republics, is the issue of State responsibility for internationally wrongful acts committed in Lithuania, Latvia and Estonia during the Soviet occupation.

Axiomatically, there is no law without responsibility, and violations of a norm with legal quality cannot remain without consequences, at least at the level of law. However, even superficial reflection upon the structure and specificities of the international community and international law reveal that establishing the principle of responsibility in the law of nations is not an easy task. Notwithstanding the evolution of customary international law of State responsibility in recent decades, Hans Kelsen's one-time critique of the possibility of responsibility in international law is still in many aspects valid.[117] It

116 M.N. Shaw, *op. cit.*, p. 132. For instance, a representative of the US National Security Council declared that the US recognized the borders of the Baltic States, as they were established on September 2, 1991. See V.J. Riismandel, 'Vaatlusi Vabadussõjast ja Tartu rahulepingust' (Observations on the War of Independence and the Tartu Peace Treaty), in: *Vaba Eesti Sõna*, December 23, 1999. For Riismandel, the position of the USA on the Russian-Estonian border question has been 'disappointing.'

117 See H. Kelsen, ‚Unrecht und Unrechtsfolge im Völkerrecht', XII *ZöR* 1932, pp. 481–606.

is clear that due to fundamental differences in the structure of international law as compared with domestic legal order, responsibility in international law is different and may appear more primitive in comparison. For several centuries after the very origin of the Westphalian system, international law doctrine remained relatively silent on the matter of State responsibility.[118]

However, during recent decades, important developments have occurred in this field. State practice and *opinio iuris* leave no doubt that the fundamental principle of State responsibility has been recognized in modern international law. Article 1 of the *Draft Articles on State Responsibility*, adopted by the ILC at the second reading on August 3, 2001, lays out this basic principle: 'Every internationally wrongful act of a State entails the international responsibility of that State.'[119]

This fundamental principle of international law was recognized in pre-World War II case law. For instance in the *Phosphates in Morocco* case, the PCIJ affirmed that when a State commits an internationally wrongful act against another State, international responsibility is established 'immediately as between the two States.'[120] Max Huber, the arbitrator in the *British Claims in the Spanish zone of Morocco* case, declared that it is an indisputable principle that 'responsibility is the necessary corollary of rights. All international rights entail international responsibility.'[121] That aggression constituted a crime triggering international legal principles of State responsibility in the World War II era, was even recognized by Soviet scholars writing on international law.[122]

Thus, the principles of State responsibility could also be applied to the case of the illegal annexation of the Baltic republics by the USSR.

b *Main Principles of the Law of State Responsibility*

The project of codifying and progressively developing international law of State responsibility, undertaken by the ILC since the early 1950s, relies on the intellectual concept applied by former ILC Special Rapporteur Roberto Ago to the context of international law: the distinction between primary and secondary norms in international law. Innumerable rules of different types place obligations on States (that is, primary rules); the secondary rules of State

118 See C. Tomuschat, *Hague Academy General Course*, p. 269–270.

119 See A/CN.4/L.602/Rev.i

120 Phosphates in Morocco (Preliminary Objections), P.C.I.J., Series A/B, No 74 (1938), p. 28. See also Case of the S.S. Wimbledon, P.C.IJ. Series A, No. 1 (1923), p. 15; Case concerning the Factory at Chorzów (Jurisdiction), P.C.IJ., Series A, No. 17 (1927), p. 29.

121 *Reports of International Arbitral Awards*, vol. II (1925), p. 641.

122 Д.Б. Левин, *Ответственность в современном международном праве*, Москва: Международные отношения, 1969; Н.А. Ушаков, *Основания международной оветственности государств*, Москва: Международные отношения, 1983, p. 137.

responsibility seek to determine 'whether that obligation has been violated and what should be the consequence of the violation.'[123] As a fundamental principle of State responsibility, States that violate primary norms of international law incur obligations of reparation *vis-à-vis* injured States. In what has probably been the most important case of State responsibility in international jurisprudence, the *Chorzów Factory* case, the PCIJ stated that

> Reparation must, as far as possible, wipe out all the consequences of the illegal act and re-establish the situation which would, in all probability, have existed if that act had not been committed.[124]

Article 34 of the Draft Articles on State Responsibility lays out the forms of reparation in international law: full reparation takes the form of restitution, compensation and satisfaction, either singly or in combination.

The general method of State responsibility is thus as follows: first, it must be established whether an internationally wrongful act has been committed. Such an act must firstly be attributable to a State under international law and, secondly, constitute a breach of an international obligation by that State. Under certain circumstances, the wrongfulness of State conduct is precluded. Such cases involve valid consent, lawful self-defence, countermeasures, *force majeure*, distress, and—subject to far-reaching limitations—necessity. When a State incurs international responsibility for wrongful conduct and fails either to cease the wrongful behaviour and/or to make full reparation, the injured State is entitled to take countermeasures against the offending State. Countermeasures are measures, constituting violations against international obligations by the State that takes them but they are justified, within limits as responses to violations of international law. They may only be taken in proportion to the injury suffered, and are subject to other conditions.

Notwithstanding important conceptual developments in the field of State responsibility, many open questions remain. For instance, Christian Tomuschat suggests on the basis of State practice that 'the principle of full reparation applies only to small-scale violations of international law.'[125] To

123 See *Yearbook of the ILC* 1970, vol. II, p. 306, para. *66* (c).

124 PCIJ, Ser. A, No. 17, 47.

125 C. Tomuschat, 'International Crimes by States—an Endangered Species?', in: *International Law: Theory and Practice. Essays in Honour of Eric Suy*, The Hague: Nijhoff, 1998, p. 2,67–8 (quoting Hold-Ferneck, an Austrian jurist who has argued that international law is 'order in small, disorder in great matters.')

the extent that this is true in reality, it is an important *de facto* qualification of the principle of State responsibility as applied in State practice. Moreover, States have not been too eager to make the ILC Articles on State responsibility a legally binding treaty.

c *On Conditions of State Responsibility in the Case of the Baltic States: The Issue of Attributability (the International Legal Status of Today's Russia)*

In the preceding chapter, the occupation and annexation of the Baltic States by the USSR were qualified as illegal acts. The USSR seized the Baltic States, and by deporting and/or murdering tens of thousands of Baltic citizens, caused considerable loss in terms of human lives, material and moral damage. As an absolute minimum, the USSR was bound by the humanitarian standards of the 1907 Hague rules in the illegally annexed Baltic States. The mass deportations and liquidations of the elite organized by the USSR government in the Baltic States manifestly violated this minimum standard set by primary norms of international law. Without due process, thousands of Balts were sentenced to long-term imprisonment in the camps of the Gulag, and were condemned to what can only be called slave labour for the USSR. Moreover, depending upon which view one takes about the extent of the legal obligations of the USSR during the annexation period, one can, in addition, qualify the damage incurred on the economy and natural environment of the Baltic republics as internationally wrongful acts. In any case, it follows from the jurisprudence of the ICJ that the State exercizing illegal control on a certain territory is responsible for violations of international law committed on that territory.[126]

Of course, the collapse of the USSR in December 1991 poses the question of attributability of internationally wrongful acts committed by the USSR. It is submitted that from the point of view of the principles of State responsibility, the Russian Federation as the continuator State of the USSR continues to be responsible for internationally wrongful acts committed by the USSR.

It is true that the international legal position of the Russian Federation after the collapse of the USSR initially elicited contradictory interpretations and theories.[127] The leaders of the newly founded CIS first declared in Minsk 'that the

126 *Namibia Opinion*, I.C.J. Reports 1971, p. 16 at 56 para 125.

127 See B. Stern, 'La succession d'États', 262 *RCADI* 1996, 2000, p. 216 *et seq. See* also I.I. Lukashuk, 'Russland als Rechtsnachfolger in völkerrechtliche Verträge der UdSSR', 4 *Osteuropa Recht* 1993, pp. 235–246; T. Schweisfurth, 'Ausgwählte Fragen der Staatensukzession im Kontext der Auflösung der UdSSR', 32 *AVR* 1994, pp. 99–129; T. Schweisfurth, 'Vom Einheitsstaat (UdSSR) zum Staatenbund (GUS). Juristische Stationen eines Staatszerfalls und einer Staatenbundsentstehung', 52 *ZaöRV* 1992, pp. 541–702.

USSR is ceasing its existence as a subject of international law and a geopolitical entity.' However, on December 21, 1991 in Alma-Ata, the Council of the Heads of the CIS States passed a resolution which reads: 'The participating States of the CIS support Russia in continuing the USSR membership in the UN, including the Security Council, and in other international organizations.' Soon afterwards, President Yeltsin wrote in a note to the UN Secretary-General that the Russian Federation was a continuator State of the USSR.[128] It may be, as Bardo Fassbender observes, that the way Russia stepped into the USSR's legal position in the UN was 'unsatisfactory from a constitutional point of view.'[129] However, such continuity was desired by Russia and supported at the time by the international community. As a consequence, the USSR did not become extinct as a subject of international law—its international legal personality was continued by Russia. Today's Russia is, as a subject of international law, identical with the USSR,[130] just as the USSR itself was in a similar sense identical with Tsarist Russia,[131] or (for instance), today's FRG with the German *Reich*.

According to the Assistant Prime Minister and Foreign Minister of the Lithuanian pro-Soviet government, Krévé-Mickievičius, Vyatcheslav Molotov told him in Moscow on June 30, 1940: 'I must point out today what will be clear to everyone tomorrow. The Russian Tsars since Ivan the Terrible have tried to reach the Baltic Sea, not because of their political desires, but because this was required for the development of the Russian State and nation. It would be unforgivable for the Soviet government not to seize an opportunity that may never present itself again.'[132]

There is a rule in customary international law according to which, in cases of State extinction, a successor State would generally not be responsible for internationally wrongful acts committed by its extinguished predecessor State.[133] A

---

128 See *Rossiiskaya Gazeta,* January 31, 1992. See also Circular of the Ministry of Foreign Affairs of the Russian Federation, Note of January 13, quoted by the President of the Russian Association of International Law A. Kolodkin in: 'Russia and International Law: New Approaches', *RBDI* 1992, p. 553.

129 B. Fassbender, *UN Security Council Reform and the Right of Veto. A Constitutional Perspective, The* Hague: Kluwer, 1998, p. 189.

130 See S.V. Chernichenko, *Teoria mezhdunarodnoga prava, Tom II, Starye i novye teoreticheskie problemy*, Moscow: NIMP, 1999.

131 E. Martynenko has argued that the link of continuity connects the present Russian Federation (through the USSR) with the Tsar's Russia. See 'Правопреемство России в отношении собственности Российской Империи на Ближнем Востоке', in: *Правоведение* No. 1 2000, pp. 237–247 at pp. 2, 46–7.

132 See Repečka, *op. cit.*, p. 69–70 and B. Meissner, *Die baltischen Staaten...*, 1995, p. 61.

133 See further W. Czaplinski, 'State Succession and State Responsibility', 28 *Canadian YBIL* 1990, pp. 339–359.

recent interpretation of the notion of State identity—that there can be continuity of a State (personality) with a transformed identity[134]—enables the argument that even in cases of continuity of State personality, a new regime, due to its new identity, would be entitled to free itself from the obligation to make reparations for the internationally wrongful acts of its predecessor. However, this perspective does not seem to be supported by *opinio iuris* in State practice.[135] Its acceptance would have enabled post-World War governments in former Axis countries to argue that State identity had changed so much as to erase responsibility for crimes committed under the Nazi and fascist regimes. (The democratic FRG of the post-World War II era undoubtedly had a very different constitutional identity from Nazi Germany.)

The Russian Federation has explicitly preferred the legal position of continuator State to that of successor State. It is therefore misleading to argue that the Russian Federation is, from the point of view of State responsibility, not the same State as the USSR.[136] International customary law does not endorse the continuator State to act according to the so-called *pick-and-choose* principle (cherry picking). The Italian international law scholar Gaetano Arangio Ruiz emphasizes that:

> ... la partie *intéressée* devrait donc faire un choix, en premier lieu, entre un *claim of identity* et un *claim of non-identity*. Si elle choisissait l'identité—et celle-ci était acceptée ou démontrée—elle devrait accepter (sauf négotiation) la continuité absolue en matiëre de *devoirs* aussi bien qu'en matiëre de *droits*. Chaque partie, en d'autres mots, serait obligée d'accepter les conséquences de l'identité "en bloc", qu'elles lui soient favorables ou défavorables.[137]

---

134 M.C.R. Craven, 'The Problem of State Succession and the Identity of States under International Law', 9 *EJIL* 1998, pp. 142–162 at 160.

135 Note, however, that similar views of 'functional splitting' and 'functionally limited identity' have recently been suggested by Wilfried Fiedler. W. Fiedler, ‚Entwicklungslinien im Recht der Staatensukzession', in: *Liber Amicorum. Professor Ignaz Seidl-Hohenveldern*, ed.by G. Hafner *et al.*, The Hague: Kluwer, 1998, pp. 133–155 at 136 *et seq.*

136 But see, inconclusively, P.P. Kremnev, *Raspad SSSR: mezhdunarodno-pravovye problemy*, Moscow: Zertsalo-M, 2005.

137 G. Arangio-Ruiz, *L'État dans le sens du Droit des Gens et la notion du droit international*, Bologna: Cooperativa Libraria Universitaria, 1975, p. 310. "The interested party should therefore choose, in the first place, between a claim of identity and a claim of non-identity. If it chose identity—and this was accepted or demonstrated—it would have to accept (unless negotiated) absolute continuity in terms of duties as well as rights. Each party, in other words, would be obliged to accept the consequences of identity "en bloc", whether favourable or unfavourable to it."

Thus, a new regime that continues to govern the same State and naturally invokes the rights of the former regime cannot simply free itself from legal obligations and responsibilities.

d *The Reparations Issue After Re-establishment of Baltic Independence*

Even during the process that re-established independence, the issue of reparations claims was intensively discussed in the Baltic States. In Estonia, a commission convened in 1991 by Supreme Soviet Chairman Arnold Rüütel compiled a damage report and concluded that '[t]he basic responsibility for damage to social, economic and cultural development is borne by those political forces which violently forced a foreign social and economic system upon Estonia.'[138] At the same time, the Estonian Commission recognized the complexity of a prolonged annexation, by concluding that '(i)n cases of damage inflicted on social, economic and cultural development, the loyally-formed party, government, administrative and judicial institutions share joint responsibility—to the extent that they carried out the policies of a foreign power.'[139]

However, so far only Lithuania has officially demanded reparations from Russia for injuries suffered under Soviet occupation. On June 13, 2000 the *Seimas* (parliament) of the Republic of Lithuania adopted the Law on Compensation of Damage resulting from the Occupation by the USSR,[140] the text of which is reprinted in an appendix to this book.

Latvia and Estonia have presented no reparations claims to Russia. When the Lithuanian law was adopted, Estonian and Latvian politicians offered differing arguments to the general public about why their countries should not issue reparations claims. In a way, these arguments reveal that the unsuccessful boundary negotiations with Russia had taught Baltic politicians a lesson. Essentially, they maintained that it was utterly unlikely that Russia would pay reparations. Although there existed a 'moral right to compensation, at least for those crimes against humanity that the Soviet regime committed', it would

138 See J. Kahk (ed.) *World War II and Soviet Occupation in Estonia: A Damages Report,* Tallinn: Perioodika Publishers, 1991, p. 29. The issue of reparations has also been discussed in the literature. See e.g. A. Susi, 'Mis on meile maksma läinud okupatsioon?' (What has the Price of Occupation been for Us), *Looming* No. 2 1990, pp. 246–251 and I. Teder, 'N. Liidu agressiooniga Eesti Vabariigile tekitatud kahjude huvitamisest' (About Compensation of Damages Inflicted upon the Republic of Estonia with the Aggression of the USSR), *ibid.*, pp. 252–254.

139 See J. Kahk (ed.), *ibid.*

140 Republic of Lithuania law on Compensation of Damage resulting from the Occupation by the USSR, June 13, 2000, No. VIII-1727, Vilnius. (See Appendix 4).

be 'unwise to present such demands to Russia from a foreign policy point of view', *inter alia* since 'Brussels is looking for opportunities to help Russia financially rather than to make demands against Moscow.'[141] These were the views expressed before the Baltic States became members of the EU in 2004.

Russia has signalled its negative opinion with respect to the Lithuanian reparations claim. Soon after adoption of the Lithuanian Law, Aleksandr Avdeev from the Russian Ministry of Foreign Affairs presented the Russian position on the matter in the Lithuanian Foreign Policy Review.[142]

> While on the subject of the main aspects of relations between Russia and Lithuania, I cannot but dwell on those that cause our biggest worry. I have in mind first of all the Law on Recovery of Damages resulting from the occupation by the Union of Soviet Socialist Republics passed by the Lithuanian Seimas (Diet) this past June. The Russian Foreign Ministry opportunely appraised it as an instrument unfriendly toward Russia. Stressing that we could not accept attempts to interpret our shared history in this unilateral and politicized manner, we elucidated the international-law grounds upon which we regarded as unfounded the claims formulated by the Lithuanian parliamentarians. *Today I would like to emphasize the main thing: This "initiative, absolutely futile from the practical point of view, hinders both the process of ratification by the Russian State Duma of the border treaties between our countries* ... It is desirable that there should be a clear realization in Lithuania of the fact that attempts to realize the "recovery of damages' law are incompatible with the purposes of good neighborly expansion of Russian-Lithuanian relations.

Following the collapse of the USSR in 1991, scholars have reflected on the continuities and changes in the Soviet and Russian approaches to international law.[143] It appears that the current Russian approach with regard to the rights and obligations resulting from the legal identity of the Russian Federation with the USSR is reminiscent of the former USSR's position with respect to Tsarist Russia's legal obligations. It can be characterized as a pick-and-choose approach

---

141 See A. Ideon, 'Eesti jätab Leedu üksi hüvitist пõudma' (Estonia leaves Lithuania alone to demand reparations), quoting interviews with Estonian and Latvian politicians, *Postimees*, 03.07.2000.

142 A. Avdeev, 'Russian-Lithuanian Relations: An Overview', *Lithuanian Foreign Policy Review* 2000 No. 2 (6), pp. 27–33 at 29. Italics added.

143 See e.g. G. Ginsburgs, *From Soviet to Russian International Law. Studies in Continuity and Change*, The Hague: Nijhoff, 1998.

to State identity. Its fundamental feature is a doctrine which in one sense (positive rights) upholds identity with the former regime, while in another sense (negative consequences; State responsibility) disavowing that very continuity. The USSR refused to honour Tsarist Russia's obligations, since it claimed to be a new State in the 'social-class sense', although it simultaneously admitted to be the same subject of international law as well. R.L. Borbov wrote in 1968 that 'to the subject of international law which is new in the social-class sense, corresponds a creative relationship to this law.'[144] Soviet scholars expressed this creativity when they reasoned that the USSR would not be bound by the obligations of Tsarist Russia. Thus, Natalya Zakharova postulated:

> The recognition of continuity of subjects in the event of fundamental alteration of the structure of a state has, however, nothing in common with the bourgeois theory of continuity which asserts that the uninterrupted nature of the existence of a state requires the recognition of all international treaties regardless of internal changes, [Soviet legal science] acknowledges that after a social revolution a state has the right to repudiate international treaties which do not correspond to the principles of the new system and to its national interests. ... denial of the right of a state to repudiate international treaties following social revolutions is a characterictic feature of bourgeois science.[145]

In a somewhat similar vein, the Russian Federation rejected, in the case of the Baltic States, responsibility for internationally wrongful acts committed by the USSR. Even when one takes into account the time factor, the *a priori* refusal to recognize responsibility for Soviet crimes shows practical limits to full application of the State responsibility doctrine in international law.

e *The Reparations Issue: Conclusions*

Although Estonia, Latvia and Lithuania have repeatedly indicated that the USSR occupied and annexed them illegally and that Russia as the continuator

---

144 Р.Л. Борбов, *Основные проблемы теории международного права*, Москва: Международные отношения, 1968, p. 80. (Translated from Russian.)

145 N.V. Zakharova, 'States as Subjects of International Law and Social Revolution' (*Some Problems of Succession*), *Soviet YBIL* 1960, pp. 157–166 at 165. Cf. for more positive aspects of this doctrine and practice in: N. Zakharova, 'Renunication by the Soviet State of Treaties of Tsarist Russia which Violated the Rights of the Peoples in Eastern Countries', *Soviet YBIL* 1962, pp. 126–136.

State of the USSR should at least apologize for Soviet crimes,[146] only Lithuania has gone as far as demanding reparations from the Russian Federation for injuries suffered under Soviet rule. However, neither Baltic claims nor rhetoric have had practical results. Furthermore, Baltic politicians have argued that the attitude of Western, in particular European partners has not been too encouraging for presentation of reparation claims. This may be because European States, including Germany, still face unresolved claims from World War II and elsewhere in Europe too, there has hardly been full responsibility for major violations of international law such as aggression, war crimes and material damage caused in World War II.

This also confirms that power politics plays an important role in the implementation of legal principles of State responsibility. The unavoidable importance of politics in matters of State responsibility was highlighted in 1936 by Ants Piip, professor of international law at Tartu University and Estonia's long-time foreign minister:

> One is generally compelled to note that in the solution of international delicts a great role is played by the factual relationship of the parties. If political and economic relations are good, even the most serious offence finds an easy solution. When the contrary is the case, even the smallest misunderstanding can be a pretext for major conflict.[147]

146 T. Sildam, 'Välisminister Ilves: ajalugu pole pudupood' (Foreign Minister Ilves: history is not a grocery store), Interview in Postimees, 02.02.2001: 'History is not a grocery store where you take one thing and leave the other. Here you cannot say selectively that in some questions we are successors, and not in others. One cannot say that the crimes that were committed are not ours, but ours is all the property which the USSR confiscated, including the embassy buildings of the Republic of Estonia. (...) In the context of this culture where we live—in the context of Western culture—there is a habit of confessing to such behaviour over a formal apology, as many States have done.' See also the remarks by Ilves on January 16, 2002, at the opening of a memorial plate for the 63 employees of the Estonian Ministry of Foreign Affairs who were executed by the Soviet government: 'If this would all be past, our feelings today would be more simple and clear. But it seems that this is not only past. Differently from Germany's exemplary politics of *Vergangenheitsbewältigung* we notice that crimes committed are not regretted but glorified. Stalin's hymn is restored. Respect for Andropov who committed murders in Hungary, has been cast into metal. The founding day of the terror organization Cheka, founded by the great murderer Feliks Dzherzhinski, is celebrated as a festive day. We are told: do not wait for an apology... We are not even particularly waiting.' (Transl. from Estonian) See A. Lõhmus, 'Ilves kritiseeris teravalt Venemaad, (Ilves sharply criticized Russia), *Postimees*, 17.01.2001.

147 A. Piip, *Rahvusvaheline õigus* (International law), Tartu: Akadeemilise Kooperatiivi Kirjastus, 1936, p. 209. Translated from Estonian.

6 General Conclusion from Practice: The Discrepancy between Status and Rights

Mainly due to differing views with the Russian Federation as continuator State of the USSR, the Baltic States have not been able to restore certain essential rights following from their claim to identity and continuity with the pre-1940 Baltic republics. For example, the Italian scholar Enrico Milano has observed that in 1991, the Baltic nations of Estonia and Latvia could revert to their original statehood but in terms of borders with Russia had to make peace with the *uti possidetis* principle.[148] The Baltic German international law scholar Dietrich A. Loeber therefore called the continuity of the Baltic republics a limping continuity.[149] But what do such qualifications mean, except to reveal the frustrations of international law scholars concerning discrepancies between legal standards and political realities? Or is it a discrepancy between theory and practice?

Rein Müllerson points out that '... theory and practice are inseparable and in the case of contradiction between them one has to become anxious.'[150] The legal positions of the Baltic States in the early 1990s were supported by powerful theory, and must have been strong enough to 'scare' an unabiding practice, to make it 'anxious' and 'obedient.' This, however, did not happen, or only in part. It follows that it may be time for the theory to become 'anxious' or at least critical, since fictions must be accompanied by at least some sort of effectiveness:

> Si le respect effectif des consequences juridiques de l'acte fictif n'est pas assure, la fiction perd son role dans l'elaboration legislative: elle devient un acte mensonger ou frauduleux, depourvu d'effets juridiques. (...) l'usage de la fiction dans l'activite juridique internationale n'est legitime que s'il repose sur 1'effectivité des consequences tirées de la fiction.[156]

The discrepancy between fiction and effectiveness should then become a clear challenge to the doctrine of international law. Otherwise, the result would be a too utopian international law which realism would again be able to disqualify

148 See E. Milano, *Unlawful Territorial Situations in International Law. Reconciling Effectiveness, Legality and Legitimacy*, Leiden: Martinus Nijhoff, 2006, p. 107.

149 See Loeber, 'Consequences of the Molotov-Ribbentrop Pact Continuing into Our Days: International Legal Aspects', in: *Latvia in WW II. Materials of an International Conference, 14–15 June 1999*, Riga, pp. 67–76 at 75.

150 R. Müllerson, *Ordering Anarchy. International Law in International Society*, The Hague: Nijhoff, 2000, p. 51.

as irrelevant, with the regret, as Hans Morgenthau put it in the context of events leading to World War II, that:

> ...it was the general attitude of the internationalists to take the appropriateness of the devices for granted and to blame the facts for the failure. When the facts behave otherwise than we have predicted, they seem to say, too bad for the facts. Not unlike the sorcerers of primitive ages, they attempt to exorcise social evils by the indefatigable repetition of magic formulae.[157]

The previous analysis revealed that the 'magic legal formula' of 'State continuity' has in practice been mixed and intertwined with political considerations and power relations. The principle of *ex injuria, ius non oritur has* been balanced by the opposite principle of *ex factis oritur ius*, and with the conditions set by (power) politics.

156 J. Touscoz, *Le principe d'effectivité dans l'ordre international,* 1964, p. 180. "If effective compliance with the legal consequences of the fictitious act is not ensured, fiction loses its role in legislative elaboration: it becomes a false or fraudulent act, without legal effects. (...) the use of fiction in international legal activity is legitimate only if it is based on the effectiveness of the consequences drawn from fiction."

157 H. Morgenthau, 'Positivism, Functionalism and International Law', 34 *AJIL* 1940, p.260.

CHAPTER 6

State Continuity in Cases of Prolonged Illegal Annexation: Status and/or Rights?

1 Introduction

The analysis of State practice in the preceding chapter revives a fundamental theoretical problem: namely, what should State continuity as a legal concept mean or imply, in particular when statehood has been *de facto* disrupted for such a long period as with the Baltic States? If power politics plays such a profound role, as suggested, how should we interpret a certain discrepancy between status and rights? Does abstract legal status have any immediate normative consequences, as suggested by Krystyna Marek and other scholars? Should abstract legal status have a separate meaning at all or should international lawyers concentrate their attention solely on concrete rights and duties?

The crux of the problem seems to be whether and, if so, how to integrate political aspects of international relations in international law doctrine, so that international law would be neither irrelevant (too utopian), nor lose its autonomy *vis-à-vis* power politics. What should be the intellectual position of the international lawyer with respect to politics?[1] To what extent should legal doctrine accommodate fluctuations of State behaviour, often caused by power politics, as 'custom'? While mainstream international legal scholarship has tended to ignore the problem altogether, critical schools of thought have provided ever more imaginative, provocative and controversial solutions to this problem. The following discusses how the conflict between international legal theory and practice in the Baltic case has been treated in the literature.

Any lawyer's discussion of delimitation of the political from the legal must start with the most challenging of those theories, namely a non-legal (and sometimes anti-legal) school of thought which broadly denies the independent value of international law and legal analysis for an understanding of international relations (realism). After having discussed realist views, we turn to some

---

1 For some classical studies, see W. Wengler, *Der Begriff des Politischen im internationalen Recht*, Tübingen: J.C.B. Mohr, 1956; F.A. Boyle, *World Politics and International Law*, Durham: Duke University Press, 1985.

 | DOI:10.1163/9789004464896_008

explanations given by the New Haven approach and New Stream scholarship which are both relatively new schools of thought that have—from the legal scholars' camp—most extensively dealt with the relationship of law to politics in international relations. Incidentally, Martti Koskenniemi, a leading New Stream scholar in international law, has—on the basis of the case of the Baltic States—given a new interpretation to the concept of State continuity.

2 Realist Critiques of International Law

For realism, in both its classic and structural interpretations, the very project of international law is inherently utopian. Without centralized power comparable to domestic legal systems, the international system of States must be characterized as anarchical. No 'legalistic-moralistic' (George Kennan) attempts to establish the rule of law in international relations can do away with the fact that power remains the main determining factor in international politics. Realism is a theory about the predominance of power politics and, consequently, about the relative non-importance of international law in international relations. Born, in its more recent version, out of the disillusionment caused by World War II,[2] realism is probably still the most influential, even archetypical, explanation of world politics within the discipline of international relations theory.

It is easy to understand that—and why—the attitudes of international law scholars towards realist arguments have been mainly rejective. If international law does not matter, then the field of study of international lawyers can only be marginal at best. Nevertheless, in certain aspects the positivist doctrine of international law and realist approach to international relations share far more common assumptions than previously recognized—such as the focus on States as main actors in international relations and law.[3]

Realists argue that if international law seeks to play a role in international relations, it cannot but acknowledge, openly or tacitly, that international

2 See e.g. M. Koskenniemi, 'Carl Schmitt, Hans Morgenthau, and the Image of Law in International Relations and International Law', pp. 17–34, in: M. Byers (ed.), *The Role of Law in International Politics. Essays in International Relations and International Law*, Oxford University Press, 2000.

3 See A.-M. Slaughter, 'International Law and International Relations', 285 *RCADI* 2000, p. 9 at 33 et seq. Cf. with S.V. Scott, 'International Law as Ideology: Theorizing the Relationship between International Law and International Politics', 5 *EJIL* 1994, pp. 313–325, and F.R. Tesón, 'Realism and Kantianism in International Law', 86 *ASIL Proc.* 1992, pp. 113–118 at 113.

relations are power relations. As Hedley Bull points out, international law would have to follow power and force:

> (...) contrary to much superficial thinking on this subject, it is not as if this tendency of international law to accommodate itself to power politics were some unfortunate but remediable defect that is fit to be removed by the good work of some high-minded professor of international law or by some ingenious report of the International Law Commission. There is every reason to think that this feature of international law, which sets it at loggerheads with elementary justice, is vital to its working and that if international law ceased to have this failure, it would so lose contact with international reality as to play any role at all.[4]

For realists then, the use of relevant international legal concepts in the Baltic case reflects changing power relations. Solemn non-recognition of annexation (the Stimson doctrine) has to yield when the changing balance of power (Yalta) dictates acceptance of a new fact constellation. Hedley Bull has highlighted the primacy of the institution of the balance of power for international order:

> Here is an institution which offends against everyday notions of justice (...) by sacrificing the interests of small states, which may be absorbed or partitioned in the interests of the balance. (...) From the point of view of a weak state sacrificed to it, the balance of power must appear as a brutal principle. But its function in the preservation of international order is not for this reason less central.[5]

In 1991, Russia lacked power to prevent the drifting away of the Baltic republics. Nevertheless, the Baltic States never had enough power to impose their legal doctrine of State restoration, supported by Western countries, on Russia.

According to the realist argument, the doctrine of continuity of the Baltic States is essentially, like all legal doctrines, a political and ideological one. Concepts such as State continuity/identity, and related debates relating to the rights of States, can be regarded as political tools for achieving certain aims within the context of *Realpolitik*. *De facto*, there is continuity only to the extent that power can guarantee it. Realism, a simple and at the same time powerful doctrine, has often been used in explaining outcome(s) in the case of the legal status of the Baltic States.

---

4 H. Bull, *The Anarchical Society. A Study of Order in World Politics,* 2nd ed., 1995, pp 88–89.

5 H. Bull, *The Anarchical Society. A Study of Order in World Politics,* 2nd ed., 1995, pp. 87–88 and 103–104.

The fact that most realist theoreticicans come from (former) superpowers demonstrates that outspoken realism has been the classic doctrine of the most powerful. Seldom, however, do foreign policy leaders of small States confess that they see inter-State relations in terms of classic realism. Nevertheless, former Estonian Minister of Foreign Affairs Toomas Hendrik Ilves expressed the disappointment of a disillusioned idealist when he acknowledged the intellectual adoption of Hobbesian-Machiavellian *Realpolitik*,[6] *mutatis mutandis* acommodated to the needs of small States:

> Those [States in Eastern Europe] which have pursued a foreign policy of "stand up, demand justice,"[7] have discovered the sad truth that between states "law" does not apply, or only very little. Law and justice can sometimes be found in an established and sometimes well-working domestic court system, but not between states. We could approach this almost mathematically. When von Clausewitz said that war is only the continuation of politics by other means, then inter-state politics is a state of war without killing. The same rules apply, the goals are achieved by those who are stronger. Among smaller and weaker states, only those win who act most prudently or cleverly. But in our region, foreign policy has nothing to do with law (...) *Quod licet Iovi, non licet bovi.*[8] In this world, the demand for justice unfortunately does not bring results.[9]

The psychological background for this view seems to be that in the post-1990/1991 euphoria, the new foreign policy elites of the Baltic States had initially almost unconstrained belief in the view that right international law positions facilitate right outcomes in State practice.[10]

But the challenge of the realist point of view for the integrity of international legal perspective remains. Realist arguments have been invoked to explain why

---

6 Machiavelli argued that a Prince, if he wants to be successful, must inevitably break the promises he has given. As small States would have little power to do that—not that small States are more moral 'by nature'—Machiavellism for small States could then be the conviction that the big States tend to behave that way. See N. Machiavelli, *Il principe,* Chapter 18 (quoted from the German edition by Parkland: Köln, 2000.)

7 'Stand up, demand justice' is an allusion to an Estonian patriotic song.

8 What Jove is allowed, for a bull is not allowed.

9 TH. Ilves, *Eesti välispoliitika minevik, olevik ja tulevik*, aulaloeng 30. aprillil 1998 (The Past, Present and Future of Estonian Foreign Policy. Lecture in the Assembly Hall of Tartu University), Tartu: Tartu Ülikooli Kirjastus, 1998, p. 5 *et seq*. Translation from the Estonian by this author.

10 Estonian President Lennart Meri, when asked in an interview in 1998 for a comment on the successful nuclear tests by India and Pakistan, argued that 'the nuclear bomb of small States is international law.'

Lithuania cannot be successful with its reparations claim. Arkady Moishes, a Russia analyst at the Finnish Institute of International Affairs, has reminded us of certain important realities of political power:

> Needless to say, such [Lithuanian] claims are unrealistic. Any negotiations on this matter would require Moscow to recognize the fact of occupation, which is absolutely out of the question for a number of reasons.(…) The only result which this legislation can bring about is to retrigger an emotional and predominantly mutually unfriendly debate of the early 1990s, ranging from general issues of interpretation of the Soviet period in Lithuanian history to very specific cases of property rights (for example, the embassy buildings in Paris and Rome).[11]

And there is more in the analysis of Arkady Moishes about the Lithuanian reparations claim—without, however, as international law students will notice, any attention to legal concepts such as 'internationally wrongful act', 'attribution,' 'circumstances precluding wrongfulness', 'lapse of time', and so on:

> Lithuania has very little leverage that it could use to exert pressure on Russia (outside the area of transit tariffs, but in that case Russian countermeasures would hit the Lithuanian economy probably harder than vice versa). Also, precedents established by Latvian and Estonian territorial claims to Russia rather demonstrated the futility of these actions: both countries had to withdraw their claims. Furthermore, engagement in such a dispute with Russia, if it receives a high profile, would hardly facilitate the task of Lithuania's accession to European institutions. (…) However, if Vilnius really tries to make it a negotiation item, as the legislation requires, negative resonance in Russia and, consequently, deterioration of bilateral relations will become unavoidable.[12]

There's nothing new under the sun—long ago Thucydides, whom realist theoreticians consider their forerunner, made Athenians tell the Melians that '(…) *we both alike know that in the discussion of human affairs the question of justice enters where there is equal power to enforce it, and that the powerful exact what they can, and that the weak grant what they must.*'[13]

11 A. Moishes, 'Russia-Lithuania: Preserving Interaction', p. 83.

12 A. Moshes, 'Russia-Lithuania: Preserving Interaction', *Lithuanian For. Pol. Rev.* 2000 No. 2(6), pp. 83–4.

13 Athenians to Melians in 416 Be, quoted from: Thucydides, *The History of the Peloponnesian War*, translated by Benjamin Jowett, 1st ed., London: Oxford University Press, 1881, p. 167.

Similar points raising the aspect of power have been advanced with the boundaries issue. As far as the boundaries are concerned, a realist would claim that legal arguments did not ultimately decide the outcome in the Russian-Baltic debate. A realist would argue that the record of Russia's territorial disputes, especially the long-lasting Kurile Islands question with Japan,[14] gave Baltic claims at the outset virtually no prospects of success. Legal arguments remained marginal, not least because initial Estonian and Latvian initiatives for legal adjudication of the frontier issue at the ICJ were rejected by Russia. And here we have again the spectre of the political that sets limits on international law and nourishes the realist viewpoint:

> In international law, all disputes are not justiciable; for no court is competent unless the parties to the dispute have agreed to confer jurisdiction on it and to recognize its decision as binding (...) There is no principle of law which enables one to decide that a given issue is suitable for treatment by legal methods.[15]

International lawyers have had difficulty with the persuasiveness of the realist outlook for the Baltic-Russian boundaries case. Classically, on such occasions, apologetic argumentation is employed. Malcolm Shaw suggests that '*...it may well be the case that considerations of international peace and security and territorial stability dictate acceptance of the 1991 boundaries as the existing international boundaries.*'[16]

Considerations of 'international peace and security and territorial stability' (Shaw) referred to the general political consensus that opening up old territorial disputes in Europe would mean opening up a Pandora's box of mutual

14 See e.g. G. Ginsburgs, 'The Territorial Question between the USSR and Japan. The Soviet Case and a Western Apercu', in: 15 *Korea and World Affairs* 1991, pp. 259–278, V.V. Ermoshin, 'The Right of Russia in respect to Southern Sakhalin and the Kurile Islands', *Russian YBIL* 1993–1994, pp. 173–195 and V.V. Ermoshin, 'On the Russian-Japanese Controversy Over the Status Quo of Southern Sakhalin and the Kurile Islands', 1 *Moscow JIL* 1995, No. 4, pp. 63–74. For the diplomatic background, see also W. Mendl, 'Japan and the Soviet Union: Towards a Deal?', 47 *World Today* 1991 (November), p. 196 *et seq.*

15 E.H. Carr, *op. cit.*, p. 194 and 199.

16 Shaw, *op. cit.*, p. 132. Shaw strongly advocates the application of the *uti possidetis* principle, writing: '*The primary justification of the principle of uti possidetis (...), has been to seek to minimize threats to peace and security, whether they be internal, regional or international. (...) Precisely the same impulse lies behind the recognition of the principle outside the purely colonial context where the same dangers resulting from the break-up of existing states are evident. (...) That uti possidetis governs colonial situations is evident, that it extends to all cases of transition to independence has, it is believed, become clear.*' See M.N. Shaw, *Peoples, Territory...* (1997), p. 503.

claims that could possibly destabilize territorial integrity. In this sense, however consequent from the legal point of view, Estonia's and Latvia's territorial claims were necessarily viewed in the general context of post-Cold War international politics. Already in the context of the Baltic States, the call for restoration of the pre-World War II boundaries could have been used by Poland (or, in another constellation, Russia) for raising the issue of the territory of Vilnius, Lithuania's capital, just as Germany could on similar lines have raised the issue of Klaipeda (Memel).[17]

Trying to explain the interchange between law and politics, especially in territorial issues, international relations scholars have sometimes employed the concept of 'peaceful change.' It may be asked whether the transformation of the Baltic-Russian borders and the concessions made by the Estonian and Latvian Governments may also be analyzed and understood by such a term.[18] Of the international lawyers, the German scholar and diplomat Wilhelm Grewe has defined peaceful change as a procedure for altering the *status quo* without recourse to the use of force.[19] Achieving change by agreement distinguishes peaceful change from two other ways that can bring along changes in the world system governed by power politics' (Grewe): *fait accompli* or war.[20] Professor Grewe notes:

> The method of *fait accompli* is closely related to the threat or actual use of force, short of formally declared war. In essence it amounts to confronting the other interested parties with accomplished facts in the expectation that they will be incapable or unwilling to use force in order to redress those new facts. This method is clearly not compatible with peaceful change (...) If the frustrated party has recourse to unilateral action, the situation is transformed into an international dispute and the procedure for peaceful change becomes a procedure for the peaceful settlement of the dispute.[21]

In the Baltic case, it was precisely the latter (a procedure for peaceful settlement of a dispute) which was employed in the Estonian-Russian and Latvian-Russian

---

17 See also J. Salmon, 'Pays baltes', 24 *RBDI* 1991, p. 267.

18 For a treatment of the international legal aspects of peaceful change, see D. Murswiek, *Peaceful Change. Ein Völkerrechtsprinzip?*, Köln, 1998. For an international relations analysis, see A.M. Kacowicz, *Peaceful Territorial Change*, University of South Carolina Press, 1994.

19 W. Grewe, 'Peaceful Change', in: *EPIL* III (1997), p. 965. See also Murswiek, p. 15.

20 W. Grewe, *ibid.*, at 967.

21 W. Grewe, *ibid.*, p. 967.

border negotiations from 1991 and onwards. The Soviet unilateral change of the borders could be qualified as a *fait accompli*, but not as a result of peaceful change. The negotiations must therefore be understood as a procedure for peaceful settlement of a dispute rather than as peaceful change.[22] However, in these negotiations Estonia and Latvia accepted the territorial *status quo* and thereby gave final legality to the Soviet *fait accompli*. One can therefore, in the context of Baltic-Russian frontiers, speak of an example of how facts can make law—*ex factis oritur ius*.

One of the founders of classic realism, E.H. Carr, has suggested that '[*e*]*very solution of the problem of political change, whether national or international, must be based on a compromise between morality and power*.'[23] It cannot be denied that the aspects of both morality and power were included in legal and political solutions in the Baltic restoration process, which *was* an issue of political change.

Political change is a reality that must sometimes be accepted by more powerful nations than the Baltic republics. The FRG considered for many years the amputation of its territory beyond the so-called Oder-Neisse line as illegal, since—*pacta tertiis nec nocent nec prosunt*—it had never consented to this transfer of territory of the German *Reich*. However, during the reunification process in 1990, Germany gave (or, in a way, was forced to give) its final acceptance to the *status quo*.[24] It has been colloqially maintained that Germany paid for its re-unification with a part of its territory. It may of course be argued that Germany in World War II was an aggressor State and thus had to accept certain negative consequences of a war that its leadership had initiated, while the Baltic States became victims of aggression. However, also in the World War II context, certain territorial changes, such as following the Finnish-Soviet war, were accomplished and recognized as a consequence of aggression.[25]

22 See generally on territorial disputes and change: N. Hill, *Claims to Territory in International Law and Relations*, Oxford University Press: London, 1945; Б. Клименко, *Государственная территория. Вопросы теории и практики международного права*, Москва: Международные Отношения, 1974, p. 125 *et seq*; S.P. Sharma, *Territorial Acquisition, Disputes and International Law*, The Hague: Martinus Nijhoff Publishers, 1997.

23 E.H. Carr, *The Twenty Years' Crisis. An Introduction to the Study of International Relations*, Macmillan: London, 2nd ed. 1946, p. 209.

24 See for discussion and differing views: C. Tomuschat, *Die staatliche Einheit Deutschlands: staats- und völkerrechtliche Aspekte*, Bonn: Friedrich-Ebert-Stiftung, 1990, p. 25 and D. Blumenwitz, *What is Germany?*, 1989, p. 69–70. See also H. Bethge, ‚Das Staatsgebiet des wiedervereinigten Deutschlands', in: Josef Isensee, Paul Kirchhof (eds.) *Handbuch des Staatsrechts*, Band VIII, Heidelberg, 1995, pp. 603–620.

25 See also for this D. Blumenwitz, 'ex factis ius oritur—'ex iniuria iu non oritur', in: D. Blumenwitz and B. Meissner (eds.) *Staatliche und nationale Einheit Deutschlands—ihre Effektivität*, Köln: Verlag Wissenschaft und Politik, 1984, pp. 43–56 at 48.

For international lawyers, the question remains: how much realism should international law theory accommodate? When does acceptance of realist presumptions and considerations abolish (the autonomy of) international law and when does it express common sense?[26] Of the German international lawyers, Wilhelm Grewe has expressed a very realist viewpoint:

> (…) ein Kleinstaat ist im allgemeinen einer Großmacht gegenüber nicht in der Lage, seine Rechtsansprüche durchzusetzen. Den Großmächten fällt es nicht schwer, Mittel, Wege und Argumente zu finden, um lastige Rechtsansprüche kleinerer Staaten zurückzuweisen. Sie unterwefen sich weder einer obligatorischen Gerichtsbarkeit noch einer zwangsweisen Vollstreckung eines Urteils.[27]

Similarly, realist considerations seem to warn of the creation of fictional States in international law. Gaetano Arangio-Ruiz—who has performed as an idealist in matters of State responsibility—has argued contrary to the normative views of Krystyna Marek, and suggested sober realism with respect to the creation of fictional States. Otherwise, international legal doctrine would only create trouble for itself:

> Tout d'abord le droit des gens n'est pas en mesure (…) de créer une personne là où en fait il n'a pas une. Pour être en mesure de poursuivre un tel

26 One attempt to include realist points in the legal discussion has been made by A. Carty, *The Decay of International Law? A Reappraisal of the Limits of Legal Imagination in International Affairs*, Manchester UP, 1986. Carty criticizes that '(a)n international lawyer will rely on the explicit, conventional prohibition of the use of force since the 1920s as proof of the completeness of his legal system. (…) The only way forward is for States to agree to changes in [the] *status quo*. Yet the basic flaw in legal theory is that States define the threats which they face, not in terms of their territorial boundaries, but in the light of their idea of themselves as States. (…) States, organised on the basis of ideologies, feel acutely threatened by one another (…)' See pp. 7–8. However, realist presumptions make this legal author conclude that it is '…necessary for doctrine to accept a subjective, personal and relative role for itself, where the authority it enjoys rests upon the quality of its argument rather than upon a pseudo-objective professionalism. Then the international lawyer may be proud that he proves able to present literature to those active in international society. The Oxford English Dictionary defines literature as "writings that are valued for their beauty of form". Could international lawyers keep better company?' See p. 131.

27 W.G. Grewe, 'Außenpolitik und Völkerrecht in der Praxis', in: 36 *ADV* 1998, p. 3. "A small state is generally unable to enforce its legal rights *vis-à-vis* a great power. It is not difficult for the great powers to find ways, means and arguments to reject the legal claims of smaller states. They are not subject to compulsory jurisdiction or to the compulsory enforcement of a judgment."

> but le droit des gens devrait "contrôler"—c'est-à-dire atteindre—le milieu interindividuel au sein duquel 1'organisation de la personne devrait se réaliser. Nous avons constate qu'il n'en est pas ainsi. (...) le maintien en vie d'une personne qui s'est dissoute n'aurait ni un sens ni une utilité pratique comparable su sens et à 1'utilité du phénomène de droit interne (identitè *légale* de la personne morale) apparemment analogue. Les règles internationales qui poursuivraient de tels buts n'auraient, directement, ni éxécuteurs ni bénéficiaires.[28]

Ethiopian and Albanian lawyers would quite likely disagree with Professor Arangio-Ruiz on the issue whether this rule would have beneficiaries or not; however, the lack of 'executors' is indeed a real problem that international law doctrine must take into account. It therefore seems wise, from a legal standpoint of view, to accept that power plays a role in the implementation of international legal norms since there exists, as Wolfgang Friedmann has put it, 'the bipolarity of politics, as resulting from a perpetual tension between "conscience and power"; between "ethical and coercive factors."[29]

But should international legal doctrine in the case of State continuity take this bipolarity between power and normativity further into account? We will proceed with a brief discussion of views from two legal schools of thought which have explicitly included political aspects in their legal analysis.

3 The New Haven Approach and New Stream: Politics in International Law

Legal academia has not wholly recovered from attacks accomplished by realism. Many lawyers turned away from positivism and suggested new ways of thinking about international law. But new ways of thinking were often at least as contested as the old positivism. The New Haven school, led by Myres

28 G. Arangio-Ruiz, ,L'État dans le sens...', 1975, p. 307. "First of all, the right of peoples cannot (...) create a person where in fact it does not have one. To be able to pursue such a goal the right of peoples would have to "control"—that is, to reach—the interindividual environment within which organization of the person is to be realized. We have found that this is not the case. (...) maintaining the life of a person who has gone would have neither meaning nor practical utility comparable to the meaning and usefulness of the apparently analogous phenomenon of domestic law (legal identity of the legal person). International rules pursuing such aims would have neither executors nor beneficiaries."

29 W. Friedmann, *The Changing Structure of International Law*, London: Stevens & Sons, 1964, p. 50.

S. McDougal and Harold Lasswell, presented their subjective vision and values in the package of an international law of an 'authoritative and controlling decision-making process.' International law was not to be 'objective' rules but was supposed to embrace and *include* politics (not surprisingly, the politics preferred by proponents of the New Haven scholars, and often the US government). The New Haven school's view on international law could thus perfectly enable one to justify all outcomes in the Baltic case as legal. Human dignity, being the ultimate goal of the international legal process according to the New Haven school, is not less problematic and open to manipulation than concepts of rigid positivism. Although influential and intellectually stimulating, the New Haven view on international law has not been deemed satisfactory by many international lawyers, at least outside the USA.[30]

For scholars of the postmodern Critical Legal Studies (New Stream) movement, international law *is* politics, a special professional culture and language for conducting international politics. With this radical identification of international law and politics, New Stream scholars have of course been at odds with positivist scholars who, at least programmatically, presume the separation of law and politics. Martti Koskenniemi has attacked 'the idea that international law provides a non-political way of dealing with international disputes.'[31] In a programmatic article, Koskenniemi has argued that '*our inherited ideal of World Order based on the Rule of Law thinly hides from sight the fact that social conflict must still be solved by political means and that even though there may exist a common legal rhetoric among international lawyers, that rhetoric must* (…) *rely on essentially contested—political—principles to justify outcomes to international disputes.*'[32]

One recognized New Stream method, also employed for demonstrating the political nature of law, is deconstruction of existing legal and intellectual concepts. French philosopher Jacques Derrida, one of the creators of the postmodern deconstruction method, has suggested that it is crucial '… *to recognize that in a classical philosophical opposition we are not dealing with the peaceful coexistence of a vis-à-vis, but rather with a violent hierarchy. One of the two terms governs the other* (*axiologically, logically, etc*) *or has the upper hand. To deconstruct the opposition, first of all, is to overturn the hierarchy at a given moment.*

30 See e.g. S. Voos, *Die Schule von New Haven: Darstellung und Kritik einer amerikanischen Völkerrechtslehre,* Berlin: Duncker & Humblot, 2000.
31 M. Koskenniemi, *From Apology to Utopia…*, p. 50.
32 M. Koskenniemi, 'The Politics of International Law', 1 *EJIL* 1990, p. 7.

To overlook this phase of overturning is to forget the conflictual and subordinating structure of opposition.'[33]

State continuity and succession are concepts well-suited to the method of deconstruction: it is hard to deny that there is a strong element of indeterminacy in those concepts, and in how they are employed in practice. Martti Koskenniemi has deconstructed the notions of State succession, continuity and identity, and argued that the conceptual distinction between identity/continuity and succession is superficial:

> It assumes status as prior to the legal relationships that relate to it. However, it is not certain that the two can be separated in a meaningful way. (...) the mere continuity or disruption of abstract statehood seems much less important for the determination of the rights and duties of the various protagonists of a normative problem than the material scope of the relevant law. Indeed the order between status and the law is now reversed: status is reduced to the sum total of the rights and obligations allocated to an entity by an overriding legal order (...) For this view, whether an entity is 'identical' or 'different' is simply a shorthand to address the continued validity—in temporal, personal, and geographical terms—of certain norms in a transformed political situation where the issue of validity has arisen.[34]

According to Koskenniemi, abstract status is not a useful analytical framework:

> The view which holds status as prior to relationships thinks of statehood as an autonomous quality possessed by certain entities *ab initio*, prior to and independently of their participation in social life. Such an approach projects a Vattelian domestic analogy that considers States as persons, writ large, and their legal relationships as extensions of their statehood. (...) the idea of a State's 'identity' as something given and pre-existing social relationships looks like a rather vulnerable piece of political metaphysics. It also undermines the degree to which an entity's 'statehood' is constructed in the process of communicative interaction between it and the external world and fails to appreciate the extent to which the talk of identity is informed by views about the *right principles* of communal policy. (...) Such analysis avoids the anthropomorphism implied in

33 J. Derrida, *Positions*, Alan Bass trans., Chicago: University of Chicago Press, 1972, p. 41.

34 M. Koskenniemi, 'The Present State of Research', *Hague Academy*, 1996, p. 154.

> thinking about status in material terms, as an inalienable 'soul' of a State. It goes directly into what for lawyers is the important issue, the continuity or discontinuity in the legal rights and obligations that existed prior to the transformations.[35]

This critique succeeds in identifying vulnerable spots in the predominant doctrine of legal status. However, Professor Koskenniemi's suggestion that rights mean status and that there is no 'status as such' has its own weaknesses as well. When deciding about the important issue, namely the fate of legal rights and obligations that existed prior to the transformation(s), only talk of status can determine *which* transformations and thus *which* legal rights and obligations are to be taken into account. By talking about the continuity of legal rights and duties in cases of illegal annexation—or by denying the illegality of annexation and/or the continuity of rights and duties—one inevitably expresses oneself about status as well. How else could one attach one's claim or position to a particular transformation? If there should not be any independent concept of status at all, how could the respective rights and duties, the (dis) continuity of which is at stake, even be identified?

When Koskenniemi argues that his interpretation is based on Marek's theory, he overlooks that Marek not only argued that rights amount to status, but also that a restored State has a basic presumption in favour of restoration of its rights. One way to bridge the gap between the two different approaches would be to argue that the *presumption* of continued validity of rights and duties in the cases of illegal annexation *signifies* status. But Martti Koskenniemi seems to argue that status amounts to those rights that will *in fact* be restored in practice, and nothing more. In this manner, an illegally annexed State whose independence is in the process of restoration would be in a difficult situation: the continuity of its pre-annexation rights and duties is somehow presumed, but at the same time the inability to restore (some of) those rights *in fact* puts the very claim of continuity under doubt. How can the material scope of the relevant law, as suggested by Koskenniemi, determine the outcome when, as for instance in the State borders issue, claims are mutually opposed? Former rights will either be restored or not. Would it be left totally to the political process to decide? For what reasons would those rights that make up identity be restored? It would be a failure of international law to contain little normative guidance for such a situation.

35 Koskenniemi, 'The Present State of Research', p. 156 and 157.

4 Doctrinal Proposal: Status Goes beyond Legal Rights and Duties

State practice in the Baltic case suggests that a distinction exists between two levels of State continuity: status and rights. This is a departure from Krystyna Marek's groundlaying proposition, the price for extending the fiction of continuity of status throughout a prolonged annexation period. Germany has recognized the identity of the Baltic States with the pre-World War II Baltic States, yet it has announced that it prefers not to reinforce pre-World War II bilateral treaties with those States.[36] According to Professor Koskenniemi, there would then, in relations with those States, be no identity of the Baltic States with the pre-1940 republics at all.

At the same time, Germany has recognized the State continuity of the Baltic States with the pre-World War II Baltic republics, and not recognized those States with a birth certificate issued in 1991. This demonstrates that, in the practice of recognition, States have paid attention to something beyond rights and duties which can properly be called status. Its symbolic nature should not be dismissed. International law has always contained doctrinal elements which satisfy legitimate social needs for symbols—for example, when it recognizes satisfaction in the form of an apology as a consequence of State responsibility for internationally wrongful acts. The recognition of status beyond rights and duties does fulfill similar functions, at least the function of recognizing illegality. By recognizing status in the cases of restoration after illegal annexation, the most important right of all States—their right to existence—is recognized. In this function, 'status' perceived as something beyond concrete rights and duties is not necessarily a 'tû-tû'—a legal concept devoid of any real meaning at all, as wittily caricatured by Alf Ross.[37] Instead, status signifies claims and recognitions by States (that is, their peoples, or their governments, or their elites) proclaimed constitutional identities or 'selves.' States do serve and presumably will, at least in the foreseeable future, continue to serve for many people as mirrors of identity, as Brigitte Stern has suggested.[38] It was thus, for example, with a certain determination that the Baltic States celebrated their 100th anniversary in 2018.

36 A similar position was taken by Japan, Italy and China. Possibly, it is also due to fundamental political changes that have taken place in those countries, i.e. not only in the Baltic republics.

37 A. Ross, 'Tû-tû', 70 *Harvard Law Review* 1956/57, pp. 812–825.

38 See B. Stern, 'How to Regulate Globalization?', in: M. Byers (ed.) *The Role of Law in International Politics*, Oxford UP, 2000, pp. 247–268 at 268.

The challenge for legal doctrine seems to be, to quote from the analysis by Paula Escarameia on the concept of self-determination, that '[l]aw has to find ways of avoiding both rigidification by rejecting concepts void of emotion and indeterminacy by rejecting the adoption of political slogans.'[39] Escarameia suggests that in legal conceptualization, goals, ideals, dreams are too precious to be dismissed because such dismissal would correspond to negation of the greatest dimension of humanity.[40] A doctrinal balance between rigidification and indeterminacy of political slogans can also be found in cases of State re-establihment after illegal annexation—in a slight modification of the classic view (as presented by Krystyna Marek). Practice in cases of restoration of States demonstrates that the identity of status is important *per se*, and should not be *in toto* equated with international rights and duties. Matthew C.R. Craven, although splitting up the concepts of State personality and identity, has rightly suggested that identity is primarily concerned with what is personal or exceptional in the nature of the subject.[41] It is therefore possible that State identity has been preserved even when all, or even many, rights and duties have not been reactivated. In such cases of illegal annexation, the problem of status is a 'whether or not' question; the problem of rights and duties is a question of degree and scale. Here lies a certain symbolism of the reconfirmation of the identity of a State whose rights and duties have not remained identical.

That, of course, would not mean that the relationship between status and rights could be abolished altogether in cases of restoration after illegal annexation. Otherwise, we would indeed have a 'tû-tû' situation, and the continuity of a restored State would lose almost any meaning beyond the symbolic. Recognition of State identity on an abstract level of status creates a presumption in favour of restoration of former rights. However, the longer and more pervasive the period of *de facto* non-existence of a since restored State, the more effect can be attributed to existing realities. It follows that restoration of rights and

---

39 P. Escarameia, *Formation of Concepts in International Law. Subsumption under Self-determination in the Case of East Timor*, Lissabon, 1993, p. 106.

40 P. Escarameia, *ibid.*, p. 161.

41 M.C.R. Craven, 'The Problem of State Succession 'and the Identity of States under International Law', 9 EJIL 1998, pp. 142–162 at 160. (' "Identity" assumes that individual states, whilst being members of a particular class of social or legal entities, also possess certain distinguishing features that differentiate one from another.') Similar ideas have been expressed by James Leslie Brierly: 'In a sense in which no individual is, every state is unique. (…) Its history and traditions, its geographical position in the world and the physical configuration of its territory, its economic development, its interests, political, strategic, cultural, and so on—all these things are particular to each individual state and are not the same for all.' J.L. Brierly, *The Outlook for International Law*, Oxford: Clarendon Press, 1945, p. 41.

duties, notwithstanding the identity of status, will be subject to a bi- or multilateral review process. It is then a tribute to the principle of *ex factis oritur ius* when changes in terms of rights and duties are taken into account. Restoration of former rights would not follow automatically. *Restitutio in integrum* would remain a normative guide for the review process, but not the absolute determinant of the further fate of all earlier rights and duties. The discontinuity of certain rights will thus not *a priori* challenge the legal status of the restored State.

Nevertheless, the proposition that the annexing State may not benefit from annexation must be upheld in international law. For instance, the annexing State's refusal to recognize the basic principle of its responsibility for internationally wrongful acts committed during an illegal annexation constitutes a violation of international law. This is *a fortiori* clear with respect to international crimes committed during illegal annexation. Applied to the Soviet annexation of the Baltic republics, it cannot be maintained that the USSR was not legally responsible for the Soviet mass deportations of civilians, which constituted crimes against humanity.

This distinction between status and rights offers more flexibility in dealing with the special circumstances of each case of illegal annexation. For instance, in the case of Austria, its legal status during the period of occupation by Nazi Germany in 1938 and liberation by the Allied Powers in 1945 coexists with the recent establishment of the General Settlement Fund, reflecting a commitment to a self-critical scrutiny of the National Socialist past.[42] Thus, a country which was illegally annexed in World War II has taken upon itself a certain responsibility for illegal acts committed during the period of annexation. In other words, legal status is not totally identical with rights and duties.

Several legal scholars have, upon analysing the case of the Baltic States, suggested splitting up the level of status and the level of rights in the State identity/continuity discussion.[43] The Baltic States may have preserved their continuity, but this does not necessarily imply *restitutio in integrum*. And *vice versa*, the fact that *restitutio in integrum* was implemented with important reservations does not suggest that continuity must be denied. Of course, by

42 See US-Austria: Joint Statement and Exchange of Notes between the United States and Austria concerning the Establishment of the General Settlement Fund for Nazi-Era and World War II Claims, January 2001, 40 ILM 565 (2001), pp. 565–566.

43 See e.g. M. Lehto, 'Succession of States in the Former Soviet Union. Arrangements Concerning the Bilateral Treaties of Finland and the USSR', in: 4 *FYBIL* 1993, pp. 194–228 at 208; M.N. Shaw, 'State Succession Revisited', in: 5 *Finnish YBIL* 1994, pp. 34–98 at 58 (the claim of State identity and its recognition is one thing, but '[t] he recognition of the consequences of such restoration is a different one.') T. Annus, *Riigiõigus* (Constitutional Law), Tallinn: Juura, 2001, p. 23.

separating status and rights in State identity analysis one brings fiction back through the back door. While this theory gives more space to the political, the danger remains that abstract words supporting the identity of status will not be covered by real action, in other words, the readiness to restore legal relations that could follow from it. However, some deviations from the principle of *restitutio in integrum* may be a necessary price for keeping the law relevant to the facts. A brief comparison with the domestic aspects of State continuity in the Baltic case reveals that a full *restitutio in integrum* has also become domestically impossible after so many years of contrary developments.

5 The Domestic Analogy of Restoration in the Baltic States: No *restitutio in integrum*

A brief analysis of the domestic aspects of State restoration already demonstrates that a purist application of the State continuity principle was also impossible in the domestic sphere. Just as it had become practically impossible and unreasonable to deny Soviet-era immigrants the right to stay in the Baltic States, the unconditional restoration of pre-1940 property rights could not occur without important exceptions and transition periods. Notwithstanding many confirmations of the principle of State continuity, its legal consequences remained a subject of political struggle.

In the Estonian parliamentary elections of 1992, the election campaign slogan of one of the winning political parties[44] was: 'Estonia will come back' (*Eesti tuleb tagasi*). This slogan demonstrates quite vividly the eagerness of the Baltic peoples to undo the foreign-imposed Soviet period. However, from the very beginning, the claim for restoration was not undisputed within Baltic societies. In 1989/1991, the restorationists, coming from outside the local communist elite, competed for the sympathy of the electorate. They held a heated intellectual and political dispute with more moderate circles that took a more evolutionary rather than revolutionary (restorationist) view. For people who had made larger compromises in terms of the Soviet regime and a career in the Soviet system, it made less sense to undo the Soviet decades as mere occupation.

Even though the 'restitutionists' tended to prevail in this debate, it became increasingly clear that after fifty-one years of foreign domination, the Baltic States could not return exactly in the form in which they had existed before

44 The Estonian National Independence Party (*Eesti Rahvusliku Sõltumatuse Partei*).

their occupation and annexation in 1940. Changes in society had been too profound for that.

The Baltic States applied a 'pick-and-choose' approach towards their pre-1940 domestic legal—including constitutional—norms. Only Latvia reinstated its pre-World War II Constitution, while Estonia and Lithuania opted for completely new basic laws (which drew on the pre-World War II constitutions, but took a more modern and liberal approach with respect to crucial issues such as separation of powers and basic rights).[45] Of other pre-World War II laws, the majority could not be reinforced automatically since they no longer corresponded to existing social, political and economic realities. Hence, the restored Baltic States temporarily continued with laws adopted by local legislative bodies during Soviet occupation, even when formally the former Soviet laws were transformed in each of the three republics.[46]

One of the most controversial—if central—issues has been restoration of pre-1940 property rights. All former communist countries in Central and Eastern Europe chose the path of (re-) privatisation of former communist era State properties.[47] However, the crucial question of how to transfer State property into private ownership was resolved differently. One of the main dilemmas was whether to restore property to its former owners (or their heirs), or to give preferential treatment to those who had used this property—sometimes *bona fide*—during the communist regime. In the Baltic States, with several noteworthy exceptions, restoration of pre-communist property rights was adopted as a general principle.

45 For an analysis in English, see C. Taube, *Constitutionalism in Estonia, Latvia and Lithuania. A Study in Comparative Constitutional Law*, Uppsala: lustus Förlag, 2001, p. 46 *et seq.*

46 Cf. U. Ziehen (1962) who explains the rational behaviour in such circumstances of *Annexionsbesetzung. 'Obwohl diese Massnahmen rechtswidrig sind, da sie sowohl gegen das volkerrechtliche Annexionsverbot verstossen als auch in die Hoheitsrechte eines anderen Staates ohne Rechtsgrund eingreifen, nimmt man also ihre Folgen im beschranktem Umfang hin, indem man auch nach der Wiedereinsetzung des verletzten Staates bestimmte—von der Okkupationsmacht erlassene—Vorschriften, Massnahmen und Entscheidungen als rechtwirkam betrachtet. Entscheidend dafur ist die Überzeugung, dass es irreal undpraktisch undurchführbar wäre, die von dem Rechtsbrecher in dem besetzten Gebiet effektiv errichtete Herrs chaftsordnung, den tatsächlichen Machtbestand, als nicht existent zu betrachten...'* pp. 95–96.

47 See generally C. Tomuschat (ed.), *Eigentum im Umbruch. Restitution, Privatisierung und Nutzungskonflikte im Europa der Gegenwart,* Berlin: Berlin Verlag Arno Spitz und Verlag Österreich, 1996. For a critical view of the economic effects of the 'restorationist' ideology on the Estonian agriculture, see I. Alanen, *Eesti põllumajanduspoliitika ja võitlus kollektiivmajandite saatuse pärast* (Estonian Agricultural Policy and the Fight for the Fate of the Collective Farms), *Akadeemia* No. 11 2000, pp. 2259–2300.

However, restoration of former property rights has sometimes been balanced with important restrictions. These were deemed necessary to avoid escalation of social conflicts, and to cope with the concrete situation. For instance, the right of landlords to demand rent from tenants living in apartments in pre-1940 buildings was temporarily restricted by the Baltic parliaments (rent control).

In conclusion, such practices in the domestic sphere demonstrate that a pure or unconditional *restitutio in integrum* after an extended period of different social, economic and political realities was both undesirable and impossible. The changes that had taken place during Soviet rule could not be ignored. This domestic parallel may usefully be kept in mind for analysis of international aspects of State continuity. Unconditional *restitutio in integrum* and the total refusal, for instance, to extend citizenship rights in Estonia and in Latvia was not, although a legally pure solution, an acceptable option for the same reason that unconditional restoration of all pre-1940 property relations was impossible.

6 Conclusions

Just as non-recognition of illegal situations must take 'human necessity'[48] into account, the restoration of a legal order in an illegally annexed State cannot ignore changes occurring during annexation, or, for that matter—human necessity. Therefore, as the Baltic case demonstrates, the principle of *ex injuria ius non oritur* is balanced by the contrary principle *ex factis oritur ius* in the restoration process. The importance of the principle of *ex factis oritur ius* can partly be explained by the realist need to acknowledge political change. Application of normative standards is balanced by the circumstances created by power politics. Once a State has been annexed for as long as the Baltic republics were, the principle of *restitutio in integrum* in the fundamentalist sense often could not be applied. Recent State practice and the views presented in the literature demonstrate that a certain separation has occurred between status and the rights of a given restored State. State identity/continuity means not only identity of rights and duties, although claims—or absence of claims—by the restored State for the restoration of former legal rights remain important guidance for the review process, creating a presumption in favour of the restoration of legal relations. Therefore, fact that *restitutio in integrum* has not been unconditionally applied in the Baltic case does not yet challenge the basic

48 *Namibia Opinion*, ICJ Reports 1971, p. 16 (56 para. 126).

principle of the continuity of Estonia, Latvia and Lithuania. Thus, the continuity of the illegally annexed States is indeed a qualified (Brownlie) or a dynamic continuity in the sense that it may not reflect the total continuity of all pre-annexation legal relations. This, however, does not call the State continuity of these States as such into question.

PART 3

Between Normativity and Power: The Implications of the Baltic Case for International Law

CHAPTER 7

The Baltic Case and Lessons from Other Cases

1 Introduction

In the first part of this study, we confirmed the triumph of normative considerations over illegally introduced facts by using the deductive approach, namely by applying general legal concepts to a particular case. The deductive method, like all individual methods of legal inquiry, should be complemented by additional methods. Christian Tomuschat has pointed out the limits of deductive reasoning: it 'can be easily overstretched and even abused. Students of international law could simply 'invent' a basic principle from which they then infer concrete conclusions.'[1] *Ex injuria ius non oritur* could potentially be such a very broad principle, open to overinterpretation. In the preceding chapters of this study, concerning restoration of legal rights, the investigation of application of the principle of *restitutio in integrum* already led to the discovery of a discrepany between a (disputable) general rule and the facts of the cases under examination. That inconsistency was resolved by this author by suggesting slight modifications in the interpretation of the general rule on the basis of recent State practice. Therefore, an inductive approach was already being taken. It may prove useful to further examine the lessons of the Baltic case in this last chapter with the help of the inductive method.

The main issue is: what ideas have crystallized, together with the Baltic case, in international law? What evidence does the Baltic case give about norms and developments in international law? What about the impact of politics which, as we have demonstrated, played an important role in crystallizing the Baltic case? It may then be helpful to employ the inductive approach once again, and compare the Baltic situation with other significant parallel cases.

As we shall see in the following, recent developments in State practice seem to have taken a more normative direction, confirming that the outcome of the Baltic case was not a purely accidental or political fiction. However, each time the international community tries to resist the pull of illegally created facts, it notices that international law cannot totally ignore the power of facts either.

1 See C. Tomuschat, 'Obligations Arising for States without or against their Will', in: 241 *RCADI* 1993, pp. 199–374 at 303.

2 Illegal Annexation and State Continuity

According to a recent rule crystallized in customary international law, the international community is obliged to refuse recognition to illegally achieved annexations. The formulation of the UN GA 1970 Friendly Relations Declaration was discussed above. The duty of non-recognition was supported by the Namibia decision of the ICJ, although this case did not involve illegal use of force against a State. In the Namibia case the ICJ stated that '[t]he Member States of the United Nations are...under obligation to recognize the illegality and invalidity of South Africa's continued presence in Namibia.'[2] The ICJ determined that official acts performed by the Government of South Africa on behalf of or concerning Namibia after the termination of the Mandate are illegal and invalid.'[3] The effectiveness arising from South Africa's continued occupation of Namibia was thus overriden.

In 1940, and in the view of some legal scholars even subsequently,[4] third States were in principle entitled to choose whether or not to recognize a new situation born of aggression. As a consequence, State practice was not uniform and authors used to point out that '[e]*ntre la théorie et la pratique de la non-reconnaissance des acquisitions territoriales effectuées en violation du droit des gens, subsiste ainsi un écart considerable.*'[5] Today, a State recognizing a situation born from violation of the prohibition of threat or use of force itself violates international law.[6]

It is true that even in 1970 several Western States expressed their doubts about the viability of the duty of non-recognition.[7] The question has therefore been debated: to what situations exactly does the duty of non-recognition apply? For example, it has been argued that the obligation to refuse recognition to situations born of violation of the right of peoples to self-determination—that is, to be differentiated from illegal use of force against another State—has

2 See Legal Consequences for States of the Continued Presence of South Africa in Namibia (South West Africa) notwithstanding Security Council Resolution 276 (1970), Advisory Opinion, ICJ Reports 1971, p. 54 (para. 118). See also p. 56 (para 126).

3 Namibia Opinion, ICJ Rep. 1971, p. 56.

4 W.G. Grewe, *Epochen der Völkerrechtsgeschichte,* Baden-Baden: Nomos, 2. Aufl., 1988, p. 710: 'Ob das Prinzip der Stimson-Doktrin (...) Bestandteil des geltenden Völkerrechts geworden ist, mag (...) zweifelhaft erscheinen.'

5 J. Verhoeven, *La reconnaissance internationale...*,1975, p. 308. "Thus a considerable gap remains between the theory and practice of non-recognition of territorial acquisitions achieved in violation of the law of nations."

6 But see A. Cassese, *International Law*, Oxford: University Press, 2001, p. 304.

7 See J. Verhoeven, *La reconnaissance internationale ...*, 1975, p. 292. See also H. M. Blix, 'Contemporary Aspects of Recognition', *RCADI* 1970-II, t. 130, pp. 567–703 at 662–664.

not yet become a part of customary international law.[8] This problem arose in the case of East Timor.

a *The Annexation of East Timor and the Uncertainties of Non-Recognition in State Practice*

On August 30, 1999, a referendum on independence was held in East Timor in which 79 per cent of the people voted for independence. On October 25, 1999, the UN SC passed resolution 1272, establishing a UN Transitional Administration in East Timor (UNTAET) 'to support capacity building for self-government.' Indeonesian rule over East Timor came to an end.

East Timor was a former Portuguese colony invaded by Indonesia on December 7, 1975 and annexed on July 17, 1976.[9] As with the USSR and the case of the Baltic States, claims by Indonesia that it did not violate the prohibition of the use of force, and was invited to intervene, were rejected by a segment of the international community. However, similarly to the Baltic case after 1940, the reaction of the State community to the annexation was not uniform.[10] Among others, several western States recognized East Timor at least *de facto* as part of Indonesia.

International legal scholars have deemed the invasion and annexation of Indonesia illegal on two grounds: illegality of the use of force and violation of the right of the East Timorese people to self-determination.[11] In its Resolution 32/34 of November 28, 1977, the UN General Assembly rejected 'the claim that East Timor has been integrated into Indonesia, inasmuch as the people of the Territory have not been able to exercise freely their right to self-determination and independence.'[12] The prevailing view among legal scholars is that, during

8 See J. Crawford, Legal Counsel for Australia, *Case Concerning East Timor,* I.C.J. Reports 1995, Public Sittings, CR 95/11, 16 February 1995, p. 45 and H. Krieger, *Das Effektivitätsprinzip im Völkerrecht,* p. 197.

9 See *East Timor* (Portugal v. Australia), Judgment, I.C.J. Reports 1995, p. 90. See also J.G. Taylor, *The Indonesian Occupation of East Timor 1974–1989. A Chronology*, London, 1990; H. Krieger (ed.) *East Timor and the International Community. Basic Documents,* Cambridge University Press, 1997; P. Escarameia, *Formation of Concepts in International Law. Subsumption under Self-determination in the Case of East Timor,* Lissabon, 1993.

10 See for overview in: Krieger, p. xxiv and xxv and S. Marks, 'Kuwait and East Timor: a brief study in contrast', in: *International Law and the Question of East Timor*, CIIR/IPJET, 1995, pp. 174–180.

11 See R.S. Clark, 'The 'Decolonisation of East Timor and the United Nations Norms on Self-determination and Aggression', in: *International Law and the Question of East Timor,* CIIR/IPJET, 1995, pp. 65–102 at 73 *et seq.*

12 Reprinted in Krieger, *East Timor...*, p. 125. For analysis, see T. D. Grant, 'East Timor, the UN. System, and Ebforcing Non-Recognition in International Law', 33 *Vanderbilt J. of Transnational Law* 2000, pp. 273–310.

the period of annexation, Indonesia acquired no legal title over East Timor,[13] and that the right of the people of East Timor to create an independent State remained unchanged. The ICJ ruled in 1995 that the territory of East Timor remained a non-self-governing territory and its people had the right to self-determination.[14] Since East Timor was, in 1975, not yet an independent State but rather a non-self-governing territory or 'self-determination unit', this case is not one about preservation of statehood, but a comparable one of continuation of illegal occupation and preservation of the claim of statehood.

When the practice of non-recognition in the case of annexation of the Baltic States contributed to consolidation of the rule by which annexations following illegal use of force must be refused recognition, the case of East Timor supported a similar rule according to which annexation violating the right to self-determination may not be recognized either. However, some international legal scholars have remained cautious when interpreting State practice.

For example, the German scholar Jochen Abraham Frowein used two qualifications when arguing that '[t]erritorial changes brought about by the use of force are *generally* seen to be unlawful and will *in most cases* not be recognized in present-day international law.'[15] Although there may still be good reasons for caution with exceptional constellations, non-recognition practice in the cases of Southern Rhodesia and the Israeli annexation of East Jerusalem and the Golan Heights[16] has overall followed the spirit of the 1970 Friendly Relations Declaration. A noteworthy exception was when the USA under President Trump recognized Israeli sovereignty over the Golan Heights in 2019. Nevertheless, overall there are indications of *opinio iuris* in State practice: the duty of non-recognition has become a rule of customary international law.[17] Non-recognition of illegal situations has become organized and in a certain sense collective in the State community—it is employed in order to maintain

13 See e.g. L. Hannikainen, 'The Case of East Timor from the Perspective of *jus cogens*', in: *International Law and the Question of East Timor*, 1995, p. 103–117 at 111 *et seq*, H. Krieger, *Das Effektivitätsprinzip*, p. 471 and C. Antonoupoulos, 'Effectiveness v. the Rule of Law Following the East Timor Case', 27 *Netherlands YBIL* 1996, pp. 75–111 ar 77.

14 *East Timor Case* (*Portugal v. Australia*), Judgment of 30 June 1995, ICJ Rep. 1995, pp. 105–106, para. 37.

15 See J.A. Frowein, 'Non-recognition', *EPIL* 10, 1987, pp. 314–316 at 315. Italics added.

16 See for East Jerusalem: UN Doc. S/Res./252 of 21.5.1961, for Golan Heights: S/Res/497 of 17.12.1981.

17 Cf. V. Gowlland-Debbas, *Collective Responses to Illegal Acts in International Law*, 1990, p. 284 *et seq*. See e.g. Judge Skubiszewski, dissenting opinion, East Timor, Judgment, I.C.J. Reports 1995, p. 224 at 261 *et seq*. paras. 122–133. See also *Conference of Yugoslavia Arbitration Commission*, Opinion No. 3 of January 11, 1992, 31 ILM 1992 p. 1488, at pp. 1499–1500.

international *ordre public.*[18] Collectivity of action by the international community in such cases is an important step—in the view of Heike Krieger even a precondition for a fiction of 'continued (non-)existence' to be consistently upheld.[19]

According to the ILC Articles on State Responsibility,[20] adopted at the second reading on August 3, 2001, States have an obligation not to 'recognize as lawful a situation created by a serious breach within the meaning of Article 40, nor render aid or assistance in maintaining that situation' (Article 41). The duty of non-recognition has been characterized as 'an early model for the consequences of the breach of an *erga omnes* obligation.'[21]

b *State Continuity as a Necessary Consequence of Illegality of Annexation*

After the end of the Cold War, the rule that illegal annexation does not extinguish the personality of the annexed State was reconfirmed following Iraq's invasion and occupation of Kuwait in August 1990.[22] The UN Security Council called upon all States not to recognize 'any regime set up by the occupying Power', and expressed its great concern about Iraq's declaration of a 'comprehensive and eternal merger' with Kuwait. It declared that the 'annexation of Kuwait by Iraq under any form and whatever pretext has no legal validity, and is considered null and void.'[23] In a later resolution the Security Council determined that the situation in Kuwait was one of continued occupation by Iraq[24] and stated that 'the Fourth Geneva Convention applies to Kuwait.'[25]

The UN and virtually all States viewed the purported annexation of Kuwait by Iraq as null and void *ab initio.* Iraq's occupation and annexation, being illegal, did not affect Kuwait's status under international law. Therefore, the Latvian international law scholar Ineta Ziemele has argued that the Kuwait crisis exemplifies that the prohibition of forcible annexation prevents extinction of the annexed State and that this rule nowadays is binding *erga omnes.*[26]

---

18 Cf. J.A. Frowein, 'Reactions by not Directly Affected States to Breaches of Public International Law', 248 *RCADI* 1994, pp. 345–437 at 431.

19 H. Krieger, *Das Effektivitätsprinzip im Völkerrecht,* 2000, p. 256 and 416.

20 See A/CN.4/L.602/Rev.i, 26 July 2001.

21 C. Tomuschat, *General Course ...,* p. 105–6.

22 See generally B. Stern (ed.) *Les aspects juridiques de la crise et de la guerre du Golfe,* Paris, Montchrestien, Cahier du C.E.D.I.N. no. 6, 1991.

23 UN SC Res. 662 (1990),) 9 August 1990.

24 UN SC Res. 670 (1990), 25 September 1990.

25 UN SC Res. 674 (1990), 13 September 1990.

26 I. Ziemele, *op. cit.,* p. 34.

Realist analysts, however, have also inferred that the speed and efficiency of the reaction by the international community in the Kuwait crisis was *inter alia* due to the strategic importance of Kuwait and its oil for the West and that, for example, a possible annexation in some parts of Africa would not necessarily be confronted with equally determined condemnation by the international community.

State continuity notwithstanding, the nullity of annexation is a function of the by now *ius cogens* nature of the prohibition of use of force in modern international law. There is evidence that a customary rule has developed as a corollary of the prohibition of the threat or use of force, a rule according to which a State would preserve its legal personality notwithstanding illegal annexation, similarly to the classic rule preserving State continuity in cases of *occupatio bellica*. This is essentially what the Baltic illegal annexation case has been about.

By supporting the continued existence of a State, the international community and international law create a legal fiction. The continued existence of an illegally annexed State is different from that of the 'normal' case of statehood where a State government exercises *de facto* power over its people on a defined territory. Such States are during the illegal annexation only 'sleeping' States, although governments in exile may exist as well. Their existence is primarily the continued existence of their rights and duties. Insistence on the continued existence of the legal personality of the State is also a protest; a condemnation and negation of a factual situation achieved by illegal means; a function of the illegality of annexation.

According to Krystyna Marek's interpretation of State practice, in the case of illegal annexation of an independent State, the latter continues to exist as ideal notion until its independence is restored:

> The essence of the matter thus lies in the affirmation of the legal existence of a State as a purely ideal notion. This point cannot be emphasized strongly enough. For the question does not concern a miraculous resurrection of a State which had once become extinct and has subsequently been restored, in which case the problem would not be one of State continuity, but one of a new State creation. On the contrary, the *punctum saliens* is the actual legal existence of the State *during* the actual period of its physical suppression which view alone allows the affirmation of continuity.[27]

27 Marek, *op. cit.*, p. 552.

Why, and on the basis of what reasoning has State practice started to make such departures from the Montevideo criteria of statehood? Departure from strict application of the Montevideo criteria by the international community has usually been accepted only when important considerations pertaining to fundamental legal rules have been present.[28] It has been noted that in order to fulfill its function of guaranteeing stability and order, the international community opposes the violent extinction of its members, which is why its laws must protect existing States.[29] On the basis of the developments analyzed above, this author cannot, therefore, support the view which tends to see mainly 'political fictions' in the continued existence of illegally annexed States.[30] They are political in the sense that *all* legal developments reflect the politics of law. They are legal fictions in the sense described earlier. But they are not fictions created by politics at odds with law—rather, they reflect the pull of international law that is based on values that are also other than classic effectivity.

On other occasions, the international community refrains from asserting that States which have sunk into chaos and anarchy have become extinct. Christian Tomuschat argues that '*Somalia has become a fictitious entity, measured by the yardstick of what is required of a State*', but that there are good reasons why Somalia should *not* easily become extinct: '*For the international community, it is much simpler to carry a man half-dead with it, contending that he is well and alive, instead of issuing a death certificate, which inevitably gives rise to struggles about inheritance.*'[31] In the case of illegal annexation, a very active wanna-be-inheriter is waiting for recognition of their right of inheritance. In that case, the question is no longer what would be simpler or more difficult for the international community to do: it may even be easier to recognize the right of the subjugator. But that the international community would not accord such recognition to the annexing State, and would 'carry a man half-dead with it', seems just to fulfill the minimum requirements of international solidarity and bear witness to the very existence of an international community worthy of

28 See also H.-J. Uibopuu, ‚Gedanken zu einem völkerrechtlichen Staatsbegriff', in: C. Schreuer (ed.) *Autorität und internationale Ordnung. Aufsatze zum Völkerrecht*, Berlin: Duncker & Humblot, 1979, pp. 87–110 at 88.

29 See e.g. H. Ruiz Fabri, 'État (création, succession, compétences). Genèse et disparition de l'état a l'époque contemporaine', 38 *AFDI* 1992, pp. 153–178 at 154–155.

30 But see H. Krieger, *Das Effektivitätsprinzip im Völkerrecht*, p. 175.

31 See C. Tomuschat, *General Course*, p. 110–111. See also Y. Osinbajo, 'Legality in a Collapsed State: the Somali Experience', 45 *ICLQ* 1996, p. 910.

the name.[32] Once aggression becomes outlawed in international law, States cannot be simply eliminated without any normative reaction.

c *Other Relevant Factors beside Illegality? Precedential Effects*

A question that must be posed, however, is: which cases do qualify under the rule of continued existence of State personality notwithstanding illegal annexation? Was the outcome in the Baltic case determined by legal and/or extralegal factors other than the illegality of the annexation?

Whether the outcome in the case of the Baltic States can signal further precedenial effects also depends on what view one takes of international law generally. The possibility of a particular case serving as a precedent seems to be questioned by the policy-oriented-approach to international law (the New Haven approach). Myres McDougal strongly criticized the traditional approach to international legal norms:

> It confuses reference to probable future decisions. It fails to distinguish between past decision and preference for future decision. It confounds statement of past trend in decision and scientific study of variables affecting decision. By overemphasis on past decision, it retards inventiveness in the creation of new situations.[33]

In short, McDougal argues that decisions taken in each case have their own unique contextual grounds, which makes it premature to insist that general legal rules offer pre-determined normative solutions in particular cases. This view is contrary to the positivist model of the rule of law which regards law as impersonal and general, dealing 'with persons and situations as examples of types and not as individual cases to be treated each according to its special circumstances.'[34] In the context of State succession and identity, the Austrian scholar Konrad Bühler has recently challenged the 'theoretical illusion that the identity of a State was "a matter of law to be determined objectively."'[35]

---

32 "The members of the family of nations cannot with honour abandon any independent free nation to international gangsters or pirates.' P.M. Brown, 'Sovereignty in Exile', 35 *AJIL* 1941, p. 667.

33 M. McDougal, 'Some Basic Theoretical Concepts about International Law: A Policy-Oriented Framework of Inquiry', in: R. Falk and S. Mendlovitz (eds.) *The Strategy of World Order, vol. III—International Law*, New York: World Law Fund, 1966, p. 117.

34 J.L. Brierly, *The Outlook for International Law*, Oxford: Clarendon Press, 1945, p. 40.

35 See K. Bühler, *op. cit.*, p. 316. See also pp. 318–319: '...in certain marginal cases the subjective factor of recognition and acceptance of a State's claim to continuity by the international community will become the ultimately decisive criterion for State identity.'

Of course, there are elements of contextuality in the case of the Baltic States, too. The Baltic case had its special features—primarily because the illegality of the use of force lay quite far back in the past, and condemnation by the State community was not collective, to the extent that several States and analysts had almost 'forgotten' the historical circumstances of the annexation. Moreover, the prolonged case of the Baltic States was partly born from the fact that comparable situations, namely Nazi and Soviet territorial seizures in World War II, were not treated in the same way or equally by the international community.

However, the present author has earlier suggested that the crucial element in the case of the Baltic States was the illegality of the annexation, based upon the illegality of the use or threat of military force. Nevertheless, it has been argued that the Baltic case was decided as much by the right of the Baltic peoples to self-determination as by the illegality of Soviet use of force in 1940.[36] However, the right of the Baltic peoples to self-determination, which Soviet Russia had recognized in the Peace Treaties of 1920, further confirms the illegality of annexation. Jorri Duursma seems to overlook this aspect when he counterposes the right of self-determination to the illegality of annexation, and argues that '...the non-recognition of the 1940 annexations was not necessarily the main legal reason for accepting the secession of the Baltic States in 1990.'[37] The Soviet violation of the right of the Baltic peoples to self-determination was just a further factor which made the annexation illegal.[38]

Due to the the right of peoples to self-determination, the non-acquiescence of the Baltic peoples to Soviet rule also acquired an important role in the preservation of the Baltic republics. Although rudimentary remnants of the Baltic State organs continued to function in exile, the illegally suppressed statehood was primarily vested in the Baltic peoples. It may be too bold to argue that, in international law, statehood can be carried on by the people of the State, even in the case of lack of an effective government.[39] Nevertheless, State peoples

36 Cf. on this aspect of self-determination in the Baltic case in A. Cassese, *Self-determination of Peoples. A Legal Reappraisal,* Cambridge UP, 1995, p. 262.

37 See J. Duursma, *Fragmentation and the International Relations of Micro-States. Self-determination and Statehood,* Cambridge UP, 1996, p. 99.

38 See e.g. the US Congress, House Concurrent Resolution 416, 22 October 1966 (pointing to 'denial of the rights of self-determination for the peoples of Estonia, Latvia, and Lithuania and calling for 'restoration of these rights to the Baltic peoples.')

39 This has been suggested with respect of Somalia in J.-D. Mouton, 'L'État selon le droit international: diversité et unité', in: *L'État souverain a l'aube du XXIe siècle. Colloque de Nancy,* Paris, pp. 79–106 at 103.

have become an increasingly important factor in determining international law issues related to statehood.

An additional criterion for legal status, besides the principle of *ex injuria ius non oritur*, is the self-understanding of the restored State.[40] A forceful claim of State continuity by the affected State seems to be a *condition sine qua non* for the affirmation of such continuity. Note, for instance, that today's Republic of Moldova, whose territory was also occupied and annexed by the USSR in 1940,[41] has not claimed restoration of its interwar legal status as a part of Romania. Correspondingly, no such status has been accorded to it by the international community.

The illegality of annexation must therefore be supported by a strongly presented continuity claim. When any one of these aspects is represented weakly, the international community is reluctant to accept State continuity. For example, State practice demonstrates that continuity claims alone, if not accepted, are not capable of according legal continuity to the claimaint. It seems instructive to compare the facts of the Baltic case with another claim to State identity that was almost simultaneous with the Baltic identity/continuity claim—but found a quite different reception in State practice, namely the case of Georgia.

i Georgia 1921–1991: A Non-Recognized Claim of State Continuity

Georgia, an independent republic in the South Caucasus has, with varying consistency, claimed to be legally identical with the independent Georgian Democratic Republic proclaimed on May 26, 1918, and occupied and annexed by the Soviet Russia in 1921.[42] In reference to the Treaty of May 7, 1920, concluded between Georgia and Soviet Russia, the Supreme Soviet of the Georgian SSR declared in the Decree of March 9, 1990, that '*the seizure of* [*Georgia's*] *whole territory in legal terms amounted to military interference* (*intervention*) *and occupation with a purpose of overthrowing the existing political order as from a*

40 Fiedler, p. 60–61. See also on 'self-understanding' in K. Schmid, ‚Gedanken zu Untergang und Entstehung von Staaten in Mittel- und Osteuropa', 69 *Friedens-Warte* 1993, pp. 72–97 at 93 *et seq*.

41 See Graham, 'The Legal Status of the Bukovina and Bessarabia', 38 *AJIL* 1944, pp. 667–673.

42 K. Korkelia, G. Lordkipanidze, 'State Succession in Respect of International Treaties in Post-Independent Soviet Union: Some Reflections on the Status of Georgia', in: *International Law Journal* (Tbilisi State University), Vol. III, 1998, No. I-II, pp. 41–50. Interestingly, after 1918 claims were made for the identity of independent Georgia with Georgia before its incorporation into Tsarist Russia in 1802. See O. Nippold, *La Géorgie du point de vue du droit international*, Berne: Bureau de Presse géorgien, 1920. For critique, see Dörr, *op. cit.*, pp. 48 and 226 *et seq*.

political point of view it turned into factual annexation![43] The Supreme Council went on to declare that it *'condemns the occupation and factual annexation of Georgia by Soviet Russia as an international crime and strives to make void the result of the breach of the 7 May 1920 Treaty and restore the rights of Georgia as recognized by Soviet Russia under this Treaty!'*[44] Most importantly, the Supreme Council of the Georgian SSR decided to *'initiate negotiations with the purpose of restoration of the independent statehood of Georgia, since the Treaty on establishing the Union of Soviet Socialist Republics of December 30, 1922, is illegal in respect of Georgia!*[45] On June 20, 1990, the Supreme Soviet adopted a Decree concerning Creation of a Legal Mechanism of Restoration of Independent Statehood, in which it recognized *'the right of Georgia to restore its State independence lost in 1921 as a result of violation of the treaty of May 7, 1920, by the Government of the RSFSR in the form of intervention, occupation and factual annexation.'*[46]

The Act of Restoration of Georgian Independent Statehood was adopted by the Supreme Council of the Republic of Georgia on April 9, 1991. In that act, not only contemporary Georgia's identity with the Georgian Democratic Republic of 1918–1921, but also the latter's identity with Georgia, subjugated by Russia in 1801, was reconfirmed.[47] The act states that:

> Georgian statehood, which originates from the depth of the centuries, was lost in the 19th century by the Georgian nation as a result of annexation by Russia and abolition of its statehood by the Russian Empire. The Georgian people never submitted to the loss of freedom. By the proclamation

43 See Sakartvelos sabchota sotsialisturi respublikis uzenaesi sabchos utskebebi/the Supreme Soviet Official Gazette of the Georgian Soviet Socialist Republic, 1990, N3 (596), March, Tbilisi, Decree of N52 on Safeguards of the State Sovereignty of Georgia, p. 9. N 214-XI S, March 9, 1990. (Quoted and translated by Korkelia and Lordkipanidze, *ibid.*)

44 *Ibid.*

45 *Ibid.*

46 Sakartvelos sabchota sotsialisturi respublikis uzenaesi sabchos utskebebi/the Supreme Soviet Official Gazette of the Georgian Soviet Socialist Republic, 1990, N6 (599), June, Tbilisi, Decree of the Georgian Supreme Soviet concerning Creation of Legal Mechanism of Restoration of Independent Statehood p. 12–13. N 218-XI S, June 20, 1990. Quoted and translated by Korkelia and Lordkipanidze, *ibid.*

47 See Sakartvelos respublikis uzenaesi sabjos mier migebuli kanonebisa da dadgenilebesis krebuli/Laws and decrees adopted by the Supreme Council of the Republic of Georgia, Act of Restoration of the Georgian Independent Statehood, N 291, April 9, 1991. Quoted and translated by Korkelia and Lordkipanidze, *op. cit.*, p. 47 *et seq.* For a critical account, see Dörr, *Die Inkorporation*, p. 48.

> of Independence Act of 26 May 1918 the abolished Georgian statehood was restored. (…)
>
> Georgia did not voluntarily join the Soviet Union and its statehood exists until today, the Independence Act and the Constitution are still legally valid since the Government of the Democratic Republic did not sign the capitulation act and continued activity in exile.
>
> The Supreme Council of the Republic of Georgia elected by multi-party, democratic vote on 28 October 1990 based on the unanimous will of the Georgian population expressed by the Referendum of 31 May 1991, states and makes publicly known the restoration of Georgian independent statehood on the basis of the Georgian Independence Act of 26 May 1918.[48]

Subsequently, in January 1992, the Military Council (Georgian provisional Government) decided to re-instate the Georgian Constitution of February 22, 1921.[49] This decision remained, as Ferdinand Feldbrugge has argued, rather a political gesture by the Gamsakhurdia government than an actual change of constitution.[50] Although on August 24, 1995, the new Georgian Constitution was adopted, its preamble reiterates the fundamental principles of the 1921 Georgian Constitution.[51]

Notwithstanding the Georgian position, its claim to State continuity has not found any specific recognition in international practice.[52] Therefore, as a general rule, Georgia was still considered to be bound by the legal obligations of the USSR.

Why was State identity recognized in the Baltics, but not in the Georgian case? This must be asked, especially in light of the fact that the duration of the incorporation of the Baltic States, fifty-one years, is not fundamentally different from the seventy-year annexation of Georgia. When a State can, as a legal

---

48 See *ibid.* (*Sakartvelos…*).

49 See Korkelia and Lordkipanidze, *op. cit.*, p. 47.

50 See F.J.M. Feldbrugge, 'The Law of the Republic of Georgia', 18 *Review of Central and East European Law*, 1992, No. 4, p. 372.

51 See Korkelia and Lordkipanidze, *op. cit.*, p. 48.

52 See C. Gray, *YBEL*, p. 487. The position accepted by State practice is that all former Soviet republics, except the Baltic States became successor States of the USSR. The Russian Federation was recognized as the State continuator to the USSR. See e.g. ILA Helsinki Conference (1996), Aspects of the Law of State Succession, *Rapport preliminaire sur la succession d'etats en matiere de traites*, pp. 13–15. See also L. Love, 'International Agreement Obligations after the Soviet Union's Break-up: Current United States Practice and Its Consistency with International Law', *Vanderbilt Journal of Transnational Law*, Vol. 26, 1993, pp. 394–395.

fiction, preserve its statehood for fifty years, why should it not be able to do so for seventy? Moreover, Georgia, too, had for a while a government in exile; for example, the legation in Paris existed until 1933.

However, the crucial differences between the Georgian and the Baltic cases seem to lie elsewhere. Why did key Western States ultimately recognize the Soviet seizure in Georgia but not in the Baltic case? The most crucial factor seems to be the legality of forcible seizure under general international law. Of course, today's Georgia has correctly argued that Soviet Russia violated the non-aggression treaty in force between Georgia and Russia when it occupied and annexed Georgia in 1921. Before that, 'Georgia possessed all the necessary attributes of a State and was rendered recognition by more than twenty States out of the total number of States that existed at the beginning of the century.'[53] At the same time, however, it played a significant role in practice that the period of Georgia's independence (1918–1921) was too short for later international recognition of the continuity link. Georgia's independence could not properly crystallize before it was taken over by Soviet Russia in 1921.

Most importantly, Soviet Russia did not violate a universal norm prohibiting the use of force when it resubjugated Georgia in 1921. For these reasons, the claim to independent Georgia's continuation as a subject of international law during the Soviet period (1921–1991) was dismissed by the international community. At the same time, no clear answers have yet been given in State practice about whether Georgia is to be treated as a classic successor State of the USSR in terms of mandatory succession to all relevant treaty obligations of the USSR.[54] As the Russian Federation recognized the 'independence' of the breakaway regions of Abkhazia and South Ossetia in 2008, both parts of the Georgian SSR, today's Russia and Georgia continue a deep conflict over the borders and geopolitical orientation of Georgia.

The case of Georgia demonstrates that State continuity in cases of annexation is never about pure symbolism of status—if it would, Georgia's identity would have been recognized as easily in 1991 as the identity of the Baltic States.

53 Korkelia and Lordkipanidze, *op. cit.*, p. 48.

54 It is interesting to note that Georgian authors K. Korkelia and G. Lordkipanidze refer to the continuity claim of Georgian constitutive acts from 1990–1992, but at the same time argue that '*the status of Georgia within the Soviet Union could match the definition of Newly Independent States given in article 16 of the Vienna Convention.*' On the basis of these two—in the view of this writer, contradictory—premises, the authors argue: '*Thus, it could be stated that the status of Georgia is different from that of the other republics (except the Baltic States) of the Soviet Union in contradistinction to the views held by some legal scholars from the former Soviet Union.*' See *op. cit.*, p. 48.

The fact that it was not demonstrates that State continuity presupposes certain important conditions set by international law.

ii The Status of Non-Recognized State Continuity Claims

It is evident that the claim to be a subject of international law identical with a previous historical State formation has no international consequences when that identity is dismissed by the State community, on the basis that the annexation was legal at the time and other States consider the former State to have become extinct. When other States deny a State's claim to identity on the ground of legality of annexation, then continuity is, from the standpoint of international legal personality, non-existent, notwithstanding the constitutional claims by the affected State. This holds especially true in the historical cases mentioned when there was no rule of *ex injuria ius non oritur* preserving the continuity of annexed States. From today's point of view of morality, the (third) partition of Poland in 1795 may be just as reprehensible as the Iraqi annexation of Kuwait in 1990, yet it was not illegal from the point of view of international law at the time.

It may be concluded that in State practice, identity *claims* can sometimes also be irrelevant for the purposes of international law. Such, for instance, is the Lithuanian claim that it was occupied between 1795 and 1918. Kazimiera Prunskiene, a former Lithuanian prime minister, enters the terrain of political rhetoric rather than international law when she argues that '[*i*]*n den letzten zwei Jahrhunderten wurde Litauen* (…) *zweimal von Russland bzw. der Sowjetunion okkupiert. Die erste Okkupation dauerte 120 Jahre und endete 1918*.'[55]

There can be no identity of two subjects of international law when the first subject has been annexed with no clear violation of the international law of that time.

What, then, is the fate and value of the identity (and continuity) claim of a State when other States reject it on legal grounds? No other actor in international relations can, of course, prohibit a State from seeing itself as it wishes. One recalls the primacy of political interest in determination of international legal status in cases of continuity/ succession.[56] However, for continuity claims

---

55 See K. Prunskiene, 'Unabhängigkeit als Option für die Selbstbestimmung—das Beispiel Litauen', in: K. Ludwig (ed.) *Perspektiven für Tibet.* (…), München, 2000, pp. 91–97 at 91. "[i]n the last two centuries Lithuania (…) has been occupied twice by Russia and the Soviet Union respectively. The first occupation lasted 120 years and ended in 1918."

56 See also P.M. Eisemann, 'Bilan de recherches…', in: *State Successsion: Codification Tested Against the Facts*, Hague Academy, 1996, p. 52: '*Face à cet événement, les États concernés vont élaborer une stratégie juridique correspondant à leurs fins politiques. Leur "politique juridique extérieure" les conduira tout naturellement à utiliser le droit international pour*

to become effective and meaningful in international relations, the recognition of such claims by substantive State practice is crucial. Indeed, such recognition, at the end of the day, becomes an additional test of identity.

Therefore, State identity in the domestic (constitutional) and international sense can also be regarded separately.[57] A State may or may not be identical with its predecessor in the sense of domestic law (the respective position of the State itself being the only decisive factor), while its status as a subject of international law can differ from that position.[58] Communist Russia after 1917 was continuous with Tsarist Russia as a subject of international law, but not in the sense of its own constitutional understanding. Poland after 1918 was regarded by its courts as the same State as pre-1795 Poland in the constitutional sense, but not by the international community, at least not in the legally relevant sense.

Although a State's self-understanding with respect to its legal personality can have a strong influence on the attitude of the international community, it does not, however, determine the identity of a subject of international law.[59] In cases when an identity/continuity claim is raised but not recognized, one can speak, not of the continuity of the State as a subject of international law, but about the historical or political revival[60] of the State, of restoration in the sense of constitutional law. The re-birth of a State, involving its political and historical—but not its legal—identity is not a case of identity in the sense of international law.[61]

The unsuccessful claim by Georgia demonstrates that the international community is willing to support claims of State continuity only when supported by elements such as a clear violation of the rule prohibiting the use of force against a State, and subsequent non-recognition of annexation. Claims that do not fit these criteria, although born in situations of considerable injustice, will likely be rejected. Such may be the issue with the argument of the precedential effect of the restoration of the Baltic States for the situation in Chechnya.

---

parvenir au but qu'ils se sont assignés plus qu'ils ne chercheront à appliquer des normes supposées "objectivement' applicables."

57 See Fiedler, *Staatskontinuität...* 1970, p. 102 *et seq.* and Fiedler, *Das Kontinuitätsproblem...*1978, pp. 38–39 and 102.

58 See the views of Kelsen, Verdross and Marek, as summarized by Cansacchi, *op. cit.* p. 19; Cf. also U. Scheuner, 'Die Funktionsnachfolge und das Problem der staatsrechlichen Kontinuität', in: *Vom Bonner Grundgesetz zur gesamtdeutschen Verfassung,* (*Festschrift für Franz Nawiasky*), München: Isar Verlag, 1956, p. 9 at 12 and 14.

59 Cf. Fiedler, *Das Kontinuitätsproblem...*, p. 69.

60 Cf. Fiedler, *ibid.*, p. 37.

61 Cf. Marek, *op. cit.*, p. 28 and 581.

iii A Case Beyond the Baltic Precedent: Chechnya

Dr Thomas D. Grant of Cambridge University has examined the question whether the restoration of the independence of the Baltic States in 1991 may have served as a legal model for Chechnya, the formerly separatist North Caucasus republic in the composition of the Russian Federation.[62] The military conflict in Chechnya and the attempts undertaken during the 1990s to achieve and consolidate Chechnya's independence have been much publicized in the mass media. Grant lays out Chechnya's tumultuous history, in particular the history of the expansion of the Russian Empire in the Caucasus during the 19th century. From 1849 to 1856 there appears to have been a Chechen State, led by Shamil.[63] Of course, this State was not recognized by European countries and did not enjoy the privileges of *jus publicum europaeum*. Grant demonstrates how Chenchnya's history in the composition of the Russian Empire and later in the USSR has been one of rebellion, resistance and repression. Even during the Soviet period, Chechnya remained a somewhat unsafe periphery of Soviet effective control with a 'diarchy of structures' where official structures such as district committees of the party, kolkhozes and courts functioned on the surface, but 'in reality all of them were no more than outward forms of the traditional Islamic structures.'[64]

On the basis of these factual assumptions, Grant discusses whether Chechnya was ever legally acquired by Russia. As the Baltic States were never legally acquired by the USSR and thus the statehood of the Baltic republics was preserved, Grant suggests that Chechnya could have cemented its independence (claim) on the same legal principle:[65]

> It may well be that it is this very status that Aslan Maskhadov would like to prove Chechnya too possesses—a territory never incorporated *de jure* into the Russian Empire and thus a territory not requiring recognition as a new state. If Chechnya could be proven to possess a status like that of the Baltic States, then the international community in treating Chechnya as a state would not effect any change in legal statuses.[66]

62 T.D. Grant, 'A Panel of Experts for Chechnya: Purposes and Prospects in Light of International Law', IX *Finnish YBIL* 1998, pp. 145–248, especially at 204 *et seq.*

63 See *ibid.* p. 174–177.

64 See *ibid.* p. 184 and 187.

65 See *ibid.* p. 195.

66 See *ibid*, p. 204.

In conclusion, Grant finds that although 'it appears plausible that the Russian Empire and its continuations, the RSFSR and the USSR, gained legal title to the Chechen lands by prescription', then, nevertheless, 'doubts surround that doctrine [of prescription].'[67] Moreover, Grant adds that recent developments in international law may suggest a 'review' of the question of prescription—Russian title may not have survived changes in international law, that is, Russia 'at some point lost title to Chechnya.'[68]

It was, however, quite doubtful whether the continuity of the Baltic States could serve as a legal model for the independence claim by the Chechen rebel movement. It appears highly questionable whether Chechnya has ever been recognized as a sovereign State, as a subject of international law. Moreover, it seems incorrect to question the existence of prescription in the case of the Russian seizure of Chechnya in the 19th century, a conquest that cannot be challenged according to the international law of that time. Chechnya became legally a part of the Russian Empire. Should Russian title to Chechnya be denied on the basis of absence of prescription, it could be denied, in a similar stretched application of the concept, in other parts of Russia and furthermore, the world. Most States treated the rebellion in Chechnya over the 1990s differently from the case of the Baltic States in 1989–1991—from the standpoint of the legal positions *de facto* as opposite examples. The analogy of Chechnya makes evident once again the importance of established statehood and of illegal annexation in the solution given to the Baltic situation.

A solution to the situation of Chechnya in the framework of international law must be found within the limits of the right of peoples to self-determination. However, according to international law today, the existence of the right to self-determination supports the claim for an independent State only in exceptional circumstances.

3 Departures from the Effectiveness Principle and Fear of Unfulfilled Fictions

Other parallel developments and cases involving State personality point to the fact that statehood in international law can no longer be understood simply as a sociological fact. When confronted with violations of peremptory norms of international law, the practice of States has started to depart from unrestricted application of the effectiveness doctrine. Similarly to the problem of

67 Grant, *op. cit.*, p. 222.

68 Grant, *op. cit.* p. 233.

extinction of States, international practice has made important qualifications to the 'three elements theory' in the question of creation of States.[69] Entities that have claimed statehood but have been created in violation of the right to self-determination or the rule prohibiting apartheid have on several occasions not been recognized as States under international law.

For instance, Southern Rhodesia had effective government, but was not recognized as State, since its government had violated the rule prohibiting apartheid and the right to self-determination.[70] The domestic effectiveness of the regime of Ian Smith, in power in Southern Rhodesia for more than fourteen years, has never been questioned. However, for the purposes of recognition, considerations of effectiveness were ignored, in order to ensure enforcement of an international norm deemed fundamental to the international community.[71]

Vera Gowlland-Debbas has argued that fourteen years of collective non-recognition of the effective situation in Southern Rhodesia did not necessarily highlight the powerlessness of legality as opposed to effectivity—on the contrary, '[*i*]*t is undoubtedly because of the general non-recognition of the effectiveness of the situation created by the illegal regime over the years, that the Southern Rhodesian case came closer to a solution than it otherwise would have done.*'[72]

The principle of effectiveness could not, however, be ignored altogether in the Southern Rhodesian case. It was in the interest of the international community to establish that during the time of its *de facto* existence, Southern Rhodesia would not, notwithstanding its illegality, stand completely outside of international law—rather, its status was characterized as that of a *de facto* regime.[73]

Similarly, the Bantustans—the South African homelands of Transkei, Ciskei, Boputhatswana and Venda—were not considered States by the international

69 See T. Darsow, *Zum Wandel des Staatsbegriffi. Unter besonderer Berücksichtigung der Lehre und Praxis internationaler Organisationen, der Mikrostaaten und der Palästinensischen Befreiungsorganisation* (PLO), Frankfurt: Peter Lang, 1984, p. 264. See also H. Krieger, *Das Effektivitätsprinzip im Völkerrecht,* 2000, p. 176.

70 UN SC Res. 217 (1965), 277 (1970), 288 (1970), 328 (1973), 423 (1978), 445 (1979), 448 (1979). See further J. Crawford, *The Creation of States…*, 1979, pp. 105–6. J. Dugard, *Recognition and the United Nations,* Cambridge: Grotius Publications, 1987, pp. 90–8.

71 See further V Gowlland-Debbas, *Collective Responses to Illegal Acts in International Law. United Nations Action in the Question of Southern Rhodesia,* Dordrecht: Martinus Nijhoff, 1990, p. 182 *et seq.*

72 V Gowlland-Debbas, *Collective Responses to Illegal Acts….,* 1990, p. 325. See also V Gowlland-Debbas, 'The Functions of the United Nations Security Council in the International Legal System', in: M. Byers, *The Role of Law in International Politics*, Oxford, 2000, pp. 277–314 at 304.

73 See H. Krieger, *Das EJfektivitätsprinzip im Völkerrecht,* p. 203 and 218.

community, since their creation by the South African regime violated the rule prohibiting apartheid.[74] Their creation was without legal effect not because they lacked effectiveness, but because their existence violated peremptory rules of international law.[75] The State community has started to deny State qualities to entities that have been created following violations of the rule prohibiting use or threat of military force. N.L. Wallace-Bruce therefore argues:

> ... if an entity emerges onto the international scene through acts which are illegal under international law, no matter how effective it might be, its claims to statehood could not be maintained. It ... cannot be clothed with legitimacy by the international community.[76]

At the same time, international lawyers sometimes express doubts about the effectiveness of such fictions, which attempt to ignore 'sociological reality.' Antonio Cassese maintains that '(i)nternational law is a realistic legal system (...) largely based on the principle of effectivity.'[77] Louis Henkin has argued that the Rhodesian case did not overhaul the usual criteria for statehood, based on effectiveness, but constituted only an exception to those criteria. However, according to Professor Henkin, '[t]hat exception may not be pragmatic or 'realistic' but it is designed for a practical end, to put pressure on the offending State to terminate the illegality.'[78] The most significant concern for international law seems to be the possibility of a situation where a fiction has been adopted, and pressure on the offending State to terminate illegal behaviour is present, but the situation has been consolidated to the extent that the fiction indeed starts to appear non-efficient and irrealistic. This, in its turn, could potentially undermine the credibility of the relevant international legal rule.

Such doubts have sometimes been confirmed in State practice. An example would be the situation in Northern Cyprus. The Turkish army invaded Cyprus in 1974—according to the Turkish position in order to protect the Turkish minority in Cyprus. On November 15, 1983, the Turkish Republic of Northern Cyprus (TRNC) was proclaimed on the 'Turkish' part of the island. Although

---

74 See UN SC Res. 402 (1976). See also J. Dugard, *Recognition and the United Nations,* Cambridge: Grotius Publications, 1987, pp. 90–98 and E. Stabreit, *Der völkerrechtliche Status der Transkei, Ciskei, Bophuthatswanas und Vendas während der Zeit ihrer formellen Unabhängigkeit von der Republik Südafrika,* Frankfurt a.M., 1997.

75 J. Dugard, *op. cit.*, p. 131.

76 N.L. Wallace-Bruce, *Claims to Statehood in International Law,* New York: Carlton Press, 1994, p. 67.

77 A. Cassese, *International Law,* Oxford: University Press, 2001, p. 12.

78 See L. Henkin, 'International Law: Politics, Values and Functions', *RCADI* 1989-IV, t. 216, p. 32.

the TRNC could today qualify as a State on the formal basis of the elements of territory, population and effective government, it has not as yet been recognized as a State by the international community, except by Turkey.[79]

However, non-recognition of the TRNC has so far not brought an end to the illegal situation. Voices demanding a political compromise between Cyprus, Turkey and Greece, and thus due attention to the principle *ex factis oritur ius,* have become increasingly audible. In the past, US President Clinton's statement on September 28, 1999 that there could be no return to the pre-1974 status of the island was regarded as a significant breakthough by Turkey and the first step to achieving some way of satisfying northern Cyprus's demand for recognition short of statehood.[80] In the legal literature, too, it has been doubted whether the initial illegality of the creation of the TRNC can stand against its statehood *ad infinitum*.[81]

The phenomenon of departure from the 'three elements theory' for the defence of illegally annexed States and against other illegally managed situations, thus continues to be accompanied by the eroding effect of the principle *ex factis oritur ius*. Moreover, legal developments cannot of course expel the political from matters of recognition and non-recognition of statehood. Often pronouncements that have been made on recognition and statehood are a mixture of political considerations and legal standards. Some non-factual criteria, as proclamied in recent State practice, may leave some space for manipulation, or maybe even for forms of modern imperialism. The December 16, 1991 EU Guidelines on the Recognition of New States in Eastern Europe and in the Soviet Union made no reference to effectiveness, but contained a long list of normative requirements, such as rule of law, democracy and human rights, instead.[82] At the same time, the EC recalled that 'its member States will not recognize entities which are the result of aggression.'[83] In another circumstance, however, a controversial statement by the EC Arbitration Commission

79 See UN SC Res. 541 (1983). (The UN SC '... 2. Considers the declaration referred to above as legally invalid and calls for its withdrawal; ... 7. Calls upon all States not to recognize any Cypriot State other than the Republic of Cyprus ...') See further K. Chrysostomides, *The Republic of Cyprus. A Study in International Law,* The Hague: Nijhoff, 2000 and for a Turkish view: Y. Altuğ, 'The Cyprus Question', in: 21 *GYBIL* 1978, pp. 311–344.

80 See R. Dwan, 'Armed Conflict Prevention, Management and Resolution', in: *SIPRI YB 2000. Armaments, Disarmament and International Security*, Oxford UP, 2000, pp. 77–134 at 122.

81 H. Krieger, *Das Effektivitätsprinzip im Völkerrecht,* 2000, p. 253.

82 See for the text e.g. in 31 ILM 1992, p. 1486. See also J. Charpentier, 'Les déclaration des Douze sur la reconnaissance des nouveaux États', *R.G.D.I.P.*, 1992, pp. 343–355 and R. Bieber, 'European Community Recognition of Eastern European States: A New Perspective for International Law?', in: *ASIL Proceedings* 1992, pp. 374–378.

83 See *ibid.*

on Yugoslavia (the so-called Badinter Commission) in its Opinion No. 1[84] still reads, in conservative fashion, that 'the existence or extinction of a State is a question of fact.'

The complex interplay between international law and politics can also be observed in the case which most genuinely resembles the legal situation of the Baltic States during their illegal annexation, namely that of the Chinese annexation of Tibet.

a *Legality and Effectiveness in Tibet*

Tibet's modern political history has certain parallels with developments in the Baltic States. Historically, Tibet in the Himalayas has always been a buffer zone between Chinese and Indian civilizations.[85] The exiled leaders of Tibet and the Chinese leadership hold opposing views about the historical relationship between China and Tibet. Tibet's status in medieval times is difficult, if not impossible to explain with the help of notions which were developed in late medieval Europe, such as sovereignty or State. In any case, international law was hardly universal at the time and in East Asia the Sinocentric system of tributary neighbours of China was the reality. In earlier centuries, Tibet appears to have been a *de facto* independent entity, with only a symbolic relationship of suzerainty with the Chinese Emperor. It has been suggested that the status of Tibet at this time was something akin to a loose protectorate or tributary State; in any case, it was not a province of China.[86] From 1912 until 1950, Tibet was *de facto* independent from China.[87] However, during its independence, Tibet followed an isolationist policy: it was a hermit State. For example, it never applied for membership in the League of Nations at the time.

China, however, has always opposed the position that Tibet was an independent State. According to the official Chinese position, Tibet has always been a part of China—with varying degrees of autonomy.[88]

The Communists, coming to power in China under the leadership of Mao Zedong, invaded Tibet on October 7, 1950. The 14th Dalai Lama, Tenzin Gyatso, sought support from other States, and wrote, for instance, to the UN that '... *there*

84 Published in R.G.D.I.P. 1992, pp. 264–269. See also A. Pellet, 'Note sur la Commission d'arbitrage de la Conférence pour la paix en Yougoslavie', *AFDI*, 1991, pp. 329–348.

85 See generally A.D. Hughes, 'Tibet', in: *EPIL* 4, 2000, pp. 858–861.

86 See International Commission of Jurists (ed.) *The Question of Tibet and the Rule of Law*, Geneva, 1959, p. 83.

87 See G. Gyaltag, 'Das Recht auf Selbstbestimmung aus historischer Sicht', in: Ludwig (ed.), pp. 49–59 at 56. See also C.H. Alexandrowicz-Alexander, 'The Legal Position of Tibet', 48 *AJIL* 1954, pp. 265–274.

88 See e.g. T.-T. Li, 'The Legal Position of Tibet', 50 *AJIL* 1956, pp. 394–404.

is little hope that a nation dedicated to peace will be able to resist the brutal effort of men trained to war, but we understand that the United Nations has decided to stop aggression whenever it takes place.'[89] However, attempts by Tibetan envoys to find support in the West and at the UN remained unsuccessful.

Initially, the Tibetan leaders were allowed by the Chinese authorities to remain formally in their positions. However, the formal annexation of Tibet to China was carried out in 1951. On May 23, 1951, the Chinese forced the Tibetan delegation in Beijing to sign an 'Agreement of the Central People's Government of Tibet on Measures for the Peaceful Liberation of Tibet' (also known as the Seventeen-Point Agreement). This agreement was not voluntary, was concluded under duress, and was therefore not ratified or sealed by the Dalai Lama.[90] Due to the violations involved, the Tibetan leadership has considered the Seventeen-Point-Agreement null and void. Complete subjugation of Tibet's autonomy by China followed in 1959, subsequent to an anti-Chinese uprising in Tibet. The Dalai Lama and approximately 100,000 of his fellow Tibetans were forced to flee the country and take refuge in neigbouring India and other countries.

Under the leadership of the 14th Dalai Lama, the Tibetan government in exile—the Kashag—was formed in Dharmsala, India. This government in exile has, however, not been recognized by other States. To the contrary, all States have formally recognized Tibet as part of China. At the same time, the attitude of third States to China's claims has sometimes been inconclusive and noncommittal.[91] The USA, for instance, seems on the one hand to recognize Chinese sovereignty over Tibet, but on the other hand, it has also condemned China's aggression and invasion of Tibet.[92] Notwithstanding Chinese protests, US President George W. Bush met with the Dalai Lama in a 'private capacity', on the 50th anniversary of the Chinese-Tibetan 17-point agreement which China claims confirmed Chinese sovereignty over Tibet.[93] Moreover, Chinese human rights violations in Tibet have several times been condemned by the GA of the UN.[94]

---

89 From the Appeal by His Holiness the Dalai Lama of Tibet to the United Nations, November 11, 1950, UN Doc. A/1549, reprinted in M.C. van Walt van Praag, *The Status of Tibet*, p. 337.

90 See Int. Com. Of Jurists, *The Question of Tibet*, p. 96 and M.C. van Walt van Praag, *The Status of Tibet. History, Rights, and Prospects in International Law*, Boulder: Westview Press, 1987, p. 147 and 157.

91 See M.C. van Walt van Praag, *The Status of Tibet*, p. 185.

92 See further van Walt van Praag, p. 186.

93 See E. Eckholm, 'A New Poke in the Eye: China Bristles Over Tibet', *NY Times*, May 23, 2001.

94 See Res. 1353 (XIV) of October 21,1959, 1723 (XV) in 1961 and 2079 (XX) of December 18, 1965 of the UN GA.

What is Tibet's status from the viewpoint of international law today? Although this issue has invoked abundant scholarly attention,[95] issues remain open. Although the exact nature of the sovereignty of Tibet between 1912 and 1950 has been debated, most Western international legal scholars agree that the Chinese invasion of Tibet in 1950 violated the prohibition of the use of force in international law.[96] Michael C. van Walt van Praag has persuasively argued that the People s Republic of China could not have obtained legal title of sovereignty over Tibet on the basis either of military invasion or of the subsequent exercise of a measure of effective control.[97] He argues that in terms of international law, the State of Tibet, supported by the continued existence and activity of the Tibetan government in exile, continues to exist:

> The continued support for the Dalai Lama among the overwhelming majority of the population, the active resistance to Chinese rule in Tibet, the successful development of Tibetan policy in exile, and the functioning of the government in exile are all factors that contribute to the continuity of the Tibetan State.[98]

If one accepts the proposition that Tibet was an independent State before the Chinese invasion, it can be concluded that legal considerations similar to the Baltic case apply in the case of Tibet as well. The challenge in the situation of Tibet, however, is similar to the Baltic States during the 1970s/1980s. One can forever insist on the illegality of annexation and on unchanged legal status, but if the illegal situation appears to be effective for so long... The main task for the government in exile remains to guarantee the survival and the safeguarding of basic interests of the Tibetan people. *Die normative Kraft des Faktischen* has caused a realization of the need for compromise among the Tibetan leaders. Until the 1970s, the Tibetan government in exile fought for the complete independence of Tibet. Recently, however, the Dalai Lama has stepped back from this demand, and has instead consented to real autonomy of Tibet within China.[99] In 1988, the Dalai Lama presented the details of his autonomy plan for Tibet to the European

95 See e.g. R. McCorquodale/N. Orosz (eds.) *Tibet: The Position in International Law. Report of the Conference of International Lawyers on Issues relating to Self-Determination and Independence for Tibet,* London, 1994; G. Schmitz, *Tibet und das Selbstbestimmungsrecht der Völker,* Berlin: Walter de Gruyter, 1998.

96 See e.g. van Walt van Praag, p. 154.

97 Van Walt van Praag, p. 187.

98 Van Walt van Praag, p. 187.

99 See His Holiness XIV Dalai Lama, 'Die Zukunft Tibets', in: K. Ludwig (ed.) *Perspektiven für Tibet. Auf dem Weg zu einer Zukunft in Freiheit und Selbstbestimmung*, München: Diamant Verlag, 2000, p. 13–23 at 13.

Parliament in Strasbourg. Nevertheless, several other Tibetan refugee groups still continue to claim the right of independence for Tibet.

It seems, however, that most States nowadays fail to condemn the situation in Tibet outright as illegal in terms of China's sovereign title. If anything, Western states sometimes point out human rights violations; not ony in Tibet but in other Chinese regions as well.

4 Concluding Observations

The discussion about the legal status of the Baltic States upon restoration of their independence led us to analyze other relevant cases in international relations such as that of Tibet. The case of the Chinese annexation of Tibet demonstrates that a legal study about the consequences of illegal annexation should not be restricted to the past—the story of the illegal annexation of the Baltic republics in 1940–1991 is today relevant elsewhere, and will very likely be relevant in the future, too. It is an inspiring story for nations whose sovereignty is temporarily suppressed.

This book highlights how the principles of both *ex injuria ius non oritur* and *ex factis oritur ius* contradict and complement each other in the practice of international law. On the one hand, international law seeks to be normative and keep its promise of distinguishing between legal and illegal acts. On the other hand, the pursuit of normativity and justice in international law has always been balanced with the principle of effectiveness. This contradiction is sometimes revealed in responses of international law to annexations following illegal use of force.

In the Baltic case, the principle *ex injuria ius non oritur* managed to keep its central promise. Already during World War II, the international community accepted the legal principle that an illegally annexed State would not become extinct as a subject of international law. Restoration of the sovereignty of Estonia, Latvia and Lithuania in 1991 reconfirmed this legal rule—notwithstanding that the Soviet illegal annexation had lasted for half a century. The case of the Baltic States therefore demonstrates that the international community and international law have taken a further step in protection of established States against illegal annexation. A rule has developed in customary international law, according to which an illegally annexed State does not become extinct, and can consequently preserve its legal personality for as long as fifty years. Before the prohibition of the use and/or threat of force, the response of international law to forcible seizure was that a State became extinct when its independent government—for whatever reasons—disappeared or ceased to exercise effective power over its territory, at least when occupation could no longer be said to be temporary. Nowadays, following illegal use of force, an illegally annexed State can survive for longer periods, and re-emerge after restoration of independence as the same subject of international law that existed *de facto* prior to annexation.

Recent State practice regarding statehood thus confirms the observation of Sir Robert Jennings that 'the law will always lean towards the principle that a wrongful act must be ineffective to change or to create legal rights.'[100] The case of the Baltic States illustrates a phenomenon which has been described as the emerging decline of the effectiveness doctrine in international law.[101] International law must be based on considerations of effectiveness, but effectiveness cannot prevail when respect for most fundamental provisions of international law is at stake. In the context of statehood, the trend has been towards overhauling the strict application of the 'purely fact-based' Montevideo criteria of statehood in cases of illegality.[102] We agree with the observation of Obiora Chinedu Okafor that 'the traditional deference of international law is slowly giving way to the incorporation of normative requirements in decision-making regarding the legitimacy or otherwise of states.'[103]

This change in international law and its practice can be appraised primarily from a historical perspective. In order to comprehend the revolutionary nature of the transformation of international *opinio iuris*, one needs only to think back to a time when even the most idealistic international lawyers, such as Walter Schätzel, did not see a chance for international solidarity with the victims of conquest:

> Vor allem muß man sich vor dem Fehlschluß hüten, daß andere Staaten und Völker für die nationalen Forderungen eines bestimmten Volkes ein besonderes Interesse hätten. Ihre eigene Ruhe und Sicherheit ist ihnen wichtiger. Bezeichnend ist die Äußerung von Proudhon: '*Qu'est-ce que le monde a perdu en laissant perir la Pologne?*[104]

100 R. Jennings, 'Nullity and Effectiveness in International Law', in: *Cambridge Essays in International Law, Essays in Honour of Lord McNair*, London, 1965, p. 64–87 at 72.

101 See also O.C. Okafor, *Re-Defining Legitimate Statehood* (…), The Hague: Nijhoff, 2000, p. 65.

102 102 See for similar conclusions: T.D. Grant, 'Defining Statehood: The Montevideo Convention and its Discontents', 37 *Columbia JTL* 1999, pp. 403–457 at 408 and 434.

103 103 See Okafor, *ibid.* p. 65.

104 W Schätzel, *Die Annexion im Völkerrecht,* 1920, reprinted in 1959, p. 175 (quoting Proudhon, *La guerre et la paix,* 1861, t. I, p. 59). "Above all, one must beware of the fallacy that other states and peoples have a special interest in the national demands of a particular people. Their own peace and security is more important to them. Proudhon's statement is significant: 'What has the world lost in allowing Poland to die?"

Compared to this earlier thinking, international law and the morality on which it is based have changed. Even though each State's own comfort and security have remained—and most likely will remain—the most important factors determining its policies, modern international law recognizes that indeed, it has something important to lose when the international community allows its members to be attacked and annexed without serious collective reaction.

But the Baltic case also reveals that facts, too, tend to have their own power, as indeed does the principle *ex factis oritur ius* in international law. While the principle of State continuity was clearly supported in State practice in the Baltic case, some consequences of this principle remained debatable. In practice, the main issue concerning restoration of the Baltic States was what the identity and continuity of those States with the pre-war Republics should *mean*. Ultimately, the Baltic States were not successful in claiming *restitutio in integrum*: the international legal relations of the pre-annexation period could not be restored in totality. The present book has suggested that international law doctrine should move closer to the facts in the cases of illegal annexation, and distinguish between the continuity of legal status as such, on the one hand, and the continuity of legal rights and duties on the other. State continuity in cases of illegal annexation of course presupposes continuity of rights and duties, but failure to restore all pre-annexation legal relations would not necessarily call into question the continuity of status as such. The concept of State continuity in cases of illegal annexation demonstrates the increasing reluctance of the international community to accept the principle of unrestricted effectiveness, and thus symbolizes a further maturing of international law.

Appendix 1

Directive No. 02622 the People's Comissar for Defence of the USSR, Marshal S. Timoshenko, and the Chief of the General Staff, Marshal B. Shaposhnikov to the Commander of the Red Banner Baltic Fleet, V. Tributski of June 9, 1940.

Source: the Central Archives of the Naval Forces of the USSR.[1]

The Commander of the Red Banner Baltic Fleet was directed (the exact translation of the document follows):

1. To transfer at 05.00 of 10 June of the current year the Red Banner Baltic Fleet into operative subordination of the Commander of the Leningrad military district, and from 12 July it be ready to perform combat tasks under his directives.
   a. To secure full alert of the naval bases and vessels of the Red Banner Baltic Fleet, situated at the ports of Tallinn, Paldiski and Liepaja.
   b. To capture, under the command of the Commander of the Leningrad military district, all vessels of the Estonian and Latvian naval forces.
   c. To capture mercantile marine and vessels.
   d. To prepare and organize the landing of troops in Paldiski and Tallinn, to seize ports and batteries of Tallinn.
   e. To block the gulf of Riga.
   f. To organize a permanent and secure patrol service: on the Gulf of Finland—from the direction of Finland, and on the Baltic Sea—from the direction of Sweden and from the south.
   g. To assist, in close collaboration with armed forces, the troops of the Leningrad military district in their advance towards Rakvere.
   h. To prevent, by using air force, the air fleet of Estonia and Latvia from flying to Finland and Sweden.
2. The Commander of the Leningrad military district shall establish the exact time of the commencement of military actions.
3. The combat plan of the Red Banner Baltic Fleet is to be elaborated and submitted by 11 June of the current year for approval.[2]

---

1 Central Archives of the Naval Forces of the USSR, C. R-92, r. 2c, f. 671, s. 1–2 R-92, r. 2c, f. 672, s. 171–252. Available on the internet, at the website of the Foreign Ministry of the Republic of Estonia, http://www.vm.ee/eng/estoday/2000/Directive.htm, visited on November 20, 2000.

2 *Ibid.* See http://www.vm.ee/eng/estoday/2000/Directive.htm, visited on November 20, 2000.

Appendix 2

Excerpts from the report of the Commander of the Red Banner Baltic Fleet, Vice Admiral Vladimir Tributs about implementation of orders.[1]

Sheet 171. According to the Directive of the People's Comissar for Defence of the USSR No-0262222 of June 9, 1940, the Red Banner Baltic Fleet was assigned the following missions:

1. To capture all vessels of the Estonian and Latvian naval forces both at bases as well as at sea, to capture the naval forces of Lithuania.
2. To capture mercantile marine and vessels of Estonia, Latvia, to disrupt sea connections between these countries.
3. To prepare and organize the landing of troops in Paldiski and Tallinn, to seize the ports of Tallinn and batteries on the islands Nargen and Vulf, to be prepared to seize the Suurupi battery from the mainland.
4. To block the Gulf of Riga and the coasts of Estonia and Latvia on the Gulf of Finland and the Baltic Sea, to prevent evacuation of the governments of these countries or troops and property.
5. To organize permanent and secure patrol service: on the Gulf of Finland—from the direction of Finland, and on the Baltic Sea—from the direction of Sweden and from the south.
6. To assist, in close collaboration with armed forces, the troops of the Leningrad military district in their advance towards Rakvere.
7. To prevent, by using air force, the air fleet of Estonia and Latvia from flying to Finland and Sweden.

Sheet 172. 120 vessels participated in the operation, include. 1 liner vessel, 1 cruiser, 2 leaders, 1 gun boat, 7 fighters, 5 guard ships, 7 base trawlers, 18 heavy trawlers, 17 submarines, 10 torpedo boats.

Air Forces of the Red Banner Baltic Fleet including:

8th air base—7 sq. 'SB' and 'DB-3'
10th air base—64 planes, 'MBR-2', 'SB'
10th air force regiment—64 planes, 'MBR-2'
73rd air force regiment—9 planes, 'MBR-2'
61st fighter base in full for purveyance of the General Naval base.

Sheet 176. During the negotiation period and after reaching the agreements between the government of the Soviet Union and the governments of Estonia, Latvia and Lithuania, the Red Banner Baltic Fleet discharged the following missions:

---

1 Central State Archives of the Naval Forces, C. R-92, r.2c, f. 672, s. 171–252. Excerpts available at http://www.vm.ee/eng/estoday/2000/Report.htm, visited on November 20, 2000.

a. Sea connection between these countries was disrupted.

b. The submarines of the 1st, 2nd, 3rd and 4th submarine brigades assumed their positions in the Baltic Sea, in the Gulfs of Riga and Finland executing the mission to prevent sea connections, sailing of vessels and evacuation of troops and property.

(…) F. The Gulf of Riga was blocked and the coasts of Estonia and Latvia were blockaded from the direction of the Gulf of Finland and the Baltic Sea. The air forces of Latvia and Estonia were prevented from flying to Finland and Sweden.

Sheet 179b. A total of 52 (Latvian, Estonian, Finnish and Swedish) vessels were captured by our ships and submarines during the blockade period.

Sheet 251. The light force unit of the Red Banner Baltic Fleet on board of the cruiser 'Kirov', leaders 'Minsk' and 'Leningrad', destroyers 'Gordyi' and 'Lenin' captured 7 Latvian and 2 Estonian transports.

Sheet 252. Due to resistance from the transports, the cruiser 'Kirov', destroyer 'Lenin' and submarine 'S-I' fired warning shots, after which the transports halted.

Appendix 3

Report of the People's Comissar for the Defence of the USSR to General Secretary of the CP of the USSR Josef Stalin and to People's Comissar for the Foreign Affairs Vyatcheslav Molotov, no. 390ss (completely secret) – 17 June 1940.

Source: VRSA, f. 4, n. 19, s 71, l 238–238 ob (Quoted in: M. Мэлтюхов, *Наращивание советского военного присутствия в Прибалтике в 1939–1941 гг.*—Отечественная история, No. 4 2000, стр. 46–70. Estonian translation by J. Isotamm in: 13 Akadeemia No. 10, 2001, pp. 2074–2095 at 2087–2088.)

'I consider it necessary in the interest of guaranteeing the quickest preparation of the Baltic war theatre (*teatr vojennogo deistvii*) to start without delay to perform the following actions in the occupied territories:

1. To occupy without delay the border with East Prussia and the coast of the Baltic Sea by our border guard military units, in order to prevent espionage and diversion.
2. To install into each occupied republic one (in the first place) regiment of the NKVD forces for the protection of the domestic order.
3. To solve as quickly as possible the problem of the "governments" of the occupied republics.
4. To start the expropriation of weapons from the armies of the occupied republics and their reformation. To expropriate weapons from the population, police and the existing military organizations.
5. To assume control of guarding and garrisoning functions by our troops.
6. To start decisively to sovietize the occupied republics.
7. To form on the territories of the occupied republics the Baltic Military Region, with headquarters in Riga. To appoint, in charge of the troops of the Region, the director of the troops in the Central Asian Military Region, general polkovnik Apanassenko. The headquarters of the Military Area will be formed on the basis of the headquarters of the 8. Army.
8. To start on the territory of the Area works for the preparation of the war theater (construction of fortifications, the change of the width of the rails, the construction of roads, stocks, the creation of reserves etc.)

I will present the plan of the preparation of the war theater in addition.'

Appendix 4

On June 13, 2000 the Seimas (parliament) of the Republic of Lithuania adopted the *Law on Compensation of Damage resulting from the Occupation by the USSR*[1] which reads as follows:

> The Seimas of the Republic of Lithuania,
>
> in line with:
>
> the universally recognised norms and principles of international law as well as the international practice of compensation of damage caused by occupations to other countries and the citizens thereof, during the World War II period,
>
> Republic of Lithunia Supreme Council-Reconstituent Seimas Resolution of June 4, 1991, 'On Compensation of the Damage inflicted by the USSR on the Republic of Lithuania and its Citizens During 1940–1990,'

the July 29, 1991 Treaty between the Republic of Lithuania and the Russian Soviet Federated Socialist Republic on the Basis for Relations between States, in which the parties declared to be 'convinced that once the Union of Soviet Socialist Republics annuls the consequences of the 1940 annexation violating Lithuania's sovereignty, additional conditions will be created for mutual trust between the High Contracting Parties and their peoples',

> the will of the people expressed by the universal vote of the Republic of Lithuania citizens in the June 14, 1992 Referendum On the Withdrawal of the Russian Army and Compensation for the Caused Damage and demand that 'the damage inflicted upon the Lithuanian people and the State of Lithuania will be compensated,' which was approved by the June 30, 1992 Resolution of the Supreme Council-Reconstituent Seimas,
>
> Article 15 of the Helsinki Summit Declaration of July 10, 1992 and the accompanying expanatory statement by the Delegation of Lithuania, which notes that the compensation of the losses experienced by Lithuania, as well as withdrawal of the russian occupation army from the territory of sovereign Lithuania, is an essential precondition for elimination of the consequences of the occupation and annexation;
>
> taking into account the fact that according to international law, the Russian Federation is the successor to the rights and obligations of the USSR, and this

1 Republic of Lithuania law on Compensation of Damage resulting from the Occupation by the USSR, June 13, 2000, No. VIII-1727, Vilnius.

it acknowledged itself by the Resolution of the Council of the Leaders of the Commonwealth of Independent States, of December 21, 1991, the letter of the president of the Russian Federation, B. Yeltsin, addressed to the United Nations Secretary General of December 24, 1991, the January 13, 1992 note of the Foreign Ministry of the Russian Federation addressed to heads of the diplomatic representations, and other documents, as well as the fact that, on December 23, 1991, the European Community and the Member States thereof, stated that, 'Russia shall be a successor to and shall implement the international rights and obligations of the former USSR';

stating that although Russia demonstrated a great deal of good will and withdrew its army in accordance with the procedure and within the terms established by the agreements of September 8, 1992, it has not yet eliminated all the consequences of the USSR occupation and annexation of Lithuania, and it still occupies the land and building belonging to Lithuania in Paris and similar issues in Rome have not been resolved as yet,

passes this law:

Article 1. Periods of Damage Inflicted by the USSR Occupation on Lithuania

The periods of damage inflicted by the USSR occupation on Lithuania shall be as follows:

1. the USSR occupation and damage during 1940–1990, including the damage caused to the Lithuania people deported and forcibly detained in the USSR territory during 1941–1945, as well as the damage inflicted by the USSR Army and repression structures during that period;
2. damages caused by the USSR, its repression structures and the army during 1990–1991, and damages caused by the Army of the USSR (the Russian Federation 1992–1993) during the period between 1991 and 1993.

Article 2. Obligations of the Government of the Republic of Lithuania

The Government of the Republic of Lithuania shall:

1. prior to September 1, 2000 form a delegation for negotiations of the Republic of Lithuania with the Russian Federation concerning the compensation of the USSR occupation damage to the Republic of Lithuania;
2. prior to October 1, 2000 in accordance with the work programme approved by Government Resolution No. 242 of February 13, 1996 'On the Work Programme on the Evaluation of the Damage Inflicted on the Republic of Lithuania by the Army of the Russian Federation during 1991–1993', specify more accurately and finish calculations of the damage caused by the USSR occupation, including payments to the Lithuanian citizens for the damage caused during the USSR occupation and its consequences, as well as expenses related to the homecoming of the deportees and their descendants;

3. prior to November 1, 2000 appeal to the Russian Federation for the compensation of the damage caused during the period of the USSR occupation, submitting the calculations of damage, also inform the United Nations Organisation, the Council of Europe and the European Union about this, and constantly seek the support of these Organisations and the member States thereof when solving the issues of the compensation of the USSR occupation damage to Lithuania;
4. initiate negotiations and constantly seek that the Russian Federation compensate to the Lithuanan people and the State of Lithuania for the damage caused by the USSR occupation;
5. accumulate funds received from the Russian Federation as the compensation of the damage caused by the USSR occupation, in the separate occupation damage compensation account in the State Treasury, and primarily allocate such funds to compensate for the damage caused to the Lithuanian people due to deportations, forced labour, occupation regime repression and lost property.

Article 3. The Fund for the Return to the Homeland of the Persons Deported by the USSR

Bearing on mind that on January 25, 1996, the Russian federation committed itself before the Council of Europe to assist the persons, previously deported from the occupied Baltic States and (or) their descendants, to return to their country according to special repatriation and compensation programmes, the Government of the Republic of Lithuania shall create a Fund for the Return to the Homeland of the Persons Deported by the USSR, and shall appeal to the Russian Federation regarding the allocation of funds for the return to the Homeland of the persons deported from Lithuania, and their descendants.

Based upon the second paragraph of Article 71 of the Costitution of the republic of Lithuania, I promulgate this law passed by the Seimas of the Republic of Lithuania.

Chairman of the Seimas of the Republic of Lithuania
Vytautas Landsbergis

Bibliography

Treatises

Abi-Saab, G., *Les Nations Unies et le droit international humanitaire. Actes du colloque international de l'Université de Genève*, Paris: A. Pedone, 1996

Ali Khan, L., *The Extinction of Nation-States. A World without Borders*, The Hague: Kluwer, 1998

Allcock, J.B., *et al.* (ed.) *Border and Territorial Disputes*, 3rd ed., Longman Current Affairs, 1992

Ando, N., *Surrender, Occupation, and Private Property in International Law. An Evaluation of US Practice in Japan*, Oxford: Clarendon Press, 1991

Annus, T., *Riigiõigus* (Constitutional Law), Tallinn: Juura, 2001

Arangio-Ruiz, G., *L'État dans le sens du Droit des Gens et la notion du droit international*, Bologna: Cooperativa Libraria Universitaria, 1975

Arend, A.C., *Legal Rules and International Society*, New York: Oxford University Press, 1999

Arendt, H., *The Origins of Totalitarianism*, London: André Deutsch, 1986

Aron, R., *Peace and War: A Theory of International Relations*, translated by R. Howard and A. Baker Fox, Garden City, NY: Doubleday, 1966

Барсегов, Ю.Г., *Территория в международном праве. Юридическая природа территориального верховенства и правовые основания распоряжения территорией*, Москва: Государсвенное издательство юридической литературы, 1958

Bedjaoui, M., *La Révolution algèrienne et le droit*, Bruxelles: Association internationale des juristes démocrates, 1961

Bekiashev, K.A. (ed.) *Mezhdunarodnoe publichnoe pravo*, 2nd ed., Moscow: Prospekt, 2003

Belgrad, E.A., *The Theory and Practice of Prescriptive Acquisition in International Law*, Dissertation at the Johns Hopkins University, Baltimore, 1967

Benvenisti, E., *The International Law of Occupation*, Princeton: Princeton University Press, 1993

Biger, G., *The Encyclopedia of International Boundaries*, Jerusalem, 1995

Bjerge, B., *Nowherelands. An Atlas of Vanished Countries 1840–1985*, New York: Thames & Hudson, 2017

Blumenwitz, D., *What is Germany? Exploring Germany's Status after World War II*, Bonn: Kulturstiftung der deutschen Vertriebenen, 1989

Bollow, U., *Die baltische Frage in der internationalen Politik nach 1945*, Berlin: Freie Universität Berlin Politikwissenschaften, 1993

Boyle, F.A., *World Politics and International Law*, Durham: Duke University Press, 1985

Борбов, Р.Л., *Основные проблемы теории международного права*, Москва: Международные отношения, 1968

Brierly, J.L., *The Outlook for International Law*, Oxford: Clarendon Press, 1945

Brownlie, I., *International Law and the Use of Force by States*, Oxford: Clarendon Press, 1963

Brownlie, I., *Principles of Public International Law*, 5th ed., Oxford: Clarendon Press, 1998

Bühler, K., *State Succession and Membership in International Organizations. Legal Theories* versus *Political Pragmatism*, The Hague: Kluwer, 2001

Bull, H., *The Anarchical Society, A Study of Order in World Politics*, 2nd ed., New York: Columbia University Press, 1995

Byers, M. (ed.), *The Role of Law in International Politics. Essays in International Relations and International Law*, Oxford: Oxford University Press, 2000

Capaldo, G.Z., *Le situazione territoriali illegitime nel diritto internazionale*, Napoli: Editoriale Scientifica, 1977

Carr, E.H., *The Twenty Years' Crisis. An Introduction to the Study of International Relations*, Macmillan: London, 2nd ed. 1946

Carty, A., *The Decay of International Law? A Reappraisal of the Limits of Legal Imagination in International Affairs*, Manchester: Manchester University Press, 1986

Cassese, A., and J.H.H. Weiler (eds.), *Change and Stability in International Law-Making*, 1988, Berlin: W. de Gruyter, 1988

Cassese, A., *Self-determination of Peoples. A Legal Reappraisal*, Cambridge: Cambridge University Press, 1995

Cassese, A., *International Law*, Oxford: University Press, 2001

Charpentier, J., *La reconnaissance internationale et l'évolution du droit des gens*, Paris: Pedone, 1956

Chen, T.-C., *The International Law of Recognition. With Special Reference to Practice in Great Britain and the United States*, London: Stevens & Sons, 1951

Chernichenko, S.V., *Teoria mezhdunarodnoga prava, Tom II, Starye i novye teoreticheskie problemy*, Moscow: NIMP, 1999

Chrysostomides, K., *The Republic of Cyprus. A Study in International Law*, The Hague: Nijhoff, 2000

Clute, R.E., *The International Legal Status of Austria, 1938–1955*, The Hague: Nijhoff, 1962

Crawford, J., *The Creation of States in International Law*, Oxford: Clarendon Press, 1979

Crawford J. (ed.), The International Law Commission's Articles on State Responsibility. Introduction, Text and Commentaries, Cambridge: Cambridge University Press, 2002

Cumper, P., and S. Wheatley (eds.), *Minority Rights in the 'New' Europe*, The Hague: Nijhoff, 1999

Cuthbertson I.M., and J. Leibowitz (eds.), *Minorities: The New Europe's Old Issue,* Prague etc: Open Society Press, 1993

Dahm, G., *Völkerrecht*, Band I, Stuttgart: Kohlhammer, 1958

Dahm, G./J. Delbrück/R. Wolfrum, *Völkerrecht*, Bd. I/1, 2. Aufl., Berlin: de Gruyter, 1989

Daillier, P., A. Pellet, Nguyen Quoc Dinh, *Droit international public*, 6e edition, Paris: L.G.D.J, 1999

Darsow, T., *Zum Wandel des Staatsbegriffs. Unter besonderer Berücksichtigung der Lehre und Praxis internationaler Organisationen, der Mikrostaaten und der Palästinensischen Befreiungsorganisation* (*PLO*), Frankfurt: Peter Lang, 1984

Debbasch, O., *L'Occupation militaire. Pouvoirs reconnus aux forces armées hors de leur territoire national,* Paris: R. Pichon et R. Durand-Auzias, 1962

Derrida, J., *Positions*, translated by Alan Bass, Chicago: University of Chicago Press, 1972

Dinstein, Y., *War, Aggression and Self-Defence,* 2nd ed., Cambridge: Cambridge University Press, 1994

Дипломатическая Академия МИД РФ et al. (соз.), *Международное право*, Издание 2е, Москва: Международные Отношения, 1998

Документы внешней политики СССР, том. I, Москва, 1957

Doehring, K., *Völkerrecht. Ein Lehrbuch,* Heidelberg: C.F. Müller Verlag, 1999

Dugard, J., *Recognition and the United Nations,* Cambridge: Grotius Publications, 1987

Dunsdorfs, E., *The Baltic Dilemma. The Case of the de jure Recognition by Australia of the Incorporation of the Baltic States into the Soviet Union*, New York: Robert Speller & Sons, Publishers, Inc, 1975

Duroselle, J.-B., *Histoire diplomatique de 1919 à nos jours,* 11e édition, Paris: Duroselle, 1993

Duursma, J., *Fragmentation and the International Relations of Micro-States. Self-determination and Statehood*, Cambridge: Cambridge University Press, 1996

Эсаян, А.А., *Некоторые вопросы теории и истории международного права*, Ереван: Издательство Ереванского Университета, 1977

Escarameia, P., *Formation of Concepts in International Law. Subsumption under Self-determination in the Case of East Timor*, Lissabon, 1993

Fassbender, B., *UN Security Council Reform and the Right of Veto. A Constitutional Perspective,* The Hague: Kluwer, 1998

Fastenrath, U., T. Schweisfurth, C.T. Ebenroth, *Das Recht der Staatensukzession.* (*The Law of State Succession*), Berichte der Deutschen Gesellschaft für Völkerrecht, Bd. 35, Heidelberg: C. F. Müller Verlag, 1996

Фельдман, Д.И., (соз.), Международная правосубьектность (некоторые вопроы теории), Москва: Юридическая литература, 1971

Fiedler, W., *Staatskontinuität und Verfassungsrechtsprechung. Zum Begriff der Kontinuität des deutschen Staatswesens, unter besonderer Berücksichtigung der Rechtsprechung des Bundesverfassungsgerichts*, Freiburg: K. Alber, 1970

Fiedler, W., *Das Kontinuitätsproblem im Völkerrecht. Zum funktionalen Zusammenhang zwischen Völkerrecht, Staatsrecht und Politik*, Freiburg: K. Alber, 1978

Fischer, A., *Teheran, Jalta, Potsdam. Die sowjetische Protokolle von den Kriegskonferenzen der 'Großen Drei'*, Köln: Verlag Wissenschaft und Politik, 1973

Fischer, F., *Griff nach Weltmacht. Die Kriegszielpolitik des kaiserlichen Deutschland 1914/18, 1. Aufl.*, Düsseldorf: Droste Verlag, 1961

Franck, T.M., *Fairness in International Law and Institutions*, Oxford: University Press, 1995

Friedmann, W., *The Changing Structure of International Law*, London: Stevens & Sons, 1964

Getman-Pavlova, I.P., *Mezhdunarodnoe pravo*, Moscow: Yurait, 2013

Ginsburgs, G., *Moscow's Road to Nuremberg, the Soviet Background to the Trial*, The Hague: Martinus Nijhoff, 1996

Ginsburgs, G., *From Soviet to Russian International Law. Studies in Continuity and Change*, The Hague: Nijhoff, 1998

Glahn, G. von, *The Occupation of Enemy Territory. A Commentary on the Law and Practice of Belligerent Occupation*, Minneapolis: The University of Minnesota Press, 1957

Gornig, G.-H., *Der Hitler-Stalin-Pakt. Eine völkerrechtliche Studie*, Frankfurt: Peter Lang, 1990

Gowlland-Debbas, V., *Collective Responses to Illegal Acts in International Law. United Nations Action in the Question of Southern Rhodesia*, Dordrecht: Martinus Nijhoff, 1990

Grabar, V.E., *The History of International Law in Russia 1647–1917. A Bio-Bibliographical Study*, translated by W.E. Butler, Oxford: Clarendon Press, 1990

Graber, D.A., *The Development of the Law of Belligerent Occupation 1867–1914*, New York: Columbia University Press, 1949

Grashoff, D., *Staatensukzessionbedingter Schuldnerwechsel. Die Teilung öffentlicher Schulden unter Nachfolgestaaten im Dismembrationsfall*, Frankfurt a.M.: Peter Lang, 1995

Grewe, W.G., *Epochen der Völkerrechtsgeschichte*, Baden-Baden: Nomos, 2. Aufl., 1988

Grotius, H., *De iure belli ac pacis*, reprinted in Aalen: Scientia Verlag, 1993

Guggenheim, P., *Traité de droit international public. Avec mention de la pratique internationale et suisse*, Avec la collaboration de D. Kappler, 2. èd., t. 1, Genève: Georg, 1967

Hannikainen, L., *Peremptory Norms (Jus Cogens) in International Law. Historical Development, Criteria, Present Status*, Helsinki: Lakimiesliiton Kustannus, 1988

Hathaway, O.A.; Shapiro, S.J., *The Internationalists. How a Radical Plan to Outlaw War Remade the World*, New York: Simon & Schuster, 2017

Henckaerts, J.-M., *Mass Expulsion in Modern International Law and Practice*, Martinus Nijhoff: The Hague: 1995

Henkin, L., *How Nations Behave. Law and Foreign Policy*, New York et al: Frederick A. Praeger, 1968

Hall, W.E., *A Treatise on International Law*, 8th ed., ed. by A. P. Higgins, Oxford, 1924, reprinted by Scientia Verlag (Aalen), 1979

Hathaway, O.A., Shapiro, S.J., *The Internationalists. How a Radical Plan to Outaw War Remade the World*, New York: Simon & Schuster, 2017

Hermelin, O., *Gerechte Ablehnung derer lassterhafften Beschuldigungen womit der moscowitische Czar seinen Krieg damit er Schweden wieder Eyd und noch neulich versicherte Treu und Glauben angegriffen zu beschönigen gesuchet hat*, Stockholm, 1701

Heumann, G., *Aspects juridiques de l'indépendence estonienne*, Anvers: Lloyd, 1937

Hill, N., *Claims to Territory in International Law and Relations*, London: Oxford University Press, 1945

Hillgruber, C., *Die Aufnahme neuer Staaten in die Völkerrechtsgemeinschaft. Das völkerrechtliche Institut der Anerkennung von Neustaaten in der Praxis des 19. und 20. Jahrhunderts*, Frankfurt a.M.: Peter Lang, 1997

Hirsch, F., *Soviet Judgment at Nuremberg. A New History of the International Military Tribunal after World War II*, Oxford: Oxford University Press, 2020

International Commission of Jurists (ed.) *The Question of Tibet and the Rule of Law*, Geneva, 1959

International Commission of Jurists (ed.), *Tibet: Human Rights and the Rule of Law*, Geneva, 1997

ILA (ed.), *Rapport preliminaire sur la succession d'Etats en matiere de traites*, (rapporteur B. Stern), in: Report of the 67th Conference held at Helsinki, Finland, 12 to 17 August 1996, London, 1996

ILA (ed.), *Rapport interimaire sur la succession en matiere de traites constitutifs d'organisations internationales et de traites adoptes au sein des organisations internationales*, (rapporteur B. Stern), in: Report of the 68th Conference held at Taipei, Republic of China, 24–30 May 1998, London, 1998

Ilmjärv, M., *Silent Submission. Formation of Foreign Policy of Estonia, Latvia and Lithuania. Period from Mid-1920-s to Annexation in 1940*, Acta Universitatis Stockholmiensis, Studia Baltica Stockholmiensia 24, Stockholm, 2004

Ilves, T.H., *Eesti välispoliitika minevik, olevik ja tulevik*, aulaloeng 30. aprillil 1998 (The Past, Present and Future of the Estonian Foreign Policy. Lecture in the Assembly Hall of Tartu University), Tartu: Tartu Ülikooli Kirjastus, 1998

Ipsen, K., *Völkerrecht. Ein Studienbuch*, 4. Auflage, München: C.H. Beck'sche Verlagsbuchhandlung, 1999

Jaakson, E., *Eestile* (For Estonia), Tallinn: SE & JS, 1995

Jellinek, G., *Allgemeine Staatslehre*, Hg. von. W. Jellinek, 3. Aufl., Berlin: Häring, 1914

Jellinek, H., *Der automatische Erwerb und Verlust der Staatsangehörigkeit durch völkerrechtliche Vorgänge, zugleich ein Beitrag zur Lehre von der Staatensukzession*, Berlin: Carl Heymann, 1951

Jennings, R.Y., *The Acquisition of Territory in International Law*, Manchester: Manchester University Press, 1963

Jessup, P.C., *The Birth of Nations*, New York: Columbia University Press, 1974

Kacowicz, A.M., *Peaceful Territorial Change*, Columbia, SC: University of South Carolina Press, 1994

Kahk, J., (ed.) *World War II and Soviet Occupation in Estonia: A Damages Report*, Tallinn: Perioodika Publishers, 1991

Kaljurand, M., *Some Aspects of Succession of Estonia to the International Treaties Concluded in 1918–1940*, Master's Thesis at The Fletcher School of Law and Diplomacy, 1995

Kasekamp, A., *A History of the Baltic States*, 2nd ed., London: Bloomsbury, 2017

Kaslas, B.J., *The USSR-German Aggression against Lithuania,* New York: Robert Speller & Sons, 1973

Kelsen, H., *Der soziologische und der juristische Staatsbegriff. Kritische Untersuchung des Verhältnisses von Staat und Recht*, 2. Aufl., Tübingen: Mohr, 1928

Kelsen, H., *Principles of International Law*, 2nd edn., rev. and ed. by Robert W. Tucker, New York: Holt, Rinehart, and Winston, 1967

Kiris, A., *Restoration of the Independence of the Republic of Estonia. Selection of Legal Acts (1988–1991)*, Tallinn: Ministry of Foreign Affairs of the Republic of Estonia and Estonian Institute for Information, 1991

Kissinger, H., *Diplomacy*, New York: Simon & Schuster, 1994

Klabbers, J., M. Koskenniemi, O. Ribbelink and A. Zimmermann (eds.), *State Practice Regarding State Succession and Issues of Recognition: the Pilot Project of the Council of Europe*, The Hague: Kluwer Law International, 1999

Klein, E., *Das Selbstbestimmungsrecht der Völker und die deutsche Frage*, Berlin: Gebr. Mann, 1990

Клименко, Б., *Государственная территория. Вопросы теории и практики международного права*, Москва: Международные Отношения, 1974

Kochavi, A.J., *Prelude to Nuremberg. Allied War Crimes Policy and the Question of Punishment*, Chapel Hill, 1998

Korhonen, O., *International Law Situated. An Analysis of the Lawyer's Stance Towards Culture, History and Community*, The Hague: Kluwer, 2000

Korman, S., *The Right of Conquest. The Acquisition of Territory by Force in International Law and Practice,* Oxford: Clarendon Press, 1996

Koskenniemi, M., *From Apology to Utopia. The Structure of International Legal Argument*, Helsinki: Lakimiesliiton Kustannus, 1989

Koskenniemi, M., (ed.), *International Law*, Aldershot *et al.*: Dartmouth, 1992

Kraus, H., *Das Recht der Minderheiten. Materialien zur Einführung in das Eiverständnis des modernen Minoritätenproblems*, Berlin: Stilke, 1927

Krause-Ablaβ, W.-D., *Intertemporales Völkerrecht. Der zeitliche Anwendungsbereich von Völkerrechtsnormen*, Hamburg: A. Metzner Verlag, 1970

Kremnev, P.P., *Raspad SSSR: mezhdunarodno-pravovye problemy*, Moscow: Zertsalo-M, 2005

Kreuzer, C., *Staatsangehörigkeit und Staatensukzession. Die Bedeutung der Staatensukzession für die staatsangehörigkeitsrechtlichen Regelungen in de Staaten der ehemaligen Sowjetunion, Jugoslawiens und der Tschechoslowakei*, Berlin: Duncker & Humblot, 1998

Krieger, H., (ed.) *East Timor and the International Community. Basic Documents*, Cambridge University Press, 1997

Krieger, H., *Das Effektivitätsprinzip im Völkerrecht*, Berlin: Duncker & Humblot, 2000

Kuznetsov, V.I., B.R. Tuzmukhamedov (eds.) *Mezhdunarodnoe pravo*, Moscow: Norma, 2007

Laar, M., *War in the Woods. Estonia's Struggle for Survival 1944–1956*, Washington, DC: The Compass Press, 1992

Laidre, M., *Domus belli. Põhjamaade Saja-aastane sõda Liivimaal 1554–1661*, Tallinn: Argo, 2015

Langer, R., *Seizure of Territory. The Stimson Doctrine and Related Principles in Legal Theory and Diplomatic Practice*, Princeton: Princeton University Press, 1947

Laun, R., *Die Haager Landkriegsordnung. (Das Übereinkommen über die Gesetze und Gebräuche des Landkrieges.)*, 4. Aufl., Wolfenbüttel: Wolfenbütteler Verlagsanstalt G.m.b.H, 1949

Laun, R. v., *Staat und Volk. Eine völkerrechtliche und staatsrechtliche Untersuchung auf philosophischer Grundlage*, 2. Aufl., Aalen Scientia Verlag, 1971

Lauterpacht, H., *Private Law Sources and Analogies of International Law*, London: Longmans, Green & Co., 1927, reprinted Archon Books, 1970

Lauterpacht, H., L. Oppenheim, *International Law. A Treatise*, 5th ed., London: Longmans, Green, vol. 1–2, 1935–37

Lauterpacht, H., *Recogntition in International Law*, Cambridge: At the University Press, 1947

Lauterpacht, H., (ed.) *International Law. A Treatise*, 8th ed., 1955

Lemkin, R., *Axis Rule in Occupied Europe. Laws of Occupation. Analysis of Government. Proposals for Redress*, Washington: Carnegie Endowment for International Peace, 1944

Lenin, V.I., *Collected works* (Сочинения), t. 30, Moscow, 1959

Ленин, В.И., *Государство и революция. Учение марксизма о государстве и задачи пролетариата в революций*, Москва: Издательство политической литерературы, 1952 (orig. 1917). (V. I. Lenin, *The State and Revolution*).

Левин, Д.Б., *Ответственность в современном международном праве*, Москва: Международные отношения, 1969

Lettland unter sowjetischer und nationalsozialistischer Herrschaft. Eine Darstellung des lettischen Okkupationsmuseums, Riga, 1998

Lewis, R., *Legal Fictions in International Law*, Cheltenham: Edward Elgar Publishing, 2021

Liebich A., *et al* (eds.) *Citizenship East and West*, London: Kegan Paul Int'l, 1995

Lieven, A., *The Baltic Revolution. Estonia, Latvia, Lithuania and the Path to Independence*, New Haven and London: Yale University Press, 2nd ed., 1994

Machiavelli, N., *Il principe*, German edition of Parkland: Köln, 2000

Made, V., *Külalisena maailmapoliitikas: Rahvasteliit ja Eesti 1919–1946* (As Guest in World Politics: the League of Nations and Estonia 1919–1946), Tartu: Tartu Ülikooli Kirjastus, 1999

Maim, N., *Völkerbund und Staat. Ein Beitrag zur Ausarbeitung eines allgemeinen öffentlichen Rechts*, Tartu: K. Mattiesen, 1932

Marek, K., *Identity and Continuity of States in International Law*, Genève: E. Dros, 1954

Marek, K., *Identity and Continuity of States in International Law*, 2e éd., Genève: E. Dros, 1968

Martens, G. von, *Précis du droit des gens moderne de l'Europe, fondé sur les traités et l'usage*, 2e éd., Göttingen: Henri Dietrich, 1801

Mattisen, E., *Searching for a Dignified Compromise. The Estonian-Russian Border 1000 Years*, Tallinn: ILO, 1996

McCorquodale, R./N. Orosz, (eds.) *Tibet: The Position in International Law. Report of the Conference of International Lawyers on Issues relating to Self-Determination and Independence for Tibet*, London, 1994

McMahon, M.M., *Conquest in Modern International Law*, Washington, DC: Catholic University of America Press, 1940

McNair, Sir A.D., *Legal Effects of War*, 2nd ed., Cambridge: University Press, 1944

McNair, A., A. Watts, *The Legal Effects of War*, 4th ed., 1966

Medijainen, E., *Saadiku saatus. Välisministeerium ja saatkonnad 1918–1940*, (The Fate of the Ambassador: The Foreign Ministry and the Legations in 1918–1940), Tallinn: Eesti Entsüklopeediakirjastus, 1997

Meissner, B., *Sowjetunion und Haager LKO. Gutachten und Dokumentenzusammenstellung*, Hamburg: Universität Hamburg, 1950

Meissner, B., *Die Sowjetunion, die baltischen Staaten und das Völkerrecht*, Köln: Verlag Politik und Wirtschaft, 1956

Melkov, G.M., (ed.) *Mezhdunarodnoe pravo*, Moscow: RIOR, 2009

Milano, E., *Unlawful Territorial Situations in International Law. Reconciling Effectiveness, Legality and Legitimacy*, Leiden: Martinus Nijhoff, 2006

Misiunas, R.A., R. Taagepera, *The Baltic States. Years of Dependence 1940–1980*, 2nd ed., Berkeley: University of California Press, 1993

Morré, P., *Die Änderung der staatlichen Gebietshoheit nach sowjetischer Völkerrechtslehre und Völkerrechtspraxis, mit besonderer Berücksichtigung des Annexionsverbots*, Dissertation, Münster, 1967

Moser, J.J., *Versuch des neuesten Europäischen Völkerrechts in Friedens und Kriegszeiten, vornehmlich aus denen Staatshandlungen derer europäischen Mächten, auch anderen Begebenheiten, so sich seit dem Tode Kaiser Karls VI im Jahre 1740 zugetragen haben*, 1777

Müllerson, R., *International Law, Rights and Politics. Developments in Eastern Europe and the CIS*, London: Routledge, 1994

Müllerson, R., *Ordering Anarchy. International Law in International Society*, The Hague: Nijhoff, 2000

Muralt, R.W.G. De, *The Problem of State Succession with Regard to Treaties*, The Hague: W.P. van Stockum & Zoon, 1954

Murswiek, D., *Peaceful Change. Ein Völkerrechtsprinzip?* Köln: Verlag Politik und Wirtschaft, 1998

Neuhold, H., W. Hummer, C. Schreuer, *Österreichisches Handbuch des Völkerrechts*, Band 1: Textteil, 2. Auflage, Wien: Manzsche Verlags- und Universitätsbuchhandlung, 1991

Nippold, O., *La Géorgie du point de vue du droit international*, Berne: Bureau de Presse géorgien, 1920

O' Connell, D.P., *International Law*, Volume One, London: Stevens & Sons Limited, 1965

O'Connell, D.P., *State Succession*, Vol. II, Cambridge: University Press, 1967

Okafor, O. C., *Redifining Legitimate Statehood. International Law and State Fragmentation in Africa*, The Hague: Martinus Nijhoff, 2000

Оленев, С., *Международное признание СССР*, Москва: Издательство социальнополитической литературы, 1962

Oplatka, A., *Lennart Meri. Ein Leben für Estland. Dialog mit dem Präsidenten*, Zürich: Verlag Neue Zürcher Zeitung, 1999

Orav, M., Nõu, E. (eds.) *Tõotan ustavaks jääda...: Eesti Vabariigi Valitsus 1940–1992* (I Swear to Remain Faithful...: Government of the Republic of Estonia 1940–1992), Tallinn: Eesti Kirjanduse Selts, 2004

Orwell, G., *Nineteen eighty-four*, London: Seeker & Wartburg, 1997

Pellet, A., *Human Rightism' and International Law*, Memorial Lecture in honour of Gilberto Amado on 18 July 2000 at the ILC's International Law Seminar

Peters, A., *Das Gebietsreferendum im Völkerrecht. Seine Bedeutung im Licht der Staatenpraxis nach 1989*, Baden-Baden: Nomos, 1995

Pictet, J.S., *Commentary to the I Geneva Convention*, Geneva: ICRC, 1952; *Commentary to the III Geneva Convention*, Geneva: ICRC, 1951

Piip, A., *Rahvusvaheline õigus* (International law), Tartu: Akadeemilise Kooperatiivi Kirjastus, 1936

Piirimäe, K., *Roosevelt, Chruchill, and the Baltic Question. Allied Relations during the Second World War*, London: Palgrave Macmillan, 2014

Pompe, C.A., *Aggressive War—an International Crime*, The Hague: Martinus Nijhoff, 1953

Pusta, K.-R., *Le statut juridique de la mer Baltique à partir du XIXe siècle*, 52 RCADI 1935, pp. 105–190

Radbruch, G., *Rechtsphilosophie*, 4. Aufl., herausg. von E. Wolf, Stuttgart: Koehler, 1950

Rauch, G. von, *Die Universität Dorpat und das Eindringen der frühen Aufklärung in Livland 1690–1710*, Essen: Essener Verlagsanstalt, 1943

Rauschning, D., *Das Schicksal völkerrechtlicher Verträge bei der Änderung des Status ihrer Partner*, Hamburg: Hansischer Gildenverlag, 1963

Rei, A., *Nazi-Soviet Conspiracy and The Baltic States. Diplomatic Documents and Other Evidence*, London: Boreas, 1948

Reinhards, A., *Lettonie-Russie. Traités et documents de base* in extenso, Lausanne, 1998. (Also available at http://www.tbw.ch/letton)

Reinisch A., and G. Hafner, *Staatensukzession und Schuldübernahme beim „Zerfall" der Sowjetunion*, Wien: Service Fachverlag, 1995

Repečka, J., *Der gegenwärtige völkerrechtliche Status der baltischen Staaten, unter besonderer Berücksichtigung der diplomatischen Vorgeschichte der Eingliederung dieser Staaten in die Sowjetunion*, Dissertation at the University of Göttingen, 1950

Ress, G., *Die Rechtslage Deutschlands nach dem Grundlagenvertrag vom 21. Dezember 1972*, Berlin: Springer, 1978

Rifaat, A.M., *International Aggression. A Study of the Legal Concept: Its Development and Definition in International Law*, Stockholm: Almqvist & Wiksell International, 1979

Rivier, A., *Principes du droit des gens*, I Tome, Paris: Arthur Rousseau, 1896

Rorty, R., *Objectivity, Relativism, and Truth*, Cambridge University Press, 1996

Rosenbusch, M., H. Schützler, S. Striegnitz (Hg.) *Schauplatz Baltikum: Szenarium einer Okkupation und Angliederung: Dokumente 1939/1940*, Berlin: Dietz Verlag, 1991

Rousseau, C., *Le droit des conflits armés*, Paris: A. Pedone, 1983

Rubin, A.P., *Ethics and Authority in International Law*, Cambridge: Cambridge University Press, 1997

Rudolf, W., *Wandel des Staatsbegriffs im Völkerrecht?*, Bonn: Europa Union Verlag, 1986

Runes, D.D., (ed.) *Dictionary of Philosophy*, Ames, Iowa: Littlefield, Adams & Co., 1958

Sarv, E., *Õiguse vastu ei saa ükski: Eesti taotlused ja rahvusvaheline õigus* (No One Can Withstand the Law: Estonia's Aspirations and International Law), Tartu: ORURK, 1997

Sassòli, M., and A. Bouvier, *How Does Law Protect in War? Cases, Documents and Teaching Materials on Contemporary Practice in International Humanitarian Law*, Geneva: ICRC, 1999

Satkauskas, R., *États baltes: succession ou identité?*, Master's thesis at the Sorbonne, 2000

Schätzel, W., *Völkerbund und Gebietserwerb*, Berlin, 1919, reprinted in: W. Schätzel, *Das Recht des völkerrechtlichen Gebietserwerbs*, Bonn: Ludwig Röhrscheid Verlag, 1959

Schätzel, W., *Die Annexion im Völkerrecht*, Berlin, 1921, reprinted in: W. Schätzel, *Das Recht des völkerrechtlichen Gebietserwerbs*, Bonn: Ludwig Rohrscheid Verlag, 1959

Schmitt, C., *Der Begriff des Politischen. Text von 1932 mit einem Vorwort und drei Corollarien*, Berlin: Duncker & Humblot, 1963

Schmitz, G., *Tibet und das Selbstbestimmungsrecht der Völker*, Berlin: Walter de Gruyter, 1998

Schnitzer, A.F., *Staat und Gebietshoheit*, Zürich: Verlag für Recht und Gesellschaft, 1935

Schweisfurth, T., *Der internationale Vertrag in der modernen sowjetischen Völkerrechtstheorie*, Köln: Verlag Wissenschaft und Politik, 1968

Scott, J.B., *The Proceedings of the Hague Conferences*, 5 volumes incl. index, New York: Oxford University Press, 1920

Seidl-Hohenveldern, I., T. Stein, *Völkerrecht*, Köln: C. Heimann Verlag, 2000

Shafirov, P.P., *A Discourse Concerning the Just Causes of the War Between Sweden and Russia: 1700–1721*, with an introduction by William E. Butler, Dobs Ferry, N.Y.: Oceana Publications, 1973

Sharma, S.P., *Territorial Acquisition, Disputes and International Law*, The Hague: Martinus Nijhoff Publishers, 1997

Silagi, M., *Staatsuntergang und Staatennachfolge mit besonderer Berücksichtigung des Endes der DDR*, Franfurt a. M.: Peter Lang, 1996

Stabreit, E., *Der völkerrechtliche Status der Transkei, Ciskei, Bophuthatswanas und Vendas während der Zeit ihrer formellen Unabhängigkeit von der Republik Südafrika*, Frankfurt a.M., 1997

Stalin, J.V., *Über die Grundlagen des Leninismus* (Orig.: *Об основах ленинизма*). Vorlesungen, gehalten an der Swerdlow-Universität Anfang im April 1924, Berlin, 1946

Starke's International Law, 11th ed. I.A. Shearer, ed., London: Butterworths, 1994

Stern B. (ed.), *Les aspects juridiques de la crise et de la guerre du Golfe*, Paris, Montchrestien, Cahier du C.E.D.I.N. no. 6, 1991

Suy, E., *Les actes juridiques unilateraux en droit international public*, Paris, Bibliothèque de droit international, Institut des hautes études de l'Université de Paris, 1962

Swettenham, J.A., *The Tragedy of the Baltic States. A Report compiled from Official Documents and Eyewittnesses' Stories*, London: Holli and Carter, 1952

Taagepera, R., *Softening without Liberation in the Soviet Union: The Case of Jüri Kukk*, University Press of America, Inc., 1984

Talmon, S., *Recognition of Governments in International Law. With Particular Reference to Governments in Exile*, Oxford: Clarendon Press, 1998

Tamman, T., *The Last Ambassador. August Torma, Soldier, Diplomat, Spy*, Leiden Brill, 2011

Taube, C., *Constitutionalism in Estonia, Latvia and Lithuania. A Study in Comparative Constitutional Law*, Uppsala: Iustus Förlag, 2001

Taylor, J.G., *The Indonesian Occupation of East Timor 1974–1989. A Chronology*, London: Catholic Institute for International Relations, 1990

The Baltic States and the Soviet Union. Reprinted from a Report of the Council of Europe, with a Preface and Supplementary Comments, Stockholm: Estonian Information Centre, Latvian National Foundation, Supreme Committee for Liberation of Lithuania, 1962

The Baltic States 1940–1972. Documentary Background and Survey of Developments Presented to the European security and Cooperation Conference, Stockholm: The Baltic Committee in Scandinavia, 1972

Thiele, C., *Selbstbestimmung und Minderheitenschutz in Estland*, Berlin: Springer, 1999

Thucydides, *The History of the Peloponnesian War*, translated by Benjamin Jowett, 1st ed., London: Oxford University Press, 1881

Toman, J., *L'Union Soviétique et le droit des conflits armés*, Thèse, Université de Genève, Institut Universitaire de Hautes Études Internationales, Genève, 1997

Tomuschat, C., (ed.), *Eigentum im Umbruch. Restitution, Privatisierung und Nutzungskonflikte im Europa der Gegenwart*, Berlin: Berlin Verlag Arno Spitz und Verlag Österreich, 1996

Tomuschat, C., *Die staatliche Einheit Deutschlands: staats- und völkerrechtliche Aspekte*, Bonn: Friedrich-Ebert-Stiftung, 1990

Tomuschat, C., (ed.), *Modern Law of Self-Determination*, Dordrecht: Martinus Nijhoff Publishers, 1993

Touscoz, J., *Le principe d'effectivité dans l'ordre international*, Paris: R. Pichon et R. Durand-Auzias, 1964

Чуев, Ф.И., *Сто сорок бесед с Молотовым. Из дневника Ф. Чуева*, Moscow: Terra, 1991

Tucker, R.W., *The Inequality of Nations*, New York: Basic Books, 1977

Tunkin, G., 'International Law in the International System', 147 *RCADI* 1975, pp. 1–218

Uhler, O.M., *Der völkerrechtliche Schutz der Bevölkerung eines besetzten Gebiets gegen Maßnahmen der Okkupationsmacht (unter besonderer Berücksichtigung der Genfer Zivilkonvention vom 12. August 1949*, Zürich: Polygraphischer Verlag, 1950

Uibopuu, H.-J., *Die Völkerrechtssubjektivität der Unionsrepubliken der UdSSR*, Vienna, New York: Springer, 1975

UNPO, *China's Tibet. The World Largest Remaining Colony. Report of a Fact-Finding Mission and Analyses of Colonialism and Chinese Rule in Tibet.* August 1997

Ушаков, Н.А., *Основания международной оветственности государств*, Москва: Международные отношения, 1983

Vattel, E. de, *Le droit des gens ou principes de la loi naturelle, appliqués à la conduite et aux affaires des nations et des souverains*, 1758. Reprinted in Tübingen: Mohr, 1959

Verdross, A., *Völkerrecht*, Wien: Springer, 5. Aufl., 1964

Verdross, A./B. Simma, *Universelles Völkerrecht*, 3. Auflage, Berlin: Ducker & Humblot, 1984

Graf Vitzthum, W., (ed.) *Völkerrecht*, Berlin and New York : Walter de Gruyter, 1997

Verhoeven, J., *La reconnaissance internationale dans la pratique contemporaine*, Paris: Pedone, 1975

Verosta, S., *Die internationale Stellung Österreichs. Eine Sammlung von Erklärungen und Verträgen aus den Jahren 1938 bis 1947*, Wien: Manz, 1947

Vierdag, E.W., *The Concept of Discrimination in International Law*, The Hague: Nijhoff, 1973

Viñuales, J. (ed.) *The UN Friendly Relations Declaration at 50*, Cambridge: Cambridge University Press, 2020

Visscher, C. de, *Les effectivités du droit international public*, Paris: Pedone, 1967

Visscher, C. de, *Théories et réalités en droit international public*, Paris: Editions A. Pedone, 4ème éd., 1970

Vitas, R.A., *The United States and Lithuania. The Stimson Doctrine of Nonrecognition*, New York: Praeger, 1990

Vizulis, I.J., *Nations Under Duress. The Baltic States*, Port Washington: Associated Faculty Press, Inc., 1985

Voos, S., *Die Schule von New Haven: Darstellung und Kritik einer amerikanischen Völkerrechtslehre*, Berlin: Duncker & Humblot, 2000

Wallace-Bruce, N.L., *Claims to Statehood in International Law*, New York: Carlton Press, 1994

Walt van Praag, M.C. van, *The Status of Tibet. History, Rights, and Prospects in International Law*, Boulder: Westview Press, 1987

We Demand Freedom for Estonia. Memoranda Presented to the Delegations at the Paris Conference (1946), London: Boreas, 1947

Wehberg, H., *Krieg und Eroberung im Wandel des Völkerrechts*, Frankfurt a.M.: Alfred Metzner Verlag, 1953

Wengler, W., *Der Begriff des Politischen im internationalen Recht*, Tübingen: J.C.B. Mohr, 1956

Whiteman, M.M., *Digest of International Law*, Vol. 2, Washington, DC, 1963

Wiewióra, B., *Uznanie nabytków terytoryalnych w prawie mizdzynarodnowym* (The Recognition of Territorial Acquisitions in International Law), Poznan: Instytut Zachodni, 1961

Woodward, Sir L., *British Foreign Policy in the Second World War*, London: Her Majesty's Stationery Office, Vol. 1–5, 1970–1976

Захарова, Н.В., *Правопреемство государсв*, Москва: Международные отношения, 1973

Ziemele, I., *State Continuity and Nationality: the Baltic States and Russia. Past, Present and Future as Defined by International Law*, Leiden: Brill, 2005

Zimmer, G., *Gewaltsame territoriale Veranderungen und ihre völkerrechtliche Legitimation*, Berlin: Duncker & Humblot, 1971

Zimmermann, A., *Staatennachfolge in völkerrechtliche Verträge. Zugleich ein Beitrag zu den Möglichkeiten und Grenzen völkerrechtlicher Kodifikation*, Berlin: Springer, 2000

Articles

Alanen, I., 'Eesti põllumajanduspoliitika ja võitlus kollektiivmajandite saatuse pärast' (Estonian Agricultural Policy and the Fight for the Fate of the Collective Farms), *Akadeemia* No. 11, 2000, p. 2259–2300

Alexandrowicz-Alexander, C., 'The Legal Position of Tibet', 48 *AJIL* 1954, pp. 265–274

Alexandrowicz, C.H., 'New and Original States. The Issue of Reversion to Sovereignty', 45 *International Affairs* 1969, pp. 465–480

Allott, P., 'State Responsibility and the Unmaking of International Law', 29 *Harvard JIL* 1988, pp. 1–26

Altuğ, Y., 'The Cyprus Question', in: 21 *GYBIL* 1978, pp. 311–344

Ammas, A., 'Gluhhov: Eesti peab Venemaad tänama, mitte ootama vabandamist', (Glukhov: Estonia should thank Russia, not wait for apology), *Eesti Päevaleht*, 15.11.2000

Anonymus, 'Non-recognition: A Reconsideration', 22 *The University of Chicago Law Review* 1954–1955, pp. 261–278

Ansbach, T., ‚Der Rechtsstatus der nicht-estnischen Bevölkerung in Estland', in: *Recht in Ost und West*, September 1996 No. 7, pp. 217–225

Antonoupoulos, C., 'Effectiveness v. the Rule of Law Following the East Timor Case', 27 *Netherlands YBIL* 1996, pp. 75–111

Antonowicz, L., 'The Disintegration of the USSR from the Point of View of International Law', 19 *Polish YBIL* 1991–1992, pp. 7–16

Avdeev, A., 'Russian-Lithuanian Relations: An Overview', *Lithuanian Foreign Policy Review* 2000 No. 2 (6), pp. 27–33

Baade, A., ‚Baltische Staaten', in: K. Strupp and H.-J. Schlochauer (ed.), *Wörterbuch des Völkerrechts*, Band I, 2. Aufl., Berlin: Springer, 1960, pp. 142–149

Barrington, L.W., 'Nations, States, and Citizens: an Explanation of the Citizenship Policies in Estonia and Lithuania', in: 21 *Review of Central and East European Law* 1995 No. 2, pp. 103–148

Barsegov, G.Y., 'On the Criticism of the "Inter-Temporal Law" Doctrine', 1985 *Soviet YBIL*, pp. 202–205

Beemelmans, H., ‚Die Staatennachfolge in Staatsvermögen in Drittstaaten, Auslandsschulden, gebietsbezogene rechtliche Regelungen und Staatsangehörigkeit—eine Problemskizze', 41 *Osteuropa Recht* 1995, pp. 73–98

Beemelmans, H., 'State Succession in International Law: Remarks on Recent Theory and State Praxis', 15 *Boston University ILJ* 1997, pp. 68–85

Bergmane, U., "The Uncerstainty That Persists': The Bank of France, the Baltic Gold and the Non-Recognition of a Forcible Seizure of Territory during the Cold War', *The International History Review* 2021 (online)

Bernhardt, R., ‚Kontinuität', in: K. Strupp, H.-J. Schlochauer (eds.) *Wörterbuch des Völkerrechts*, Band 2, 1961, 2. Aufl., pp. 295–297

Bethge, H., ‚Das Staatsgebiet des wiedervereinigten Deutschlands', in: J. Isensee, P. Kirchhof (Hg.) *Handbuch des Staatsrechts*, Band VIII, Heidelberg, 1995, pp. 603–620

Bieber, R., 'European Community Recognition of Eastern European States: A New Perspective for International Law?', in: ASIL *Proceedings* 1992, Washington, DC, pp. 374–378

Bilfinger, C., ‚Vollendete Tatsache und Völkerrecht—Eine Studie', 15 *ZaöRV* 1953/54, pp. 453–481

Bindschedler, R., ‚Die Anerkennung im Völkerrecht', in: BDGV, Band 4, Karlsruhe: C. F. Müller, 1961, pp. 1–27

Bindschedler, R.L., ‚Annexation', in: R. Bernhardt (ed.) EPIL, 1992, Inst. I, Amsterdam: North Holland, pp. 168–172

Blackman, J.L., 'State Successions and Statelessness: the Emerging Right to and Effective Nationality Under International Law', 19 *Michigan* JIL 1998, pp. 1141–1194

Blix, H.M., 'Contemporary Aspects of Recognition', 130 RCADI 1970, pp. 567–703

Blumenwitz, D., 'ex factis ius oritur'—'ex iniuria iu non oritur', in: G. Ziegler and B. Meissner (Hg.) *Staatliche und nationale Einheit Deutschlands—ihre Effektivität*, Köln: Verlag Wissenschaft und Politik, 1984, pp. 43–56

Bojārs, J., 'The Citizenship and Human Rights Regulation in the Republic of Latvia', 39 *Osteuropa Recht* 1993, No. 2, pp. 132–145

Bokor-Szegö, H., 'Questions of State Identity and State Succession in Eastern and Central Europe', in: M. Mrak (ed.) *Succession of States*, The Hague: Martinus Nijhoff, 1999, pp. 95–108

Bothe, M., 'Occupation, Belligerent', in: R. Bernhardt (ed.) EPIL, Inst. III, pp. 64–67

Bothe, M., et Schmidt, C., 'Sur quelques questions de succession posees par la dissolution de l'URSS et celle de la Yougoslavie', 96 RGDIP 1992, pp. 811–841

Brakas, M., 'Lithuania's International Status: Some Legal Aspects', 38 *Baltic Review* (August 1971)

Briggs, H.W., 'Non-recognition of Title by Conquest and Limitations of the Doctrine', 34 *Am. Soc'y Int'l L. Proc.* 1940, pp. 72–82

Briggs, H.W., 'Non-recognition in the Courts: the Ships of the Baltic Republics', 37 AJIL 1943, pp. 585–596

Brown, P.M., 'Sovereignty in Exile', 35 AJIL 1941, pp. 666–668

Brownlie, I., Recognition in Theory and Practice, in: 53 BYBIL 1982, pp. 197–211

Brunner, G., ‚Die rechtliche Lage der Minderheiten in Mittel-, Ost- und Südosteuropa', in: 40 *Osteuroparecht*, September 1994, pp. 157–177

Bungs, D., 'Joint Political Initiatives by Estonians, Latvians, and Lithuanians as Reflected in Samizdat Materials 1967–1987', in: D. A. Loeber, S.V Vardys, L. P. A. Kitching (eds.) *Regional Identity under Soviet Rule—the Case of the Baltic States*, 1990, pp. 429–462

Burdeau, G., 'Money and State Succession in Eastern Europe', in: B. Stern (ed.) *Dissolution, Continuation and Succession in Eastern Europe*, The Hague, 1998, pp. 35–66

Busygina, I., 'Russia, the Baltic States and the European Union', in: T. Jundzis (ed.) *The Baltic States at Historical Crossroads*, Riga: Academy of Sciences of Latvia, 1998, pp. 502–519

Bychkov Green, S., 'Language of Lullabies: The Russification and De-Russification of the Baltic States', 19 *Michigan Journal of International Law* 1997, pp. 217–294

Cansacchi, G., 'Identité et continuité des sujets internationaux', 130 *RCADI* 1970, pp. 1–94

Castrén, E.J., 'Aspects recents de la succession d'états', 78 *RCADI* 1951, pp. 379–506

Charpentier, J., 'Les déclaration des Douze sur la reconnaissance des nouveaux États', 96 *RGDIP* 1992, pp. 343–355

Chemillier-Gendreau, M., 'Origine et rôle de la fiction en droit international public', in : 32 *Archives de Philosophie du Droit* 1987, pp. 153–162

Chemillier-Gendreau, M., 'Le droit international et la protection d'un peuple contre l'annexion', in: *Revue d'études Palestiniennes* No. 34, 1990, pp. 63–73

Chernichenko, S., 'Ethnic Russians in the Baltics', in: 44 *International Affairs* (Moscow) 1998, pp. 118–123

Clark, R.S., The 'decolonisation' of East Timor and the United Nations norms on self-determination and aggression, in: *International Law and the Question of East Timor*, London: CIIR/IPJET, 1995, pp. 65–102

Condorelli, G., 'Ex facto jus oritur', *Rivista internazionela di filosofia del diritto*, 1931, pp. 115–139

Crawford, J., 'The Criteria for Statehood in International Law', 48 *BYBIL* 1976/77, pp. 93–182

Crawford, J., 'State Practice and International Law in Relation to Secession', 69 *BYBIL* 1998, pp. 85–117

Crawford, J., 'Democracy and International Law', 64 *BYBIL* 1993, pp. 113–133

Craven, M.C.R., 'The Problem of State Succession and the Identity of States under International Law', 9 *EJIL* 1998, pp. 142–162

Cybichowski, S., ‚Das völkerrechtliche Okkupationsrecht', XVIII *Z. für VR* 1934, pp. 295–322

Czaplinski, W., 'International Legal Aspects of Polish-Lithuanian Relations', 19 *Polish YB of Int'l Law* 1991–1992, pp. 31–48

Czaplinski, W., 'La continuité, l'identité et la succession d'états—évaluation de cas récents', 26 *RBDI* 1993, pp. 374–392

Czaplinski, W., 'State Succession and State Responsibility', 28 *Canadian YBIL* 1990, pp. 339–359

Dalai Lama, His Holyness XIV, ‚Die Zukunft Tibets', in: K. Ludwig (ed.) *Perspektiven für Tibet. Auf dem Weg zu einer Zukunft in Freiheit und Selbstbestimmung*, München: Diamant Verlag, 2000, pp. 13–23

Damrosch, L.F., 'Enforcing International Law Through Non-Forcible Measures', 269 *RCADI* 1997, pp. 9–250

Degan, V.D., 'Equity in Matters of State Succession', in: R.St.J. Macdonald (ed.) *Essays in Honour of Wang Tieya*, The Hague: Nijhoff, 1993, pp. 201–210

Degan, V.-D., 'Création et disparition de l'État (À la lumière du démembrement de trois fédérations multiethniques en Europe)', RCADI 1999, pp. 195–376

Doehring, K., 'Effectiveness', in: R. Bernhardt (ed.) EPIL, Inst. 7, Amsterdam: North Holland, 1984, pp. 70–74

Doehring, K., 'State', in: R. Bernhardt (ed.) EPIL 10, Amsterdam: North Holland, 1987, pp. 423–427

Dwan, R., 'Armed Conflict Prevention, Management and Resolution', in: *SIPRI Yearbook 2000. Armaments, Disarmament and International Security*, Oxford University Press, 2000, pp. 77–134

Ebenroth C.T., and D. Grashoff, ‚Öffentliche Schulden im Prozeβ desintegrierender Staatensukzession—die Zuordnung von Staatsschulden auf Nachfolgestaaten', 92 *ZVglRWiss* 1993, pp. 1–28

Eckholm, E., 'A New Poke in the Eye: China Bristles Over Tibet', *NY Times*, May 23, 2001

Eidintas, A., 'The Meeting of the Lithuanian Cabinet, 15 June 1940', in: J. Hiden and T. Lane (eds.), *The Baltic and the Outbreak of the Second World War*, Cambridge: Cambridge University Press, 1992, pp. 165–173

Eisemann, P.M., 'Bilan de recherches de la section de la langue française du Centre d'étude et de recherche de l'Académie', in: *Académie de Droit international de la Haye. Centre d'étude et de recherche de droit international et de relations internationales*, 1996, pp. 17–88

Elagab, O.Y., 'The Law of Belligerent Occupation versus the Law of Annexation of Territories: A Case Study of the Golan Heights', 6 *Development of Peace* 1985, pp. 118–128

Elias, TO., 'The Doctrine of Intertemporal Law', 74 AJIL 1980 pp. 285–307

Ermoshin, V.V., 'The Right of Russia in respect to Southern Sakhalin and Kuril Islands', *Russian* YBIL 1993–1994, pp. 173–195

Ermoshin, V.V., 'On the Russian-Japanese Controversy Over the Status Quo of Southern Sakhalin and the Kurile Islands', 1 *Moscow* JIL 1995, No. 4, pp. 63–74

Fastenrath, U., 'States, Extinction', in: R. Bernhardt (ed.) EPIL 10, Amsterdam: North Holland, 1987, pp. 465–467

Feldbrugge, FJ.M., 'The Law of the Republic of Georgia', 18 *Review of Central and East European Law* 1992, No. 4, pp. 367–375

Feldman, D.I., 'Illegality of the Hallstein Doctrine', *Soviet* YBIL 1962, pp. 158–165

Ferencz, B.B., 'Aggression', R. Bernhardt (ed.) EPIL, Vol. I, Amsterdam: North Holland, 1992, pp. 58–65

Fiedler, W., 'Continuity', R. Bernhardt (ed.) EPIL 1, Amsterdam: North Holland, 1992, pp. 806–809

Fiedler, W., ‚Entwicklungslinien im Recht der Staatensukzession', in: G. Hafner *et al.* (eds.) *Liber Amicorum. Professor Ignaz Seidl-Hohenveldern*, The Hague: Kluwer, 1998, pp. 133–155

Fiedler, W., ‚Der Zeitfaktor im Recht der Staatensukzession', in: *Staat und Recht. Festschrift für Günther Winkler*, Wien: Springer, 1997, pp. 217–235

Fleischhauer, C.A., ‚Prescription', R. Bernhardt (ed.) *EPIL* 10, Amsterdam: North Holland, 1987, pp. 327–330

Franck, T., 'The Emerging Right to Democratic Governance', 86 *AJIL* 1992, pp. 46–91

Franck, T.M., 'Are Human Rights Universal?', in: *Foreign Affairs* Jan/Feb 2001, pp. 191–204

Franckx, E., 'The 1998 Estonia-Sweden Maritime Boundary Agreement: Lessons to be Learned in the Area of Continuity and/or Succession of States', 31 *Ocean Development & International Law* 2000, pp. 269–284

Franckx, E., and A. Pauwels, 'Lithuanian-Russian Boundary Agreement of October 1997: To Be or Not To Be?', in: V. Götz *et al.* (Hg.) *Liber Amicorum Günther Jaenicke*, Berlin: Springer, 1998, pp. 63–95

Frowein, J.A., ‚Die Abmachung von Evian und die Entstehung des algerischen Staates', in: 23 *ZaöRV* 1963, pp. 20–48

Frowein, J.A., 'Non-recognition', R. Bernhardt (ed.) *EPIL* 10, Amsterdam: North Holland, 1987, pp. 314–316

Frowein, J.A., 'Reactions by not Directly Affected States to Breaches of Public International Law', 248 *RCADI* 1994, pp. 345–437

Fuller, L.L., 'Legal Fictions', 25 *Illinois Law Review* 1930–1931, pp. 513–546

Gerson, A., 'War, Conquered Territory, and Military Occupation in the Contemporary International Legal System', in: 18 *Harvard ILJ* 1977, pp. 525–556

Ginsburgs, G., 'The Territorial Question between the USSR and Japan. The Soviet Case and a Western Aperçu', in: 15 *Korea and World Affairs* 1991, pp. 259–278

Gowlland-Debbas, V., 'The Functions of the United Nations Security Council in the International Legal System', in: M. Byers, *The Role of Law in International Politics*, Oxford, 2000, pp. 277–314

Graham, M.W., 'The Legal Status of the Bukovina and Bessarabia', 38 *AJIL* 1944, pp. 667–673

Grant, T.D., 'East Timor, the U.N. System, and Enforcing Non-Recognition in International Law', 33 *Vanderbilt J. of Transnational Law* 2000, pp. 273–310

Grant, T.D., 'Defining Statehood: The Montevideo Convention and its Discontents', 37 *Columbia Journal of Transnational Law* 1999, pp. 403–457

Grant, T.D., 'A Panel of Experts for Chechnya: Purposes and Prospects in Light of International Law', 9 *Finnish YBIL* 1998, pp. 145–248

Gray, C., 'Self-Determination and the Breakup of the Soviet Union', 12 *YBEL* 1992, pp. 465–504

Greenwood, C., 'The Administration of Occupied Territory in International Law', in: E. Playfair (ed.) *International Law and the Administration of Occupied Territories. Two Decades of Israeli Occupation of the West Bank and Gaza Strip*, Oxford: Clarendon Press, 1992, pp. 241–266

Grewe, W., ,Völkerrechtliche Umschau—Europa nach dem Waffenstillstand', in: 7 *Monatshefte für Auswärtige Politik* 1940, pp. 686–692

Grewe, W., 'Peaceful Change', in: R. Bernhardt (ed.) *EPIL* III, Amsterdam: North Holland, 1997, pp. 965–971

Grewe, W.G., ,Außenpolitik und Völkerrecht in der Praxis', in: 36 *ADV* 1998, pp. 1–18

Gureckas, A., 'Lithuania's Boundaries and Territorial Claims Between Lithuania and Neighboring States', 12 *N.Y.L. Sch.J. Int'l & Comp.L.*, 1991, p. 107–121

Gyaltag, G., ,Das Recht auf Selbstbestimmung aus historischer Sicht', in: Ludwig (ed.), *Perspektiven für Tibet. Auf dem Weg zu einer Zukunft in Freiheit und Selbstbestimmung*, München: Diamant Verlag, pp. 49–59

Hafner G., and E. Kornfeind, 'The Recent Austrian Practice of State Succession: Does the Clean Slate Rule Still Exist?', 1 *Austrian Review of International and European Law* 1996, pp. 1–49

Hannikainen, L., 'The Case of East Timor from the Perspective of *jus cogens*', in: *International Law and the Question of East Timor*, London: CIIR/IPJET, 1995, pp. 103–117

Hazard, J.N., 'Soviet Republics in International Law', in: R. Bernhardt (ed.) *EPIL* 4, Amsterdam: North Holland, 2000 (first published 1987), pp. 525–529

Henkin, L., 'International Law: Politics, Values and Functions, General Course on Public International Law', in: 216 *RCADI* 1989, pp. 9–416

Herz, H., ,Beiträge zum Problem der Identität des Staates', 15 *ZöR* 1935, pp. 241–268

Hough, III, WJ., 'The Annexation of the Baltic States and its effect on the Development of Law Prohibiting Forcible Seizure of Territory', 6 *New York Law School Journal of Interational Law* No. 2, 1985, pp. 301–533

Hughes, A.D., 'Tibet', in: R. Bernhardt (ed.) *EPIL* 4, Amsterdam: North Holland, 2000, pp. 858–861

Hummer, W., ,Der internationale Status und die völkerrechtliche Stellung Österreichs seit dem Ersten Weltkrieg', in: H. Neuhold *et al*, *Österreichisches Handbuch des Völkerrechts*, 3. Aufl., Wien: Manz, 1997, pp. 452–497

Huntzinger, J., ,La renaissance des États baltes', in: *L'État souverain a l'aube du XXI siècle. Colloque de Nancy*, Paris: A. Pedone, 1994, pp. 39–60

Ideon, A., 'Eesti jätab Leedu üksi hüvitist nõudma' (Estonia Leaves Lithuania Alone to Demand Reparations), *Postimees*, 03.07.2000

Ilves, TH., 'Eesti välispoliitika peegelmaastikul' (Estonian Foreign Policy on the Mirror-Landsacpe), *Postimees*, 07.08.2001

Jakusch, W., ,Okkupationstheorie, Annexionstheorie und das ius postliminii', 25 *ÖJZ* 1970, pp. 258–263

Järve, P., 'Ethnic Democracy and Estonia: Application of Smooha's Model', *ECMI Working Paper* No. 7, Flensburg, 2000

Jennings, R., 'Nullity and Effectiveness in International Law', in: *Cambridge Essays in International Law, Essays in Honour of Lord McNair*, London, 1965, pp. 64–87

Johnson, D.H.N., 'Acquisitive Prescription in International Law', 27 *BYBIL* 1950, pp. 332–354

Juda, L., 'United States' Non-recognition of the Soviet Union's Annexation of the Baltic States: Politics and Law', 6 *Journal of Baltic Studies* 1975, pp. 272–290

Juviler, P., 'Are Collective Rights Anti-Human? Theories on Self-Determination and Practice in Soviet Successor States', in: 11 *Netherlands Quarterly of Human Rights* 1993, pp. 267–282

Kaasik, N., 'L'Ultimatum soviétique à l'Estonie', in: *Annexation of the Baltic States*, Stockholm: Baltic Humanitarian Association, 1946

Kahn, M., 'Les Russes dans les ex-républiques soviétiques', in: *Le courrier des pays de l'Est* No. 376, 1993, pp. 3–20

Kamminga, M.T., 'State Succession in Respect of Human Rights Treaties', 7 *EJIL* 1996, pp. 469–484

Karpov, V.P., 'The Soviet Concept of Peaceful Coexistence and its Implications for International Law', in: H. W. Baade (ed.) *The Soviet Impact on International Law*, Dobbs Ferry, NY: Oceana, 1965

Kelly, M.J., 'Non-Belligerent Occupation', 28 *Israel YB on Human Rights* 1998, pp. 17–35

Kelsen, H., ,Unrecht und Unrechtsfolge im Völkerrecht', XII *ZöR* 1932, pp. 481–606

Kelsen, H., 'The Pure Theory of Law and Analytical Jurisprudence', 55 *Harvard Law Review* 1941–42, pp. 44–70

Kelsen, H., 'The Legal Status of Germany to be Established Immediately upon Termination of War', 38 *AJIL* 1944, pp. 680–694

Kelsen, H., 'The Legal Status of Germany According to the Declaration of Berlin', 39 *AJIL* 1945, pp. 518–526

Kennedy, D., 'Theses about International Law Discourse', 23 *GYBIL* 1980, pp. 353–391

Kerikmäe, T., H. Vallikivi, 'State Continuity in the Light of Estonian Treaties Concluded before World War II', *Juridica International* No V 2000, pp. 30–39

Kherad, R., ,La reconnaissance internationale des États baltes', 96 *RGDIP* 1992, pp. 843–872

Клапсас, И., 'П띂авопреемство и континуитет в международном праве', *Moscow JIL* 1992, No. 4, pp. 22–35

Klein, E., ,Die Rolle der Staatengemeinschaft beim Kampf um die Selbstbestimmung für Tibet', in: K. Ludwig (ed.) *Perspektiven für Tibet. Auf dem Weg zu einer Zukunft in Freiheit und Selbstbestimmung*, München: Diamant Verlag, 2000, pp. 60–76

Клименко, Б., 'Проблемы правопреемства на территорий бывшего Союза CCP', in: *Moscow JIL* 1992, No. 1, pp. 3–24

Kohen, M., 'Le droit international et le temps', in: *Societé française pour le droit international, Colloque de Paris*, Paris: Pedone, 2001, pp. 129–157

Kolodkin, A., 'Russia and International Law: New Approaches', 26 *RBDI* 1993, No. 2, pp. 552–557

Kordt, E., ‚Ungleicher Vertrag und Annektion im sozialistischen Völkerrecht und in der Staatenpraxis sozialistischer Länder', in: *Festschrift Hermann Jahrreiss*, Köln: Carl Heymanns V., 1964, pp. 201–220

Korkelia, K., G. Lordkipanidze, 'State Succession in Respect of International Treaties in Post-Independent Soviet Union: Some Reflections on the Status of Georgia', in: *International Law Journal* (*Tbilisi State University*), Vol. 3, 1998, No. I–II, pp. 41–50

Korovin, E.A., 'The Second World War and International Law', 40 *AJIL* 1946, pp. 742–755

Koskenniemi, M., 'The Normative Force of Habit: International Custom and Social Theory', 1 *Finnish YBIL* 1990, pp. 77–153

Koskenniemi, M., 'The Politics of International Law', 1 *EJIL* 1990, pp. 4–32

Koskenniemi, M., 'The Future of Statehood', 32 *Harvard ILJ* 1991, pp. 397–410

Koskenniemi, M., and M. Lehto, 'La succession d'états dans l'ex-URSS, en ce qui concerne particulièrement les relations avec la Finlande', 38 *AFDI* 1992, pp. 179–219

Koskenniemi, M., 'The Wonderful Artificiality of States', in: 88 *ASIL Proc.* 1994, pp. 22–29

Koskenniemi, M., 'The Present State of Research', in: *State Succession: Codification Tested Against the Facts*, Hague Academy of International Law. Centre for Studies and Research in International Law and International Relations, 1996, pp. 89–168

Krassilnikow, A., ‚Die Staatsgrenzen der Republik Lettland nach dem Stand vom Sommer 1993', 39 *Osteuropa Recht* 1993, No. 4, pp. 281–286

Krieken, P. van, 'Estonia's Minorities and Aliens: Time for a 'Yes-Campaign', in: S. Trifunovska (ed.) *Minorities in Europe. Croatia, Estonia and Slovakia*, 1999, pp. 105–122

Krüger, H., ‚Das Prinzip der Effektivität, oder: Über die besondere Wirklichkeitsnähe des Völkerrechts', in: D. S. Constantopoulous *et al.* (Hg.) *Grundprobleme des internationalen Rechts, Festschrift für Jean Spiropoulous*, Bonn, 1957, pp. 265–284

Крылов, С.Б., 'Борьба СССР за мир', (The Fight of the USSR for the Peace), in: В. Н. Дурденевски, С. Б. Крылов, *Международное право*, Институт права Академий Наук СССР, Москва: Юридическое издательство, 1947

Kunig, P., ‚Postliminium', in: R. Bernhardt (ed.) *EPIL* 4, Amsterdam: North Holland, 1982, pp. 140–141

Kunz, J.L., 'Identity of States Under International Law', 49 *AJIL* 1955, pp. 68–76

Lange, F., ‚Die baltischen Staaten und die KSZE', in: 44 *Osteuropa*, März 1994, pp. 232–241

Lapidoth, R., 'The Expulsion of Civilians from Areas which came under Israeli control in 1967: Some Legal Issues', 2 *EJIL* 1990, pp. 97–109

Laserson, M., ‚Das Minoritätenrecht der baltischen Staaten', 2 *ZaöRV* 1931, pp. 401–429

Laski, P., *The Prescription in International Law—Some Remarks*, 23 Polish YBIL 1997–1998, pp. 219–227

Lauterpacht, H., ‚Règles générales du droit de la paix', 62 *RCADI* 1937, pp. 95–422

Lehto, M., 'Succession of States in the Former Soviet Union. Arrangements Concerning the Bilateral Treaties of Finland and the USSR', in: 4 *FYBIL* 1993, pp. 194–228

Li, T.-T., 'The Legal Position of Tibet', 50 *AJIL* 1956, pp. 394–404

Liivak, A., 'Soviet Responses to Western Nonrecognition of Baltic Annexation', in: Loeber/Vardys/Kitching (eds.) *Regional Identity Under Soviet Rule*, 1990, pp. 375–394

Lindpere, H., 'Evaluation of the Soviet-German Pacts of August 23 and September 28 1939 from the Standpoint of International Law', 1 *Finnish YBIL* 1990, pp. 415–439

Loeber, D.A., 'Language Rights in Independent Estonia, Latvia and Lithuania, 1918–1940', in: S. Vilfan (ed.) *Ethnic Groups and Language Rights*, Vol. 3, 1990

Loeber, D.A., ‚Die baltischen Staaten vor völkerrechtlichen Problemen: Kontinuität oder Staatennachfolge in bezug auf Staatsverträge, Staatseigentum und Staatsschulden', in: B. Meissner, D.A. Loeber, E. Levits (eds.), *Die Wirtschaft der baltischen Staaten im Umbruch*, 1993, Köln, pp. 26–32

Loeber, D.A., 'The Russian-Latvian Territorial Dispute Over Abrene. A Legacy from the Times of Soviet Rule', *The Parker School Journal of East European Law* 1995/Vol. 2 Nos. 4–5, pp. 537–559

Loeber, D.A., 'Consequences of the Molotov-Ribbentrop Pact for Lithuania of Today International Law Aspects', *Lithuanian Foreign Policy Review* 1999 No. 4, pp. 95–105

Loeber, D.A., 'Consequences of the Molotov-Ribbentrop Pact Continuing into Our Days: International Legal Aspects', in: *Latvia in WW II. Materials of an International Conference, 14–15 June 1999*, Riga, pp. 67–76

Loeber, D.A., 'Forced Incorporation: International Law Aspects of the Soviet Takeover of Latvia in 1940', in: R. Clark F. Feldbrugge, S. Pomorski (eds.) *International and National Law in Russia and Eastern Europe*, The Hague: M. Nijhoff, 2001, pp. 225–259

Love, L., 'International Agreement Obligations after the Soviet Union's Break-up: Current United States Practice and Its Consistency with International Law', *Vanderbilt Journal of Transnational Law*, Vol. 26, 1993, p. 394–395

Lukashuk, I.I., ‚Russland als Rechtsnachfolger in völkerrechtliche Verträge der UdSSR', 4 *Osteuropa Recht* 1993, pp. 235–246

Lõhmus, A., 'Ilves kritiseeris teravalt Venemaad' (Ilves criticized sharply Russia), *Postimees*, 17.01.2001

Makarov, N., ‚Die Eingliederung der baltischen Staaten in die Sowjet-Union', 10 *ZaöRV* 1941, pp. 682–707

Mälksoo, L., 'Language Rights in International Law: Why the Phoenix Is Still in the Ashes', 12 *Florida Journal of International Law* 2000, pp. 431–465

Mälksoo, L., 'Professor Uluots, the Estonian Government in Exile and the Continuity of the Republic of Estonia', 69 *Nordic Journal of International Law* 2000, pp. 289–316

Mälksoo, L., 'Soviet Genocide? The Communist Mass Deportations in the Baltic States and International Law', 14 *Leiden Journal of International Law* 2001, pp. 757–787

Mälksoo, L., 'Which Continuity: The Tartu Peace Treaty of 2 February 1920, the Estonian-Russian Border Treaties of 18 May 2005, and the Legal Debate About Estonia's Legal Status in International Law', 10 *Juridica International* 2005, pp. 144–149

Mälksoo, L., 'The Soviet Approach to the Right of Peoples to Self-Determination: Russia's Farewell to *jus publicum europaeum*', 19 *Journal of the History of International Law* 2017, pp. 200–218

Mälksoo, L., 'The European Court of Human Rights and the Qualification of Soviet Crimes in the Baltic States', 39 *Human Rights Law Journal* 2019, pp. 19–22

Mälksoo, L., 'The Treaties of Brest-Litovsk, Versailles and Moscow: Contesting Sovereignty and Hegemony in Eastern Europe in 1918–1939', 62 *German Yearbook of International Law* 2019, pp. 189–209

Mälksoo, L., 'International Law and the 2020 Amendments to the Russian Constitution', 115 *AJIL* 2021, pp. 78–93

Mälksoo, L., 'Post-Soviet Eurasia, *uti possidetis* and the Clash Between Universal and Russian-led Regional Understandings of International Law', 53 *NYU Journ. Int'l L. and Pol.* 2021, pp. 787–822

Mark, H., 'Vabariigi President ja Vabariigi Valitsus Eksiilis 1988–1992' (The President of the Republic and the Government of the Republic in Exile in 1988–1992), *Akadeemia* 1997 No. 7, p. 1443 *et seq*

Marks, S., 'Kuwait and East Timor: a Brief Study in Contrast', in: *International Law and the Question of East Timor*, London: CIIR/IPJET, 1995, pp. 174–180

Марочкин, С.Ю., 'Вопросы эффективности норм международного права' Questions of Effectiveness of International Law Rules), *Soviet YBIL* 1988, pp. 12–22

Мартыненко, Е., 'Правопреемство России в отношении собственности Российской Империи на Ближнем Востоке', in: *Правоведение* No. 1 2000, pp. 237–247

Mattson, T., T. Sildam, 'Venemaa välisministeerium peab Eesti presidendi ametitunnuse tagastamise küsimust praegu lahendamatuks' (In the View of the Russian Foreign Ministry, the Question of the Restitution of the Official Regalia of the Estonian President is Currently Unsolvable), *Postimees*, 06.10.1996

McDougal, M., 'Some Basic Theoretical Concepts about International Law: a Policy-Oriented Framework of Inquiry', in: R. Falk and S. Mendlovitz (eds.) *The Strategy of World Order, vol. III—International Law*, New York: World Law Fund, 1966

Meissner, B., ‚Die sowjetische Stellung zur Annexion und zur Ersitzung', in: *Int.Recht und Dipl.* 1964, pp. 96–100

Meissner, B., ‚Die Souveränität der baltischen Nationen' (1980), in: B. Meissner, *Die baltischen Staaten im weltpolitischen und völkerrechtlichen Wandel. Beiträge 1954–1994*, Hamburg: Bibliotheca Baltica, 1995, pp. 174–195

Meissner, B., ‚Baltic States', *EPIL* 1, 1992, pp. 328–337

Meissner, B., ‚Die Russische Politik gegenüber der Baltischen Region als Prüfstein für das Verhältnis Russlands zu Europa' (1994), in: B. Meissner, *Die baltischen Staaten im weltpolitischen und völkerrechtlichen Wandel. Beiträge 1954–1994*, Hamburg: Bibliotheca Baltica, 1995, pp. 273–319

Meissner, B., 'The Occupation of the Baltic States from a Present-Day Perspective', in: T. Jundzis (ed.) *The Baltic States at Historical Crossroads. Political, Economic, and Legal Problems in the Context of International Cooperation on the Doorstep of the 21st Century. A Collection of Scholarly Essays Published in Remembrance of Senator August Loeber and the 75th Birthday of Professor Dietrich Andre Loeber*, Riga: Academy of Sciences of Latvia, 1998, pp. 473–488

Мэлтюхов, М., 'Наращивание советского военного присутствия в Прибалтике в 1939–1941 гг.'—*Отечественная история*, No. 4 2000, стр. 46–70

Mendl, W., 'Japan and the Soviet Union: Towards a Deal?', 47 *World Today* 1991 (November), p. 196 *et seq*

Miehsler, H., C. Schreuer, ‚Austria', in: R. Bernhardt (ed.) *EPIL* 12, Amsterdam: North Holland, 1990, pp. 28–33

Misiunas, R.J., 'Sovereignty Without Government: Baltic Diplomatic and Consular Representation, 1940–1990', in: Y. Shain (ed.) *Governments-in-Exile in Contemporary World Politics*, New York and Lodnon: Routledge, 1991, pp. 134–144

Morgenthau, H., 'Positivism, Functionalism and International Law', 34 *AJIL* 1940, pp. 260–284

Moshes, A., 'Russia-Lithuania: Preserving Interaction', *Lithuanian Foreign Policy Review* 2000 No. 2(6), pp. 79–86

Mössner, J.M., 'Non-Aggression Pacts', R. Bernhardt (ed.) *EPIL* III, Amsterdam: North Holland, 1997, pp. 596–600

Mouton, J.-D., 'L'État selon le droit international: diversité et unité', in: *L'État souverain a l'aube du XXIe siècle. Colloque de Nancy*, Paris, pp. 79–106

Мюллерсон, Р.А., 'Советско-Германские договоренности в аспекте международного права', in: *Советское государство и право* но. 9 1989, pp. 105–109

Mullerson, R., 'New Developments in the Former USSR and Yugoslavia', 33 *Va. J. Int'l L.* 1993, pp. 299–322

Müllerson, R., 'The Continuity and Succession of States by Reference to the Former USSR and Yugoslavia', 42 *ICLQ* 1993, pp. 473–493

Mutua, M., 'What is TWAIL?', in: *ASIL Proceedings of the 94th Annual Meeting*, April 5–8, 2000, pp. 31–38

Niitsoo, V., 'Rahvuslik vastupanuliikumine aastail 1955–1962' (The National Resistance Movement in 1955–1962) *Akadeemia* No. 12, 1994, pp. 2513–2539 and No. 1, 1995, pp. 58–71; 'Eesti rahvuslik vastupanuliikumine aastail 1968–1975', No. 9–10, 1993, pp. 1819–1833 and 2905–2110.); 'Avalik vastupanuliikumine aastail 1977–1984', No. 9–10, 1992, pp. 1917–1933 and 2180–2194

Oberhammer P./A. Reinisch, 'Restitution of Jewish Property in Austria', 60 *ZaöRV* 2000, pp. 737–761

O'Connell, D.P., 'Recent Problems of State Succession in Relation to New States', *RCADI* 1971, vol. II, 1972, pp. 95–206

Osinbajo, Y., 'Legality in a Collapsed State: the Somali Experience', 45 *ICLQ* 1996, pp. 910–923

Ottolenghi, G., 'Il principo di effectività e la sua funzione nell'ordinamento internazionale', 15 *Rivista di diritto internazionale* 1936, pp. 3–33

Pellet, A., 'Note sur la Commission d'arbitrage de la Conférence pour la paix en Yougoslavie', 37 *A.F.D.I.* 1991, pp. 329–348

Picciotti, R.A., 'Legal Problems of Occupied Nations after the Termination of Occupation', 33 *Military Law Review* 1966, pp. 25–57

Popovski, V., 'Citizenship and Ethno-politics in Lithuania', 33 *International Politics* March 1996, pp. 45–55

'Посёл Литвы Зенонас Намавичюс: Российской военной угрозы не существует', *Izvestia*, 20.02. 2001 (No. 30), p. 9

Prunskiene, K., ‚Unabhängigkeit als Option für die Selbstbestimmung: das Beispiel Litauen', in: K. Ludwig (ed.) *Perspektiven für Tibet. Auf dem Weg zu einer Zukunft in Freiheit und Selbstbestimmung*, München: Diamant Verlag, 2000, pp. 91–97

Pullat, R., 'The Restauration of the Independence of Estonia', 2 *Finnish YBIL* 1991, pp. 512–529

Quigley, J., 'Mass Displacement and the Individual Right of Return', in: 68 *BYBIL* 1997, pp. 65–126

Raestad, A., 'La cession des États d'après le Droit des Gens', 66 *Revue de droit international et de législation comparée* (RDI), 1939, pp. 441–449

Ramishvili, T., 'Latvia and Estonia: Human Rights Violations in the Center of Europe', 44 *International Affairs* 1998, pp. 116–127

Randelzhofer, A., 'Commentary to Article 2(4)', in: B. Simma (ed.) *The Charter of the United Nations. A Commentary*, Oxford: University Press, 1994, pp. 111–128

Rich, R., 'Recognition of States: The Collapse of Yugoslavia and the Soviet Union', 4 *EJIL* 1993, pp. 36–55

Riismandel, V., 'Kersten'i komisjoni töötulemusi' (Work Results of the Kersten Committee), in: *Võitlev Eesti* (Fighting Estonia), Nr. 6, 1956, pp. 35–42

Riismandel, V.J., 'The Continued Legal Existence of the Baltic States', 12 *Baltic Review* (7 November 1957), pp. 48–68

Riismandel, V.J., 'Nõukogude Liit oli agressor' (The Soviet Union was an Aggressor) in: *Vaba Eesti Sõna* (Free Estonian Word), February 26, 1998. No. 9 (2508)

Riismandel, V.J., 'Vaatlusi Vabadussõjast ja Tartu rahulepingust' (Observations regarding the War of Independence and the Tartu Peace Treaty), in: *Vaba Eesti Sõna*, December 23, 1999

Roberts, A., 'What Is a Military Occupation?', 55 *BYBIL* 1984, pp. 249–305

Roberts, A., 'Prolonged Military Occupation: the Israeli-Occupied Territories Since 1967', 84 *AJIL* 1990, pp. 44–103

Roosaare, E., 'Consular Relations between the United States and the Baltic States', 27 *Baltic Review* (June 1964), pp. 23–32

Ross, A., 'Denmark's Legal Status During the Occupation', 1 *Jus Gentium* (*Nordisk Tidsskrift for Folkeret og International Privatret*) 1949, Vol. 1, pp. 3–21

Ross, A., 'Tû-tû', 70 *Harvard Law Review* 1956/57, pp. 812–825

Rousseau, C., 'Syrie', 33 *RGDIP* 1962, pp. 413–417

Ruiz H., Fabri, 'État (création, succession, compétences). Genèse et disparition de l'état à l'époque contemporaine', 38 *AFDI* 1992, pp. 153–178

Salmon, J., 'Pays baltes', 24 *RBDI* 1991, pp. 261–267

Saxer, U.W., 'The Transformation of the Soviet Union: From a Socialist Federation to a Commonwealth of Independent States', in: 14 *Loy. L.A. Int'l & Comp. L.J.* 1992, pp. 581–715

Schachter, O., 'The Decline of the Nation-State and its Implications for International Law', in: J.I. Charney, D. K. Anton, M.E. O'Connell (eds.) *Politics, Values and Functions. International Law in the 21st Century. Essays in Honor of Professor Louis Henkin*, The Hague: Nijhoff, 1997

Schätzel, W., ‚Die Annexion im Völkerrecht', 2 *AVR* 1950, pp. 1–28

Schaumann, W., ‚Exilregierung', in: K. Strupp and H.-J. Schlochauer (Hg.) *Wörterbuch des Völkerrechts*, Band I, 2. Aufl., Berlin: Walter de Gruyter, pp. 498–499

Scheuner, U., Book review of K. Marek, 17 *ZaöRV* 1956/57, pp. 173–175

Scheuner, U., ‚Entstehung, Altersstufen und Untergang von Staaten im Lichte des Rechts', in: 4 *Kölner Zeitschrift für Soziologie* 1951/52, pp. 208–221

Scheuner, U., ‚Die Funktionsnachfolge und das Problem der staatsrechlichen Kontinuität', in: T. Maunz (Hg.) *Vom Bonner Grundgesetz zur gesamtdeutschen Verfassung*, (*Festschrift für Franz Nawiasky*), München: Isar Verlag, 1956, pp. 9–48

Schmid, K., ‚Gedanken zu Untergang und Entstehung von Staaten in Mittel- und Osteuropa', 69 *Friedens-Warte* 1993, pp. 72–97

Schram, S.R., ‚L'Union soviétique et les Etats baltes', in: J.-B. Duroselle (ed.) *Les frontières européennes de l'U.R.S.S. 1917–1941*, Paris: Librairie Armand Colin, 1957

Schreuer, C., 'The Waning of the Sovereign State: Towards a New Paradigm for International Law?', 4 *EJIL* 1993, pp. 447–471

Schulz, G., ‚Die Entwicklung des völkerrechtlichen Annexionsverbots', in: *Jahrbuch der Albertus-Universität zu Königsberg/Preußen*, Band XII, 1962

Schulz, L., 'The Relationship of the Union to the Republics in Soviet Constitutional Law', in: D. A. Loeber, S.V Vardys, L. P. A. Kitching (eds.) *Regional Identity under Soviet Rule—the Case of the Baltic States*, 1990, pp. 351–354

Schweisfurth, T., 'Germany, Occupation After World War II', in: R. Bernhardt (ed.) *EPIL* 3, Amsterdam: North Holland, 1982, pp. 191–197

Schweisfurth, T., ‚Ausgwählte Fragen der Staatensukzession im Kontext der Auflösung der UdSSR', 32 *AVR* 1994, pp. 99–129

Schweisfurth, T., ‚Vom Einheitsstaat (UdSSR) zum Staatenbund (GUS). Juristische Stationen eines Staatszerfalls und einer Staatenbundsentstehung', 52 *ZaöRV* 1992, pp. 541–702

Schweisfurth, T., 'Soviet Union, Dissolution', in: R. Bernhardt (ed.) *EPIL*, Vol. 4, Amsterdam, 2000, pp. 529–547

Sciso, E., 'Dissoluzione di stati e problemi di successione nei trattati', in: XLIX *La comunità internazionale* 1994, pp. 63–115

Scott, S.V., 'International Law as Ideology: Theorizing the Relationship between International Law and International Politics', 5 *EJIL* 1994, pp 313–325

Seidel, G., ‚Die Völkerrechtsordnung an der Schwelle zum 21. Jahrhundert', 38 *AVR* 2000, pp. 23–47

Senn, A.E., 'What Happened in Lithuania in 1940?', in: *Lithuanian Foreign Policy Review* 2000, pp. 179–195

Shaw, M.N., 'State Succession Revisited', in: 5 *Finnish YBIL* 1994, pp. 34–98

Shaw, M., 'The Heritage of States: The Principle of Uti Possidetis Juris Today', 67 *BYBIL* 1996, pp. 75–154

Shaw, M.N., 'Peoples, Territorialism and Boundaries', 8 *EJIL* 1997, pp. 478–507

Shinkaretskaya, G., 'Succession and the Borders of the Russian Federation', in: 1 *Moscow JIL* 1995, No. 4, pp. 50–62

Sildam, T., 'Välisminister Ilves: ajalugu pole pudupood' (Foreign Minister Ilves: History is not a Grocery Store), an interview in *Postimees*, 02.02. 2001

Simma, B., 'Comments on Global Governance, the United Nations Reform and the Place of Law', in: 9 *Finnish YBIL* 1998, pp. 61–66

Skubiszewski, K., 'The End of Yalta', in: K. Wellens (ed.) *International Law: Theory and Practice. Essays in Honour of Eric Suy*, The Hague: Nijhoff, 1998, pp. 107–119

Slaughter, A.-M., 'Governing the Global Economy through Government Networks', in: M. Byers (ed.) *The Role of Law in International Politics*, 2000, pp. 177–205

Slaughter, A.-M., 'International Law and International Relations', 285 *RCADI* 2000, pp. 9–250

Smirnov, I.A., 'The Legal Qualification of the Documents on Security and Cooperation in Europe', *Soviet Journal of International Law*, No. 2, 1991, pp. 111–120

Smith, G., A. Aasland, R. Mole, 'Statehood, Ethnic Relations and Citizenship', in: G. Smith (ed.) *The Baltic States. The National Self-Determination of Estonia, Latvia and Lithuania*, London: Macmillan, 1994, pp. 181–205

Smith, G., 'When Nations Challenge and Nations Rule: Estonia and Latvia as Ethnic Democracies', in: 33 *International Politics*, March 1996, pp. 27–43

Stone, J., 'What Price Effectiveness?', 50 *ASIL Proc.* 1956, pp. 198–206

Stern, B. 'La succession d'Ėtats', 262 *RCADI* 1996, The Hague, 2000, pp. 9–438

Stern, B., 'How to Regulate Globalization?', in: M. Byers (ed.) *The Role of Law in International Politics*, Oxford UP, 2000, pp. 247–268

Sur, S., 'The State between Fragmentation and Globalization', 8 *EJIL* 1997, pp. 421–432

Susi, A., 'Mis on meile maksma läinud okupatsioon?' (What has the Price of Occupation been for Us), *Looming* No. 2 1990, pp. 246–251

Szafarz, R., 'The Practice of Poland as the „Other State Party" and as a Depositary—as Regards Succession of Recently Established States in Respect of Treaties (a Case Study)', 22 *Polish* YBIL 1995–1996, pp. 221–235

Syatow, J.J.G., 'Old and New States—a Misleading Distinction for Future International Law and International Relations', in: *Le droit international demain*. Université de Neuchatel, Série juridique No. 8, Neuchatel: Éditions Ides et Calendes, 1974

Tarand, K., 'Kasvuraskused' (Difficulties of Growing), in: *EÜSi Album* XVIII, Tartu, 2000, pp. 53–60

Tchernichenko, S.V., 'State as a Personality, Subject of International Law and Bearer of Sovereignty', *Russian* YBIL 1993–1994, pp. 13–46

Teder, I., 'N. Liidu agressiooniga Eesti Vabariigile tekitatud kahjude hüvitamisest' (About Compensation of Damages Inflicted upon the Republic of Estonia with the Aggression of the USSR), *Looming* No. 2, 1990, pp. 252–254

Tesón, ER., 'Realism and Kantianism in International Law', 86 *ASIL Proc.* 1992, pp. 113–118

Tichy, H., 'Two Recent Cases of State Succession—An Austrian Perspective', 44 *Austrian Journal of Public International Law* 1992, pp. 117–136

Tomuschat, C., 'Ethos, Ethics and Morality in International Relations', in: R. Bernhardt (ed.) *EPIL* 9, Amsterdam: North Holland, 1986, pp. 127–134

Tomuschat, C., ‚Staatsvolk ohne Staat? Zum Teso-Urteil des Bundesverfassungsgerichts (BverfGE 77, 137)', in: *FS Karl Doehring*, Heidelberg: Springer, pp. 985–1008

Tomuschat, C., 'Obligations Arising for States without or against their Will', in: 241 *RCADI* 1993, pp. 199–374

Tomuschat, C., 'International Crimes by States—an Endangered Species?', in: *International Law: Theory and Practice. Essays in Honour of Eric Suy*, The Hague: Nijhoff, 1998, pp. 253–274

Tomuschat, C., 'International Law: Ensuring the Survival of Mankind on the Eve of a New Century. General Course on Public International Law', 281 *RCADI* 2001, 438 pp

Torrecuadrada, S., 'Le rôle du consentement dans la succession d'États aux traités', 23 *Polish* YBIL 1997–1998, pp. 127–170

Trapans, J.A., 'The West and the Recognition of the Baltic States: 1919 and 1991. A Study of the Politics of the Major Powers', 25 *Journal of Baltic Studies*, 2, pp. 153–173

Tunkin, G., 'International Law in the International System', 147 *RCADI* 1975, pp. 1–218

Uibopuu, H.-J., ‚Gedanken zu einem völkerrechtlichen Staatsbegriff', in: C. Schreuer (ed.) *Autorität und internationale Ordnung. Aufsätze zum Völkerrecht*, Berlin: Duncker & Humblot, 1979, pp. 87–110

Uibopuu, H.-J., 'Minorities and their Rights in the Baltic States', in: 35 *AWR-Bulletin* 1997, pp. 189–197

Uibopuu, H.-J., 'Dealing with the Minorities—a Baltic Perspective', in: 48 *The World Today* 1992 (June), pp. 108–112

Uschakow, A., ‚Die Wiederherstellung Polens im Lichte des Völkerrechts', in: B. Meissner, G. Zieger (Hg.), *Staatliche Kontinuität unter besonderer Berücksichtigung der Rechtslage Deutschlands*, Köln: Verlag Wissenschaft und Politik, 1983, pp. 107–128

Vadapalas, V., V. Žalys, 'Secret Protocols to the Soviet-German Treaties of 1939 and the Problem of Prescription in International Law', in: *Proceedings of the Estonian Academy of Sciences. Social Sciences*. 1990, 39/2, pp. 126–134

Vallens, D., 'The Law on Aliens Controversy in the Baltic States', in: *The Review of the International Commission of Jurists*, No. 54 June 1995, pp. 1–28

Varennes, F. de, 'Non-Citizens and Minorities in Estonia and Their Economic and Social Opportunities', in: S. Trifunovska (ed.) *Minorities in Europe. Croatia, Estonia and Slovakia*, The Hague: Asser Press, 1999, pp. 123–142

Verdross, A., ‚Die völkerrechtliche Identität der Staaten', in: R. Braun, A. Verdross, L. Werner (Hg.) *Festschrift Heinrich Klang*, Wien: Springer Verlag, 1950, pp. 18–21

Verdross, A., ‚Untergang von Staaten', in: K. Strupp, H.-J. Schlochauer (eds.) *Wörterbuch des Völkerrechts*, 2. Aufl., Band III, Berlin: Springer, 1962, pp. 479–480

Verhoeven, J., ‚La reconnaissance internationale: déclin ou renouveau?', 39 *AFDI* 1993, pp. 7–40

Visek, R.C., 'Creating the Ethnic Electorate through Legal Restorationism: Citizenship Rights in Estonia', 38 *Harvard JIL* 1997, pp. 315–376

Warma, A., 'Pensées, sur l'identité et la continuité de l'Etat. (Situation juridique de la République d'Estonie.), in: J.G. Poska (ed.) *Pro Baltica. Mélanges dédiés á Kaarel R. Pusta*, Stockholm: Comité des Amis de K.R. Pusta, 1965, pp 219–228

Waitz von Eschen, F. Frhr., ‚Zur internationalen Lage der baltischen Republiken nach Erlangung der Unabhängigkeit', in: 42 *Osteuropa* 1992, pp. 319–328

Whomerslay, C., 'The International Legal Status of Gdansk, Klaipeda and the Former East Prussia', 42 *ICLQ* 1993, pp. 919–927

Wright, Q., 'The Goa Incident', 56 *AJIL* 1962, pp. 617–632

Yakemtchouk, R., 'Les républiques baltes en droit international. Echec d'une annexion opérée en violation du droit des gens', 37 *AFDI* 1991, pp. 259–289

Young, R., 'The State of Syria: Old or New?', 56 *AJIL* 1962, pp. 482–488

Zakharova, N.V., 'States as Subjects of International Law and Social Revolution (Some Problems of Succession)', *Soviet YBIL* 1960, pp. 157–166

Zakharova, N., 'Renunication by the Soviet State of Treaties of Tsarist Russia which Violated the Rights of the Peoples in Eastern Countries', *Soviet YBIL* 1962, pp. 126–136

Žalimas, D., 'Legal and Political Issues on the Continuity of the Republic of Lithuania', in: *Lithuanian Foreign Policy Review* 1999 No. 4, pp. 104–116

Ziemele, I., 'The Application of International Law in the Baltic States', 40 *GYBIL* 1997, pp. 243–279

Ziemele, I., 'The Role of State Continuity and Human Rights in Matters of Nationality of the Baltic States', in: T. Jundzis (ed.) *The Baltic States at Historical Crossroads.*

Political, Economic, and Legal Problems in the Context of International Cooperation on the Doorstep of the 21st Century. A Collection of Scholarly Essays Published in Remembrance of Senator August Loeber and the 75th Birthday of Professor Dietrich André Loeber, Riga: Academy of Sciences of Latvia, 1998, pp. 248–271

Ziemele, I., 'The State Border Between Latvia and Russia and the Doctrine of the Continuity of the Republic of Latvia', 9 *Baltic* YBIL 2009, pp. 95–132

Index of Modern Authors

Index of Subjects

www.ingramcontent.com/pod-product-compliance
Lightning Source LLC
LaVergne TN
LVHW020633300926
849161LV00004B/690

* 9 7 8 9 0 0 4 4 6 4 8 8 9 *